THE LAST DAYS OF THE HIGH SEAS FLEET

REVIEWS OF

JUTLAND: THE UNFINISHED BATTLE

The best narrative account of the battle currently available.
Prof Eric Grove, Navy News, May 2016

'… closely reasoned, fair-minded and thoroughly readable.'
Allan Mallinson, The Times, July 2016

A compelling and dramatic account…scrupulously accurate and fair.
Robert Massie (Pulitzer prize-winning author, *Castles of Steel*, *Dreadnought*)

Thoroughly researched and absorbing…an excellent addition to the vast
array of literature about the epic clash.
Warships, International Fleet Review, June 2016

A lively and engaging analysis of the controversial Fleet action that
combines new material with the sympathetic but not uncritical
perspective of the British Commander-in-Chief's grandson.
Rear Admiral James Goldrick, RAN (Author, *Before Jutland*)

A dramatic, often gripping, and surprisingly objective, look at the battle,
any student of naval warfare will find this a rewarding read.
The NYMAS Review

This whole package, book and companion website, is a must for serious
naval historians. But, Jellicoe's writing is entertaining enough to engage
anyone simply looking for a delightful read.
Commander Stephen Philips, USN Naval Historical Foundation

A superb analysis…A balanced, measured and yet nuanced account of
the greatest sea battle of World War 1.
Prof Holger Herwig (*Luxury Fleet*), Naval War College Review, Autumn 2016

A worthy addition to the enormous Jutland literary compendium. The author's familial links to Admiral Jellicoe, his graphic website supporting the book and his balanced, objective treatment of the subject make this book well worth reading.

Tim Coyle, Australian Naval Institute

This is a marvelously enthralling account of the battle that combines academic thoroughness with a unique element of personal observation. I found it totally absorbing and cannot recommend it highly enough.

Warship World, May/June 2016 – PW-M. Commodore Peter Wykeham-Martin, Chairman *Friends of the NMRN*

An exceptionally well written and researched account which provides an insight into the relationship between high ranking officers of that era. All-in-all this is a good read and is very highly recommended.

Richard Osborne, Marine News, June 2016

The best account I have read about this greatest of sea battles.

Capt Don Walsh USN ret'd

A book not to be missed by serious scholars and students of the Great War at sea – his evidence and argument 'finish the battle'.

International Journal of Maritime History, February 2017

His description of the battle itself is a masterpiece of historical writing.

Prof Dr Michael Epkenhans, Centre for Military History and Social Sciences of Bundeswehr, Potsdam

To the memory of nine German sailors who never made it home.

And to my family, my wife Patricia and our two talented daughters, Zoë and Francesca. Always, for their love and support.

THE LAST DAYS
OF THE
HIGH SEAS FLEET
From Mutiny to Scapa Flow

NICHOLAS JELLICOE

Foreword by PROF DR MICHAEL EPKENHANS

Seaforth
PUBLISHING

First published in Great Britain in 2019 by
Seaforth Publishing,
A division of Pen & Sword Books Ltd,
47 Church Street,
Barnsley S70 2AS

www.seaforthpublishing.com

British Library Cataloguing in Publication Data
A catalogue record for this book is available from the British Library

ISBN 978 1 5267 5458 5 (HARDBACK)
ISBN 978 1 5267 5460 8 (KINDLE)
ISBN 978 1 5267 5459 2 (EPUB)

Pen & Sword Books Limited incorporates the imprints of Atlas, Archaeology, Aviation, Discovery, Family History, Fiction, History, Maritime, Military, Military Classics, Politics, Select, Transport, True Crime, Air World, Frontline Publishing, Leo Cooper, Remember When, Seaforth Publishing, The Praetorian Press, Wharncliffe Local History, Wharncliffe Transport, Wharncliffe True Crime and White Owl.

Typeset and designed by Mousemat Design
Printed and bound in Great Britain by TJ International Ltd, Padstow

CONTENTS

LIST OF ILLUSTRATIONS

ABBREVIATIONS

BCF	Battle-Cruiser Fleet (Schlachtkreuzerflotte)
BCS	Battle-Cruiser Squadron (Schlachtkreuzergeschwader)
BS	Battle Squadron (Schlachtgeschwader)x
C-in-C	Commander-in-Chief (Befehlshaber)
CS	Cruiser Squadron (Kreuzergeschwader)
CNO	Chief of Naval Operations (USN)
DF	Destroyer Flotilla
FKpt	Commander (Fregattenkapitan)
Hf	Half-flotilla (Halbflottille)
HMS	His Majesty's Ship (Seiner Majestät Schiff)
HSF	High Seas Fleet (Hochseeflotte)
IGS	Instructions for German Ships
IKD	Internationale Kommunisten Deutschlands
KKpt	Lieutenant-Commander (Korvettenkapitän)
LC	Light Cruiser (Kleiner Kreuzer)
LCS	Light Cruiser Squadron
MK	Marinekabinett (German Naval War Cabinet)
OK	Oberkommando der Marine (German Naval High Command)
RMA	Reichsmarineamt (The German Navy Office)
SG:	Scouting Group (Aufklärungsgruppe)
SKL	Seekriegsleitung (German Naval High Command)
SMS	Seiner Majestät Schiff (His Majesty's Ship)
SNOAS	Senior Naval Officer Afloat, Scapa
TBF	Torpedo Boat Flotilla (Torpedoboote Flottille)
USPD	Unabhängige Sozialdemokratische Partei Deutschlands
1SL	First Sea Lord
2iC	Second-in-command

RANK EQUIVALENCY

Admiral of the Fleet	Groß Admiral
Admiral	Admiral
Vice Admiral	Vizeadmiral
Rear Admiral	Kontreadmiral (Konteradmiral also used)
Commodore*	Kommodore
Captain	Kapitän zur See
Commander	Fregattenkapitän
Lieutenant-Commander	Korvettenkapitän
Lieutenant	Kapitänleutnant
Lieutenant (senior)	Oberleutnant zur See
Lieutenant (junior)	Leutnant zur See
Naval Cadet / Midshipman	Seekadette / Fähnrich zur See

*Commodore is technically a function not a rank.

Other ranks mentioned in the text

Bootsmaat	Boatswain
Heizer	Stoker (Oberheizer, leading Stoker)
Machinistmaat	Engineer (Obermachinistmaat, senior engineer)
Matrose	Seaman (Obermatrose, leading seaman)

A note on ships' name spelling

I have used Reinhard Scheer's *Germany's High Sea Fleet in World War One* as the reference for all spellings. For example, *Köln* and not *Cöln*, and *Hindenburg*, *Nürnberg* and *Königsberg*.

Digital resources

 A digital animation of the events of 21 June 1919, the circumstances surrounding the scuttle and the salvage as well as a large amount of other reference materials, are available to view online at www.ScapaFlow1919.com.

Please note that traditional naval parlance would have it that someone serves 'in' a ship and not 'on' a ship. I hope I can be forgiven for occasionally using 'on' when it reads more easily for non-naval readers.

FOREWORD

O N 28 JUNE 1919 the German government grudgingly signed the Treaty of Versailles. With the signatures of both the German and the Allied representatives in the symbolic Hall of Mirrors in the splendid palace once built by Louis XIV the Great War finally came to an end.

One event that preceded this remarkable ceremony at Versailles is often forgotten: the scuttling of the German High Seas Fleet at Scapa Flow the week before. This fleet, built to challenge Britain's supremacy on the oceans of the world, had fought bravely in the battles that had taken place in the four years of the war at sea. However, contrary to all hopes before the war, it had failed to achieve this aim. The superiority of the Grand Fleet and Britain's decision to establish a distant blockade rather than seeking a battle under the guns of Helgoland had rendered all German plans of a battle under favourable circumstances useless. As a result it had stayed on the defensive. Hopes to lure out only parts of the Grand Fleet and thus perhaps whittle down British naval strength in smaller skirmishes had also proved ineffective. The Battle of Jutland on 31 May 1916, the result of one of those sorties into the North Sea had, despite all tactical successes, again emphasised that the High Seas Fleet, at least in this war, would not be able to break Britain's supremacy. Promises of forcing Britain to her knees by waging unrestricted submarine warfare had not only also failed but also led to the entry of the United States of America into the war, thus improving the strength of Britain and her allies even more.

In the event, when it was clear that Germany had lost the war in autumn 1918, plans for a suicidal raid against Britain at the last moment to save the honour of the German Navy officers had led to a mutiny of the navy's sailors and finally a revolution that overthrew the Imperial government. On 11 November 1918 the war ended with Germany signing the Armistice at Compiègne in France.

What followed was *Der Tag* – a deep humiliation for the officers who had hoped that they would be the victors and not the defeated. In a long line of warships, Germany's High Seas Fleet, disarmed and accompanied by British warships on both sides, sailed into internment in Scapa Flow, Britain's main naval base. When it became clear, however, that the Allies would not grant a moderate peace that would even allow the return of the fleet, the Commander-in-chief of the interned fleet, Rear Admiral Ludwig von Reuter, decided to scuttle his ships instead of handing them over to the victorious Allies. After all the deep disappointments in the years before the German Navy would achieve at least a small triumph over its enemies.

Nick Jellicoe describes all the events and developments surrounding this triumph by beginning with Germany's decisions to build a fleet, to go to war with it and to finally scuttle it. What makes his book most remarkable is, however, that based on new documents he paints a vivid picture of the main actors on both sides, the decisions and aims of the politicians and the admirals involved, the life on board during the internment and the final scuttling on 21 June 1919. It is a book written with the intention to give an unbiased report and thus enable the reader to better understand an event with all its repercussions on British and German naval policy that is unfortunately often only a footnote in all the accounts of the Great War.

PROF DR MICHAEL EPKENHANS,
Centre for Military History and Social Sciences of the Bundeswehr, Potsdam

ACKNOWLEDGEMENTS

MANY ORCADIANS HAVE left their mark on this book. I was lucky to meet historian Tom Muir when he was planning the Jutland exhibition in 2015. We became close friends and shared a continued interest in telling the story of the scuttle with as much of the Orcadian side as we could. His help has been immeasurable. Others in Orkney have warmly welcomed me and helped me where they could: Fionn McCartney, Morag Robertson (Orkney island Council Business Development), David Mackie (Orkney Library and Archives), Jude Callister (Lyness Visitor Centre) and, of course, the Lord Lieutenant, Bill Spence. On every trip I have been graciously and generously looked after in Harray by Ray and Shona Gould.

I have always tried to tell the German side of the story. It is a truism that to the victor belong the spoils. The truth of war is so often buried in that process. Many Germans have continued to help me. Foremost are Dr Stephan Huck, Director of the German Naval Museum and the author of this book's foreword (and *Jutland*'s), Prof Dr Michael Epkenhans. Both are colleagues and, I would like to say, friends. And talking of friends, new ones have been made: Rear Admiral von Reuter's descendants, Yorck-Ludwig and Marc-Derfflinger. Dr Jann Witt (German Naval Association) has, as he did on *Jutland*, allowed me to spend days in the Association archives hunting for photographic materials.

One project that was related to Scapa Flow was the search for the salvaged bells. The search took me to Somerset to visit Robert McCrone's granddaughter, Helena; to the island of Eriskay, where SMS *Derfflinger*'s bell keeps the vigil opposite the skerries at the church of St Michael where Father Ross met me; to the National Museum of the Royal Navy in Portsmouth and the Imperial War Museum's storage in Duxford. Nick Hewitt helped me in both cases find the bells for which I was looking.

My ties to Scandinavia have grown closer and I'm lucky to count among my friends Gert Normann Andersen, who has so generously supported the search for the continuing naval history of both Jutland and Scapa Flow. The Seawar museum, which hosts most of his collection of artefacts, was also able to help me considerably in the search for photographic records of the scuttle and the ships that were present.

There have been many others whom I should thank. In closing, any of the mistakes made in the text are of my own doing and hopefully will be revised and corrected in due time.

NICK JELLICOE

Jongny, Switzerland, January 2019.

INTRODUCTION

T O THE PACKED onlookers crowding the waterfront, the names brought back memories of distant but better days. On the sterns could be seen the names of 'Kings and Generals who had shaped [Germany's] destinies through two centuries':[1] *von der Tann, Seydlitz, Moltke.*

These once-feared ships were now rusting, bedraggled hulks, nothing more than the 'shabby symbols of the Kaiser's naval ambitions'. Long, ugly rust stains scarred the hulls. No brass glinted in the sunlight, white paint had long since turned flat grey on the skins of these towering monsters.

There were no cheering crews lining the rails. Instead of coloured flags and bunting, now all that could be seen were red revolutionary flags or small firs tied to the masts as a sign of peace, like on the *Derfflinger*. The crews lounged around, seemingly without a care in the world. Their faces, however, wore sullen looks and expressions of bitter resignation and anger. Even, maybe, amongst the younger ones, bewilderment.

The great procession of ships was already two hours late, the crisp November day starting to chill as the sun cast shadows across the still, muddy waters of the Jade basin. On the bridge of the once-proud Fleet flagship, *Friedrich der Größe*, stood a solitary figure. Rear Admiral Ludwig von Reuter. A capable and proven commander, but now a man shouldering the heavy and unwanted burden of commanding the Fleet on its last sortie.

He had no idea of what fate awaited him, his men or the ships themselves. He'd only had three days to ponder the responsibilities of his

---

* SMS *von der Tann* was not ready initially as the battle-cruiser had not been able to raise enough steam fast enough. Its signals department had not been manning their posts when the orders for sailing had been sent. Some ships of the II Torpedo Boat Flotilla and the III Half Torpedo Boat Flotilla did not have officers. The VII Torpedo Boat Flotilla stayed and re-joined the Fleet on the evening of 20 November. They had stayed to bring the Fleet mail.

new command. All he knew was that it was his duty to deliver the core of Germany's navy into allied hands, to be interned as Germany's guarantee of her commitment to the peace negotiations that would soon start in Paris. It was not a surrender but it certainly felt like one.

A deep and painful sense of humiliation and frustration hung over the officers and many of the men. While the German Navy was largely still physically intact – the ships themselves, although in increasingly poor condition, still represented a formidable fighting machine – few retained any semblance of a will to fight. Few of the men shared their officers' sense of duty or felt that risking the Armistice terms made any sense.

Three days earlier the Fleet Commander, Franz Ritter von Hipper, had asked – not *ordered* – Reuter to take on the onerous task of leading the Hochseeflotte into internment.* Reuter had weighed the difficult decision. He was caught between duty to Germany, the honour of the Fleet and his responsibility to his own family. With no Kaiser, a new revolutionary government in power and the Fleet riddled with agitators, the choices weren't that clear. Could he even trust the crews to get the ships there? And what would the consequences be for Germany if they didn't do what the allies demanded? Reuter's son, Yorck, remembered seeing his father pacing up and down the garden as he weighed his options.

It was barely three days since the British had issued their orders for the Fleet's internment. The men were informed that the time away from their homeland would be less than forty days. In the time left before their departure, ammunition, mines and torpedoes had been offloaded and the firing mechanisms on all the guns' breech-blocks and sensitive equipment such as range-finders removed or rendered unusable.† Even valuable navigation equipment was left behind. Less was restocked and brought back on board: the ships took on less coal and water than normal as the crews had been radically cut down. It was small wonder why these great leviathans seemed to be riding so high in the water. They carried none of the tools of war and still fewer of the men who would have employed them. Not carrying out the British instructions to the letter risked an allied occupation of the island fortress of Helgoland and possibly an even costlier close blockade of Germany's seaports.

As the ships faded from sight, the last dark plumes of funnel smoke

---

* Franz Ritter von Hipper had commanded the battle-cruisers at Jutland and took over command of the High Seas Fleet from Reinhard Scheer on 12 August 1918 after Scheer had been promoted to head the Naval Staff.
† In the case of the large, integrated turret range-finders, the Zeiss optics were removed.

fading on the horizon, those that were left returned to the daily struggle of survival that had now become their lives. The allied naval blockade had denied civilians food and industry the raw materials on which the economy had depended.

It seemed only yesterday that these very same ships had passed through these waters as conquerors. Today, they were the conquered. Fourteen months later, most of the sailors would return: the ships wouldn't.

1

GERMANY AND ITS NAVY

Many of the great ships that ended their lives so ignominiously in the cold, grey waters of Scapa Flow in June 1919 belonged, generationally speaking, to an adolescent navy. A few had been in service less than three years. Only two decades before, these steel leviathans had merely been the proverbial 'twinkle in the eye' of their creator, Alfred von Tirpitz, and the German Emperor, Kaiser Wilhelm II.

Today, the fundamental role that the new German Navy played in leading the two strongest European nations to war has been largely forgotten. The new navy had threatened the stability of early twentieth-century Europe. The wealth of Europe's two leading economies had been poured into steel. The Anglo–German naval arms race would be the first great arms race of the new century.

In the early years, however, 'the German Imperial Navy was subordinated to the land-based military strategy of the German Army'. The navy's task was mostly mere coastal defence.[2] In Norman Friedman's description, 'Germany was an army with a country attached'.[3] Germany was a land power on the European continent and its army's position was paramount: 'That the German unification was based on six years of success on the battlefield earned enormous admiration and prestige for the army leadership, not only in Prussia but among a large section of the German population.'[4]

Despite the intervening years of Germany's first great navy, the creation of its second Navy, the Kriegsmarine, with its association to legendary names like *Bismarck*, *Scharnhorst* and *Tirpitz*, this orientation to the land never changed. It should hardly be surprising, then, to learn that the first two significant commanders of its Navy were both army officers. Albrecht von Stosch pushed the nascent Navy into profound modernisation immediately after the end of the Franco–Prussian war in 1872. He created a new naval academy in Kiel and founded two new corps, indicative of the new industrial times: the Machine Engineer Corps and the Torpedo Engineer Corps. Before he left office in 1873, he had embarked his navy on a ten-year building programme that his successor, Leo von Caprivi, continued.[*]

Caprivi maintained the navy's focus on the torpedo and introduced the first torpedo division in Wilhelmshaven in October 1897 and then a second in Kiel. He is also credited with the foresight of initiating the work on the Kiel Canal, completed ten years later, in 1895, though the story of the canal has been somewhat mythologised. It was just as much commercial pressure that led to its rebuilding and rerouting, rather than only a case of innovative and far-sighted naval planning.

When Kaiser Wilhelm came to the throne, the Germany he inherited was changing rapidly. Its economy was taking off and its economic muscle was starting to be felt overseas. With growth came demand for raw materials and markets. Wilhelm felt it was high time for Germany, like the other great European nations, to have its 'place in the sun'. 'He was convinced of the relationship between naval power and world power, which was the prerequisite of national prestige, economic wealth and social stability.'[5]

In 1889, Wilhelm reorganised the navy's management. The old imperial Admiralty was dissolved and in its place two new agencies created. The Oberkommando der Marine, would report directly to him on operational matters. The second, the Reichsmarineamt (the Imperial Navy Office or RMA), the more administrative office, was led by a Secretary of State for the Navy and then shared answerability between both the emperor and the chancellor. Differences of opinion and policy quickly developed into a strong rivalry between the two organisations.

Two years later, Wilhelm met a young naval officer, Alfred Tirpitz. The Kaiser was facing constant frustrations over the navy's development. The chief of the admiralty, Count Alexander Monts, was of the old school. Wilhelm asked Tirpitz, whose torpedo boats Monts regarded as 'mere show'[†], for his opinion and was immediately impressed by the latter's fluency and strength of conviction.

Wilhelm wanted to build a cruiser fleet as an instrument that would not only carry Germany's flag around the world, but could also counter

---

[*] Georg Leo, Graf von Caprivi de Caprera de Montecuccoli (1831–99) a general, became German chancellor after Prince (*Fürst*) Otto von Bismarck in 1890–94.

[†] Alexander Graf von Monts de Mazin (1832–89) had been in the Prussian Navy before he became Chief of the Imperial Navy Admiralty after von Stosch in 1888. Monts's attitude no doubt played a part in Tirpitz taking the decision to leave torpedo boats to take a command on the SMS *Preußen*.

British dominance of world trade. Increasingly, he felt that Britain was thwarting Germany's ambitions, limiting her potential, 'The Germans, and especially the leading personalities, had the feeling that Britain was in the way of the developing German Empire.'[6]

The naval reviews at Spithead were more than just the pomp and ceremony of polished decks, shining brass and massed bands; they were designed to send the very powerful and intimidating message that Britain's maritime dominance was there to stay. And anyone challenging that would do so at their own peril. But what neither Wilhelm nor Friedrich von Hollman, the head of the Imperial Navy Office, seemed to have grasped was that it was almost impossible to pursue a global naval presence without the accompanying infrastructure of coaling, supply stations and docks.* Germany's total lack of any of these would prove to be a critical weakness.

It only needed a small, nevertheless fundamental shift from thinking about trade and the bettering of German citizens' welfare, to thinking about the power that protected that trade from rivals. Britain's maritime supremacy had done just that and Germany's increased economic ambitions set the two on a collision course.

Tirpitz's ideas could not have been further from Hollmann's thinking. In one of his most important writings, the so-called Service Memorandum (*Dienstschrift IX*) penned in 1894, he argued that 'a state which has sea interests or – what is equivalent – world interests must be able to represent them and to make its power felt beyond territorial waters. National world trade, world industry, and to a certain extent, high seas fisheries, world transportation, and colonies are impossible without a fleet capable of taking the offensive.'[7]

Tirpitz not only seemed now to accept the inevitability of the emerging conflict of interests with Great Britain (which, at this stage, the High Command did not envisage), he wanted to put a larger challenge on the table. He instinctively felt that, as Mahan had written, Germany needed a battle fleet. The *Dienstschrift* recommended a battle fleet of two squadrons, each made up of eight battleships. Furthermore, this fleet's purpose was not defensive. Quite the opposite. In one section of the *Dienstschrift* entitled 'The Natural Purpose of a Fleet is the Strategic Offensive', he wrote: 'Those who consistently advocate the defensive often

---

* Friedrich von Hollmann (1842–1913) served as State Secretary of the German Imperial Naval Office, the *Reichsmarineamt* (RMA) as part of the Cabinets of Leo von Caprivi, 1890–94, and Prince Chlodwig von Hohenlohe-Schillingsfürst, 1894–1901.

base their argument on the premise that the offensive enemy will present himself to do the decisive battle wherever that might suit us.'[8]

He believed that the purpose of the new fleet was the annihilation of the enemy, nothing less. It sounded very much like Nelson who, on the eve of Trafalgar, told his officers, 'I don't want victory. I want annihilation.'

Hollmann had supported the ideas of the *Jeune École*. Like them, he believed that second-tier naval powers could use the likes of cruisers, submarines and torpedo boats to challenge a leading naval power like Great Britain.* Tirpitz, the chief of staff to the High Command, didn't share these views. Gradually, the Kaiser came closer to sharing Tirpitz's views, focusing on the need for a fundamentally different expression of naval strength: 'Only he who dominates the sea can effectively reach his enemy and maintain, undisturbed by him, the freedom of military operations.'[9]

Wilhelm needed a long-term strategy to exploit Britain's diplomatic weaknesses while the instrument to challenge the former's maritime dominance was still being built in great secrecy. For that task, Wilhelm would rely on two men. One, Bernard von Bülow would, as Secretary of State for Foreign Affairs, steer Germany through the shifting sands of politics, diplomacy and alliance while Tirpitz built the navy that would liberate Germany from Britain's maritime shackles.

When, yet again, Hollmann failed to persuade the Reichstag to support his new naval vision, Wilhelm turned to Tirpitz. On 31 March 1897 Tirpitz received the Kaiser's telegram asking him to head up the Imperial Navy Office, opening the so-called *Ära Tirpitz*. He would remain the Navy's State Secretary until March 1916.

If Germany embarked on this path, however, there would inevitably be a period during which she would be in extreme danger. The navy that she was building would be seen as a threat long before it was powerful enough to actually deliver.

With the passing of the so-called First Navy Law, 'aimed at emancipating the fiscal foundation of the Imperial Navy from the budgetary control of the Reichstag', Tirpitz laid the cornerstone of the new Navy in 1897.[10] The Fleet that he would build would be one suited for

---

* The *Jeune École* was a school of naval officers, primarily French, who advocated the use of small, powerfully equipped vessels like torpedo boats to counter the larger nations' battleship fleets. Much of their thinking was drawn from the successes their navy had with torpedo boats in the 1883–85 war against the Chinese. In the same way, France was an early proponent of the submarine or armoured cruisers to hamper a larger nation's commerce.

'home-water', North Sea operations rather than for far-flung colonial expansion and support. The weight savings benefits from building smaller-range ships could be directly transferred to heavier armour and a wider beam, providing his ships with both more stable and better protected gunnery platforms. As far as armament was concerned, rather than compete on gunnery calibre, Tirpitz's focus would be on the gun's muzzle velocity and the design of munitions. His preference would pay handsome dividends.

Tirpitz's goal was to build a fleet that, by 1905, would consist of nineteen battleships and forty-six cruisers. Based on a seven-year construction programme, and knowing that eight older battleships would still be operational, he needed eleven new ships, two ships in each of the first two years, one in the third, and so on (the schedule is often presented as 2:2:1:2:1:1:2). The task was huge, not least because a naval construction and armaments infrastructure hardly existed in Germany.

Tirpitz wanted a fleet that would represent enough of a threat to the Royal Navy by its mere existence. All the so-called 'fleet in being' threat had to accomplish was to tie up British resources, manpower and focus, not necessarily threaten the Royal Navy's existence. At this point, it was positioned as a defensive fleet.

The threat to Britain's maritime supremacy did not necessarily come from just one rival naval power alone. Hence, the British started to use a new metric to measure her navy against other naval adversarial threats: the 'two-power standard'. The British position of superiority was henceforth to be measured against the strength of the next two foreign fleets combined, while looking to add a margin of at least 10 per cent advantage over this combined, two-navy threat. From the German side, Tirpitz saw this threat as part of what he called his 'risk theory' (*Risikotheorie*). Britain would not risk a conflict with the fleet of one of its two next rival naval powers if, weakened by an engagement with one, it would find itself at risk from the other.

Tirpitz's concept was workable when tensions between Britain and Germany's potential naval partners, either the French or the Russians, ran high. With the signing of the Entente Cordiale in 1904 and the Anglo–Russian Entente of 1907, his approach seemed less realistic. At that point, Germany had no real potential naval allies.

The British might not and, as it turned out, did not oblige by fighting the battle where Tirpitz wanted. In fact, as the war progressed the Royal Navy held back in a playing field that was increasingly distant, further to the north. When the war started, the Royal Navy did not put in place a 'close blockade' where Tirpitz could fight the battle in home waters, close to the Helgoland. When the British adopted a distant blockade, it proved to be a fatal flaw: 'Geography, which Tirpitz had always neglected when planning his fleet, now turned out to be a serious disadvantage.'[11]

The 'stopper' was put in the North Sea 'bottle', at the north by naval forces based in Scapa Flow in Orkney and in the south by locking down the Strait of Dover.* The decreasing importance in British naval strategy of a 'close blockade' of European waters was reflected in the increasing importance of Scapa Flow. Despite the role of neutrals, the effect on Germany's war economy was brutal. The country, 'had depended heavily upon international trade. Half of its raw materials and about one-third of its manufactured goods were sold abroad. The imposition of the British blockade deprived Germany of all but 20 per cent of its export market.'[12]

It was possibly during the Boer War that Wilhelm had started to understand the importance of sea power. He had strongly, although only vocally, supported the Boer leader, Krueger:† 'I realised that unless I had a Navy sufficiently strong that even you would have to think a little bit before you told me to 'Go to hell out of it' my commerce would not progress as I wanted it to, and so I determined to build a Navy which would at least command respect.'[13]

As the new century began, the British stopped and searched three German steamers, suspecting that they were carrying supplies to the rebel forces. British behaviour so enraged German public opinion that Tirpitz was able to get all the political mileage he needed from this growing Anglophobia to put a second Navy Bill on the table, 'Now we have the wind we need to blow our ship into port; the Navy Law will pass.' Managing public opinion in Germany was important and this was a heaven-sent opportunity.

In Britain, some people finally started to pay attention. Lord Selborne, at the time First Lord of the Admiralty, was one:‡ 'The result of this policy will be to place Germany in a commanding position if ever we find ourselves at war with France and Russia...Naval officers who

---

* Scapa Flow seems first to have been described as 'the stopper in the North Sea bottle' in an article in the *Daily Mail* in 1909.
† Stephanus Johannes Paulus 'Paul' Kruger (1825–1904) was president of the South African Republic from 1883–1900.
‡ William Palmer, 2nd Earl of Selborne (1859–1942), became First Lord of the Admiralty in 1900.

have seen much of the German Navy lately are all agreed that it is as good as can be.'[14]

Before long, he saw in German naval construction a more significant threat than that of either France or Russia. The numbers spoke for themselves: German naval construction costs were increasing. The 1897 Estimates had totaled 118 million marks, reached 146 million in 1900 but by 1905 topped 223 million.[15] 'The more the composition of the new German fleet is examined, the clearer it becomes that it is designed for a possible conflict with the British fleet.'[16]

After positive diplomatic moves towards the French, the British were secure enough to redistribute their ships to counter a growing German North Sea threat. Sir John Fisher* regarded the North Sea as Britain's backyard, 'a defeat in the North Sea would be catastrophic; in foreign waters a mere setback'.[17] Furthermore, the Anglo–Japanese Naval alliance in 1902 gave the British breathing space in the Pacific, reducing the pressure on a portion of Britain's imperial naval resources.†

A new Atlantic Fleet was created from the former Channel Fleet and moved to Gibraltar, a pivotal geographic location. From there, it could either reinforce the North Sea or send ships east into the Mediterranean. The new alignment of forces was not popular and some felt that Fisher had been distracted from other threats. Admiral Beresford, for example, maintained that a Franco–Russian naval alliance was a greater danger to Britain than Germany's growing power in the North Sea.‡

At this point, Tirpitz wanted to be as unostentatious as possible. Before the new German Navy gained a certain size, the only threat it represented was against itself. It was more provocation than deterrent. It could be seen as being large enough to raise alarms with the British but not large enough to dissuade the British from considering a pre-emptive strike against an emergent but still weak rival. Jacky Fisher raised the idea of a 'Copenhagen' strategy, attacking a 'holed-up Fleet in a pre-emptive Pearl Harbour-like stroke' as Nelson had done in 1807. Even the King said that such ideas were madness.[18]

---

* Admiral, Sir John 'Jacky' Fisher (1841–1920) is often regarded as the father of the modern Royal Navy. Under his watch, the Royal Navy was significantly reformed, old ships cut, new designs, like the dreadnought (named after HMS *Dreadnought*) and the battle-cruiser introduced, while the geographical allocation of fleets was reoriented to face the growing challenge of Germany's High Seas Fleet in the North Sea.
† Despite its short-term benefits, the alliance would increasingly irritate America, a source of conflict that became apparent after the end of the First World War.
‡ Admiral Lord Charles Beresford (1846–1914) became an outspoken critic of Jacky Fisher.

Fisher's privately held thoughts were voiced publicly in February 1905 by the Lord Commissioner, Arthur Lee.* He argued that Britain should 'get its blow in first, before the other side had time even to read in the papers that war had been declared'.[19] So, when in June 1904, the Kaiser hosted Edward VII for the Kielwoche (Kiel Week), Tirpitz was furious that the Kaiser put on a show of German naval strength.† It was 'unnecessarily provocative', particularly given that the British had pulled off a diplomatic coup, the same year signing the *Entente Cordiale* with France in April.‡ For the same reason, Tirpitz had decided against sending a large naval force to China four years previous during the Allied actions against the Boxers.

Fisher also worked decisively to rationalise the ships that he had. For him, less could be better. Ships that were 'too weak to fight and too slow to run away' were simply cut. At the stroke of a pen ninety ships crews were paid off and another sixty-four put into reserve.

Arguably, the British now badly stoked the fire and gave Tirpitz all the ammunition that he needed to openly accelerate German fleet construction. The Admiralty Committee on Designs spearheaded the two great innovations with which Fisher's name has come to be associated: the revolutionary new battleship, HMS *Dreadnought*, and the equally dramatic development, the battle-cruiser, HMS *Invincible*.[20] §

Britain's, or more precisely Fisher's, naval construction programme was, in Lloyd George's mind, 'a wanton and profligate ostentation'.[21] The Admirals were able to win the budget battle but the hostility it created would haunt Jellicoe.¶ *Dreadnought* also had one fatal flaw as it: '... put Britain and Germany on an equal footing, as it made Britain's power – partly based as it had been on the sheer numbers of ships available – obsolete'.[22]

---

* Arthur Lee, 1st Earl of Fareham (1868–1947) became a civil member of the Admiralty in 1900.
† Regatta week in the northern German port of Kiel is still known as *Kielwoche*.
‡ The Entente Cordiale, signed in April 1904 between Great Britain and France, was the first stepping stone to improved Franco–British relations that, while it was originally focused on colonial issues, soon took on an anti-German tone and became the cornerstone of the Allied alliance against Kaiser Wilhelm.
§ This committee was formed at the end of 1904 to push forward the design of new battleships. Its members included Philip Watts (Director of Naval Construction), Lord Kelvin, RE Froude of the Admiralty Experimental Works, Henry Gard, Sir John Thornycroft, Prince Louis of Battenberg, John Jellicoe, Reginald Bacon, Captain Henry Jackson and Rear Admiral Alfred Winslow.
¶ John Jellicoe worked closely with Sir John Fisher in this period while he was 3rd Sea Lord. It was his and Fisher's pushing for more dreadnoughts that earned JRJ Lloyd George's longer enmity and made their working together in 1917 even more difficult.

Tirpitz now had the perfect rationale for accelerating, and qualitatively improving, his own shipbuilding programme, although the costs were fast becoming politically problematic. When the German response to *Dreadnought*, SMS *Nassau*, was being planned, the costs were put at 20 per cent less than the year end estimate of 36.5 million marks. The costs – without even considering the additional burden of widening the Kaiser Wilhelm Kanal – were going to be very high.[23] The cost of the new German battle-cruiser, *von der Tann*, had increased from the 27.5 million mark appropriation to a cost of 34.5 million based on approved designs.[*] While Tirpitz worried about the parliamentary reaction to these costs, the Kaiser seemed all too oblivious, to the point where Tirpitz felt he had lost his support and offered his resignation. In fact, the Allmächtige actually felt that Tirpitz's parliamentary demands had been too small. The only way that Tirpitz could navigate the Reichtag's treacherous budgetary waters was to hold off some of the costs until the 1906 Estimates.[†]

Britain, encumbered by the Liberal Government's priorities for welfare reform, was in danger of losing the race and two of the four capital ships in the British 1907–08 building programme had to be cancelled.

Germany saw that there was a chance now to pull ahead. Fisher had effectively annulled the huge superiority that Britain had previously held in pre-dreadnoughts and levelled the playing field in Germany's favour. It was clear that the massive naval arms race was racing ahead and out of control. 'In the short term, Fisher's innovation paid dividends. By November 1909, Britain had seven commissioned dreadnoughts; Germany had two and Japan one. But Germany had eleven in building against Britain's projected ten.'[24]

'The huge British superiority in pre-dreadnoughts would become increasingly irrelevant as both sides built more dreadnoughts.'[‡] The United States, Russia, France and Italy were all increasingly sensitive to the new naval landscape and were all contemplating dreadnought building programmes. In 1916, the United States Congress passed legislation to build a navy 'second to none' and Japan, unaffected by the war in Europe,

---

[*] In May 1906, Tirpitz learned that the British planned to use 34.3cm guns on the new battleship and 30.5cm guns on the battle-cruisers (see Seligmann, Nägler and Epkenhans p. 160).
[†] The expansion of the torpedo boat arm and the establishment of the submarine service were two items held off.
[‡] Arthur Marder maintained that there was not 'a scrap of evidence' indicating that Fisher had pushed the dreadnought project in order that Germany would be obliged to widen the Kiel Canal.

was building a new fleet of heavily armed ships, to eventually expand across the Pacific.

New intelligence suggested that Germany was stockpiling nickel, an essential ingredient of hardened armour steel, and the pace of turret and gun barrel manufacture at Krupp's Essen works hinted at a much higher hull building programme than the politicians – notably Lloyd George – believed. In fact, he was contemptuous of the navy's intelligence and made it plainly obvious. The friction between him and the Admiralty was palpable: 'It looked like the ratio between the British and German Fleets could by 1912, optimistically, be 18:13. But if the Germans had reduced construction time they could have as many as eighteen or even twenty-one ships. Britain would be at a severe disadvantage.'[25]

The public clamoured for more, 'We want eight and we won't wait'. The press whipped up the frenzy, the *Observer* announcing, 'The Eight, the whole Eight, and nothing but the Eight'.* In Germany, too, the public became increasingly anti-British so that the January 1907 polls 'put a halt to the seemingly unstoppable rise of the Social Democrats, removed the Centre Party from the centre stage and gave birth to the "black-blue bloc", as the alliance of liberal and conservative parties were dubbed'.[26] It was a situation in which, ironically, Tirpitz felt that he was being pushed to go faster than he thought advisable.

The British looked to her empire for help which came in the form of new ships: HMS *Australia*, HMS *Canada* (acquired later, and paid for by the Dominion) and HMS *New Zealand*. The new relationship with France also helped. The French fleet was moved from Brest to Toulon in 1912. What the Germans had earlier only suspected was now confirmed: the British and French had divided the zones of major naval responsibility between them: the British the North Sea, the French the Mediterranean.

---

* The cry came about because of a mounting fear in the Admiralty that Germany was accelerating her shipbuilding programme. According to a memo from the Sea Lords to Sir Reginald McKenna, the First Sea Lord, 'We concur with the statement of the First Lord that there is a possibility that Germany, by the spring of 1912, will have completed 21 dreadnoughts (including large cruisers) and that there is a practical certainty that she will have 17 by that date; whereas, presuming we lay down six in the coming year, we shall only have 18...We therefore consider it of the utmost importance that power should be taken to lay down two more armoured ships in 1909–1910, making it eight in all.' (Memorandum, Sea Lords to McKenna, BL, Add. MSS 48990). Seligmann, Nägler and Epkenhans (pp. 349–351) cite recent evidence of intelligence being received from German sources (from a competitor to Krupp, Erhardt) as being the ironic truth behind Lloyd George's claim that the scare was 'contractor's gossip'.

At the point when German naval budgets continued to climb (from 259 million marks in 1906 to 419 million marks in 1909), the Tirpitz–Bülow partnership fell apart with the latter now pushing for Tirpitz to make naval concessions to the British.[27] Even Bethmann-Hollweg, Bülow's replacement as the new chancellor in July 1909, pushed for compromise with the British. With opposition from the chancellor and a fear that parliament would not fund his building programme, Tirpitz started to feel that his grand plan was falling apart. He complained to Bethmann-Hollweg, reminding him that: 'When the current naval policy was embarked upon all relevant decision-making factors were clear about the fact that we would have to pass through a danger zone. Then [as now] the ultimate question was: either to abdicate as a world power or to take risks.'[28]

In October 1913, at a time when the politicians were looking for compromise, he would voice a similarly proactive position in a speech to officers at the Imperial Navy Office:

> The General question of whether Germany should fight England for its position in the world if necessary – with the great commitment that this fight would involve – or whether it should content itself from the beginning with the position of a second-rate European continental power is in the end a matter of political belief. After all, it seems more worthy of a great nation to fight for the supreme objective and maybe perish with honour rather than to relinquish its future ingloriously.[29]

The German Army's head, General Helmuth von Moltke, regarded war as inevitable. He had worried about Russian recovery and wanted to strike before her navy could again pose a threat after the modernisation of her military. It was through Moltke that Germany found herself locked in to a two-fronted war on land. He had thought it possible to knock out Russia (whom he regarded a long-term threat) in a lightning strike before turning what he thought would now be his freed-up armies westwards to face France.*

In the years leading to the outbreak of war, Tirpitz felt 'isolated, misunderstood and sometimes lonely'.[30] The army was increasingly listened

---

* When Germany found herself locked in the two-front war, she tried once again, in 1917, to knock Russia out of the picture, this time by actively aiding the revolution. Lenin was allowed to travel across Germany in a sealed wagon to re-enter Russia through Sweden.

to by the Kaiser, who would launch Tirpitz on the preparation of a new budget amendment only to almost immediately drop his interest. The army's budgets now took increasing priority for the Kaiser. So much so that Tirpitz confessed to Captain Hopmann that he though the Kaiser looked upon the navy merely as 'a mechanical toy'.[31]

Despite the size of the fleet, the major fleet components, the battle fleet, was used sparingly during the war. In fact, on two important occasions, at the battle of the Helgoland Bight in August 1914 and at the battle of Dogger Bank in January 1915, 'isolated German forces were surprised and badly mauled by the British owing to the lack of battleship support . 1 he rest ot the tleet started calling them 'kennel hounds'.

When the naval war came, it was the battle-cruisers that took the brunt of the action. *Moltke* and *Seydlitz* were at all four actions: Yarmouth, Hartlepool, Dogger and Jutland. *Von der Tann* was at three, *Derfflinger* at two and even *Lützow* only at one, unfortunately Jutland, where she had to be scuttled by two of her own torpedo boat escorts. *Hindenburg* wouldn't be commissioned until May 1917.

The first two Commanders-in-Chief of the High Seas Fleet, von Ingenohl and von Pohl, were both timid and over-keen to follow the Kaiser's lead in not committing the battle fleet if it might put it at risk. Not so for Reinhard Scheer who challenged the British at Jutland.[*]

Much of the war's impact would be felt from actions taken below the waves, from submarines or minefields. Germany unleashed two unrestricted submarine campaigns against Great Britain and the second, launched on 1 February 1917, nearly crippled her though it greatly influenced the American entry into the war on 6 April. America's entry gave Britain the crucial additional destroyer resources needed to protect convoys coming from America through the Western Approaches without cutting back the Grand Fleet's Battle Squadrons' own protective destroyer screens.

Sea power would turn out to be a deciding factor in the war. The British blockade would gradually cut off Germany from vital resources and the Allies would be able to bring in fresh troops from the USA at the

---

[*] Jutland, what the Germans call Skagerrakschlacht, was the first and only battle fleet engagement of the war. I have written extensively about the battle in *Jutland. The Unfinished Battle* and don't wish to replicate what I wrote here. Some 150 British and ninety-nine German ships clashed in a major conflict on the North Sea, unforeseen by both sides until the last moments. While British losses were heavy, twice as much tonnage sunk and three times more sailors killed, the German fleet only ventured out on to the North Sea in strength one more time, on 18 August 1916, although it returned to port immediately the British were sighted.

moment they were most needed. Try as Tirpitz might to delay the war, events in Sarajevo took control. His new navy was not yet prepared. The High Seas Fleet failed to achieve its primary wartime goal, the breaking of British maritime supremacy.* Blockade was, though still largely un-recognised, 'one of the decisive weapons' of the war.[32]

---

* That supremacy helped Britain win the war against Germany, leading some to call Jutland the battle that 'won the war'. It was, rather, part of the Navy's role that *helped* win the war.

2

THE WAR'S CLOSING DAYS

IN SPRING 1918, Germany launched its final gamble. The second period of unrestricted submarine warfare that had started so well had by now burned itself out. On 21 March a massive German offensive involving 4 million men, 2,800 guns and 1,400 mortars was launched. Ludendorff's forces pushed 60km through the Allied lines but soon ground to a halt as transport problems beset them.* In July, the Allies counter-attacked and on 29 September broke through the Hindenburg Line into Germany. 'The soldiers, undernourished and physically and mentally exhausted, deserted in droves.'[33] German military resistance was in free fall.

However, the German Army's retreat turned into a 'scorched earth policy'.[34] 'The devastation was deliberate and systematic': mines were flooded, railway lines torn up and farms razed. At sea, the murder of civilians and neutrals continued.

Many soldiers returning to their homeland at the end of 1918 could scarcely recognise what Germany had become. It might not have been as bad as 1945 would be, but the country was in an almost complete state of collapse as revolution challenged and, in some instances, replaced the established political order. The Kaiser's departure on 9 November deepened the political vacuum and the sense of doom.

After the Pyrrhic victory at the Skagerrakschlacht, service on board one of the Emperor's ships quickly started to lose its attraction. For most officers and many of the men, sea duty was steadily replaced with the tedium of lying at anchor, imprisoned in the protective confines of the Jade river. While their countrymen were dying by the thousands in the grime and filth of the trenches, the navy only had to put up with endless days of routine. Inaction had killed its *ésprit de corps* and will to fight.

---

* Erich Ludendorff (1865–1937) was the German general who won the victories at Liège and Tannenberg. In August 1916 he was appointed to the position of Quartermaster General, putting him on a near equal footing to Field Marshal Paul von Hindenburg.

The Kaiser recognised their plight. It was 'the most thankless' of tasks that the Kaiser 'had been obliged to bestow upon his officers' in the Imperial Navy.[35]

It was clear what impact this kind of duty would have on officers wanting to prove the worth of their service, all too aware of the conditions under which civilians were having to live:

> ...to refuse you the bold offences for which you are consumed within with impatience...the task of my Fleet is therefore provisionally defence and preparedness that means abnegation and self-denial, all the more so since in defending against the enemy – unlike the army – it is not granted to have the enemy at sword point. What demands I make of officers and men by that, I ask of you in strain and strength will, be assured, I am fully aware.

Already in 1917, there had been stirrings in the ranks. At the start it was about the amount and quality of the mostly turnip-based rations. Mid-year, on 6 June, what had been the discontented mutter of complaint broke out into the first hunger strike. Sailors not only refused to eat, they also refused to work. Continued overt resistance was only averted, however, when the State Secretary for the Navy, Capelle, ordered that Menagekommission (rations committees) be established on the battleships. Not only was the order deeply unpopular with the officers (Prince Heinrich, for example, simply refused to implement it) the committees provided the discontent with an organisational structure in which it could grow: 'From these arose small cells of resistance, often politically sympathetic to the independent social democratic party, the USPD.'[36]

While this might have reduced the pressure from the ranks, the officers tightened political control. Distribution of left-wing propaganda, while forbidden by an order from Admiral Bachmann, started to grow, and on many ships, clandestine sailors' councils, fashioned along the lines of revolutionary Russian soviets, were created often with the Menagekommission that Admiral Capelle had created in June acting as the incubating vessel.*

Feelings on the lower deck were running high but most senior officers

---

* The staffing of a ship's Menagekommission usually consisted of 'men elected from the lower deck and were usually headed up by the ship's executive officer, with the paymaster and warrant officer from the ship's catering department' (Woodward, p. 68).

seemed to be completely unaware. Hipper only became aware through the most circuitous of routes. On the fast minelayer *Bremse*, a lowly sailor, Konrad Lotter, took it upon himself to make the situation known to him. He turned up one day at Hipper's house in Wilhelmshaven, requested to speak to the admiral, and astonishingly, was granted an audience. '*Es stinkt in der Flotte, Excellenz*', Lotter declared. Hipper listened, then confirmed his standing and story with his commanding officer, Bülow. Lotter's story didn't end there. He wrote to his father about what he had done. His father, concerned for his son, wrote to the Dean of Cologne Cathedral, who passed it to the Catholic Party's naval spokesperson, Dr Pfleger, who in turn passed the letter on to Admiral Capelle. What was happening in the fleet had made its way from the lower deck to the top of the Admiralty.* Capelle thought he had taken appropriate action when he appointed a commission, headed by Rear Admiral Hebbinghaus, to investigate but it turned out to be a sham. Hebbinghaus did not bother to talk to a single man from the lower decks.[†]

The diaries of Matrose Richard Strümpf, a sailor on the SMS *Helgoland* recorded that conditions were already so bad that they could explode without additional external encouragement: '*Kluft war, so dass es keiner Agitation von Außen bedürfte! Unsere herrliche Flotte ist tatsächlich an innerer Fäulnis zusammengebrochen.*' (roughly, 'The divisions were so great that no agitation from the outside was needed. The Fleet was rotten to the core.')[37]

On the fleet's flagship, *Friedrich der Große*, affectionately known by her crew as the 'Big Fritz', a supreme council was elected. One of the ship's stokers was elected chairman. It was hardly surprising that the core revolutionary leadership should be recruited from these men. Theirs was a thankless, back-breaking toil in scorching heat in the very bowels of the ship. It wasn't uncommon to hear of stokers coming up for air and passing out on deck.

In June, the coaling gear on *Prinzregent Luitpold* was sabotaged. The lines were cut and the blocks thrown overboard. Later, on her way to Wilhelmshaven through the Kiel Canal, her engines were shut down, causing her to drift and block the waterway. On the 6th, the stokers announced they would not eat the dried vegetables that had been prepared for their mess (On *Helgoland*, a similar situation occurred when

---

* Pfleger had heard rumours and reports of the same discontent on *Friedrich der Große*, *Prinzregent Luitpold*, *Pilau* and *Thüringen*, where officers sitting in the wardroom had had water poured on them (Source: Woodward, p. 70).
[†] Hebbinghaus was Head of the Admiralty's General Department.

sailors refused to load flour that had gone bad). In July, it all blew up again. Sailors on *Friedrich der Große* had been in a night-firing exercise and afterwards had eaten some bread earmarked for the following day. When they were refused bread the next day, they in turn refused to work and the situation was only righted when an officer arranged for them to receive porridge. It wasn't complicated; it was a basic lack of respect or concern by the officers for their men's well-being. On the 19th, men on *Prinzregent Luitpold* called a hunger strike. Worms had been found in the soup. There were similar food issues – this time related to the turnips – on *Posen*. On the next day, 137 sailors walked off *Pillau* when their leave had been cancelled. When they were persuaded back on board, the sailors finished the work that had been interrupted to show their continued good faith. Most disturbing, on the *König Albert*, the captain, Kapitän Thorbecke, had fallen overboard and drowned. He 'had a reputation in the Fleet of great severity' and his death, on 25 July, was just days after he had punished a sailor for having copies of the socialist newspaper, *Vorwärts*, on board. Surely his death could not have been co-incidental.[38]

Some of the movement's leaders were clearly of an extreme left-wing political hue: Beckers and Köbes were probably anarchists, Sachse a 'radical of the left', Reichpietsch 'inclined to the USPD' and Weber SPD. But Sachse's 'ingrained sense of contrariness' took him from one extreme to the other, the extremes of the left to right-wing National Socialism. In 1944, ironically, he was executed by the Nazis for being a member of the communist Uhrig group.* Nevertheless, the vast majority of men saw these events in a different light, 'more akin to a strike than a mutiny':

'The sailors, in the spirit of trade unionism, were concerned with small tangible improvements in their daily lives, not lofty political ideals.'[39]

The sailors had been holed up in Wilhelmshaven for months and, in these conditions, bad personnel management fed on the already exceedingly low morale: '...*wobei Langweile und schlechste Menschenführung die Moral der Besatzung zerrütteten* (boredom and the worst personnel management destroyed the crews).[40]

On *Prinzregent Luitpold,* lying at anchor in the lower Elbe river, the order was given to weigh anchor to get under way. Not only were the

---

* There were probably some *agents provocateurs* amongst the revolutionaries: Matrose Adams on *Westfalen* was probably one. Others complained that they were simply bullied into compliance with the revolutionaries.

orders ignored, the stokers supposedly extinguished the bunker fires.* Woodward disputed that the stokers put the bunker fires out saying that if this happened, it would have signalled a new and dangerous escalation:

> It has become a part of left-wing legend that the engine-room complements of the big ships of the High Seas Fleet extinguished the fires in their boilers during these mutinies so that they could not put to sea. The story was given worldwide publicity by a highly inaccurate play called *Draw the Fires* by Ernst Toller,[†] but in fact only once were fires drawn in a ship and this was on 1 November, when the engine room complement of the *Friedrich der Große*, protecting the minesweepers off Borkhum, did do so.[41]

A week later, there was a more serious incident. On 31 July, a group of sailors on the *Prinzregent Luitpold* had wanted to see a film. It was to be shown aboard, which was 'something of a novelty at the time', when shore-based training had been cancelled because of bad weather. When the weather improved and the training re-instigated, the film was cancelled. On 1 August, a group of stokers walked off the ship. They tried to hold a meeting in a freight yard aboard a rail wagon, were refused and escorted back. The ship's captain, *Kapitän zur See* Karl von Hornhardt, however, decided to make an example and arrested eleven of them.

The rising tension could not be contained any longer. The next day, 2 August, tenfold the original number, between 350 and 600 sailors, left the ship, forced their way past the armed sentries and went to the dyke at Rusterstiel.[‡] The sight of sailors thronging through Wilhelmshaven streets had never been seen before and the event would become known as '*der großer Ausmarsch*'.

They held a small meeting outside the guesthouse *der weißer Schwan* at which one of the speakers was the young, twenty-five-year-old politically driven sailor, Albin Köbes, supported the USPD position.[§]

---

* Horn (p. 417) talks of other occasions when stokers took decisive action in their engine rooms. He says that the boiler fires were put out on the *Strasburg* on 26 October 1918 when the crew had 'tried to sink the ship by opening the flood gates'. I think he meant 'sea-cocks'.
† Toller, Ernst. *Draw the Fires! An Historical Play* (John Lane, 1935). Meurer had been in command and ended the protest with a promise of no punishment.
‡ The numbers are not exact. Kinzler and Tillman (p. 78), for example, just state '*über 400*'.
§ Carsten (p. 119) mentions that there were a number of meetings being held on 2 August in Wilhelmshaven pubs. At one, twenty sailors who had been listening to a presentation on the causes of war, were arrested. In another, six. Albin Köbes (1892–1917) had volunteered for naval service on the battleship *Prinzregent Luitpold*. He gradually became more embittered by the war and the treatment of the lower deck.

Another was Johann Beckers. It did not take much to whip the mood of the sailors who were already angry. On the surface, the protest did not seem to be about a major issue. However, it was not really just about what had happened that day, it was about the rights of ordinary sailors, and in particular the rights of a stoker, to enjoy, like any officer, the simple pleasures of visiting a cinema. For crews that had been so thoroughly badly treated, it was the last straw. That gesture was symbolic of the manner in which they were viewed, valued and treated.

A sergeant of the Marine Artillery was sent to close down the meeting but the men insisted that they go back without an escort. The result was that they were shadowed the whole way back until one of the ship's officers, Lieutenant-Commander von Wiehe, joined them, pedalling along on his bike. As quickly as possible, seventy-five sailors were arrested and *Prinzregent Luitpold* was sent to the Schillig Roads to isolate the ship.* But the fuse had already been lit. Demonstrations and work stoppages followed on *Friedrich der Große* and *Kaiserin* and early on 5 August, *Kaiserin*, *König Albert* and *Kaiser* were sent to join *Prinzregent Luitpold* at the head of the Jade basin and from there to the Kiel Kanal locks at Brunsbüttel.

Despite these actions, trouble continued. It was now clear that the feelings of resentment and the shared commitment to do something about it were spreading to other ships. On *Rheinland*, after leave had been cancelled, a protest broke out on 16 August. On *Westfalen*, orders were openly refused and up to forty men left the ship in protest against extra rations not being handed out after coaling. In October, one of *Moltke*'s crew was arrested for shouting peace slogans. Other ships, apparently, were also involved. It may be difficult to rely on Willi Sachse's account (known to be 'very much an exhibitionist, greatly exaggerating the entire scale of events in the Fleet and his own share in them')[42] but, he reported the occurrence of similar instances on *Große Kurfürst*, *Helgoland*, *Ostfriesland*, the patrol vessel *Zieten* and *Schwaben*.

---

* Again, while numbers are not precise, directionally this seems correct. Rackwitz, for example, says that seventy-six were arrested (p. 19). Woodward is by far the most precise (p. 77): 200 were arrested and jailed, 150 more were demoted, seventy-seven were found guilty and five were sentenced to death. Two of these sentences (Köbes from *Prinzregent Luitpold* and Reichspietsch from *Friedrich der Große*) were carried out. Of those remaining, eight received ten to fifteen years' penal servitude, eleven between five to ten years, four were imprisoned from five to ten years, two were imprisoned from two to five years, twenty-one were imprisoned from one to two years and twenty-four were imprisoned for more than a year. On *Helgoland*, Richard Linke received ten years' penal servitude. Petty Officer telegraphist Franz Schlegel on *Zieten* and *Bieber* on *Helgoland* each received ten-year sentences (reduced to six on appeal) and Bräumer on *Kaiserin* received twelve years (reduced to ten on appeal).

It went on for three days. The fleet was in turmoil. Scheer had to step in to bring about the end to the spiralling chaos, and he had to be seen to do so without wavering. The unrest 'was put down with an iron hand and extremely severely punished'. ('*die mit eisener Hand unterdrückt und furchtbar bestraft worden waren*'.)[43]

The actions might have been harsh but, given what happened later, did Scheer have much choice? Maybe he had but he seemed out of touch and needed to better understand conditions on the lower deck and he needed to better understand the varied motivations of the 'mutineers'. An Oberheizer from *Friedrich der Große*, Willy Weber, said that 'nobody wanted a revolution, we just wanted to be treated more like human beings'.[44] The officers' strategy should, at the very least, have tried to divide the true revolutionaries from the merely demoralised, downtrodden or embittered. Weber was lucky to have his death sentence commuted. Another sailor on *Westfalen* agreed: 'I never thought that this could be dangerous to the ship or to state.'[45]

Despite the severity of local reaction, it also seems clear now that the fast-emerging danger was not recognised or understood for what it would become. Gustav Stresemann, later to be chancellor and foreign minister, commented at the time: 'We knew what had happened at Wilhelmshaven, and we knew that it was comparatively unimportant.'[46]

However, it must be said that Scheer's own report:

> ...stands up well as a reasonably accurate account of what happened, a reasonably accurate diagnosis of the causes of the troubles and an intelligent programme of reform. Only in his account of the USPD involvement does he seem to have been wildly astray, while his theory that there was a USPD conspiracy is matched by the claim of the communists that there was such a conspiracy, not by the USPD but by a party still further to the left, the Spartacists, who were the forerunners of the communists in Germany.[47]

The ships on which it seemed that discipline had most broken down were sent off to the Schillig Roads, at the North Sea entrance to the Jade basin. It was hoped that this would isolate them and put an end to the contagion. Interrogation of the ringleaders immediately got under way.

Two of the most vocal were quickly confirmed as the main ringleaders: twenty-five-year-old Albin Köbes and Max Reichpietsch, aged twenty-three. Under questioning, Reichpietsch eventually admitted to having met with the USPD in Berlin in June 1917. In fact, he had already been a party member for five years who, with his fellow conspirators, had succeeded in collecting 4,000 signatures of support (about seven per cent of the crews of the Fleet).[48] The young sailor had visited USPD politicians in Berlin and with only a vague promise of support from one party member, the cautious Wilhelm Dittmann, made out that the USPD had given the sailors their full backing.* It was more likely Luise Zietz, 'a short, vehement woman', who gave him the encouragement he needed.[49] She might have fallen for Reichpietsch, 'the fair-haired, blue-eyed young sailor'. The young sailor had gradually fallen from being regarded as 'top notch' after being demoted to seaman second class when he'd been accused of theft. The Party Secretary, Haase, warned Reichpietsch about the consequences of over-promising: 'that he might make rash remarks which could be used against him'.[50]

On 5 September, at Wahner Heide, near Cologne, a twenty-man firing squad was drawn up and the two sailors Reichpietsch and Köbes executed.† Others escaped execution. Weber, Johann Beckers, Willy Sachse, the youngest, plus three others, all had their sentences commuted to fifteen years' penal servitude in Rensburg prison. The harshness of the sentence remains controversial till today. Dr Stephan Huck, the Director of the German Naval Museum at Wilhelmshaven and a former officer, called it a singular and unprecedented case in German military history: 'beispielloser und einmaliger Vorgang in der Militärjustiz der Kaiserlichen Marine im Ersten Weltkrieg'.[51]

In the end, it was Sachse who buckled, saying that he'd been led astray by left-wingers but that he had worked very closely with Reichpietsch. The two of them had formed the food committee on the Friedrich der Große and had both redirected and politicised its role. Sachse, however, was clearly as committed as Reichpietsch. The twenty-one-year-old had been in the Social Democratic Youth movement even before the war. Although he managed to escape a death penalty, the Nazis would later execute him for his alleged involvement in the July plot against Hitler. He died on 21 August 1944 in Brandenburg prison.

* Wilhelm Dittmann (1874–1954) was a German Social Democrat and writer who split with his former party and joined the ranks of the USPD. He was imprisoned the following January, 1918, for his part in the Berlin munition factory strikes. He was released in October 1918 by Prince Max von Baden under a general amnesty.
† Reichpietsch and Köbes became martyrs for the new East German Communist state. The DDR Navy named two patrol vessels after the executed sailors.

Another, Beckers, was lucky to get off. He and Köbes had not been convinced of the value of a food committee and far preferred the idea of setting up a sailors' council, a soviet. When Dittmann would not meet them, their mistrust was confirmed. The possibility of having the death sentence commuted was dangled before him, to try to gain more information on the structure of the revolutionary machine in Berlin.*

What Hipper feared most at this point was a loss of face. He felt that the shame of the fleet and its officers would be far worse without a last fight. 'What I fear is that when peace comes all the blame will be heaped on the Navy and nobody will have a good word to say for it, and it will be all the worse if the Fleet, the big capital ships, have never been in action.'[52]

The army was crumbling. In the last months of the war 'up to a million men went voluntarily into captivity or deserted' in a 'cloaked military strike'.[53] By September, the military knew the game was up and put its voice behind a ceasefire. The navy, on the other hand, was still a force to be reckoned with. Scheer and von Trotha thought like Hipper: it was 'better to go down with honour'.[54]

Against this background, Prince Max of Baden was trying to negotiate an end to the war. He'd been appointed chancellor on 4 October and had written to the US president seeking an end to the war. Woodrow Wilson had, in 1916, already positioned his country as the arbiter of a European peace. In May, he outlined his ideas for a 'League of Nations' and in December Wilson sent an 'Appeal for Peace' without Allied knowledge. 'The note had been sent out only one week after German Chancellor Bethmann-Hollweg had offered a peace note on behalf of the Central Powers, and consequently the Allies suspected the USA of acting in co-operation with Germany.'[55]

Ths late in the war, however, Britain was heavily dependent on the Americans for resources, both financial and material. Nitro-cellulose, 40 per cent of its flour imports (according to the food controller), lubricating oil and petrol were all primarily sourced from the Americans.

These were years of privation for both Britain and Germany – particularly for Germany. German agriculture was 'severely handicapped by lack of labour', while its importation of Chilean saltpetre and raw phosphates (an essential chemical ingredient for fertilizers) had been cut drastically by the blockade.[56] The winter of 1916/17 became known as the 'Turnip Winter': the weekly potato ration was reduced

---

* The possibilities were either fifteen years' penal servitude or duty at the Western Front with a naval brigade.

to 500 grams with one kilogram of turnips as a supplement. The meat ration was reduced to 400 grams and ersatz butter, margarine, was introduced.

The continued sinking of American cargo and passenger ships with its consequent loss of life, and the revelations of the Zimmerman telegram, helped secure Wilson's entry of his country into the war.* In the end, it was Germany's resumption of unrestricted submarine warfare on 1 February 1917 that broke the diplomatic deadlock with the United States.

America's declaration of war on Germany had its most immediate effect on bolstering Allied naval resources, allowing for the introduction of the convoy system.† While the Flanders flotilla could claim enormous success in the Channel, only 138 of 16,539 vessels in convoy across the Atlantic were sunk from June 1917 to November 1918.[57]

Wilson was now within the Allied camp and, consequently, in a better position to push his version of peace terms. The note that Prince Max sent to Wilson assumed that the president's 'Fourteen Points' (unveiled on 8 January 1918) would be the basis of peace negotiations. French intelligence intercepted the communication.

The British never accepted the first two points of Wilson's declaration. The idea that they could not enter into secret agreements or that they should bow to outside pressure to reduce their maritime control in time of war was anathema. The British had used their naval and maritime strength across the world's oceans as a means to grow and defend their empire for decades. Any weakening of its independence in this sphere, any compromise to Wilson's second point, that of freedom of the seas, had dire consequences for a sea power such as Great Britain. Together with the French, they felt that Wilson's proposals, '...might give away at the peace table what the soldiers had been fighting for so bitterly – a settlement that would put an end to future German aggression.'[58]

Soon after, on 7 October, the Allied powers held an unofficial meeting in which the United States was not asked to participate. Eight principles of negotiation were drawn up. Despite some detailed proposals from Admiral GPW Hope representing the Admiralty, he mentioned nothing

---

* The Zimmerman telegram was a secret German Foreign office communication in January 1917 to Mexico proposing a military alliance between the two countries and German support in any effort to regain territories annexed by the United States in the nineteenth century (Texas, California, Arizona and New Mexico) if America entered the war on the Allied side. It was intercepted by British intelligence and passed to the Americans.
† Already by May 1918, around one million American troops would be serving in France.

about the disposal of either the German or Austrian surface fleets.* Around this time, on 13 October, an Admiralty memorandum titled 'The Case for Surrender of the German Fleet as an Article of the Armistice' started to circulate. Its author was and remains unknown. It argued that no improvements could be made in its naval forces while the negotiations were under way and, moreover, the Germans should be pressured in a way 'that would preclude refusal of the final Peace settlement'.[59] Surrender of their fleet would achieve that.

Wilson's position on 'freedom of the seas' was found by the British to be equally dangerous. Wemyss presented the Admiralty position on 17 October:

> It would prevent us from using our strongest weapon and place in the hands of our enemy a power which he does not possess. The value of military power, both for attack and defence, would be enhanced, and a radius of action increased, while the value of naval power for attack and defence and its radius of action would be correspondingly diminished.[60]

Britain's position was significantly different:

> The British idea of the Freedom of the Seas is free and unfettered access in time of peace, to all the seas by all who wish to cross them 'upon their lawful occasion'; in time of war this privilege must be fought for by belligerent navies, causing as little inconvenience as possible to neutrals, but maintaining the rights of capture of belligerent merchant ships and of searching neutral merchant ships in order to verify their nationality and prevent their aiding a belligerent...Acceptance of this proposal (Wilson's) would result in making sea-power of little value to a nation dependent upon it for existence whilst providing a military power with free lines of overseas communications.[61]

The military men on both sides – American and British – at least the ones who had been on the front line, were wary of the politicians. Admiral Sims

---

* Admiral Sir George Price Hope (1869–1959) was made Deputy First Sea Lord in 1918 and joined the Armistice talks in Compiègne. His points included the following (see Trask, p. 315): cessation of submarine warfare; return to home harbour of all submarines; assembly of surface fleet at specified ports; submission of details on minefield locations; surrender of enemy forts such as Helgoland.

expressed his reservations strongly to Admiral Bayley: 'You may be sure that we military men will do all we can to keep the politicians from letting us down.'[62]

In Germany, Scheer 'violently opposed' the idea that the unrestricted submarine campaign should be suspended as the basis for talks to start. He had, '...put all his hopes for the future into U-boats and...still believed that the campaign should be kept going, as a means of keeping pressure on the enemy for milder terms.'[63]

Within two weeks of Prince Max's original note, the American position had toughened. In Germany the proposals were rejected by all except the Independent Socialists. On 14 October, Wilson issued another note. It was shortly after the torpedoing of the Leinster with the loss of more than 500 of the 720 on board.* Scheer backed down and on 20 October a note was sent to Wilson: 'In order to avoid anything that might hamper the work of peace, the German Government had caused orders to be dispatched to all submarine commanders precluding the torpedoing of passenger ships.'[64]

Despite backing down, the damage had been done, a direct result of the Navy's stubbornness. Two weeks now passed between the initial contact and Wilson's new, much tougher, position for Germany's uncon-ditional surrender, stated on 23 October. Scheer, however, looked at the episode in an entirely different light from those around him. He saw it as freeing up the fleet for major independent action, that it 'had regained its liberty of action' in no longer needing to support the U-boat campaign.[65] The British were able to pull destroyer submarine protection back up to Rosyth for the Grand Fleet, making it more likely that a sortie of the Grand Fleet could be undertaken and – ironically – that Scheer would start thinking of renewed action by the High Seas Fleet (HSF). It would be the genesis of Plan 19 – the last sortie – that Scheer now started to formulate with his chief of Staff, Magnus von Levetzow.†

The European leaders of the Allied alliance were furious about Wilson's meddling: 'Lloyd George and Clemenceau vie with each other in scoffing at the President, and Sonnino‡ is almost openly apprehensive of allowing him to interfere in European politics.'[66]

---

* Rackwitz (p. 27) cites a substantially different death toll: 501 out of a total of 771 passengers and crew.
† Magnus von Levetzow (1871–1939) was Chief of Staff of the Seekriegsleitung in 1918 and the planning mind behind Operation Albion in 1917 and the relaunch of unrestricted submarine warfare.
‡ Sidney Costantino, Baron Sonnino (1847–1922) was the Italian Minister of Foreign Affairs during the war.

In some sense, it might have been that since 'there was by no means a close identity of interests' among the Allies, some of the thornier issues were purposely left alone so as not to split the Allied front at the start of negotiations.[67] The British Admiralty's position was the opposite. While their views might have 'disturbed' the War Cabinet, Beatty believed that the terms of Armistice should closely resemble what eventual peace terms would likely be. The American interpretation, again, was that, 'If we are to get a fair and permanent peace, we do not want Germany beaten any worse than she is. If she should be reduced to a point where England and France should think they did not need our help any more, they would rub it in beyond reason.'[68]

But it wasn't entirely because of wanting to keep Britain down, it was also that the Americans were frightened of the spectre of Bolshevism. From that point of view, the American approach was actually far-sighted.

Things got so bad that, when asked if America might seek a separate peace if Wilson's Fourteen Points continued to be frustrated, Colonel House, his closest confidant and advisor* answered: 'It might'.[69] Britain's insistence on keeping its version of 'freedom of the seas' did not waver, and now Britain also supported the demands for compensation, mainly from the French and Belgians. It was only Wilson's diplomatic intervention at this point that held things together. He wrote soothingly to Lloyd George that: 'There is no danger of it [blockade] being abolished' and the prime minister reciprocated, saying that he would agree to discussion of the 'freedom of the seas' but not its principle.

While the British Admiralty did not think there was any danger of continued German fleet action, Marder cited Sir Henry Newbolt, who would complete Sir Julian Corbett's official history of the naval war, in saying that Hipper and Scheer were both 'striving with the greatest energy to provoke a Fleet action whilst the negotiations were proceeding'.[70] Scheer was not necessarily of the opinion that such an action could 'decisively influence the course of events' but that it was important 'from the moral point of view, a question of the honour and existence of the German Navy to have done its utmost in the last battle'.[71] Von Trotha agreed. A last symbolic battle was the only way to lay the foundations for a new German Navy. It would remove the stain of defeat and strongly support Germany's right-wing storyline of 'stab in the back'.

* Edward M House (1858–1938), usually known as Colonel House even though he had never held a military position, was a Texas politician and diplomat. He became an influential personal advisor to Woodrow Wilson on European issues and the peace conference.

'Operational Plan 19' was the result. The Navy's plan might have been around since April 1918, but now it was made public (on 22 October) when Kapitän von Levetzow, the Admiralstab's Operations Division Chief of Staff, announced that: 'The forces of the High Seas Fleet are to be employed to strike a blow against the English Fleet,' and the U-boats were to play an important role. It led Hipper to end the unrestricted submarine war.

On the 20th a recall order went out to the U-boats to return to harbour. At this point, only a small number of boats were affected. The Naval Staff had other ideas for how the seventeen boats could be better employed.[72] Preparations for the final battle necessarily brought about an end to unrestricted submarine warfare. The fleet had a new role, one in which Hipper even seriously considered asking the Kaiser to personally participate.[73]

Six boats were reassigned to patrol British North Sea bases and a further twenty-four sent from Germany to reinforce the submarine trap. The subsequent performance of these thirty boats was unimpressive: two were sunk on 28 October (*U.78* by British submarine *G.2* and *UB.116* by a controlled minefield in Scapa Flow)

The plan called for a dual attack by light cruisers and destroyers on both the Flanders coast and the Thames Estuary, with von Reuter's battle-cruisers in support for an attack on Thames shipping.* The aim was to draw the Grand Fleet (which in April had moved south, from Scapa to Rosyth, a redeployment unknown to Scheer) towards the awaiting High Seas Fleet at Terschelling.

The officers developed the plan in such secrecy that neither the Kaiser nor the chancellor were told. Such behaviour earned it the apt description *'Meuterei der Admirale'* (the admirals' mutiny).

On 28 October initial arrangements were made to bring the attacking elements together, ready for the planned sortie on the following day. Some of the destroyers and cruisers were sent off to the Jade basin, at the Schillig Roads, to await further orders. Rumours of an impending action started to spread. Light cruisers of the 4th Scouting Group were in Cuxhaven, loading mines, 'something that was never done unless a real operation was planned'.[74] Another good indication was when *Moltke's* second funnel was painted red (painting the funnels red and yellow were to aid night

---

* The battle-cruisers were to wait for the Thames attack at Black Deep, 18 miles north of Margate and 20 miles east of Foulness Point. Four of the Jutland veterans would be joined by the new SMS *Hindenburg*, which would be von Reuter's flagship.

recognition). Two days before, *Strasburg's* crew had put out the boiler fires. As the ships of the 4th Scouting Group (Aufklärunggruppe) started to take on oil and coal, *Regensberg's* sailors refused to clear away mess equipment, while others came on deck dressed not in their engine room uniforms but for shore leave.

HIGH SEAS FLEET SCOUTING GROUPS DURING MUTINY

Group	Ships	Officers
First Scouting Group (Erste Aufklärungs-gruppe)	*Seydlitz, Derfflinger Moltke, von der Tann, Hindenburg*	Kontreadmiral Ludwig von Reuter, Kapitän Carl Feldmann
Fourth Scouting Group	*Stralsund, Brummer, Bremse, Regensburg, Strasburg, Frankfurt*	Kontreadmiral Johannes von Karpf

As ships gathered at the Schillig Roads, readying for their departure on the 30th, it was clear that few of the men shared Hipper's enthusiasm for the plan described by the German historian Wilhelm Diest as 'not a militarily necessary operation but [it was] a political demonstration'.[75] Hipper noted that fifty-eight men were absent without leave on *von der Tann*, while on *Derfflinger* it was closer to one hundred.[*] *König* wasn't even able to leave her dockside berth before 'mutinous dockyard workers had swarmed on board and torn down the war flag'.[76] Neither did it help the mood on the ship when the rumour went around like wildfire (*'ging wie ein Lauffeuer durch ganzes Schiffe'*) that the captain, Kapitän zur See Hans-Carl von Schlick, had 'done a runner'.[77]

The sailors believed that Scheer's planned action could have a very negative impact on the peace process. 'Not only were the crews faced with defeat and death but they believed that, if the Germans did attack, the Allies would break off the Armistice negotiations.'[78]

Even Holtzendorf, the architect of the submarine campaign, thought the plan 'adventurist'. Most of the ranks just wanted the war to come to an end. Living in barracks on shore, the privations that the civilian

[*] See Wolz (p. 177). Between 200 and 300 men from *Derfflinger* and *von der Tann* left their ships at the lock gates and temporarily vanished. While they were successfully rounded up, it gave a sense of what might be to come.

population was suffering were all too clear. Under Hipper and his officers in Wilhelmshaven, the ground was becoming unsteady. Political power, particularly in north Germany, was decisively shifting to the left. Two days before, on 28 October, the city of Wilhelmshaven fell under the control of the Workers' and Soldiers' Council (Arbeiter und Soldatenrat).

On the ships, the mettle of the officers was being tested. It was not just the ships that were in bad condition, their officers no longer felt the same pride and confidence as they had at Jutland. Most had 'requested or had been transferred to more productive duties' to serve on destroyers and submarines.[79] This drain left the fleet devoid of the best deck officers, and without the kind of leadership that would inspire men to willingly go back to war. There were, of course, notable exceptions. One was Wilhelm Tägert, *Seydlitz*'s commanding officer. 'The men are standing by me and are showing it to me in (a) touching manner and I definitely believe I can get them through this honourably.'[80]

A few threw in the towel, like the captain of the 2nd SG *Nürnberg*, who lowered his own pennant when the red flag went up and left the ship, declaring that he no longer felt responsible for the men. '*Der Kommandant des Kleinen Kreuzers Nürnberg holte bei Setzen der rote Flagge seinen Wimpel nieder und erklärte sich für nicht zuständig – er verließ das Schiff.*'[81] ('The commander of the light cruiser *Nürnberg* struck his pennant in place of the red flag and left the ship, declaring that he no longer felt responsible.')

In the ships, many of the sailors were now actively resisting any actions that could prolong the war. On the *Thüringen* a representative from the lower deck went to see the first officer: '*...und erklärte, dass der geplante Flottenverstoß wohl nicht in Sinne der neuen Regierung.* To which the officer replied '*Ja, das ist Ihre Regierung!*' (words to the effect that 'the planned Fleet sortie was not in line with the new government's wishes', to which the officer replied, 'it is against *your* government's wishes').

This was significant because it meant that the sailors felt a legitimacy for what they were doing. Resistance to continued war was supporting the (not just their) government's position. Gone was the idea of blind obedience to any order from a superior, a kind of obedience that Matrose Strumpf labelled *Kadavergehorsam* (corpse-like obedience).[82] It was the officers who were out of sync, not the men: '*Wie sie es sahen, übten sie legitime Staatsnotwehr und verteidigen das höhere Recht; wenn sie meuterten, dann meuterten sie gegen Meuterei.*' (Roughly, 'As they saw it, they were practising a legitimate state emergency and protecting a higher right. If they were mutineers, then they were in mutiny against other mutineers.')[83]

The officers tried to keep the battle-planning secret, telling the men that it was only an exercise that was in the offing. What made the men suspicious was that far too much ammunition was being brought on board.

HIGH SEAS FLEET BATTLE FLEET SQUADRONS DURING MUTINY

Squadron	Ships	Officers
First Squadron (Erste Geschwader)	*Ostfriesland, Oldenburg, Thüringen, Helgoland, Posen, Nassau, Rheinland, Westfaleng*	Vizeadmiral Friedrich Boedicker, Kontreadmiral Johannes Hartog (2iC)
Third	*Prinzregent Luitpold, Große Kurfürst, Markgraf, Kronprinz Wilhelm, Dayern*	Vizeadmiral Hugo Kraft, Kontreadmiral Constanz Feldt (2iC)
Fourth	*Kaiser, Kaiserin König Albert Prinzregent Luitpold, Friedrich der Große*	Vizeadmiral Hugo Meurer, Kontreadmiral Ernst Goette (2iC)

As the ships overnighted on 29 October, the unrest on the five battleships of the III Battleship Squadron was almost tangible. On a significant number of ships, crews refused to raise anchor, while the stokers threatened to put out the boiler fires.

When the crews of ships from *Thüringen* and *Helgoland* refused orders, the taste for a last, *Götterdämmerung*-like foray finally evaporated. *Thüringen's* captain had talked of going down fighting in apocalyptic terms: '*Wir verfeurern unsere letzten 2000 Schuß und wollen mit wehende Fahne untergehen.*'[84] ('We will keep firing to the last round and will go down with our flags flying.) However, the day nearly ended in disaster, a bloodbath. As she was about to get under way on 31 October, the ship's electricity was cut, causing the anchor lift to fail. An officer tried to go below decks to find out what was happening but found his way blocked by a crowd of yelling sailors. At the same moment the captain on the bridge heard that the stokers had put out the ship's fires. The '*Pestschiff*' (plague ship), as some of the officers knew her, wasn't going to go anywhere fast.* The captain ordered his officers to the bridge and then, as a group, they went down into the ship: '*In den vollständig dunkeln Gängen und Räumen standen die Matrosen und Heizer herum, schweigend und wohl auch selbst bedrückt von dem Gefühl, das ganz unerhörtes vor sich ging.*'[85] ('Sailors and stokers were standing around, silent in the blacked out corridors and cabins. While they were silent, they must have been under the impression that something unheard of was going on.')

They couldn't do anything as the culprits had locked themselves behind bulkheads. Four hundred or so sailors had joined the action, a third of the ship.

Hipper ordered an armed response. He sent a submarine, the *U.135*, commanded by a veteran, Lieutenant-Commander Johannes Spiess, to make it clear to the mutineers that they would be fired upon if they did not back down. Spiess had been Otto Weddingen's first lieutenant and a man Hipper trusted, however, Spiess did not reciprocate the trust that had been placed in him: he asked for written orders, which both Hipper and Commodore Michelson, his senior officer, refused to give him.

Nevertheless, Spiess undertook his task in full faith of its validity. His submarine approached the *Thüringen* along with five torpedo boats from the 4th Half-Flotilla (*B.109*, *B.97*, *B112*, *B.110* and *B.111*) and two transports with 250 armed marines aboard. *B.97* slowly passed down the battleship's hull, from bow to stern, threatening to torpedo it if the mutineers did not fall in line within ten minutes. From the mast, the Stander-Z, the attack flag, fluttered.[†] It was clear that they meant business. When the torpedo boat got amidships, the pennant dipped and the boat turned away. A message had been sent to hold fire when a signal was received saying that the mutineers were backing down.

Helgoland's crew were dealt with in the same manner. There, the crew even manned some of the main batteries and threatened Spiess and *B.97*. Spiess would have fired on *Thüringen*. He later maintained that, 'If we had fired into the forward battery of the *Thüringen,* where the mutineers were, discipline would have been re-established in the Fleet.'[86]

According to Hipper, 'the order to fire had already been given when the mutineers finally came up and were taken away without

---

* *Kapitänleutnant* Johann Heinemann, on the *Köln*, was close by and watched the drama unfold. He was able to see the radio traffic sent back to Hipper and consequently was completely informed of what was happening (RM/44 p. 33).
† The *Stander-Z* is the German Navy's red pennant, hoisted to signal 'Attack!'

offering resistance'.[87] ('*gaben diese auf und ließen sich schließlich wider-standlos festnehmen*').[88]

Once back in harbour, *Thüringen's* mutineers were taken ashore to be sent to Oslebshausen barracks near Bremen. They would not be alone. Others followed. Revolutionary elements were sent ashore from *Helgoland, Markgraf, König* and *Friedrich der Große*. Also included were twenty stokers from *Oldenburg*. They had been ordered to go over to *Thüringen* to work her boilers.* Their officer tried to help their cause by saying that they had not wanted to exchange their proud cap tallies with those of a disgraced ship. It did not work. The fact that Scheer had not informed others of his intentions made them feel that they were actually following the government's line, which in turn made their actions patriotic not mutinous.

Levetzow was a hardliner. When he read the reports of the incident, he recalled Sir John Jervis's threat to HMS *Marlborough's* crew at the 1797 Spithead mutiny. He had been fully in favour of a more overt, more aggressive stance: his marginalia accused Hipper and Trotha, whom he said had 'completely failed'. 'Where was Lord (sic) Jervis?' he asked.[89]

Hipper had little choice now. He gave the orders for the sortie to be cancelled under the face-saving pretext that bad weather was closing in. Scheer was furious: 'There was no doubt that despite the greatest secrecy, the men had been told about an operation in preparation, and in the belief that they were going to be sacrificed for nothing...[they] would apparently refuse orders at the decisive moment... .'[90]

Back in port, things were stirring on other ships. The crews had been pent up and rumours were running wild. The mass arrests and offloading of crews had been witnessed and word of the *Thüringen's* near-fatal stand-off had passed around. Shore meetings were called.

Preparations for mass resistance now got underway and the Sailors' Committee passed a message around the ships: 'Guarded meeting after dark at the New Soldier's Cemetery. Send delegates from every unit.'†They came to the meeting individually, in one's and two's, to avoid attracting attention. They gathered around the tombstones and, one by one, the

---

* Horn (p. 419) put the number of arrests as follows: *Thüringen* 600, *Helgoland* 150, *Große Kurfürst* 200 and *Markgraf* 150. Compared with other reports, these seem to be exaggerated. Wolz (p. 178) puts the number for *Thüringen* at 300, for *Helgoland* at 100, Koop and Mulitze (p. 169) at, respectively, 350 and 150.

† The account of the November Kiel uprising was written by a communist union organiser, Ernst Schneider. He had been a member of a number of left-wing groups such as the IKD, the KPD and the KAPD. He escaped from Germany in 1939, the manner of his escape being rather spectacular and earning him the *nom de plume* Icarus (Quoted in Kuhn, p. 9).

names of the ships were called out and a roster taken. After the decision to both occupy the ships as well as the signal station had been reached, the men slipped back into the night.

As the delegates from the cemetery meeting made their way back to the ships, the 'heavy tramp of marching troops' could be heard.[91] A column of three hundred men from *Thüringen* and another hundred from *Helgoland* were being marched off to the train bound for Oslebshausen barracks prison.

The returning delegates cheered the column of prisoners, and shouts of 'Down with the war' broke out. Warning shots rang out from the guards. It didn't make any difference. As the column passed the Admiralty building, the sailors broke ranks and seized the guardhouse along with fifteen machine guns. They then continued to the main gate, Gate A, of the Kaiserliche Werft (the Imperial Dockyards) and, seeing that it was already under revolutionary control, they went on to the *Baden*. Even there, the officers had lost control. During the night the revolutionaries sat down and elected a new commander, one of their own, a member of the committee.

The night was coming to an end and as dawn broke, all the ships – except the *Hindenburg* – were in revolutionary hands, their white ensigns struck and replaced by red flags. After a struggle on deck, *Hindenburg*'s Imperial flag also came down. *Baden*'s crew had threatened to open fire if they didn't comply. It happened so fast that additional help from *Baden*'s sailors, mainly a detachment of stokers and firemen, wasn't even needed. With the red flag being hauled up above the decks of ships of the cruiser squdron, the take-over seemed complete. The sailors were changing their headbands, either blacking out the SM if the cap tally was that of a particular ship (so that the result would be S *Helgoland*, no longer SMS *Helgoland*) or if the text was Kaiserliche Marine, the end result would be Erliche Marine (the honest navy). Either way, the reference to the Kaiser disappeared.

A demonstration outside the Admiralty was organised. A huge group of around 20,000 sailors and civilians responded to the call and a march around the naval base organised. At the head were sailors from the 15th Torpedo Half-Flotilla. Throughout the day, the revolutionaries continued to organise themselves and by evening had elected a council of twenty-one sailors, over which a 'body of five members with executive powers' was established. The former was supposed to be the core body in the naval revolution but it soon became known that, of the five members on the executive group, four were not even hard-core socialists.

It was more than just mere symbolism that the Council of 21 would headquarter itself among the sailors on the *Baden*, while the supposed Executive Council of Five chose the more luxurious officers' casino. It gave the impression that they both lacked revolutionary commitment and credentials. Between the two groups, nothing was really well-defined as to what powers and responsibilities each had and how they were to work together.*

That night, 30 October, the III Squadron, with more than 5,000 crew on board its ships, was sent out into the North Sea, past Cuxhaven, to Kiel, where *König* was undergoing dry dock repairs. The Seekriegsleitung (SKL) gave the order as it believed the move would stop the resistance jumping from one ship to another but it caused the opposite.† It gave the mutiny the means to spread from the naval port of Wilhelmshaven to the more politically fertile ground of the industrial city of Kiel.‡ Vizeadmiral Hugo Kraft would have to deal with the 'important decision which was to have fatal consequences'.[92]

Markgraf and the other ships of her squadron got under way. En route, at Brunsbüttel, the western opening to the Elbe and the Kaiser Wilhelm Kanal, the most vocal mutineers were taken off. Initially, the order affected only forty-seven sailors, but three days later another fifty-seven were added. To try and calm the situation, more crew were given shore leave. It was another mistake. It merely gave the disembarking sailors the opportunity to establish contact with shore-based marines and war-weary workers in Kiel (*Kriegsmüden Kieler Arbeitern*)[93] where around 50,000 marines and infantry were based.

That evening, 31 October, one of the III Geschwader's staff officers, Commander Meusel, went ahead to give Admiral Souchon his impressions. Souchon had only recently arrived, having been recalled from Istanbul, to take up the posting of Kiel Naval Garrison commander.§ The rumour mill was out of control and the tension rising. Both men expected there to be dangerous demonstrations of solidarity in Kiel on either 5 or 7 November. After all, it was the one-year anniversary of the Russian Revolution. It was obvious that

---

* The Council of 21 could also be referred to as the Twenty-first Committee of the Workers' and Soldiers' Council.
† At the end of the war, on 27 August 1918, Reinhard Scheer, would create the Seekriegsleitung (SKL) to streamline the various staffs running the operations of the navy.
‡ On 11 August 1918, Reinhard Scheer was nominated to head up the newly formed Seekriegsleitung (SKL).
§ Vizeadmiral Wilhelm Souchon (1864–1946) claimed fame when he succeeded in taking the SMS *Goeben* and SMS *Breslau* through the Mediterranean to Istanbul at the outset of the war. He had been appointed head of the Baltic Naval station and Governor of the City of Kiel but had arrived at his new post only days before, on 30 October.

the sailors should have been kept at greater distance from the workers but, at this point, Kraft seemed confident that he could maintain order on his ships.

Arriving in Kiel late in the night of 31 October/1 November, the ships of the III. Geschwader – a squadron that had not been tainted with mutiny up to this point – were met by the highly politicised dock workers. They had come through the Holtenauerschleuse that morning at 0145. In Kiel, both the men who had been given shore leave and the sailors who had been arrested on *Markgraf* were dropped off, but as a precaution Kraft had wanted to have a further 180 sailors taken off *Markgraf* and put into detention.

Kiel was a city created by the German economic boom of the 1890s where, despite the creation of a new middle class, hardly anything had changed in its moribund social structure. It was still dominated by the aristocracy and the military. Kiel was so much a navy city that the sailor's suit was even called 'the Kiel suit'. Kiel occupied an important place in the German naval armaments industry and its workers were heavily unionised. Here were the large Germaniawerft and Kaiserlichewerft shipyards as well as the Friedrichsort Torpedowerkstatt. Ships such as the armoured cruiser *Blücher* and the battleships *Kaiser, Prinzregent Luitpold and Kronprinz Wilhelm* had been built in these yards.[*] In May 1917, the USPD already had a membership body across the city of more than 1,000 and held the majority of the shop stewards in the Torpedo works.[94]

The impact of these industrial workers had already been felt on the war effort. On 25 January 1918 around 3,000 of the 4,500-strong Friedrichsort Torpedowerkstatt workforce downed tools.[95] Within days, thousands more from the Germaniawerft and the Kaiserlichewerft joined in. At the highpoint, 30,000 demonstrators gathered on the Wilhelmsplatz on 29 January. There they passed a resolution to send to the chancellor, Count von Hertling, to push for serious negotiations to end the war and to bring about a new electoral system. The same energy could be seen in Berlin. There, around 400,000 workers had ceased work. It was only the threat of sending strikers to the front that got them back to the workplace.

In Berlin, however, little notice was taken of the events in either Wilhelmshaven or Kiel. At the 2 November cabinet meeting, hardly any time was given to the Secretary of State for the Navy's report. Vizeadmiral Ritter von Mann was given seven lines on the agenda. Berlin was being

[*] SMS *Kronprinz Wilhelm* was originally named SMS *Kronprinz*. In January 1918 the Kaiser decided that she be renamed after his son and that June the ship's name was duly changed. I was contacted by someonewho had one of the ship's life rings with the new name painted over the old.

overwhelmed. The discussions covered other pressing issues such as the possible Armistice terms, the fact that Bavaria might be looking for a separate peace, the demands for constitutional reform and how to bring back German troops from the fronts that were collapsing all around them. Mann, however, wanted a representative from the central government to go to talk to the revolutionary sailors and Gustav Noske, a Social Democrat naval expert, and Conrad Haußmann, a secretary of state, were selected for the task.* Oscar Kürbis, the Social Democrat party secretary in Schleswig-Holstein, would accompany them. Their task was to calm the situation and bring some order back to the navy by validating the actions that the officers had taken. Above all, they made it clear that they '…were not putting an end to the war between the nations in order to start a Civil War'.[96]

When the three arrived in Kiel, Noske was immediately collared by one of the firebrand sailors and USPD member Karl Artelt, who tried to push them into a more visible show of support for the mutiny. Noske was cautious as his agenda was completely different. Most important, he did not see significant danger in what was happening: 'there was no impression that a great revolution had broken out', he wrote.[97]

When the remaining mutineers were taken off *Markgraf*, waiting dock-workers cheered them. The first thing the sailors had to do was to send a delegation ashore to demand their release. They were refused.

That same evening, Artelt organised a meeting at the trades union headquarters. Around 250 sailors from *Markgraf*, *König* and *Bayern* came to the gathering where Artelt exhorted them: '*Nieder mit den Lumpen.*' It was a general cry against those in authority, *den Lumpen*.

Another meeting was called for the next day by the local USPD leader Lothar Popp, but Souchon got wind of the plans and had the union headquarters locked. The meeting moved to the Harmonie Café on the Faulstraße but was again thwarted when the owner refused them entry. From there the throng moved to the Waldwiese, the open common on Kiel's outskirts. The crowd was getting angry and vindictive as its ranks swelled to around 600. With growing numbers, a sense of impunity was created. Matrose Strumpf described the change. He said that he 'was able to observe the gradual rise of bestiality (in the mob). Every woman was greeted with coarse remarks and whistles.'[98] Soon the police started to make arrests.

* Conrad Haußmann (1857–1922) and Gustav Noske (1868–1946) were members of the government, the former a Progressive, the latter a Social Democrat.

Earlier that day, following Kraft's orders, around seventy more sailors had been escorted off the *Markgraf* by thirteen marines. Souchon had heard that their fellow sailors had been hesitant about confronting the guards and ordered Kraft to take the battleship out again. Kraft refused as he doubted his orders would be obeyed. He was right, and on the morning of 3 November he and his officers were thrown off their own ship.

Another meeting was scheduled for the Waldwiese but this time Souchon decided that it should be banned outright. Despite his troops going through the streets announcing the ban with fanfare, '…if the drums and bugles served any purpose at all it was to advertise the forthcoming meeting'.[99] The meeting, already 3,000 strong, took place. The local SPD leader, Garge, tried to aim the meeting but, despite his appeals, the sailors and workers moved off en masse to the Feldstraße barracks. As they marched, their ranks swelled. By the time they arrived, they numbered 20,000. On the way, any officer risked having his rank epaulettes and dirk forcibly removed. As they rounded the corner on Brunswickerstraße and Karlstraße, they ran into a wall of forty-eight armed sailors.

It was this confrontation that really set things off. The loyalist sailors could not get the oncoming crowd to disperse. Their officer ordered them to fire over their heads and when this didn't work – and when fire was returned – the young lieutenant, Oskar Steinhäuser, ordered his men to level their shots into the crowd. His impetuous orders led to the death of nine sailors and wounded twenty-one more.[*] The dead and wounded were taken into a local café, the Kaiser. Steinhäuser was immediately set upon and killed, 'it is said by his own men'.[100] He was shot in the back. More than any other single incident, this was the moment that triggered the German revolution. '*Plötzlich erkannten alle: nun gibt es kein Zurück mehr, und plötzlich wußten auch alle, was jetzt zu tun sei.*' ('At that moment everyone recognised that there was no going back, indeed they finally understood what needed to be done').[101]

Surprisingly, Souchon now cancelled an earlier request for support from the Altona command, saying that he felt the situation to be under control. It was anything but.

During the night of 3 / 4 November, the sailors armed themselves while

---

[*] Exact numbers are difficult to find. Kuhn (p. 20), like Woodward (p. 144) stated eight killed in one reference, seven in another (p. 3). Ulrich (p. 29) states nine, as does Wolz (p. 179). Kuhn maintained that there were 'women and children' in the group fired upon. Nordwoche, 27 June 1969, Arnim von Manikowsky, *Was geschah wirklich in Scapa Flow?*, put the number of wounded at twenty-one.

at the same time disarming their officers. High up above the moored ships the red flag fluttered. On shore most of the significant buildings in Kiel had been occupied. On only one ship, *Schlesien*, was the flag absent. It was out at sea and found itself under threat from the guns of a sister-ship.

The day started with a crowd of 10,000, headed by Obermatrose Artelt marching on the Wik barracks and demanding the release of those arrested the day before.

When Artelt and his followers reached the barracks a list of demands was drawn up and a Soviet elected. The list included freeing those imprisoned from the III Geschwader, all political prisoners and those who had been jailed a year before in the 1917 food riots. They also called for the Kaiser's abdication, universal suffrage and the conclusion of an immediate peace. The barracks commander, Kapitän Bartels, felt totally powerless and now elevated Artelt to be the principal spokesperson. He sent him and a stoker from the *Große Kurfürst*, Podolski, to see the governor. Souchon agreed to only what he could control: the release of all prisoners connected with both the Wilhelmshaven and Kiel mutinies. The military prison had been occupied by the revolutionary sailors without any substantial resistance and by evening Kiel was under revolutionary control.

The sailors had little idea of what else to do when the representatives of the Berlin government arrived. After Souchon had finally asked for help – something he was loathe to do – Noske and Haußmann were sent.

When they arrived by train on the evening of 4 November, Noske and Haußmann were welcomed and when the two made it clear that the sailors' mutiny was seen by the government as an act carried out in legitimate support and not one determined to undermine it, the sailors cheered them on. However, Noske's role would be to steer the movement back to the mainstream, away from the more left-leaning revolutionaries.

From the deck of a moored battleship, standing on a gun platform out over the ship's slanting steel sides, Noske addressed a group of recently returned submariners gathered on the quay below him. It was not a large crowd but Noske's and Haußmann's presence in Kiel was 'the first act of SPD infiltration of the revolutionaries' ranks'.[102] It was an important moment.

Souchon had survived the first four days of the Kiel naval mutiny. Now the city was in the hands of more than 4,000 sailors and marines and during the night of the 4/5 November his garrison fortress commander, Kapitän Haine, was shot. Souchon's new status was clear when, on the morning of 5 November, he was taken to a second-class railway waiting room whilst outside the red flags flew over the city.

Back in Berlin, Mann now not only talked of blockading Kiel by laying an armed cordon across the peninsular of Schleswig-Holstein, he also threatened to bombard the town. Luckily, he was overruled in cabinet, where Haußmann had previously pointed out the potential for huge loss of innocent life.

One solitary Imperial flag still fluttered over the battleship *König*, where it had been protected by its captain, Kapitän Weniger, and two officers, Commander Heinemann and Leutnant Zenker. When a rating tried to haul up the red flag, Weniger shot him. Miraculously, despite being shot five times, he survived. Heinemann and Zenker did not. *König* was the only case where an officer put up resistance to protect the Imperial flag.

Newly proclaimed governor of Kiel on 7 November (and under whom Souchon and his staff agreed to served), Noske was starting to feel that things had gone too far: 'This bloody business must end. You must put an end to the shooting,' he implored Artelt.[103] Noske's evaluation of the seriousness of what was happening in Kiel is not that easy to come to terms with. Clearly, he did not think that Artelt could control the storm he had unleashed and he had told officers to get out of Kiel, in disguise if needed. At the same time, he found it necessary to complain of the exhaustion of attending so many speeches.

Noske had to work fast. The day before, workers at both the Germaniawerft and the Torpedowerkstatt had 'downed tools' and on 5 November, industrial action spread and a general strike was declared in the city. A soldiers' council was elected,with Noske elected as its chairman, followed a few hours later by a workers' council.

While still governor, Souchon had been powerless to act, feeling he had no choice but to negotiate with the new forces. Not only had they succeeded in being heard, he had also agreed to their major negotiating points. The so-called 'Kiel Fourteen Points' included the agreement to the release of imprisoned sailors and political prisoners, the involvement of the soldiers' council in all-important decision-making and, finally, a declaration that the fleet would not now be employed for any further belligerent purposes.

In less than two weeks, the German Navy's purpose had deteriorated from a force designed to deliver 'Operational Plan 19' to a force bound by the renunciation of war. The disgust among some officers was tangible: 'We are all deeply upset over the disgraceful mutiny in the Fleet. We are preparing ourselves for self-defence. Naval command is wilting, not daring to intervene any more. It is reported that Souchon has been negotiating with the refractory ratings and has given in to them.'[104]

Included in the Fourteen Points were changes that went to the very essence of the divide between the officers and men: the manner in which lower ranks were treated and viewed. The proposed changes called for 'the correct handling of ratings by superiors' and for the end to blind obedience in off-duty hours. To Strumpf it was a long overdue recognition of the lower deck: 'Now at last, after many years, the suppressed stokers and sailors realise that nothing – no, nothing – can be accomplished without them.'[105]

In the following months Noske started to win the navy's trust. The ranks trusted him because of his position within the SPD and he was able to use this to win election to the chairmanship of the soldiers' council. But Noske was more concerned with regaining order within the navy and, together with his close friend, Ebert, used the paramilitary power of the newly created Volksmarinedivision to suppress communist agitation.

His recommendations for leniency and an amnesty for the revolutionaries was supported in cabinet. Despite the idea there that this might allow more in the military to feel that they had been released from their oaths of allegiance, the growing feeling now was that the Kaiser had to abdicate if any progress was going to be made.

In the ships of the fleet, revolutionary action continued partly because Hipper now decided to also move the I Squadron from Brunsbüttel. Many of the naval mutineers were meeting in the Café zum Guten Eck in Westerbüttel, in the northern part of the town. The sailors raced back, one group clashing with a shore party and then ransacking an armoury en route, while another freed some of their imprisoned comrades. They arrived at the shorefront just as *Oldenburg* was trying to get through the gates. *Posen* had already passed through and beside her *Oldenburg* reversed engines. Beside her, as *Nassau* went forward, *Ostfriesland*'s searchlights picked up the gangways that had been laid down to connect her with the shore. The sailors swarmed aboard and thence on to *Oldenburg*. *Posen* was given a signal that, if she did not return, fire would be opened. She complied. By 0400 it was over and the crews went to sleep.

After much hesitation, Kraft decided to move the III Squadron back out of Kiel and take his ships further down the coast, south to Travemünde, from where sailors took local transport into Lübeck in order to agitate. They encountered no resistance but, knowing that it was in Kiel where decisions were being made, now wanted the ships to be sailed back. It was a plan with which their officers refused to comply.

Aircraft were sent over the small estuary town of Brunsbüttel by Hipper, and the pilots reported back that the mutineers had also taken control of one of the other squadron ships, the *Nassau*. Swarms of sailors from *Ostfriesland* and *Oldenburg* had gone ashore and were marching with their bands through the town with red flags flying.

Later that night there was a commotion aboard *Ostfriesland* when rumours that the officers were planning to blow her up whipped up tension. On both her and *Oldenburg* the officers barricaded themselves in and would only come ashore when Boedicker ordered them to do so. On *Nassau*, one officer shot himself rather than submit.

Scheer now went to see the Kaiser in Spa. He wanted Souchon (who by now was reporting to Noske) replaced by someone who, in his mind, would bring order back to the fleet. He succeeded in getting the Kaiser to agree that the Flanders commander, Admiral Ludwig Schröder, who had a reputation for harshness, should be appointed. At 0200 on 6 November, he received his orders and made ready his men – a battalion of naval shock troops, a machine gun company, twenty naval policemen and artillery.

The cabinet rescinded Schröder's appointment on 7 November. Neither Mann, nor the acting Chief of Staff, Kapitän von Restorff, nor Prince Max von Baden had been informed by Scheer. They objected, one and all, to appointing a man known to be 'a ferocious disciplinarian, a hot-head and ardent proponent of the most extreme right-wing points of view'.[106]

On 7 November, Noske announced that the mutineers were safe from outside intervention. No troops would be sent in and those already there would be withdrawn. He told Berlin that any troops would not stand a chance against the armed sailors. He was also able to 'buy' the sailors' confidence and allegiance, telling them that they would be paid as he had sent an aircraft to Berlin to secure the necessary money.

Hugo Meurer's IV Squadron was mostly at sea during the initial events but early in the morning of 9 November, at 0400, he heard that there was trouble on *Kaiserin*. He managed to avoid open insurrection breaking out by promising to 'consider their grievances on the ship's return to Wilhelmshaven'.[107]

They would not get back until the next day. When the Kaiser's abdication was announced on 9 November, celebrations broke out in Wilhelmshaven. Signal flares provided an impressively memorable fireworks display as ships' sirens wailed in the background.

Order was finally coming back to the navy. Ritter von Mann managed to get cabinet approval to have a new decree issued. Among the decisions agreed was that a superior officer's orders were, henceforth, to be unconditionally followed. Officers would also be allowed to wear their side arms and symbols of rank. The cabinet made it clear that it was in the interests of peace: 'We must all work together to see that the conditions of the Armistice are speedily and effectively carried out. The Navy must recognise that upon the conscientious execution of the Armistice everything depends.'[108]

*   *   *

The fires that had been sparked into life in Wilhelmshaven and Kiel now took on more vigour and spread, with the sailors fanning out to the south. Shock columns of revolutionary sailors were sent out to bolster the left-wing throughout Germany.

Twenty or so sailors arrived in Hamburg on the evening of 4 November and, together with a sailor on his way from Flanders, Friedrich Zeller, were able to enlist the help of the light cruiser *Augsburg*, and they would be joined by soldiers billeted in the city and workers from the great shipbuilding yards of Blohm & Voss. On 6 November they were sufficiently well-organised to be able to put on a 40,000-strong demonstration on the Heiligengeistfeld in St Pauli.

That same day, Lübeck, Brunsbüttelkoog and Bremen all joined when the spark of revolution arrived. The next day, 7 November, it reached Hannover, Oldenburg and Cologne. In Munich, at the very southern end of Germany, though not directly a result of the events on the northern coast, the local anti-monarchist putsch added to the overall political turmoil of the country. There, the Bavarian USPD leader, Kurt Eisner, ousted Prince Ludwig III and declared a republic.* On 8 November, the cities of Leipzig and Magdeburg fell victim to the revolutionary wave and even Berlin erupted in a general strike.† One objective for the naval revolutionaries was the radio station at Nauen, just outside the capital Berlin. It was an important means of establishing close communications with

---

* Kurt Eisner (1867–1919) was a journalist and a key player in the revolution that overthrew the Wittelsbach monarchy in Bavaria in 1918.
† The fact that a rating, Oberheizer Bernhard Kuhnt, was elected as the president of the government of the Oldenburg Republic underlines the importance of the navy as the source of political change. His self-proclaimed position, however, was rescinded by Oldenburg.

Kronstadt, the nearest radio station in soviet hands to Wilhelmshaven. At that point Nauen was in the hands of the Ebert government. The sailors' attempt to take it over did not succeed and they continued on to the capital instead, forming the Volksmarinedivision under the leadership of a young revolutionary lieutenant close to Karl Liebknecht, Heinrich Dorrenbach.* In Cologne, the future German chancellor, Konrad Adenauer, initially tried to prevent the sailors getting into the city but when they did, put the town hall at their disposal.

A leading stoker, Bernard Kuhnt, declared himself head of the newly independent state of Oldenburg, where Friedrich August, the Grand Duke, had been deposed. Kuhnt's declaration was premature as Oldenburg rejected his pronouncement. Some of the towns, like Cuxhaven, openly declared their willingness to surrender to the Allies, saying that they 'reject the idea of national defence and would therefore hoist the white flag if the English were to come'.[109]

*   *   *

The actions in Kiel and Wilhelmshaven effectively brought about the end of naval command of the Imperial High Seas Fleet. Tirpitz's dream of a navy that would lead Germany to greater glory and supremacy had been shattered. He could only blame others: 'It was the men who had refused, not the ships that had failed.'[110]

Korvettenkapitän Ernst von Weizsäcker, whose son would be destined to become a future president of the eventual German Federal Republic, summed up the final contribution of the Kaiser's fleet:[†] 'This Navy! It was spawned by world power arrogance, ruined our foreign policy for twenty years, failed to keep its promises during the war and has now kindled revolution.'[111]

For Scheer, the navy would long carry a bitter responsibility for what befell Germany: 'A curse lies on the Navy because out of its ranks Revolution first sprang and spread over the land.'[112] The navy became the critical element that sparked revolution in Germany. What started in Wil-

---

* Karl Paul August Friedrich Liebknecht (1871–1919) was a founding member, along with Rosa Luxemburg (1871–1919), of the Spartakist movement, the forerunner of the German Communist Party. Heinrich Dorrenbach (1888–1919) helped put together a naval brigade in Berlin despite never having been in the navy.
† Ernst von Weizsäcker (1882–1951) had been at Jutland and later served in the Foreign Office. He was the father of Richard von Weizsäcker (1920–2015), who became president of Germany from 1984–1994.

helmshaven as mutiny morphed into revolution in Kiel and then spread through the country with a speed and ferocity that few could have foreseen: 'War-weariness and hunger had already provided plenty of incendiary material, but it was the naval mutinies which set fire to it.'[113]

It was not a revolution in the style of that which had happened in Russia a year earlier but it was a revolution, nevertheless: '*Was aber zwischen der 4. und 10. November über das westelbische Deutschland rollte, war eine echte Revolution, nämlich der Sturz der alten Obrigkeit und der Ersatz durch eine neue.*'[114] ('But what had rolled through West Elbe between 4 and 10 November really was a revolution, namely, in involved the overthrow of the old authorities and its replacement by a new one.')

In January, the murder on the 15th of the two leading Spartakists, Karl Leibknecht and Rosa Luxemburg, by supporters of the Ebert government created a potentially explosive turning point.* They had been apprehended, killed and their bodies thrown into a Berlin canal. Throughout the fleet, red flags flew at half-mast in solidarity, while on the streets of Wilhelmshaven bitter armed struggle erupted.

Germany's political future was in the balance, swinging erratically between the extremes of socialism and communism, the fleet caught in the middle of something which it had helped spark but now could no longer control.

---

* Friedrich Ebert (1871–1925) was a Social Democrat and the first president of Germany from 1919–25.

3

ARMISTICE

'THE FATE OF the German Kaiser Reich was sealed in two railway coaches.'[115] One was at Compiègne, where the centrist politician Matthias Erzberger and the German delegation met on 8 November with Allied commanders to be handed the Armistice terms.* The other one was a train heading towards the Dutch border. The fifty-nine-coach train only had one passenger: the ex-Kaiser. It was heading north, taking him into exile.†

The speed of Germany's final collapse came as a surprise. Not many felt at the start of 1918 that this would be the final year of the war. Consequently, little had been done to prepare for the historic moment. Right into the last months, significant orders were being made by the Royal Navy for more ships from American yards. Ironically, the only nation that had taken steps to plan for the post-war world was America, the country that was last to enter into the fray and was least impacted by the gigantic scale of death and destruction that had been wreaked on most of Europe, and which had been making overtures to Berlin without even consulting her European partners. It was understandable how bitterly they reacted to Woodrow Wilson's arrival in Europe.

'What brings you gentlemen here?' asked Foch as the German delegation presented themselves. It was all he could bring himself to say by way of a mocking acknowledgement.

---

* Hitler ordered the original railway carriage to be returned to the same location so that he could sign the Armistice with France on 22 June 1940 with the full symbolism of a France defeated twenty years after having imposed its terms on Germany. Matthias Erzberger (1875–1921), Catholic Centre party politician, who signed the Armistice for Germany, had spoken against the war since 1917.

† The Kaiser would live in the house of Baron Bentick in Utrecht for the next year and a half before Doorn House was purchased from Audrey Hepburn's great aunt near Amerongen. The Kaiser would not go wanting. Not only did he receive a special payment from the new German government of 80 million marks as compensation for confiscated Hohenzollern properties, the special train brought with him all his personal possessions – art, furniture and anything that could be moved from his former estates.

The Armistice was to be put into operation for thirty-six days. Germany would be obliged to immediately withdraw to a line set at 30 miles east of the Rhine as well as to pull back from the important bridgeheads at Koblenz, Mainz and Cologne.

The Armistice terms were harsh. The terms might have been based on President Wilson's Fourteen Points but there had been considerable changes made. At 'the insistence of Lloyd George', their severity had been ratcheted up:

> Further, in conditions of peace laid down in his address to the Congress of January 8, 1918, the President declared that invaded territories must be restored as well as evacuated and freed. The Allied Governments feel that no doubt ought to be allowed to exist as to what this provision implies. By it they understand that *compensation will be made by Germany for all damage done* (my italics) to the civilian population of the Allies and their property by the aggression of Germany by land, sea and from the air.*

The initial terms were later viewed as less harsh by the difficult additional burdens that were added. Because of 'delays' the Germans would also be required to deliver 500 locomotives and 19,000 rail wagons. The Allies rejected 3,100 of the surrendered 4,900 locomotives on the grounds that they weren't good enough and, when Germany couldn't find enough rolling stock, the locomotives were replaced with 58,000 pieces of agricultural equipment and 400 steam ploughs.[116]

The country was being stripped down to the bare bones and it made little economic or long-term diplomatic sense. The politicians were more focused on short-term political gains. It made economists such as John Maynard Keynes question the logic of seemingly destroying Germany's ability to generate enough economic growth to fund future reparations.[†] To men such as Balfour, the terms were so humiliating that 'a people with any self-respect would not grovel to sign a document like this Armistice'.[117]

In the context of what Germany's own war aims had been, however, the terms were a mirror of what she had intended to levy on France had she won.

---

* Tampke p. 88. The Lansing note was written up by US Secretary of State Robert Lansing.
† John Maynard Keynes (1883–1946), a journalist and economist who wrote extensively on the causes of unemployment.

France was to be weakened to such an extent that it would cease to be a leading power. In addition to its territorial losses (the annexation of Belfort, the western Vosges, the coastal region from Dunkirk to Boulogne and the iron-ore region of Briey being the minimum demands) France was to pay an indemnity large enough to cripple its armaments production for the next 18 to 20 years... to make the country economically dependent on Germany.[118]

The question of what to do with Germany's navy became one of the major points in the negotiations, in fact *the* major stumbling block in the progress of intra-Allied negotiations.

Naval power was seen as the yardstick of a nation's power and prestige. British maritime dominance had helped build the country's empire, its source of wealth. For centuries, the Royal Navy had ruled the world's oceans, undefeated and, in the last century, unchallenged. That is until Germany's desire for a 'place in the sun' and a navy to rival Britain's put the two nations on a path to war. Now America, seeing before her a bankrupt and war-weary Britain, was claiming her own naval rights. It would set her on a collision course with her former ally.

Already at the Paris Allied Naval Council meeting in late October the British position of what to do with the German fleet was at odds with the American one, particularly that of Admiral Benson, the US Chief of Naval Operations (CNO), the head of the national navy. Sir Sydney Fremantle, known among the men as 'Frowsy Fred', later revealed what had happened at these discussions.* Writing in 1953, he said that the Admiralty proposal 'had received full consent with the partial exception' of the American admiral, who 'wished only for the internment of the 10 battleships'.[119] Beatty, the Commander-in-Chief of the Grand Fleet after Jellicoe, and the British Admiralty wanted the German fleet surrendered 'to enable the Allies to enforce the Armistice – should coercion become necessary'.[120] Benson, on the other hand, suggested that 'it was not desirable to risk German refusal of the Armistice by insistence on the ten battleships being surrendered instead of interned'.[121] At this point, Foch asked, 'Why we should be so exacting, as the (German) ships had never been used, and when both Mr Lloyd George and M. Clemenceau persisted, the Marshal said that the "action of the British fleet was virtual

---

* Admiral Sir Sydney Fremantle (1867–1958) took over as senior officer at Scapa on 18 May 1918. He arrived with the 1st Battle Squadron and replaced Vice Admiral Sir Arthur Leveson (1868–1929). The reference to his nickname is from de Courcy-Ireland, p. 57.

ABOVE: A defaced Cap tally from SMS *Braunswchweig* after removal of the letters SM to take away the reference to the Kaiser (SM, *Seiner Majestät*). Sailors added red armbands to their uniforms to show revolutionary solidarity. Red ink has been used to paint on red flags and to delete SM from a contemporary postcard of *König Albert*.

Cap Tally / armband: Author's collection, postcard: Deutsche Marinemuseum, Wilhelmshaven)

RIGHT: Unloading munitions from the High Seas Fleet flagship, SMS *Friedrich der Große*, Wilhelmshaven 17 November 1918. Any valuable technology, like range-finding equipment, was also offloaded. (Deutsche Marine Bund)

BELOW: The railway car at Compiègne with the representatives of the Allies. Among others, at the meeting were Admirals Wemyss and Hope (left), in front of them is German Secretary of State Matthias Erzberger. Standing at the table is General Foch beside whom sits General Weygand. Painting by Maurice Pillard. (Public Domain)

HMS *Cardiff* leads the German internment fleet into Rosyth, 21 November 1918. (© National Maritime Museum, Greenwich, London)

The internment terms being handed to Rear Admiral von Meurer and his staff by Admiral Sir David Beatty aboard HMS *Queen Elizabeth*. Painting by Sir John Lavery. (Imperial War Museum)

Rear Admiral von Reuter being taken aboard a British
drifter after failing to sink his own ship, SMS *Emden*.
(© National Museums of Scotland)

Beatty (Admiral Sir David). Sir John Jellicoe's successor as C-in-C of the Grand Fleet and the man who unsuccessfully lobbied for the complete surrender of the High Seas Fleet in November 1918, an act that would have probably avoided a scuttle. (Author's collection)

Meurer (Rear Admiral Hugo von) was sent by Hipper to meet with Admiral Sir David Beatty and his staff to organise the internment planning aboard HMS *Queen Elizabeth* which he is shown boarding here. (Unknown)

Madden (Admiral Sir Charles). Sir John Jellicoe's brother in law, C-in-C of the Grand Fleet after Sir David Beatty and then Atlantic Fleet where he was Sir Sydney Fremantle's senior officer. (Madden Family)

Fremantle (Rear Admiral Sir Sydney). C-in-C 1st Battle Squadron, Atlantic Fleet and responsible for the guarding of the interned German Fleet at Scapa Flow. (Fremantle Family)

Reuter (Rear Admiral Ludwig von). Former C-in-C of the battle-cruisers and then of the interned German fleet at Scapa Flow appointed by Franz Hipper. (von Reuter Family)

Trotha (Admiral Adolf von). Head of the German Admiralty and the man many believe ordered Reuter to proceed with the scuttling of the interned German Fleet. (Unknown)

Cox (Ernst Guelph) & McKenzie (Commander Tom, RN). The founder of Cox & Danks (sitting) and Tom McKenzie, both engineers but it was the latter who brought salvage experience to the team.
(Kirkwall Library & Archives)

McCrone (Robert W). Chairman of Metal Industries and the man who continued Cox's work but did so with greater financial success.
(Courtesy of Ian Buxton, Metal Industries)

SMS *V82*, painted by William Wyllie. *V82* was scuttled by her crew with the rest of the interned German fleet, but she was one of the ships on which the British intervened and beached her before she sank. She was later refloated and towed to Portsmouth, and is depicted here beached on the mudflats to the west of Fountain Lake. She was broken up at Portsmouth in 1922. (© National Maritime Museum, Greenwich, London)

Some of the crew of *V82*, photographed in Bruges (below), and the vessel herself alongside the quay at Calais. (Deutsche Marine Bund & SeaWar Museum, Denmark)

and not actual, and were we to continue the war solely to suppress the virtual influence".'[122]

The Supreme War Council sided with Benson and Foch.

Germany's U-boat fleet, on the other hand, was to be surrendered and disarmed. One hundred and sixty submarines were to be handed over to the Allies for destruction.* Their use was seen as a war crime by both Britain and, more importantly, America, whose exports had largely sailed under British flag and where losses had been keenly felt by business and Wall Street.

A decision on the fate of the main fleet itself – under Article XXIII – was not going to be so easy: The warships of the German High Seas Fleet indicated by the Allies and the USA will at once be dismantled and then interned in neutral ports, or in default, in ports of the Allied Powers.' The Allies demanded that this be made up of ten battleships, six battle cruisers, eight light cruisers, of which two were minelayers, and fifty destroyers. It was Wemyss who managed to get what turned out to be the crucial clause 'or in default, in ports of the Allied Powers' inserted. Scapa Flow was his harbour of choice. With Admiral William S Sims chairing the meeting, the new approach was agreed to on 13 November.

Beatty never fully agreed with these suggestions. The day before he had written to the First Lord saying that the Royal Navy's role in Germany's defeat would only be validated 'if the Sea Power of Germany is surrendered under the eyes of the Fleet it dared to encounter, and in the harbours of the Power that swept it from the sea'.[123] It goes without saying that this would also be a validation of his own role in Germany's defeat.

Alternatives to Scapa were few. At least two were considered: one in Spain, one in Norway. Both were turned down. The British were unlikely to have strongly supported efforts to house the interned fleet in ports other than its own. First, the facilities needed would be significant but, more important, there would be little benefit for them. Friedrich Ruge maintained that Beatty and the Admiralty acted 'contrary to the wishes of the British Prime Minister', Lloyd George but he presents scant evidence.† He similarly concluded that the Allies 'made no inquiries in

---

* Under Article XXI.

† Vice Admiral Prof Friedrich Ruge joined the service in April 1914 and served on the torpedo boat B.110, living through the internment at Scapa Flow. He was Senior Officer of Minesweepers 1940–41 and was responsible for strengthening German West European coastal defences. He was promoted to vice admiral in 1943. After the war he lectured at Tübingen University, where he was given an honorary professorship. He visited Orkney again in 1982 and was interviewed by Orkney Radio on his wartime experiences.

Holland, Sweden, Norway, Denmark or Spain'. [124] On two of those, Roskill disagreed, stating that it was 'Spain and Norway [that] declined to accept' the German fleet.[125] Ruge disagreed about Norway. The country had, apparently, already started preparing and were 'surprised to get no inquiries'.[126]

Whether or not any of these countries were actually asked by the Allies about whether they would take the German Fleet into one of their harbours for internment is difficult to confirm. It is unlikely, however, given the number of ships involved, whether any other harbour other than the eventual choice, Scapa Flow, would have even possessed adequate facilities. And, in any case, if the Armistice terms could not be worked out, the Allies wanted to be in a position to be able to seize these ships quickly. Even then, the threat of scuttling was consciously anticipated for without an actual *surrender*, it would be impossible to place guards on the German ships and, therefore, difficult to prevent.

But should these ships even be allowed to continue their lives as machines of war? Article XXXI specifically referred to their destruction.

Beatty felt that after having been actively at war with the German Navy for the past four years, his opinions about how the service should now be treated were especially important and should be listened to. On 21 October, he put his case to the War Cabinet. It was a beautifully concise piece of writing:

1. I assumed the object of the war was the destruction of German militarism. From a naval point of view, the destruction of German sea power.

[...]

6. To achieve the destruction of German sea power and reduce Germany to the status of a second-rate Naval Power, it is necessary to lay down in the Naval Terms of the Armistice conditions which would be commensurate with the result of a Naval action, i.e. the result of the Armistice should be what we expect would be the result of a Naval action as regards the relative strength of the two forces.[127]

Madden felt that their destruction 'admittedly assists the United States to become the premier naval power with the least possible delay'.[128] Beatty came perilously close to breaking the very strong working relationship that he had established with the First Sea Lord, Jellicoe's successor, Sir Rosalyn Wemyss. 'Rosy', as all his friends called him, was not known for his intellect but, as the King pointed out, was both diplomatic and easy to work with.* Beatty felt that the Supreme Council was being far too lenient on the issue of the naval terms. When writing to Wemyss, he did little to hide his anger:

> I was very perturbed at the underlying tone of your letter, which indicated that the Supreme Council might override the Naval Council. You speak about 'If we are obliged to ease up our Naval terms', also 'If our terms are put down by the Supreme War Council, we can do nothing but enter a protest.'[129]

The night of 13/14 November, Beatty signalled Germany's Naval Command. He asked that a representative of flag seniority be sent on a light cruiser to meet and to work through the arrangements for the German fleet's transfer to Internment. Hipper's choice was Rear Admiral Hugo Meurer.† He was asked to go to sea as quickly as possible.

Three days after the Armistice had been signed, in the afternoon Meurer set off in the light cruiser SMS *Königsberg*. His ship had to weave and skirt around the numerous minefields leaving German waters. She was given a salute from a Danish ship but had not been able to answer as she had been disarmed. En route, *U.67* surfaced and Meurer brought her captain and crew up to date with the latest war news.

Fifty miles off May Island, *Königsberg* was met by the British light cruiser, HMS *Cardiff*.‡ With her were the squadron's five other light cruisers and an escort of ten destroyers. It was, of course, like everything that was to take place over the next forty-eight hours, an exaggeration designed solely to put the German 'negotiator' in his place. Commodore Hodges, Admiral Sir Charles Madden's Chief of Staff, came across to the *Königsberg* to be met by three sailors, who announced that they were the

---

* Phipps Hornby, whose family knew Wemyss well, said that 'he may not have been the outstanding intellect in the service of that era' (Marder Papers, UCI, letter dated 24 October 1966).
† Rear Admiral Hugo Meurer (1869–1960) had been at Jutland. After he joined the navy in 1886 he was Captain of the SMS *Deutschland* in May 1916. He'd gone on to command *König* and was then promoted to rear admiral in 1917 when he became the second in command of the 4th Battle Squadron. After the war he was promoted to vice admiral. He died in Kiel.
‡ 6th Light Cruiser Squadron (LCS).

appointed delegates of the workers' and soldiers' council and that the officers were merely their 'technical advisors'.[130] Very promptly they were put in their place.

Everything had been designed to make the Germans feel unwelcome and inferior. Beatty had, he said, arranged a most beautiful setting. 'My dramatic sense was highly developed at the moment.'[131] So much so that he even noted that he had wished Madden had shaved off his beard. Beatty did not think he looked stern enough.

At 1930 on the evening of the 15th, Meurer was taken across to Beatty's flagship by destroyer, the *Oak*. It was dark and a thick fog cloaked them. Beatty joked that the German had no idea of the power of the battleships that he'd unknowingly passed by. 'The heavy fog had caused a delay of some three hours in the arrival of the Germans. Since about 5 p.m., men had been waiting around expectantly, over and over again peering into the gloom hoping to catch some sight of the little destroyer *Oak* which was to bring the party from *Königsberg*... .'[132]

Finally, a figure stepped off and slowly came up *Queen Elizabeth*'s gangway. It was Meurer, followed by four other officers. The ship's lighting was as bright and powerful as possible – Beatty mentioned that they were 'the strongest electric sunlights'[133] – so that Meurer had to squint as he came aboard the British flagship.* 'As [Meurer] stepped aboard, he saluted the quarter deck. A moment's pause and hesitation, and he turned and saluted the Captain of the Fleet and the officers with him. The salute was returned.'[134]

The Germans were met on board by marine guards, bayonets fixed to 'impress the visitors as to the exact nature of their mission'. It was not a Guard of Honour, nor were arms presented. Once on board he was met by Rear Admiral Hubert Brand, the Captain of the Fleet, and Captain Chatfield.[†] Both were in dress uniform and wore their swords. They were, in Beatty's words, 'frigidity itself' and Fremantle, 'courteous in the extreme but firm as a rock'.[135] Vice Admiral Sydney Fremantle, a descendant of one of Nelson's favourite captains, Thomas, would later be

---

* Beatty had moved his flag to the faster and more powerful battleship after dropping the *Iron Duke*, declaring that there was 'too much of Jellicoe in her' but, more fundamentally, since he wanted a faster ship than the older *Iron Duke*. HMS *Queen Elizabeth* was armed with 15in guns and could steam at around 24 knots.

† Captain Ernle Chatfield (1873–1967), later Admiral of the Fleet, Baron Chatfield, had been Sir David Beatty's flag captain on HMS *Lion* at Jutland. Admiral Hubert 'Tommy' Brand (1870–1955) served as Chief of Staff to the senior officer (SO) commanding the Battle-cruiser Squadron in 1916.

ordered to guard the interned fleet in Scapa Flow with the 1st Battleship Squadron.

The artist, Sir John Lavery, was also on board, furtively hidden in the shadows and disguised as a naval officer, there to record the moment for posterity.* His painting evocatively captured Meurer's lonely mission, his insignificance on *Queen Elizabeth*'s quarterdeck. Another witness was one of the marine guards, who said that he had seen a German steal some cheese. He had been looking through a keyhole. 'A subsequent search of the greatcoat revealed a large lump of cheese.'[136]

Meurer was then escorted to Beatty's cabin, where he was met by British Admirals Brock, Tyrwhitt and Madden.† They were sitting behind a cloth-covered table, maps strewn across, a large 9in brass doorstop on the table in the form of a crouching lion. Behind Beatty, on the wall, was a full-length painting of Nelson. Every last detail was stage-managed to add symbolism to the moment. Even the courtesies that normally existed between officers were tightly reined in.

With a cold, belittling manner bordering on a charade, Meurer and his four staff officers were told to present their credentials. With Meurer were a submarine officer and a Zeppelin commander. Another group was obliged to stay on the *Königsberg*. Beatty flatly stated that he would have nothing to do with the three members of the Committee of 21 that the sailors' council had sent along with Meurer. They had been appointed by a government that was not recognised by Great Britain. Nevertheless, Beatty would only deal with Meurer once he had received confirmation that he had been, '...sent by Admiral Hipper as his plenipotentiary to arrange the details for carrying out the terms of the armistice which refer to the surrender of the German Fleet'.[137]

Meurer did not, as it turned out, have the official documentation that Beatty had asked for. A signal was immediately sent to Admiral Hipper. Over the next three sessions, it became clear that Beatty had never

---

* Sir John Lavery (1856–1941) was a renowned Irish painter, mainly now remembered for his wartime paintings. He would paint Meurer's arrival aboard HMS Queen *Elizabeth* and the meeting with Beatty and his staff.

† Sir Charles Madden was Jellicoe's brother-in-law. He had become Sir David Beatty's 2nd in command when Jellicoe went to the Admiralty to become First Sea Lord in December 1916. He'd been Jellicoe's Chief-of-Staff at Jutland and served in *Iron Duke* with Osmond Brock (1869–1947), Beatty's Chief of Staff. Also present were Captain Ernle Chatfield and Rear Admiral the Hon. Hubert 'Tommy' Brand, both of whom met Meurer on deck. With them also were Commander R.M. Bellairs and Commander WT Bagot (the interpreter) and, for some of the time, Vice Admiral Sir M. Browning and Rear Admiral Sir Reginald Tyrwhitt, commander destroyers at Harwich at the time of Jutland.

intended for these talks to be anything more than a means of conveying his orders to the Germans. They were not to be given any concessions whatsoever. Hipper's confirmation of Meurer's credentials eventually arrived while the third session was in progress.

Beatty had always fought hard for the actual 'surrender' of his enemy's fleet but the word had become a sticking point in the Armistice negotiations and British naval hardliners lost out.* The original phrasing of Articles XXII and XXIII had included the word 'surrender'. Not surprisingly, it had stuck in the throats of the German negotiating delegation. There would be no formal surrender of the *surface fleet* until the Armistice terms were agreed. Article 184 of the eventual terms makes that *very* clear.

Both Wemyss and Admiral de Bon felt that they were within their rights to insist on the surrender of the German Navy. Admiral Benson argued – against David Lloyd George, Clemenceau and Foch – for internment. He wanted the blood-letting halted. Haig, always one to look out for his own interests, supported Benson.† He saw no reason why he should let the navy's role in delivering victory take any of the spotlight away from him.

Article XXIII was amended to read: 'The following German surface warships…shall forthwith be disarmed and thereafter interned…and placed under the surveillance of the Allies and the United States of America, only *caretakers* (my italics) being left on board… .'

Articles XXII was not changed and a large portion of the German submarine fleet was surrendered to Rear Admiral Reginald Tyrwhitt at Harwich. He had been waiting in his flagship, the light cruiser HMS *Curaçao*, 35 miles offshore.

On 20 November, at 0445, the first German submarines appeared off Lowestoft. 'Disposed in four divisions of five boats each,' the first batch represented twenty of Germany's 'latest type of U-boat'.[138] A British airship, the Harwich-based R26 (accompanied by three flying boats and a blimp) escorted them on the last leg of the journey. The next day, twenty more would follow. On each a prize crew was put on board, the white ensign run up and the submarines taken into Harwich. Eventually

---

* The British Admiralty formalised its initial position in a paper published in 13 October 2018, 'The Case for the Surrender of the German Fleet as an Article of the Armistice' (See Trask p. 319. USNSF, TX File). On 17 October Admiral Wemyss issued the formalised position on Freedom of the Seas, 'An Inquiry into the Meaning and Effect of the Demand for "Freedom of the Seas"'.

† Douglas Haig and Robertson, so often supported in War Cabinet by Jellicoe, particularly on the central issue of the need to focus on one front, the Western Front, would similarly support Jellicoe's removal from office, despite Lloyd George constantly belittling the field marshal in front of War Cabinet colleagues.

Germany would surrender 176 submarines.* The sight of their arrival must have been particularly poignant for many of the locals with memories of the April 1916 Lowestoft raid still vivid.†

The first group nearly did not sail at all. German sailors were deeply suspicious of the Allies and worried that they would be arrested as 'war criminals'. The submarines' continued existence had been seen in a very different light from that of the surface fleet. They had been used by Germany, so the argument went, for a criminal war that was often waged against civilians and neutrals in disregard of the established rules of war. Meurer is supposed to have specifically asked for a guarantee of the safety of submariners surrendering their boats. Not unnaturally, there was considerable anxiety that they would be treated as war criminals.‡ Beatty answered his concerns, saying, rather sanctimoniously, 'Admiral Tywhitt will guarantee their safety, but their honour is entirely in their own hands.'[139]

In the end, 'Only the payment of cash bonuses of 500 Marks, and a Life Insurance Policy of 10,000 Marks for each man, had restored their willingness to deliver the boats.'[140]

On two evenings – 15 and 16 November – Meurer had met Beatty and his staff on HMS *Queen Elizabeth* to hear the terms. Given Beatty's approach, it was small wonder that the meetings between himself and Meurer didn't proceed smoothly. Some of the preparations were understandable but Beatty's desire to humiliate his enemy wasn't productive and, arguably, laid the seeds for some of the problems down the road. In victory, he lacked the equanimity needed to empathize with Meurer's position. Back on their own ship, the Germans discussed the terms passionately until the early hours. Men on one of the British launches, silently patrolling the enemy cruiser's anchorage 12 miles from *Queen Elizabeth*, could quite clearly hear 'voices raised in argument, coming from the open scuttles of the *Königsberg*'s wardroom, and not until 0500 were the lights put out'.[141]

When the German group were handed the documents outlining the orders for the transfer, Meurer was given until 0930 the following morning to prepare his response. The documents were so detailed that it was clear that they had taken a lot of work by Beatty's staff. At best, the lack of time they

* Numbers differ. Temple Patterson states 170 (p. 210), George states that by 20 November 129 submarines 'had been escorted into harbour' (p. 20).
† While absolutely minimal damage was caused, with only three civilians and nineteen wounded, the coastal raids forged public opinion and gave birth to the 'Baby Killer' label that would be associated with the German Navy.
‡ It is sobering to point out the massive losses that those serving in U-boats also suffered: of the 374 put into service, 228 were sunk. 5,249 submariners lost their lives (see Witt, p. 55).

were given was both unseemly and manifestly unfair, and Meurer was visibly insulted. 'All questions were decided in his [Beatty's] favour without question.'[142]

Meurer, of course, asked for more time. He was especially concerned for the morale of the men as they were still in a visibly mutinous mood. He wouldn't be the one to have to deal with the longer term; that would be left to others. Most of the men simply wanted to avoid a resumption of hostilities even if there were deep doctrinal and ideological divisions in their ranks. Insultingly harsh terms would risk alienating the officer leadership, making implementation even more difficult than it needed to be.

Beatty would brook no delay and, at midnight 16 November, the terms were signed. It was hardly an 'agreement'.

Exhausted and – one would imagine – deeply depressed, Meurer was taken back at 0330 to his own ship. An hour later, on 17 November, *Königsberg* set course for Kiel with *Cardiff*'s squadron and her destroyers acting as a guard escort 'to a point halfway between Kirkaldy and Aberlady Bays, east of Inchkeith'... while 'the destroyers went to the Haddington shore, by Cockenzie'.[143]

As soon as Meurer departed, Beatty signalled the Admiralty, '...the representatives of the High Seas Fleet were prepared to agree to any demands we made and...they preferred their Fleet being moved to a safe place to the alternative of it being controlled by the Workmen's [sic] and Soldiers' Council.'

He also said that the German officers were 'pleased' by the fact that Beatty had refused to see anyone else but Meurer and his officers. There was little else about which they could be 'pleased'.

Beatty was dead-tired, but on top of that he'd also just received the news from Osbourne College that his son, David, had come down with pneumonia. He'd only just got through a case of the measles. If that weren't enough, the King and Queen would be visiting Rosyth on 20 November, the day before the German fleet's arrival. Testily, he complained: 'in the middle of it, the Monarch buts in under the auspices of the little ray of sunshine'.[144]

Beatty may have been exhausted, but he also seemed to be basking in the importance of it all. He was now, as he rather flamboyantly explained it to Eugénie on 19 November, 'in the position of commanding the High Sea Fleet as well as the Grand Fleet, which is a big business'.*

---

* Beatty must have been rather busy juggling his relationships during these weeks. He met his 'beloved Tata' at Inverkeithing (sp) railway station around the same time that he was writing to Eugénie. Eugenie was married to the King's Equerry, Bryan Godfrey-Faussett. She was described by Bob Massie as in her early thirties 'with long golden hair'.

4

ON TO INTERNMENT
– ROSYTH

To sail with the fleet into internment was, as anyone could imagine, not the kind of duty that many sailors would have relished. No one knew where they would be sent, what the conditions would be like, or, for the married ones who had left families behind, whether they were risking a lasting sense of guilt.

Karl Heidebrunn, a cook on one of the destroyers, *B.110*, had initially wanted to stay at home. Fellow sailors encouraged him to come, saying 'it won't take long. You'll be back home soon'.[145] In the end a bonus of 'several hundred marks' was too tempting an offer to pass up.[146] Like the submariners who had been offered cash and a life insurance policy, financial incentives often worked.* The guilt of leaving loved ones behind was offset by the help they could provide for them with much-needed cash.

Many doubted that the ships would be ready on time. There was a huge amount to be done, both in disarming as well as victualing them. With the rumours circulating that Helgoland would be seized by the British if the fleet wasn't ready, there was genuine encouragement from the revolutionary committees to get the work done as fast as possible. Often, it was the simple things that got in the way: store rooms had been seized and getting them opened up to supply the ships wasn't always as straightforward as it should have been.

All shell, ammunition and torpedoes had to be removed. Anything mechanically useful or potentially dangerous was stripped off: breech-block firing mechanisms, range finders, small arms or flares. It was work that many sailors found to be almost therapeutic, even cathartic. Small wonder that for some of the more extreme elements, the work gave them an 'inordinate enthusiasm for ...destruction'.[147]

---

* Woodward (p. 179) is more precise: 500 marks if married, 300 if single. He says that each man was insured for 1,000 (not 10,000) marks.

The man Hipper wanted take charge of the last sailing of the *Hochseeflotte* was Rear Admiral Ludwig von Reuter. He was well-known to Hipper: he'd been appointed in 1918 to command the battle-cruisers, torpedo boats and light cruisers that made up the fleet's scouting forces, the appropriately named Aufklärungsgruppe.* Reuter came from a thoroughly military family: both his brothers were generals and his father had commanded a regiment in the Franco–Prussian War.

The decision could not have been easy for Reuter. What had so recently been experienced in Kiel and Wilhelmshaven had left deep scars and divisions amongst the crews. Reuter's son, Yorck, eighteen at the time, remembered the day: 'I remember he went through our garden, back and forth, back and forth…he was thinking about this problem. Not all agreed what should [be] done with the Fleet and what not. He thought there was a possibility of saving it for Germany, or at least a part of the Fleet.'[148]

What kind of man was Reuter? He was born in 1869, the year before the Franco–Prussian War, the 'fifth child and the third son' of an army colonel who died while serving as a regimental commander.[149] The family was steeped in the military tradition and while he would rise to the rank of vizeadmiral, his elder brothers both became generals. Until Scapa Flow, he was described by van der Vat as an officer who was slightly past the prime and one having a 'good war'. His son, Yorck-Ludwig, described his father as 'Prussian', full of military values of discipline, duty and honour but he was a kind man, had a good sense of humour and an eye for the ladies. The Dutch writer was able to spend time with his son, coming away with a very personal and intimate portrait of the man who would shape one of the most decisive days in Germany's naval history. He was 'a man of action with the capacity, rare enough among such people, for reflection and even doubt, yet in the end decisive and responsible'.[150]

At midday, 18 November, Reuter took command of the fleet. It was on that day that it was supposed to have set sail but it couldn't because *von*

---

* Van der Vat maintains that Meurer himself was Hipper's first choice but his delay in getting back to Germany caused him to appoint another, more readily available officer, von Reuter. The ship Meurer had taken across the North Sea, SMS *Königsberg*, had been delayed getting back because of minefields. He'd become the Commodore of the IV *Aufklärungsgruppe* after he left the SMS *Derfflinger* in September 1915, taking his flag to SMS *Stettin*. While he was in command of *Derfflinger*, Reuter was present at the Scarborough bombardment. At Jutland, *Stettin, Munchen* and *Rostok* engaged HMS *Southampton* in the fierce night action. In September, von Reuter was given command of the II *Aufklärungsgruppe* and promoted to rear admiral, with his flag on the light cruiser, SMS *Königsberg*. He would often serve as the second in command of the I *Aufklärungsgruppe*, a position that was solidified in August 1917 when he was made the senior officer in command. The Second World War would wreak a terrible price on the family.

der Tann was running behind schedule. Later that day, the flagship, *Friedrich der Große*, arrived in Wilhelmshaven and, along with his new Chief of Staff, Fregattenkapitän Iwan von Oldekop, Reuter moved his flag to the 'the Big Fritz'.* He also took Lieutenant-Commander Angermann, an interpreter, Kapitänleutnant von Freudenreich, and two flag-lieutenants, Wehrman and Tapolski. Elsewhere, Fregattenkapitän Cordes took command of the fifty torpedo boats that were to accompany the main fleet and moved his staff on to the *S.138*.†

Through written orders, Reuter addressed all those who would be sailing with him. He said that he was 'at one with the crew [in] that every man on this transfer voyage will so fulfil his duties that the Fatherland will attain an early peace'.[151] His light, diplomatic touch was able to win him some important concessions at the first meeting of the Committee of 21. It was agreed that it would be the officers alone who would have responsibility for seamanship and navigation, secondly that the revolutionary soldiers' council would participate in all decisions in the day-to-day running of the ships; thirdly that officers would have independence in their own affairs; fourthly and most importantly, it was agreed that the right to refuse an officer's orders was now formally withdrawn.

Reuter had also worked out a plan for the revolutionary representatives of all the ships to meet at 0800 on the day of sailing to elect a three-man soldiers' council for the formation. To this group, the sailors' council added one of their own, a rating who had never even been on a battleship, let alone been at sea. Signalman Keller managed to get on board with forged papers and then, still casually smoking a cigarette, introduced himself to Oldekop, announcing that he was now the latter's 'technical advisor'.‡ It didn't take long before Keller was taken down a couple of pegs. Since few of the ratings could navigate, these duties were gradually taken back by the officers.

In the few days that the fleet had for the preparations on board, politicians like Noske attended the many formal meetings that took place ashore. He admitted that he'd become achingly tired with the absurd make-believe of it all:

---

* Oldekop would later be promoted to fleet commander, 1926–30.
† Former commander of the 7th Torpedo Boat Flotilla.
‡ Keller had been a shore-based signaller in Wilhelmshaven at the mouth of the 'third channel'. By this I think he is referring to '*Weg blau*', the extreme eastern channel that was kept swept for the HSF. The other two, from east to west, were '*Weg braun*' and '*Weg gelb*'.

The ship's band played light music, as an accompaniment to sandwiches and beer.... If the occasion had not been so grave, I would have burst out laughing at the speech of the little Chairman.... Ending up, this revolutionary said that he agreed with Bismarck: 'We Germans fear God alone, and nothing else in the world.'[152]

On 19 November, at midday, the transfer formation was to be ready to go to sea. The formation commanders – those of the III and IV Battle Squadrons and the 1st and 2nd Aufklärungsgruppen (The Scouting Forces or SGs) – were told to assemble on the flagship to receive their final sailing orders from Reuter at 0900. But as the allotted hour arrived, delays cropped up, one after the other. Eventually the ships left only two hours late, at 1400.

Part of the problem was the *von der Tann*. When the time came, she had not been ready as she couldn't raise enough steam. Her crew had been late getting started as her wireless operators were not at their posts when sailing orders had been transmitted. The light cruiser *Köln* also announced that she was having problems with her condensers. The decision was taken to put to sea but she would steadily fall behind the other ships. It was then discovered that there were no officers on some ships of either the II Torpedo Boat or III Half-Torpedo Boat Flotillas. Tired of waiting, Reuter left the officers behind. The VII Torpedo Boat Flotilla stayed behind to re-join the fleet a few days later, on the evening of 20 November.*

Friedrich der Große hadn't even reached Helgoland (it was off Wangeroog, one of the East Frisian Islands) when Oldekop ordered the red flags be taken down from the yardarm. He succeeded in unnerving the civilian chairman of the supreme soviet by informing him that if the red flag flew it would be seen as an invitation to be fired upon as it was, he lied, the international sign of piracy.

The internment group would be led across the North Sea by the veteran battle-cruiser, SMS *Seydlitz*. She was flying the broad pennant of Kommodore Wilhelm Tägert, who had been at the centre of the Wil-helmshaven unrest when almost sixty of his crew walked off. The ship was centre-stage at Jutland and had acquitted herself well but now her speed was limited to a paltry 12 knots.

---

* With the fleet sailed forty-nine destroyers. These came from the 1st, 2nd, 3rd, 6th and 7th Flotillas.

Ludwig Freiwald later wrote nostalgically about the line of great ships as they put out to sea,* 'In this symbolic train, Germany was leading into captivity the kings and generals who had shaped her destinies through two centuries.'[153]

Germany's generals *Moltke, von der Tann, Derfflinger*; and her monarchs *Friedrich der Größe, Kaiserin, König Albert, Prinzregent Leopold*. Magical names imbued with the past glory of the nation, names now besmirched with peeling paint, rust, dried out teak and oil stains.

There was something else about how the ships looked that didn't feel quite right. They were riding too high. After hundreds of tons of ammunition and coal had been offloaded, the great leviathans were sailing light. They were also steaming very slowly – at around 11 knots – conserving as much fuel as possible. They'd been asked by Reuter to take only enough food and water to last for the estimated internment period, at that point only thought to be the original thirty-six days, until 17 December.

Few on board had any idea of their final destination.† They only knew that they were to rendezvous off May Island and proceed to the Firth of Forth with a British escort. From there, they might go anywhere. Most German officers still had no indication that Scapa or any other Allied port would be the final destination. Rosyth, the first port of call, was, in Reuter's mind, only a brief stop-over 'to prove their (ships') disarmament'.[154] However, in the newspapers the rumour that it was going to be Scapa Flow was starting to circulate. One particularly astute observer on the *Orkney Herald* of 20 November, three days before the first advance units arrived in the Flow, got it spot on. 'Although nothing is known officially as to Sir David Beatty's intentions, it is probably (says a special correspondent of *The Scotsman*) that Scapa Flow will be selected as an appropriate and convenient harbour.'[155]

'There was no thought in our heads, no idea at all, that we might attack or anything like that,' said Karl Heidebrunn. Rather, 'We went across proudly and happily' (*stolz und fröhlich*). For many, there was a continued pride in the ships that had proven their prowess, fighting the mightiest Fleet on the seas: '*die vor 3 Jahren in ehrliche Kampfe mit die*

---

* The German author Ludwig Freiwald (1898–1945 missing) was a writer and propagandist, an early recruit to the NSDAP (Nazi party) which he joined in 1922.
† Reuter had actually been warned by von Meurer that he (the latter) was convinced that the Allies would not allow the German transfer formation to head to a neutral port (See van der Vat, p. 113).

mächtigsten der Feinde siegreich die Klinge kreutze'.[156] But for most, that wasn't the case. It was 'because we thought that for all of us and for our families at home things would start to look up now that the situation had almost calmed down'.[157]

There should have been four more ships, seventy-four in total. After the Helgoland Bight, the Germans crossed what should have been a swept channel to avoid mines.* However, one torpedo boat, the *V.30*, had strayed off course and paid for her mistake by striking a mine and sinking on the open sea. Two boats from the 3rd Torpedo Boat Division were able to rescue most of her crew but two men died and three were badly injured in the explosion. Reuter sent a signal informing Beatty of the loss at 0654, 20 November. On the 22nd the British admiral asked for a replacement.

There were a number of other ships missing. In Kiel, *König* and *Dresden* were still in dry dock and would only be able to follow in December. The new heavy-gunned battle-cruiser *Mackensen* was not ready (and none of her class would ever be built). She would later be replaced by *Baden*.

There were also some additional, unforeseen passengers aboard, a group of twenty British prisoners of war. They had, it was reported, 'made their way to Wilhelmshaven, and having heard that the German ships were to sail to Scapa they boarded the vessels and defied the Germans'.[158]

Though they clearly knew nothing about Scapa, they were happy to be home and were entertained in Inverness.

Throughout, signals were coming through from the Grand Fleet requesting continual updates on exact position and course. The formation was still under Reuter's operational command but it was to hand over command to Admiral Sir David Beatty after it arrived in British waters.

Early on the morning of Thursday, 21 November, the rendezvous point, 50 miles off May Island, was reached. The small island was the gatekeeper to the Firth of Forth. The time was 0800. The searchlight of a British destroyer was spotted from a German battle-cruiser and reported by signal at 0830. Overhead flew a British airship, the NS.8. The conditions were slightly closed in: the light was hazy and visibility was between 2 and 4½ miles.[159] The German ships continued looking for the *Cardiff*, which was to act as their leader into Rosyth. To be more easily spotted, she would be flying a Blue Ensign.

For the moment, the weather held. From the bridge of *Australia*,

---

* In documentation, the channel was referred to as 'channel 400'.

Captain James looked out: 'It was a beautiful day for the North Sea in November, a haze with a visibility of four miles, the sun trying its best to dispel the mist, a slight breeze with a calm sea.'[160]

The line of ships – battleships, battle-cruisers, light cruisers and torpedo boats – stretched out for nearly 19 miles.[161] Four battle-cruisers followed Tägert's lead, 'looking for all the world like a school of Leviathans led by a minnow', *Cardiff*, which was towing a captured balloon. Admiral Rodman had a similar picture. It reminded him of 'a little child leading by the nose a herd of fearsome bullocks'.[162] They were led by *Seydlitz, Moltke, Derfflinger, Hindenburg* and, finally, *von der Tann* followed.

Next in line was Reuter on *Friedrich der Größe* with nine battleships: *König Albert, Kaiser, Kaiserin, Prinzregent Leopold, Bayern, Kronprinz Wilhelm, Markgraf* and the *Große Kurfürst*. HMS *Phaeton* steamed in between the two large concentrations of ships and behind came *Kommodore* Harder leading the light cruisers, *Karlsruhe, Emden, (II), Frankfurt (II), Nürnberg, Brummer, Köln* and *Bremse*. In the second gap an auxiliary vessel, HMS *King Orry*, positioned, followed by the forty-nine torpedo boats, the latest from the 1st, 2nd, 3rd, 6th and 7th Flotillas.* A British destroyer was specially assigned for 'photographic duties'.

A great armada of Allied ships had gone to sea around 0400 that same morning, following Vice Admiral Sir Charles Madden's 1st Battle Squadron in his flagship, HMS *Revenge*:

> The fog had lifted, after five days, and the lower air was clear, but clouds hid the moon and stars and made the night dark. Silently through the darkness ship followed ship down in the open sea, an ominous awe-inspiring procession of black shapes, each indistinctly silhouetted against the sky and canopied with a smudge of smoke. The *Queen Elizabeth* took her place near the end of the line.[163]

At daybreak and now at sea 'in the grey morning mist', the fleet formed two parallel lines, 'from end to end, [it] measured at least 15 miles'. Meurer had been told by Beatty that 'a sufficient force will meet the German ships and escort them to the anchorage' (at the Firth of Forth), but Reuter could not have imagined for a moment anything like what he saw that day. It

---

* George (p. 21) mis-states, I believe, the last flotilla as the 17th not the 7th.

was the 'largest assemblage of sea-power in the history of the world'.[164] A massive mixed force of ships, mostly British, spaced 6 miles apart, two great lines of armoured jailers approaching from the north. In total, there were forty-four capital ships, of which thirty-four were battleships. There were two of the new aircraft carriers, forty-six cruisers and eight twenty-strong destroyer flotillas.

Placed amongst the British ships, were various Allied contributions: two destroyers from the French Navy and ships of the American 6th Battle Squadron. Vice Admiral Hugh Rodman proudly led the five American ships, the USS *New York*, *Texas*, *Arkansas*, *Wyoming* and *Florida*.*

It was a scene of epic proportions. 'Vast' (*eine unüberseebare Flotte*) was how one sailor on the *Kaiser*, described it. Werner Braunsberger and his fellow sailors were 'astonished' (*erstaunt*). *The Orcadian* quoted one man's impression: 'So vast was the area they covered that both the head and the rear of the columns stretched away into the haze and were lost to sight.'[165] But to many German officers, the fact that Beatty had put to sea with such a large force only strengthened their belief that they had not only not been defeated at sea, they were still a formidable and dangerous foe that the British respected. What Beatty had intended as their humiliation was taken as a compliment. It showed the seriousness with which the threat of their navy was seen.

To port, fifteen battleships held station. They were supported by four battle-cruisers, twelve cruisers and the two aircraft carriers, *Furious* and *Vindictive*. On the starboard, where Admiral Beatty watched over the gigantic procession from the bridge of *Queen Elizabeth*, came eighteen other battleships, a further five battle-cruisers and eighteen other cruisers. In the centre, behind the German torpedo boats, were seven lines of British destroyer flotillas, five Grand Fleet Half Flotilla leaders screened by the flotillas of the Grand Fleet.

The display was so impressive that a commemorative print, showing the position on the sea of all the ships involved that day, was specially commissioned and given as a gift to many officers. Across the top was emblazoned, with great irony, the words '*Der Tag*' in Gothic script.

After the meeting, the two lines of Allied ships turned 180° in the final custodian act to head back towards the Forth. The time given was 0943.[166] 'On coming abreast of the German Fleet, the British Fleet turned

---

* While only HMS *Caroline* still exists from the ships that had been at Jutland in 1916, and is today berthed in Belfast behind the great *Titanic* museum, the USS *Texas* still proudly flies her flag and serves as a floating museum.

by squadron, 16 points outwards, wheeling, that is to say, back on their own track, retaining positions on both sides of the Germans to escort them to their anchorage.'[167]

The scene was illustrated from one of *Cardiff*'s escorting cruisers: '*Cardiff* then turned about, 'marked time' as the German ship approached, took station on her and then the great trek to captivity started. The remaining four ships of our squadron steamed on past the German battleships and battle-cruisers.'[168]

Some German sailors were able to make out red flags on some of the British ships. The ones on the starboard side. Rather naïvely, they concluded that they were revolutionary flags and that what they had been told by some of their own revolutionaries – that there was also mutiny in the Royal Navy – must have been true. It was, of course, nothing of the sort. For the day, Allied ships had been divided into two forces, 'red' and 'blue'.

As Beatty steamed out in front of his fleet's ships, ratings gave 'Three Cheers'. From her halyard hung the same tattered white ensign that had flown from HMS *Lion* at Jutland.

Under the trained guns of the Royal Navy, the German fleet sailed towards captivity still unaware of their final destination.* The German ships, despite *Cardiff*'s continual requests to maintain 12 knots, slowed to around ten, so badly maintained and in such great need of repair were their propulsion systems. Much to the embarrassment of the officers (and, for *any* sailor, it would have been embarrassing), the ships bunched up, some even breaking formation to heave out of line.

A British dirigible flew overhead, photographing the seemingly never-ending line disappearing into the haze of the North Sea. Two aircraft were sent up to offer a completely unnecessary protective screen. Unluckily one, an Avro 504K, crashed into the sea near some of the escorted German destroyers, causing a good deal of mirth amongst the watching sailors.[†] The incident probably went a long way to relieving the tension.

Reuter did not want the British to feel as though they were paid any homage or honour. His sailors were not lining up along the decks as they would have done at a fleet review. Though he had ordered that the

---

* The detailed orders for the guard ship formation was called 'Plan ZZ'. It was meant to signify the very last operation of the war but I can't help thinking that there was an element of humour tucked away there.
† With almost 9,000 produced in the war, the Avro 504K was probably the type produced in the highest quantities. The small biplane continued to be produced until 1932.

traditional blue uniform be worn by all, many didn't bother. Most of the sailors lounged about on deck, smoking and chatting in small groups, visibly ignoring the great parade that Beatty had arranged for their arrival.

As the German ships entered the penultimate leg of their journey, the Firth of Forth, visibility started to deteriorate. Mist, fog and drizzle formed a cloak. It gave the Germans a welcome reprieve. Reuter was thankful that '...heaven conferred a certain mantle upon our shame in the form of a light veil of mist and the most tremendous tragedy ever enacted at sea was thereby softened to the view'.[169]

The British media also felt that the weather had diminished the pomp of the occasion. *The Orcadian* report tried to make light of it: 'From a purely spectacular point of view the pageant was robbed of some of its splendour by the low mist, which blurred all outlines and refused to yield to the cold brilliance of the sunshine. But the significance of the meeting and the procession was more important than its appearance.'

The British admiral, however, took no chances: this was not the surrender of the German fleet. It was a voluntary internment while the final terms of surrender were being worked out under the protection of the Armistice. This very fundamental point – though seemingly legalistic – is still misunderstood. Neither Beatty nor the vast majority of Allied naval officers wanted some small incident to blow up into a full-fledged confrontation. Any small incident could have quickly spun out of control. That nearly occurred when one of the German destroyers lowered a boat without permission. It was dealt with without incident but there were obviously some who wanted to see the Germans provoked enough to bring about their total destruction. After four years of war, with the loss of friends and family, there was a desire for vengeance that is difficult to comprehend today.

The British ships that awaited the arrival of the Germans were all prepared for action, despite the fact that their counterparts' had been stripped bare of the smallest means of self-defence, let alone aggression. The slightest hint of resistance would have been met with overwhelming and decisive firepower.

High above, in the director towers, binoculars and rangefinders carefully tracked the German ships, ready for instant action should it be needed. Secondary armament was fully loaded and trained. Rounds had been chambered and the guns were ready to fire. The main armament might have looked less menacing. The guns were trained fore and aft and not, as some later mistakenly reported, directly aimed at the German ships. But the heavy guns remained ready for action, nevertheless: inside the main turrets, rounds lay ready to chamber and the turrets were not locked. Mechanical gun-layers were 'up and loaded, ready for ramming home'.[170] Torpedoes were also trained and ready for launch. Torpedo officers kept constantly updating range and bearing data. Deep below the decks, the stokers kept the boilers ready to raise steam for an immediate execution of 'full speed'.

Both inside and outside their turrets, gunnery crews, gas masks ready, were all wearing anti-flash protection. A contemporary postcard shows British sailors wearing their white asbestos flame-retardant headgear, with a tagline, 'they would not trust the Hun even at the last'. The tension was palpable: 'It just needs a shot from either side to start the whole show off again,' remarked a marine major, Rendell.[171]

Again, like the gigantic demonstration of sea power on the open sea, many Germans often interpreted these precautions in a different light. Like Karl Heidebrunn, 'You really had to laugh...fully armed and guns cleared. Well, I think they were scared.'[172]

Each escorting ship was assigned an enemy ship for which she was temporarily responsible until their 'target' was handed over to another. Jellicoe's old flagship, *Iron Duke,* was at one point responsible for *Seydlitz* and then handed over to *Marlborough*. German ships were escorted into captivity by their old rivals: *Seydlitz* beside *Princess Royal, Moltke* beside *Tiger, Derfflinger* beside *Lion*. What happened with the Australian ships was interesting: HMS *Melbourne* was assigned *Nürnberg* but HMAS *Sydney,* having sunk her predecessor, was symbolically given the new *Emden*.*

As the once-proud German ships passed down the lines, sailors on each of the ships of the two great naval powers eyed each other, stern brass nameplates bringing to mind the fierce action of past battles. 'Old antagonists, victors and vanquished'.[173] From the high yard arms above *Friedrich der Größe* a white flag, a sign of surrender and shame, fluttered, 'That day hit within its bosom the most shameful act in all the history of the sea. The voluntary surrender of the German Fleet.'[174]

On the stern of his flagship, HMS *Queen Elizabeth*, Beatty stood and took the salute, lifting his cap and waving to the cheering sailors of the Grand Fleet, anchored on each side of Forth Bridge. He was in his element, adored by his men and worshipped by his officers.

Then Beatty did something that many – British and German alike –

---

* HMAS *Sydney* sunk the first SMS *Emden* off the Cocos Islands in November 1914.

still regard as 'bad form'. He ordered the German flag to be hauled down at 1557 and that 'it was not to be hoisted again without permission'. For many German officers it was not merely 'high-handed', it was extremely insulting.[175] These were flags that, for the Germans hitherto 'no British guns had been able to lower'.[176] Reuter protested saying that he was 'of the opinion that the order to strike the flag is not in keeping with the idea of chivalry between honourable opponents'.[177] Beatty stuck to his guns, refused to debate the issue and simply said that no German ship could be allowed to keep its flag in a British port. More than anything else, this one act stuck in the gullet of many a German and built a deeply held and persistent grudge against Beatty that still lasts today in German naval circles.*

He once again took the salute from the fleet, in the middle of which he turned around and quipped: 'I always told you they would have to come out.' A service of Thanksgiving was ordered to be held at 1800. It was, in Marder's words, 'reminiscent of Nelson's after the Nile', a man who had always been Beatty's guide and hero.[178]

Before continuing on from Rosyth, the German ships were first assigned positions at Inchkeith. The real work of the day, to make sure that the ships were completely disarmed, would take place while the Grand Fleet took up guard positions north and south of the bridge. An Australian midshipman, John Armstrong,† described how 'the Huns anchored in the form of a square about 20 miles up the Forth and below the Fleet anchorage' where the 1st Battle Squadron and 2nd Battle Cruiser Squadrons acted as the guard ships.[179] Ships of all size and description watched as the defeated fleet was shepherded to their assigned buoys by their new jailors.

The final sortie of the German fleet had been designed by Beatty and the British in such a way as to bring about the maximum humiliation of the enemy. Wolz described what unfolded that day as 'more humiliating than defeat in an action at sea could ever have been'.[180] It was clearly designed to bolster British naval prestige. Neither the American nor French navies had any particular axe to grind. At that moment, Beatty's feelings for the Germans were quite clear: '...the only thing is to sail into their poisonous country, wreck it and take what we want and put the fear of God, Truth and Justice into them... .'[181]

---

* Reuter thought about raising the Ensign on 22 November but decided that it would be too provocative (see van der Vat, p. 125).
† The three predominantly Australian-crewed ships were HMS *Australia*, HMS Sydney and HMS *Melbourne*.

It was not just for David Beatty's own personal need that the 'conspicuous proof' of the Royal Navy's superiority be so publicly paraded on this day. It was also there to bolster the morale of the service.

The planning for Operation ZZ, the Great War's last massed gathering, was focused on bringing one point across to the British public: the magnitude of the Royal Navy's achievement:

> By all thinking persons, the part played by the British Royal Navy and the British Mercantile Navy in attaining this consummation is recognised, but it is likely that the full significance of the final victory at sea, obtained by the British, unmarked as it has been by any dramatic episode such as would appeal to popular imagination, may for that reason achieve something less than its proper share of attention.[182]

It was not unnatural that a man of David Beatty's character would think that the outcome of the naval war should reflect on him, on the way he commanded the Grand Fleet, and he would forever chafe at not having achieved the decisive Nelsonian-like victory to which he had always aspired.

In many ways, however, it was not Beatty's 'lowering of the flag' order or the heavily stage-managed procession to Rosyth that was the basis of the German Navy's sense of humiliation, but rather, the intimacy of the ensuing inspection of the ships. It was the intrusion in to personal space that brought home the sense of powerlessness. It was also the way in which German officers were treated by the men, in front of those who should have been their common enemy. It was the sense of arrogance, insult and hatred that permeated the proceedings as Allied boarding parties went through their ships, from top to bottom, completely unimpeded.

It certainly did not help when Lady Beatty decided to cruise up and down the lines of defeated German ships in her yacht, the *Sheelah*. It was an enormous vessel, so large that it had served as a hospital ship.[†] When she sailed too close to the *Seydlitz*, she was received with a derisive crescendo of catcalls and jeers. It not only showed remarkably little respect or even good sense, it also could have easily turned nasty.

The first inspections of the German ships, carried out as darkness was

---

[*] The *Sheelah* was a 700-ton yacht that Ethel Beatty owned. The yacht was loaned to the navy by Lady Beatty from 1914–23 to serve as a hospital ship. At her own expense, the boat had been fitted out with an operating theatre.

falling, were superficial. It was to make sure that their disarmament had been correctly carried out. A longer inspection was planned for the following day.

Beatty had departed Rosyth, leaving Admiral Sir Charles Madden, his 2iC, behind. Madden went aboard SMS *Friedrich der Größe* accompanied by Commodore Michael Hodges, two staff officers and an interpreter. After an 'extremely cool' initial meeting, Hodges handed Reuter a thick package that contained the minutely detailed British orders for how German ships were to conduct themselves during internment. Reuter was ashamed of how bedraggled and dirty his men looked in 'the most unkept and filthy attire', how they had called out to the British and asked for cigarettes. He said it was a 'picture cut deep into my soul and will never fade from my memory'.

As more parties boarded German ships, two things were immediately apparent: that 'all the senior officers had been left behind' and that those remaining had little authority. *Australia*'s Captain James took Rear Admiral Halsey around on an inspection of some of the German ships the next day and noted that 'nearly all the sailors wore a little red ribbon to show they were revolutionaries and there were men with white armlets with 'Soldier & Workmen's Council' on them in all ships'.[183] Some sailors had – following the Kaiser's flight to the Netherlands – changed their cap tallies by cutting out or covering over some of the lettering: taking the 'SM' from their cap tallies, so that SMS *Prinzregent Luitpold* would now only be '*Schiffe*' ('the ship'), or 'S *Prinzregent Luitpold*' and no longer '*His Majesty's* Ship'. Others had painted the entire black, white and red cockade on their caps red. German officers had been ordered to take off their rank insignia and those that did not had them torn off by 'the dehumanised revolutionaries'.[184]

A *New Zealand* crewmember described one of the visits: 'The Germans had manned ship all around their guard rails and the Captain was in tears on the quarter deck, where also were Commissars or ratings acting as such.'[185]

Armstrong, like Captain James, said he saw much the same on the *Hindenburg*. There he described how 'a couple of petty officers wearing armlets with *"Arbeiter und Soldaten"* on them seemed to have equal control…(as) the officers,' although he added that the crews were 'very orderly and saluted our officers when passing'. James agreed: 'there was no case of actual disrespect towards us, but great curiosity,' and that, as he and other officers went through the German ships, they were saluted. Robert Willan, later Rear Admiral Willan, remembered more smaller details of the individuals, 'the stiff Prussian lieutenant' and with him, 'the entirely friendly and professional engineer'.[186]

On *G.91*, the suspicion and dislike with which each side viewed the other was obvious. Leutnant Fritz von Twardowski's torpedo boat had been boarded by an officer from HMS *Speedy*. Twardowski decided to keep him waiting while he finished shaving. It was, at best, a petty show of defiance. When he appeared on deck, he was smoking and had his hands in his pockets. Small wonder that the possibly already disagreeable British officer (for whom he later learned, even the British had low regard) and he both took umbrage with one another. The British lost face when their own ship then had engine problems immediately after the inspection of the German destroyer. They had said that they were 'most impressed' with what they saw, especially because of the 'quality of their ships and their armament'.[187] In the embarrassed confusion, *G.91*'s ensign remained flying and had not been taken down as ordered. A British PO came back on board to tear it down. The German crew merely laughed at him.

Friedrich Ruge was a young officer on another torpedo boat. He would later return to Orkney and write about his experiences on Scapa Flow.* For him these inspections went too far. Rifling the men's personal lockers for arms and ammunition was, simply put, 'exaggerated'. Furthermore, the fact that nothing was mentioned in the Armistice terms about inspections made them completely questionable in his opinion.

It was not just small arms and ammunition for which the boarding parties were looking. There were significant medical concerns as well. Doctors were included in the boarding parties. In August, there had been an outbreak of influenza in the fleet and the Allies were taking no chances that this could be an unwelcome addition to their worries. Spanish flu had broken out earlier in the year and was scything down large swathes of the world's population.†

Beatty did not invite many outsiders to this important moment. It was, after all, the *finale* to four bitter years of struggle. As the German ships slowly inched their way into the Forth, they were watched by Beatty alone. Neither Jellicoe or Churchill had been invited. Nor Fisher or Battenberg, for that matter. The naval historian, Oliver Warner, later said that had such an invitation been extended, it would have been, a 'gracious gesture'. Fisher,

---

* Friedrich Ruge, *Scapa Flow 1919*.
† The virulent influenza affected almost 500 million people, 10 per cent of whom are estimated to have died. Already in 1917 the virus was thought to have passed through fourteen American military camps.

apparently, felt the lack of an invitation 'keenly'.[188] Charles Beatty it seems, mistakenly wrote that Fisher 'took no umbrage'. Jellicoe's reactions are not known but he was far too modest to have publicly voiced his displeasure or hurt. He probably felt it, seeing at how badly he had been treated at the end of 1917. The rather implausible reason put forward, and one for which Charles Beatty said the basis for his concern was 'obvious', was that he was worried about the possibility of hostilities breaking out and feared the responsibility should one of the three be killed.[189] It was much more likely that his vanity got the better of him and he simply did not want anyone 'to rain on his parade'. It was a very vain and needlessly offensive gesture. This was not the glorious shining moment of which David Beatty dreamt; that of the returning, conquering hero.

Van der Vat captured the emptiness that Beatty must have felt on the day:

> The most spectacular moment in his career, when the disarmed bulk of the German High Seas Fleet accepted defeat without a shot being fired and presented itself for internment under his tutelage, was the hollow climax to an extraordinary career which he completed as First Sea Lord after the war.[190]

I do not think that this was far from the truth. Beatty wrote to his mistress, Eugénie Godfrey-Fawcett: 'The Fleet, my Fleet, is broken-hearted.... All suffering from a feeling of something far greater than disappointment, depressed beyond measure.'[191]

He also wrote to his wife: 'Well, Pansy, we have met the High Seas Fleet at last...It has been misty all day and that rather impaired the spectacle...and could never see more than half a dozen big ships and a dozen or so destroyers at one time.'

He concluded: it was an 'unutterably dull and monotonous day'.[192] Was this just 'folie de grandeur'?* I think Wemyss came closest to describing how unsatisfactory the end was. Wemyss said that it was 'a frame of mind which can readily be understood'.[193] I think he hit the nail on the head:

> There was a marked disposition on the part of the Commander-in-Chief and his officers to regard the climax [the Armistice] as

---

* The historian Sir Henry Newbolt (1862–1938) called it 'an act of administration hardly worth describing'. Quoted in Ruge, p. 53.

unworthy…What they got was a victory far more crushing than any Trafalgar and with none of its attendant losses on our part – but also without any of the *personal glory* [italics my own] which would have been attached to the survivors.

A young lieutenant on the *Inconstant*, Ouvry, found himself thinking that it was sad that the German fleet internment could not have been just a month earlier, 21 October, Trafalgar Day.[194] Maybe the same thought passed through David Beatty's mind that evening as he attended the service.

Beatty never once visited the interned fleet at Scapa – perhaps for the same reasons. It would have felt like a hollow occasion, a reminder that he had not achieved the kind of victory that his hero Nelson had.

Throughout the first two days, emotions ran high. Everyone had been waiting for this day to arrive. For four long years they had tried to defeat their enemy at sea. Here he was now, almost within arm's reach. It seemed unreal. Captain James remarked: 'It made one rub one's eyes and ask if it was really true and not a dream that this formidable Fleet was steaming into our anchorage without giving a shot to uphold its vaunted boastfulness, *"der tag"* indeed!.'[195]

Whatever the hidden feelings were, the day was unforgettable. There can be no question of how electric and emotionally charged these moments were, albeit that they were so varied – shame at surrender, relief that the war was over, lingering anger at the proximity of an enemy, fear of what lay ahead, bitterness at the loss of friends.[196]

A deafening noise was carried across the water. British sailors could hear German bands 'playing lively music…They must have been just as pleased as we were that all was over'. Aside from the music on the German ships, 'the crews got hold of anything that would make a noise and bashed it to hell'.* All along the shores civilians lined the banks of the Forth and clambered over the Forth Bridge to be a witness to this historic moment.

The surrender of the German Navy was the best experience I ever had in the Royal Navy. We were allowed up one at a time from our action stations and we could not believe our eyes; it was like a wild dream, just miles of ships. That day, of course, all leave was stopped. Officers and petty officers all got tight that evening…[197]

---

* Brown and Meehan, p. 126, quoting Sydney L Hunt.

5

ON TO INTERNMENT
– SCAPA FLOW

Torpedo tubes empty
Gun chambers empty
So, we went on, an unarmed army
And brought our ships,
By our own hand
To Scapa Flow
And like that we lay there, day after day
But come what will or come what may
Our power is broken
Yet our pride stands good
We're certainly carved from a very tough wood,
We Germans

KARL HEIDEBRUNN, COOK ON DESTROYER *B.110*

Rosyth was but a short stop en route. It was a fleeting interlude of public ceremony, mixed with behind-the-scenes ship inspections carried out with curt aggression. Although Scapa had already been decided upon as the final destination, the British had still not been officially confirmed or communicated their decision. Although British Admiralty directives started to hint, the German Armistice Commission, like the sailors, was also still in the dark. Transports accompanying the German Fleet – there to take men back to Germany – were now ordered to make for the Pentland Skerries south-west of Orkney. Rumours started to circulate on German ships.

Not surprisingly, an increasingly angry tension filled the air. Some even pointed to being kept in the dark as being the cause of the later scuttle. Officers such as Ruge, for example, justified the later action by saying that 'failing to carry out honourably the few obligations that he had accepted, the enemy himself had paved the way for the scuttling'.[198]

It is surprising, however, that Reuter seemed to have been in the dark. But, had he known about the transports going to the Pentland Firth, might he have guessed? And, would it have made any difference at this point?

In hindsight, it should have been all too obvious that Scapa would be the final choice. Most other ports would not have had anything near the infrastructure needed to house ships of this size and on this scale. Scapa Flow, however, was: 'the answer to a naval strategist's prayer...the rock-bound entrances are few and narrow but deep and made even more formidable to those who don't know them by vicious tides and frequent storms'.[199] It was Jellicoe's immediate successor at the Admiralty, First Sea Lord (1SL) Sir Rosslyn Wemyss who had first suggested the Orkney base.

The value of Scapa Flow had been recognised for centuries. The 80-square mile body of water was a natural harbour.* Its importance in both wars was that it became the natural choice for a fleet anchorage that would dominate the North Sea. First Lord, Churchill put it this way: 'In a war with Germany, Scapa Flow is the true strategic point from which the British Navy can control the exits from the North Sea and enforce blockade.'[200]

The special trains that ran between London and Scapa with troops and supplies echoed this importance.† Hewison quoted the claim that: '... the *Jellicoe Express* became 'the longest distance train ever run in the British Islands and probably the most punctual'.[201]

Being placed precisely where needed for its strategic role did not, however, guarantee that the governments of the day would correctly develop and protect the location:

> Given the supreme importance that Scapa Flow represented as a naval base, it was, however, inexcusable that its defences were so weak at the outbreak of war. Sir George Callaghan, the Grand Fleet's Commander-in-Chief before Jellicoe, described it as 'practically defenceless'. It prompted Churchill, then First Lord of the Admiralty, to write in 1914 that 'the Grand Fleet is uneasy. She could not find a resting place except at sea.'[202]

Churchill was one of the few to recognise the problem, saying that: 'nothing should stand in the way of the equipment of this anchorage with

---

* Its use for a naval base by the Royal Navy was first suggested in 1812 by Graeme Spence.
† Robert Foden is a railway historian based in Orkney with a particular interest in the *Jellicoe Express*. Quite correctly, I got into trouble for calling it as Hewison had, the *Jellicoe Special*!

every possible means of security. The First Lord and the First Sea Lord [Fisher] will receive a report every third day until this work is completed and the C-in-C [Jellicoe] is satisfied.'[203]

Jellicoe, true to his nature, was extremely anxious and moved the fleet's base to the west coast of Scotland, to Loch Ewe, for many of the initial months of the war, and even, for a short while, over to Ireland.

During the war, Scapa was not as well developed as it should have been. In fact, many of Scapa's more notable defences – including the famous Churchill Barriers – were only completed at the end of the Second World War.

Concerted construction on the oil facilities that were eventually built above Lyness did not start until war's end. Ships of the Grand Fleet would coal from tenders in the harbour. That also tied up shipping that could have been used elsewhere.* In 1916, the SNOAS (Senior Naval Officer Afloat, Scapa) recommended that the Admiralty purchase the land in Lyness for oil facilities. They wanted the land near Rysa Lodge. The Admiralty baulked at the costs. In January 1918, the funds were finally released and compulsory land purchases started under the auspices of the Defence of the Realm Act.

You can still see one external oil tank.† The L-shaped stone wharf is the First World War one and fuel lines up to the six external oil storage tanks were run across it. Down by the shoreline, huge depots were built for paravane and torpedo support as well as what now looks like a fairly derisory building that was the 'officers' quarters'. Sadly, much of the site was badly damaged by gales in the winter of 2016. The visible signs of Scapa Flow's naval heritage are fast disappearing.

The outline of the first naval base was completed in 1920 but mothballed until 1936, when the Royal Navy renewed its interest. It would not be until January 1939, however, that a decision was formally made to use Scapa as a major naval base again.‡

---

* *Prudentia* was HMS *Iron Duke*'s oiler. Her wreck is at the bottom of the flow. She sank in a gale when *Iron Duke* collided with her.
† During the Second World War an additional six external oil storage tanks were built, each with a 12,000-ton capacity– giving a supply for a month's typical operations. In 1938, work began tunneling into the hillside located above where the naval cemetery is to house a huge underground storage facility (to stock around 105,000 tons). The whole crown of the hill was hollowed out to hide the tanks from aerial reconnaissance and bombardment.
‡ The concrete slab that runs down from the Lyness Visitor Centre was laid to support all the facilities for the harbour's boom defences and as you walk into the centre you still see piles of torpedo netting rusting away. You can also just make out the net troughs along which the nets were hauled into the Flow.

Extensive anti-aircraft facilities were built including searchlight, radar and anti-aircraft gun emplacements as well as hydrogen production facilities for the balloons. Training programmes in specialties including radar and ship firefighting were established. Repair shops were everywhere.

The old paravane depot became a 900-seat cinema, the other half a training facility. Playing there became a star attraction for performers and artists from Vera Lynn to Yehudi Menuhin. After the end of the Second World War, the site was scaled down but remained operational until around 1957. The oil was shipped out and the Orkney Island Council (OIC) purchased the site to create the visitor centre.

The irony in choosing Scapa cannot be overlooked. The Germans had looked longingly at the number and strength of the ships that were at anchor there. For both the Kaiser, whose naval ambition knew few boundaries, and for Tirpitz, who became the architect of that ambition, entering Scapa as victors would have been a crowning moment. 'Probably to no place in the world did the enemy look to with more longing eyes than on this isle-girt stretch of water in the northern mists. Attempts by submarines – and perhaps by other craft as well – may have been made to penetrate to its recesses, and to strike a blow at Britain's vitals.'[204]

Now the Germans came into the great harbour aboard ships that were, to paraphrase Hewison, 'dirty, disarmed, dishonoured and defeated'.[205] Many contemporary commentators were struck at just how run-down this once-mighty Fleet looked.

> The German Fleet, by all accounts, is in an appalling state: both ships and crews. The vessels are dirty, foul-smelling and ill-found. Their speed, owing to the lack of lubricating oil, had to be reduced to 10 or 12 knots – and of the crews, no better description can be given than that of a naval rating who took part in the surrender. 'I never saw anything' he said, 'in such an absolute state of de-composition.' 'What do you mean? The ships?' he was asked 'Yes; and the crews, too. Absolutely awful! No paint, filth everywhere... .'[206]

The first ships to leave Rosyth for internment in the Flow were the torpedo boats, some of which left on 22 November. Two further groups followed on the 23rd and 24th, 'escorted by an equal number of British destroyers'.[207] Friedrich Ruge was on one of the first group of roughly forty ships – twenty German and twenty British destroyers.[208]

Reuter stayed on for a couple more days, only finally leaving four days after his arrival, on 25 November. An equal number of British battleships escorted him, and again an equal number of British light cruisers shadowed the three German LCs that left Rosyth two hours after the flagship. One of these, *Köln*, straggled along behind, her condensers continuing to hold her back. In early December the last of the internment force, which had arrived at Rosyth on 21 November, left for their new home: Scapa Flow.

CHRONOLOGY OF ROSYTH DEPARTURES & SCAPA ARRIVALS

Leave	Arrive	
22/11		Torpedo boats leave Rosyth (van der Vat).
23/11 Sat	23/11 Sat	First group of twenty arrive in Scapa Flow (Burrows, Ruge, and George, p. 22). The second group of torpedo boats leave Rosyth (van der Vat). This must be the second group of roughly twenty boats.
24/11 Sun	24/11 Sun	Second group of twenty torpedo boats arrive in Scapa Flow (Burrows, George, p. 22). Torpedo boats leave Rosyth (van der Vat). Battle-cruisers leave Rosyth (Wiki.de).
25/11 Mon	25/11 Mon	Five battle-cruisers and ten destroyers arrive in Scapa Flow under escort by HMS *Lion* and the British 1st Battle Squadron (George, p. 22) and ten torpedo boats (Burrows). *Friedrich der Große* leaves Rosyth with German 4th Battle Squadron (van der Vat). *Köln* plus two LCs two hours later (van der Vat). Since only forty-nine torpedo boats came across (*V.30* struck a mine) the precise numbers are clearly wrong.
	26/11 Tue	Five German battleships and four German light cruisers arrive under escort by five ships of 2nd Light Cruiser Squadron (LCS) (Burrows).
	27/11 Wed	Four German battleships and three German light cruisers arrive under escort by four ships of 1st Battle Squadron (BS) (Burrows) and four from 3rd LCS (George, p. 22).

	6/12 Fri	*König* arrives at Scapa directly from Germany with the heavily-leaking light cruiser *Dresden* and the *V.129*, which has been sent as the replacement for the *V.30* after the latter hit a mine (van der Vat).
	9/1 (1919)	The last ship to arrive is *Mackensen's* replacement, the *Baden*, which does not arrive until after Christmas, on 9 January 1919 (van der Vat).

The first German ships to arrive in the Flow were the torpedo boats that had left the day before. Ruge, on board *B.110*, described how they arrived in the early morning of 23 November. It was a Saturday, 'just after daybreak'.[210] The weather had been a 'grey November morning'.[211] He described Scapa at the time as being 'mostly dark'.

Over the next few days, more torpedo boats followed with the battle-cruisers, battleships and light cruisers of the High Seas Fleet. Great warships such as *Moltke* steamed into the flow, dirty and bedraggled, her magazines 'full of potatoes'.[212] Her officers later admitted that they had not been sure they would make the journey alive and that they had 'feared they would probably be "blotted out by the ship's crew on the way over"'.[213] A British admiral, Parry, commented that the *Karlsruhe* was 'filthy and couldn't have been cleaned in weeks'.[214]

Specific anchorages were assigned to each of the German ships as they

ARRIVALS BY WARSHIP TYPE

Vessels / Date	23/11	24/11	25/11	26/11*	27/11	6/12	9/01
Battleships				5	4	1	1[†]
Battle-cruisers			5				
Light cruisers				4	3	1	
Destroyers	20	20	9[‡]			1	

[*] This column indicates arrival of *V.129, König & Dresden*.
[†] *Baden* arrived from Cromarty.
[‡] Last group indicates missing torpedo boat, *V.30*.

arrived. The Flow had been divided into three sections around an imaginary line between the lighthouse on Cava and what was then the Houton seaplane base (and what is now where the Hoy ferry docks). This line was the dividing point between the two northern sections where the battleships, battle-cruisers and cruisers lay. The smaller craft, the torpedo boat flotillas, were to the south, in Gutter Sound. The eight cruisers were to the east.

British ships were normally at anchor north of Flotta and just to the east of Fara. Most of the destroyers to the south were out of line of sight from *Friedrich der Größe,* where Reuter had his flag (before he was forced to move to the *Emden*). This disposition of forces was not ideal for either the British or Germans. It put many ships out of the signalling line-of-sight. In fact, the island of Cava lay directly in the path of that line.

North of Rysa and to the east of Cava were locations for ships in Section 1. Battleships anchored here included *Bayern, Große Kurfürst, Kronprinz Wilhelm, Markgraf* and *König. Other ships included Emden, Köln, Frankfurt, Bremse* and *Dresden.*

Section 2, to the west of a line running north from Cava, was for the battle-cruisers (*Seydlitz, Moltke, von der Tann, Derfflinger* and *Hindenburg*) and the battleships (*Friedrich der Große, König Albert, Kaiserin, Kaiser* and *Prinzregent Luitpold*). Other ships assigned into Section 2 included *Karlsruhe* and *Nürnberg.* Each ship in the two northern sections was given a degree bearing and a distance from Cava Light, the most distant being *Friedrich der Große*, at just under a mile away (1,480yds) from the lighthouse at a bearing of 331°.

Section 3, between Rysa and Fara, was reserved exclusively for the torpedo boats in an area of the Flow known as Gutter Sound. *S.138* was designated the senior officer's (Cordes) boat and allocated anchorage P.2.

Orkney is actually a collection of sixty-seven islands, of which only seven surround Scapa Flow itself. Scapa Flow can be a very desolate spot but it can also be gloriously beautiful. Its waters can be mirror-like and calm, or thrashing, white-capped in the fury of a winter gale. For around three weeks a year, gale force winds howl across from the vast stretch of the Atlantic. The Flow is unpredictable. To any sailor going into what amounted to captivity, the Flow's beauty remained elusive. One seaman from the *Kaiser*, Braunsberger, summed up only what he saw: 'the bight was surrounded by treeless hills and was desolate and cheerless'.[215] For the most part, Orkney has no trees, and the land is flat.

Locked into a life aboard their rusting ships, they immediately understood just what a tough posting Scapa Flow had been for their adversaries. *G.91*'s captain, Leutnant Fritz von Twardowski, concluded that his enemy's lot must have been 'thoroughly frightful'.[216] Most German officers would also have understood the additional pressure that being based in Scapa would have put on any commander. In Kiel and Wilhelmshaven, the sailors could not only go ashore, but most were barracked on dry land. Not so for the sailors of the Grand Fleet.

As Reuter himself came into the Flow, he wrote about his first impressions:

> The lower parts of the land showed signs of rude cultivation, trees and shrubs were nowhere to be seen. Most of it was covered in heather, villages were just in sight on the land in the far distance – apart from which here and there on the coast stood unfriendly-looking farmhouses built of grey local stone. Several military works, such as barracks, (air)plane sheds or balloon hangars, relieved the monotonous sameness; in ugliness they would beat even ours at a bet.[217]

Reuter himself may have loved the sunsets and the stunning experience of seeing the Northern Lights, but it was hardly any just compensation for the months of relentless and repetitive monotony.

Most British sailors who had been at Scapa would agree. Beatty joked that he hoped that the 'Hun' would enjoy its hospitality as they themselves had. The British had an expression for any sailor visibly suffering the effects of Scapa's desolation. They called it the 'Scapa tap'.[218] The mental condition that many sailors suffered might have been 'treated with levity' by their pals but it was a 'serious situation' for people 'with a nervous temperament'. Cases of depression were frequent.

It was hardly surprising that the British saw the Germans' internment in Scapa as some sort of payback. 'To the British officer, the fact that the Germans are being forced to live at Scapa Flow in their own ships is one of the most perfect examples of poetic justice in the whole war... .'[219]

What Friedrich Ruge really thought is difficult to know now. He was a young, twenty-four-year-old first lieutenant serving as the officer of the watch on the torpedo boat *B.110*. His half-flotilla of four boats was 'to be their home for an indefinite amount of time' during their stay in Scapa.[220] The 4th joined together with the 3rd Half-Flotilla and the ten ships formed the 11th Torpedo Boat Flotilla under a single command ship.*

---

* Three had remained in Germany, eight sailed to Scapa Flow.

Aboard the first torpedo boats to arrive in the Flow, Ruge's own, *B.110*, would have arrived just after first light had broken. Out over the waters, it would have been almost completely silent, hardly a ripple disturbing the black, mirrored calm. The view across to Hoy, the Norse-named island meaning 'high island', is breathtaking, but its hills are also bleak, steep and covered in dark scrub. Arriving on a wintery day, there is often a mix of blue skies and dark low-hanging cloud that drifts threateningly over the low hills. Through this, rays of sunlight burst through in long shards, sprinkling the dark, cold grey-blue waters with slivers of sparkling silver. After a few months, the poetry would have long worn thin. Those first feelings of elation at the sheer beauty of the Flow would have been replaced by deep feelings of loneliness, of having become the forgotten sailors of Germany's navy.

By the end of November, Reuter and his men were finally established on the Flow. But the Seekriegsleitung, German Naval High Command, had no idea where they were, literally – a signal was sent to the C-in-C of the Grand Fleet: 'Where are the interned ships?' The afternoon of 10 December, at 1453 – almost three weeks after the first arrivals – they got their answer: 'Vessels are interned at Scapa Flow.' Meurer had been right all along. The British had deceived them.

It was difficult to get troops to serve in Orkney, even as part of the ground defences. Royal Marines were given extra pay by being able to count their duty there as 'sea time'.[221] Activities were severely limited by the special terms of the Defence of the Realm Act, rather endearingly known as DORA. Photography or sketching of any coastal landscape was forbidden.

It was very easy for the Germans, after four years of fighting in a war in which millions had been lost or maimed, to become the object of British hatred but, for the most part, British efforts were solely geared to the purposes of security and nothing more. Officers were instructed to be minimally courteous, and not to forget how the German Navy had behaved (particularly its submarine arm) and that they were technically still at war. As one midshipman wrote: 'It is as well to treat them as lepers after the way in which they have conducted the war for which they longed so much.'[222] It is hard now to write about these deep feelings without carrying the obvious contemporary concern for peacetime relations and the renewed friendship between the two countries. But it is important to realise that these enmities were completely understandable, and had purposefully been whipped up by the wartime press and propaganda machines of both nations.

How would it have felt to be on the receiving end, to be the object of so much blind hatred? Many German sailors felt that they had been gravely insulted:

> The British Fleet received us with the greatest mistrust, cleared for action and torpedoes in tubes… . There were still some men who, together with their officers, felt deeply this day of ignominy and humiliation… . Polite, cold, scornful regards greeted us, with no remnant of esteem for the past.[223]

But some of the Germans also took it in their stride. Sub Lieutenant Yates asked that the band on the SMS *Kaiser* play 'The Hymn of Hate'. He recalled that they told him 'they never play *Gott strafe England* now as they had been too much 'straffed (punished) by both Gott and England'.*

Here and there one can detect a real note of sympathy for the German sailors' – or their officers' – plight. Articles in *The Orcadian* wrote about these issues on a number of occasions '…Still one does not expect to see an officer forced to push his way through two lines of lounging seamen before he can reach the side of his battleship'.[224] Although there was never any likelihood of mutiny in the Royal Navy at the time, one could imagine British officers seeing this and thinking of their own circumstances. 'The sight of efficiency and discipline gone to pot' reported one officer, who came back depressed after a visit to a German ship. He went on: 'The mess decks were in appalling condition and the officers were dumb with shame when our men came aboard.'[225] The fact is that the British had taken great care to maintain good morale among crews, especially when the Grand Fleet had used Scapa Flow as the main fleet anchorage.

What about the islanders, the Orcadians? From the adults, there likely was an equally large amount of anger. Not only had they lost many of their own during the war, there were also many British naval officers and men lost who would have been known to, and friends with, Orcadians. Just from the ships lost at the Battle of Jutland (if one subtracts the losses on HMS *Invincible* as Horace Hood's 3rd Battle-cruiser Squadron flagship was only temporarily in the Flow for gunnery exercises), around 428 left the evening of the 30 May 1916 never to come back from ships that included the destroyers *Spitfire*, *Sparrowhawk*, *Fortune* and *Ardent*. The price

---

* The meaning of the hymn was 'God Punish England'. Quoted in Marder, *FDTSF*, Vol. 5, p. 272.

paid by British sailors during the war would have been keenly felt by Orcadians.

But with the younger ones, the children, it was different. For those married sailors, with children of their own, the sight and sounds of Orcadian children playing on the shores could only have sharpened their own sense of profound loneliness. German sailors would while away the hours of boredom by whittling down wood and sending small ships floating across the water, across to land on the shores nearby as gifts to the children.

John Tulloch recalled the magic of these small model boats.* A great deal of time was spent walking the shores just looking for these special items of interest. Here 'jetsam that floated ashore from the interned German Fleet was a great source of wonderment' to the small boy.[226] He said that he collected a large number of items on Cava's shores:

> These I had anchored in our duck pond that had become a miniature Scapa Flow. There were battleships, destroyers, coal boats, tankers, schooners, tugs, submarines and even seaplanes. Most of these ships were made to perfection and I have never seen anything to match them in a toy shop window since, in fact, they were masterpieces of craftsmanship that would have delighted the heart of any small boy.[227]

Tulloch also said that he had a collection of other German artefacts that was large and diverse: 'Caps and their name ribbons from practically every ship that ever entered the Flow, badges and gold braid of all descriptions, buttons, scarves, cords and numberless other things of all descriptions.'[228]

Tulloch must have wondered, 'Were these people as bad as I've been told?' He said that they (his family or friends, presumably) 'often watched German sailors dive over the side of their ships and swim around for a while as their mates shouted and cheered them on'. Empathy is found in proximity. The sounds of their daily lives, carried across still waters, surely would have touched many ashore. The words of one ten-year-old girl is

---

* John Tulloch's family lived in a small house on the west side of the island of Cava. Neither his father nor his grandfather had returned from the war and the house was shared with three uncles, Bill, John and Eric, though the last was still in Germany. I've never seen one of the models that Tulloch references in Orkney but I imagine that they are there. Many of the other artefacts can be seen today in Stromness museum.

a reminder: 'As a child I thought, why shouldn't they go down with their flags flying, even though they had been conquered. We felt sorry for them, you see – we felt sorry for those that were in the sea and the struggle with the ships. Being children, we didn't think of them as being an enemy.'[229]

In a document running to around 10,000 words, the British outlined how they expected the German ships and crews to behave during the internment. The 'Instructions for German Ships' (IGS) were meticulous and often harsh. Reuter was to be the sole point of communication between the British senior naval officer, the so-called SNOAS or 'Senior Naval Officer Afloat, Scapa'. During the time that the Germans were to be interned, the British had two interlocutors: Reuter and (when he went back briefly to Germany over Christmas) Kapitän zur See Hugo von Dominik, Captain of the SMS *Bayern*. Meanwhile, Reuter had to work with five different men during his time in Orkney, each one a delegated operational commander appointed by Admiral Madden: Packenham, Oliver, Leveson (who did two tours of duty), Keyes and, finally, Sydney Fremantle.*

At first it was with the battle-cruisers that the British guarded the Germans, then the 2nd Battle Squadron under Leveson and finally, the 1st Battle Squadron under Fremantle. Maybe Madden had specifically done this to avoid the possibility of any sense of camaraderie building up between the two senior officers of the interned and guard fleets. British sailors or personnel boarding German ships were not allowed to shake hands with the Germans or accept or eat any food while on board. Reuter, in fact, developed quite a close relationship with Fremantle, even if the latter had to publicly decry Reuter's later actions. But when he talked of Madden, the German had a slightly different tone. He noted that Sir Charles would accompany him to his drifter, 'The formality observed

---

* Admiral William Packenham (1861–1933) had commanded one of Beatty's battle-cruiser squadrons at Jutland. Rear Admiral Leveson (1868–1929) had been 2iC of the 2nd Battle-Cruiser Squadron at Jutland and given command of the 2nd BS in April 1919. Admiral Sir Henry Oliver (1865–1965) commanded the 1st BCS in 1918. Roger Keyes (1872–1945) had planned the raids on the Ostend and Zeebrügge submarine pens and in March 1919 took a short command of the Battle Cruiser Fleet with the acting rank of vice admiral. Sir Sydney Robert Fremantle (1867–1958) joined the Royal Navy in 1881 and would become the overall commander at Scapa Flow when the scuttle occurred in June 1919. He had served in the Dardanelles as commander of the 2nd Cruiser Squadron in 1916, the 2nd CS the following year and the Aegean Squadron from 1918–19. He served in the Admiralty as Deputy Chief of Naval Staff (DCNS) in 1918 and became vice admiral commanding the 1st Battle Squadron in 1919, a post he held until 1921. He retired in 1928.

towards me was of a cold nature but not without a certain courtesy.'* Madden's behaviour followed the spirit of his own orders:

> It is to be impressed upon all officers and men that a state of war exists during an Armistice. Their relations with the officers and men of the German Navy, with whom they may be brought into contact, are to be of a strictly formal character. In dealing with the late enemy, while courtesy is obligatory, the methods with which they have waged war must not be forgotten. No compliments are to be paid and all conversation is forbidden, except in regard to the immediate business to be transacted.[230]

The Imperial flag was not allowed on any ship (although it later became clear that many had been kept hidden aboard). Reuter was happy at least that the command flags and pennants were allowed. His own pennant taken from the SMS *Emden,* with a black cross on a white flag with a single black circle in the lower left quadrant, is now in the National Maritime Museum collection at Greenwich. On the *S.138*, the Führer der Torpedoboote, Cordes, would have also flown his command pennant.

To underline the legal independent sovereignty of the German ships, the British were not allowed to place guards on the ships themselves since the German fleet had not surrendered and were still, therefore, to be regarded as German territory.[†] Even after as qualified a writer as Captain Geoffrey Bennett explained that the word 'surrender' was taken out of the amended Article XXIII of the Naval terms, he still went on to say that 'it is not often that the Fleet of a great power *surrenders to*, or submits to internment by, another Fleet'.[231] With such ambiguity in the written word, it is no wonder that there continues to be little understanding of how difficult it was for the scuttle to have been prevented.[‡] Politicians so often sign up to agreements that military men find impossible to entertain. It was no different then. Beatty certainly did everything he could to sound as loud a warning as he could.

---

* A drifter was a fishing boat 'specifically designed to allow their nets to drift with the current, unlike trawlers, which pull their nets at deep levels beneath the sea' (Booth, p. 8).

† Writers such as George (p. 26) did make a point of underlining this.

‡ Later in the same article Bennett makes the position on internment and surrender clearer when he says that Fremantle 'expected the peace terms to [finally] require the surrender of the German ships' (Bennett, *Scapa Scuttle*, p. 537).

When the inevitable scuttle took place, the British were quick to point fingers. The Secretary of the Allied Naval Council's opening lines of the 23 June enquiry were direct:

> It will be seen that the British and French Naval Delegates never wavered from their opinion that the German surface warships should be surrendered and not interned, and only accepted the Internment finally as a decision of the Heads of their Governments and after reiterated protests.[232]

This single clause made any effective prevention of scuttling almost impossible. Under the heading, German Surface Ships (GSS), the details for how British personnel should behave was outlined. Eight drifters, scattered around the interned fleet keeping a close eye on any suspicious activities, would work in shifts and would be relieved each morning at 1000. Aboard each drifter an armed boarding party, defined as three officers, forty-five sailors and marines, would be on ready watch. They were armed, revolvers and swords for the officers, two Lewis machine guns and rifles with bayonets at the ready for the men. Each man was issued ten rounds of ammunition. The guarding light cruisers and battleships had to have steam ready for 8 knots at one hour's notice. And they also had to have boarding parties of two officers and thirty men at the ready.

German sailors were not allowed to board any interned ship (other than the one they crewed) unless for specific official business and then only with prior permission from the British. Only three people in the German Fleet had any permanent freedom of movement. Reuter himself and his two fleet chaplains – the Evangelical Lutheran Pastor Friedrich Ronnenberger and the Roman Catholic priest, Father Esterkand.*

Ronnenberger's activities in the fleet were heavily controlled by the soldiers' councils which regarded him with deep suspicion: 'His activities extend only to purely Church and instructional subjects. Politics are forbidden him by us. The Soldiers' Council exercises the sharpest control in this connection and is authorised to refuse him permission to speak in case of non-compliance with their injunction... .'[233]

---

* Friedrich Ronnenberger (1886–1968). Ronnenberger came as the pastor to the Garrison church (*Garnisonskirche*) in Wilhelmshaven in October 1915. He came back shortly before the scuttle and worked with Marinepfarer Müller. In 1926 a new altar painting was installed in the church. It was by the painter Schnars-Alquist and showed a cross floating above the North Sea grave of the 2,000 German sailors who died. The message was still '*Gott mit uns*'. He went on the 1928 world cruise of the *Emden*.

He was not even allowed on board four of the twenty-six interned battleships and cruisers. It's interesting that – like morale – religious participation was apparently higher on the destroyers than on the battleships.[*]

At first, Reuter was allowed to use his own pinnace to travel between his ships and this he did. Of course, he had to let the British know which ships he was planning to visit. He could only do so between 0900 and 1500, when his pinnace would fly the international 'F' flag. When Reuter realised that its crew had been infiltrated with revolutionary sailors and that messages were being passed between the anchored ships, fuelling the crisis of discipline on board, he stopped the practice altogether and, instead, started using a British drifter. (At night, however, Reuter's pinnace was sometimes secretly used by the sailors' council to visit ships of the fleet under cover of darkness.)[†] There were some others who could move around the interned fleet. Usually, for example, the drifters were accompanied by a German officer and a doctor. The arrival was eagerly awaited, not only for news from other ships, but also for some new jokes that might bring some welcome levity to the awful tedium.

Crews were not allowed off their own ships, nor were they able to travel between others. One might understand them not being allowed on to inhabited islands, but they were not even allowed on to the small, uninhabited tufts of land on the Flow. That did not seem to stop the sailors. There were reports of sheep raids on Flotta and that 'some of them did land on Hoy, and had to be hunted back to their ships by armed patrols'.[234] When the ships arrived for internment, it was reported that quite a number had gone ashore on one of the islands but 'were turned back by a picket boat'.[235]

If they were caught they would have been liable to have been shot. In fact, as soon as the fleet arrived for internment, German sailors had taken to their boats and come up alongside RN ships desperately seeking food. It was lucky that this did not spark an incident right at the start. The British would allow two drifters to carry traffic between the German flagship and British flagship. However, as time passed German sailors swam between ships that were close by, and in the German Naval Association archives there are photographs of sailors on the Flow in a

---

[*] It was a curious statistic but Ronnenberger maintained that 95 per cent of the destroyer crews attended services, while only 75 per cent did so on battleships.

[†] There was even a session of the council with representatives from other ships on the *Friedrich der Größe* (see Ruge, p. 79).

small row-boat. As a nine-year-old living on the island of Cava, John Tulloch grew up with the German fleet 'at his door':

> Some of them were so near to my home that on a calm day we could hear sailors talking or singing quite clearly. On a Sunday a brass band on the SMS *Friedrich der Grosse* used to play their German military tunes when weather was good, so those great ships became a part of my childhood days, a source of jetsam that was picked up wandering around the shore of my island home.[236]

His memories give us a glimpse of what life might have been like:

> Then one fine day when the patrol drifter was away up around the north side of the ships, a sailor dived over the side of the SMS *Nürnberg* and doing an overhead stroke swam across to the SMS *Moltke*, where ready hands helped him aboard. Many times, afterwards I saw sailors swim from ship to ship until to me the occurrence became a commonplace thing of which I thought nothing.[237]

The daily routine of the light cruiser *Bremse* gives a good idea of how precisely structured the daily routine was: 0730 wake up, 0830 breakfast, ship duty 0900 to 1100, meal preparation 1130, ship duty 1400 to 1730, evening 'tea' 1745, cleaning the decks and, finally, 1945 rounds. Sundays were still special: the crew got an extra half an hour sleep-in but would still be expected to dress in their Sunday best (*Sonntagsanzug*).

There was no formal radio link between the Flow and Germany but it is difficult to believe that there were no clandestine radio receivers. They would not have been hard to set up. Written communications were taken back by the supply ships that dropped off food deliveries or by the designated mail ships, including *B.98*. News from home took a long time to reach the sailors as both the newspapers and their letters had first to be censored by the British.* That step usually added more than a week. Then more delays had to be factored in: getting from the flagship to the individual fleet ships once the materials had passed the censors.

---

* At one point, the British insisted that letters and correspondence from Germany be written in Latin script instead of the extremely difficult to read (and now defunct) Fraktur Gothic text to make it easier and faster for the censors.

The Germans still bore the responsibility of keeping their ships serviceable. The readiness of German ships was defined as being able to manoeuvre when needed in stormy conditions, and to run generators to support daily routine on board. This was easier said than done. Extra precautions were taken to make sure boats were securely fastened to the buoys. On B.110, for example, Ruge described how 25m of chain was cut and doubled to make the fastening as secure as possible. Each ship was to display three bow lights and two stern lights at night. A British destroyer was moored close by so that they 'were under observation the whole time'.[238]

The currents in the Flow were unpredictable. They could change dramatically and sometimes seem to be running simultaneously in two directions, even within the confines of a couple of destroyer lengths, and again Ruge described how the sterns of his boat, B.110, and B.112 could end up facing each other. The destroyers were always at anchor, tied one to another, so both crews usually stayed on one ship at night to keep oil and generator usage to a minimum.*

Imprisoned on their ships, the men developed all sorts of diversions. Not really with the leadership and help of their officers as would have, most likely, been the case on British ships – their diversions were more their own initiative. One torpedo boat's crew modelled a primitive crossbow and managed to kill seals and seagulls.[239] Like other prisoners of war, taking care of the mind was paramount. On B.110, for example, there were lessons in 'English, Geography, Mathematics and Chemistry'.[240] English was popular as the drifter visits meant an opportunity to talk to the boarding parties, even if the colloquialism or heavily accented conversations were sometimes barely intelligible, even utterly confusing. Chemistry would have required too many additional materials for any worthwhile lab demonstrations but, after the engine room crew made the request, algebra was added to the boat's curriculum.

But it wasn't all lessons. Ruge remembered: 'then we even played tag around the funnels and the bridges – a destroyer is quite good for playing tag'.[241]

Ruge complained that the British were incapable of organising something as simple as a film hall. Additionally, though he didn't say this, films would have tremendously helped maintain morale, and, therefore Reuter's position. ('und etwas wie ein Kinovorstellung auf einem der englische Versorgungsschiffe wagte man bei uns gar nicht zu denken, obgleich das ohne

---

* On B.110, the crews from two other destroyers – B.109 and B.111 – bunked down at night. Ruge said it was manageable but 'things got rather tight in the wardroom ...at mealtimes'.

besondere Schwierigkeiten zu organisieren gewesen wäre.' ('Something like a cinema show on one of the English supply ships was not even thought of for us even though it would not have been difficult to organise.)[242] The young officer would while away the hours listening to opera, often Caruso, playing from a nearby ship. He said later, in a radio interview, that he and his fellow officers 'wanted completely to avoid giving the British any reason to interfere with our privacy, if I may say so'. One got the impression, years later, that there was little love lost between Ruge and his former captors.

Some of the projects were quite unique. On the *Seydlitz*, the crew even spent time building a carousel and a model cable railway. More often, sailors would spend hours, days and months fishing off the sides of the great rusting hulks of their once proud ships. 'What an end to it all!' summed up the feeling at seeing 'along the quarter-decks, in a row by the taffrail... a collection of German seaman with bamboo poles and lines attached'.* The reporter was struck by the condition of their uniforms, 'variegated, ragged and dirty' and their 'extremely youthful appearance'.[243] The few photographs of those days depict sailors fishing while others stand about, hands in their pockets, with nothing better to do. The body language is almost zombie-like.

Generally, it was the case that the smaller the ship, the better the morale and discipline. Where the officers and crew messed together, such as on a destroyer, morale and respect were usually higher than on the capital ships where, ironically, more space meant more comfort on board but their size also meant that crews had been more radicalised earlier in the war. Both the *Von der Tann* and *Derfflinger* had equally bad reputations as far as the agitation of the soldiers' and workers' councils was concerned, and ships that had been based at Kiel – mostly those of the III and IV Battle Squadrons – were rife with agitators. *Kaiserin* was full of 'evil elements', *Friedrich der Größe* was, in Reuter's words, a 'madhouse' and a 'hornets' nest'.[244] It was where the supreme sailors' council was headquartered and its revolutionary zeal was most fully felt. It got so bad that, in March 1919, he moved his flag to the *Emden*. *Größe Kurfürst* was one of the worst turned-out ships in the fleet, while on the *Bremse*, there was even a plot to kill the captain, Oberleutnant zur See Schacke. Van der Vat concluded that the light cruisers were probably the best place to be – a compromise between added space and limited crews.

* The ship's taffrail is the handrail around the poop or afterdeck.

It was a dangerous environment and very stressful for Reuter's officers. There was little or nothing to do to blow off steam. In Matrose Braunsberger's words, there were 'always the same comrades round you, always the same ships round you, always the same view of land…'.[245] Hermann Cordes had an interesting metric. Given the deck layout of a torpedo boat, the maximum a man could walk in one direction along a 5ft wide path was forty paces. That was one advantage the large battleships had where, for example on *Kaiser*'s decks, 100m running races were possible and you could even walk a good 172m from bow to stern. Despite all those advantages, Cordes recorded that the weather in the Flow in the spring of 1919 was so bad that walking outside was only possible, anyway, for two days in the whole month of March. Life must have been miserable.

In these circumstances, an officer's responsibility to look after his men's interests was paramount. Most were either not up to the task or simply didn't care. The winter of 1918–19 was made worse by its severity. Scarce coal supplies and the gradual breakdown of ships' boilers made the ships' frigid steel casing icy. It was especially bad on the torpedo boats as they had no dedicated boiler for heating or light, so only a complete shutdown was possible if fuel were to be saved.

Admiral Sir Charles Madden saw first-hand how badly the chain of command had been affected on the German ships. Already on 29 November, only days into internment, Madden wrote of the collapse of morale and the aggression that existed between ranks: 'All proposed orders are considered and countersigned by the men's committee before they are executed and then they are carried out as convenient.'[246] ('*Alle geplanten Befehle werden von der Mannschafts Vertretern geprüft und gegenzeichnet. Dann werden Sie ausgeführt, wie es gerade paßt).'*[247]

In many ways the breakdown was inevitable. It had already been put in motion in Kiel and Wilhelmshaven; now it was deepening. The social hierarchy between the officers and men was stark and, even within the officer class there were unnecessary distinctions: 'Engineering officers…occupied a lower social status within the officer corps than the Seamen officers.'[248] Ober-maschinist Müller on the *Friedrich der Große* was only accepted once Reuter had actually specified, in a written contractual form, what his reduced powers were ('*nachdem Reuter in einem schriftlichen Vertrag seine Berfugnisse beschnitten hat*').[249] Even between the men, the more technically oriented tended to come from the industrial areas and were more likely to be unionised, while the rest of the crew were made up from the more traditional sources that included those living on the coasts, sailors and fishermen.

As repatriations to Germany started, manpower was gradually reduced. By December, their number had shrunk from 20,000 to just under 5,000.* It meant fewer mouths to feed but also fewer men to administer. The figure of 5,000 can only, at best, be an estimate.† No truly accurate records were kept. The British had encouraged the reduction, allowing for only minimal skeleton 'caretaker' crews to remain on the ships: 200 for a battle-cruiser, 175 for a battleship, 80 for a light cruiser and 20 for a destroyer, leaving a nominal total of 4,565, plus 250 officers and warrant officers (although the exact figures are thought to be higher). The British did not roll-call the ships or really bother to count. Roughly 1,000 men remained to man the battle-cruisers, 1,925 the battleships, 640 the light cruisers and another 1,000 the destroyers.

The repatriation routine was to fill the supply ships with men for the return trip to Germany each time they had dropped off their cargoes. Before the end of December, there were three such visits. The men who were going back to Germany were told to bring back as much as they could: bedding, eating utensils, bunks, tools, chronometers, binoculars and anything that was made out of copper. It was left up to their initiative or based on what the soldiers' councils told them. ('und der Heimkehrern wird befohlen, Kojenzeug, Eßgeschirr und Hängematten mitzunehmen. Kriegs-flaggen, Werkzeuge, Chronometer, Ferngläser auch alles, was auf Kupfer ist, packen sie von sich aus ein oder auf Anregung einzelner Soldatenräte').[250] Given the limited space available on the transports, it made Reuter's task even more difficult. But it was completely understandable. Supplies and resources were severely limited in Germany; why should anything of value be left for the Allies? While the British didn't particularly care about the numbers, they went through the sailors' kit bags meticulously, searching for anything they could pilfer.

The first exodus from the Flow was on 3 December. Two ships, the SS Sierra Ventana and the SS Graf Waldersee, arrived with supplies in the usual way. The Sierra Ventana was tasked to take twenty-five officers and 1,000 men, the Graf Waldersee more, roughly 150 officers and 2,200 men.

---

* The calculations of repatriations and the remaining balance differ slightly between sources. Around 4,000 sailors returned to Germany on 3 December, 6,000 on 6 December and 5,000 on 12 December, leaving 4,815, of whom approximately a hundred continued to be repatriated each month (see Massie, p. 784 and p. 786). By June 1919, there were around 1,700 sailors (Hewison, p. 128).
† Krause (p. 209) points out the difference in the calculations in von Reuter's report (where he states 5,900) and Ruge's (where the figure is given as 4,700). In my own calculations, I end up with 5,025.

Although the ships should have only stayed for six hours, the *Sierra Ventana* did not leave until the morning of 4 December and with more than 600 extra crewmen than planned for. A total of around 3,975 men.

The next two homeward transport ships, the SS *Pretoria* and the SS *Bürgermeister*, arrived two days later, on St Nicholas Day, 6 December. Each took 250 officers. The former took an additional 4,000 men to Kiel, the latter 1,500 men to Wilhelmshaven. With these additional 6,000 men the total sent home had now reached almost half the original crew complement: 9,975.

A week later, on 13 December, it was the turn of two more ships, the SS *Batavia* and the SS *Bremen*.* The former took 200 officers and 2,800 men to Kiel, the latter a further 500 officers and 1,500 men to Wilhelmshaven. *Bremen* eventually arrived in Kiel on 14 December, although, ignominiously, she ran aground at Wangeroog and was delayed from entering the harbour for several hours. The total exodus from Scapa now totalled almost 15,000 men. This included Reuter, who not only wanted to get back to see his family in Wilhelmshaven, he also needed to see the Fleet Command (Flotteleitung). He planned to stay in Germany for around a month. Whom he saw and what he discussed would later become a source of considerable speculation.

To help understand these numbers, normally the complement of these ships would range from five to twenty times the current complement present on the Flow: On battle-cruisers, roughly 1,130 men, battleships 1,120, light cruisers 500, destroyers 95.

Reuter used the transfers carefully. It was a way of purging the more politically unreliable elements from the ships. The core of troublemakers was probably not more than 150-strong, but it was essential to get rid of them if he were to have to completely rely on his men one day. He also got rid of officers in whom he had lost confidence, officers who were 'useless or little respected' (*unbrauchbare oder unbeliebte*).[251] Another way of getting the troublemakers weeded out was to send them back on *B.98*, the torpedo boat that delivered the mail. De Courcy-Ireland said that Reuter 'took advantage of the return trip' to ship additional men back to Germany.[252] Between the various repatriations, almost 1,400 officers were sent back.

---

* The *Batavia* had an interesting history. In the thirty years of service taking the rich and famous across the Atlantic to America, she had set the record for the highest number of passengers arriving at Ellis Island in a day and counted among them one special name on its passenger manifest, the writer Mark Twain. *Bremen* had passed through the wreck field after the *Titanic* disaster, though she had not stopped to pick up bodies. There was another White Star liner there specifically for that purpose.

		Low	High	Average
Battle-cruisers	*von der Tann*	923	1,174	1,049
	Derfflinger	1,112	1,182	1,147
	Moltke	1,053	1,355	1,204
				1,133
Battleships	*König*			1,136
	Friedrich der Große (Flagship)			1,084
	Bayern			1,136
				1,119
Light Cruisers	*Nürnberg*			475
	Köln			559
	Emden			475
				503
Destroyers	*V.45*			83
	S.138 (Cordes' command boat)	80	84	82
	B.110			114
				93

On 9 February, Reuter was back with the fleet for his fiftieth birthday. Though some of the ships had made a special effort to put together a choral performance in his honour, it must have been a thoroughly depressing time for him. (It was around then, on 25 March, that he had transferred his flag). Things had become so intolerable on the *Friedrich der Große* that it was the only way he could get some sleep. Reuter's appraisal of the 'the big Fritz', Scheer's former flagship, was that it was a 'mad house' ('*tollhaus*'). *Große Kurfürst* was the same. It was totally run down and looked neglected ('*vernachlässigte*').

A group of sailors who called themselves 'the red guard' used to jump up and down on Reuter's cabin roof each night, denying the poor man any sleep and roller-skating around on the after deck above the officers' cabins solely with the intent of harassing their commander and his staff. No wonder that the officers felt they were fighting a war on two fronts – one against the British, the other against communist agitators. The light cruisers, *Bremse* and *Emden*, were considered some of the quietest ships in the interned fleet.

So, even with these pretty drastic manning reductions, Reuter's objective of shipping out the worst offenders was not completely met. Even the British wanted Reuter to go further – for different reasons – certainly.

What was officially recommended and what the men actually received for their daily food allowance, were very different: 140 grams fresh meat, 30g sausage or bacon, 30g of vegetables, 20g sugar, 600g bread, and 50g milled or pasta products.[253] Although food was sent twice a month from Germany, it was barely sufficient. It was not only in short supply but it was also, invariably, monotonous: 'mediocre potatoes, jam made from root vegetables, and barley and bread with a strong addition of potato flour formed the main part'.[254] In this case, 'root vegetables' meant beets.

The deliveries and logistics weren't well organised either. Ruge gave an example: 'The entire list of articles which the ration office in Wil-helmshaven could deliver in February consisted of soup flavouring, salt, mustard cucumbers in glass jars or kegs, pickles in jars and tins, preserved fruit, wine, cigars and cigarettes as always.'[255]

It wasn't long before two of the most important staples were in critical supply. Soap ran out in February and in April cigarettes ran out as well. As there was an excess of fat – completely appropriate during high-calorie activities such as battle – there were quite a number of cases of jaundice. Other items always seemed to be in short supply – writing paper, toothpaste, lighters, toothbrushes and pens in particular – while items like rat poison for the infested ships was in constant demand. The British flotilla commander of the destroyers sent special packages of soap and cigarettes when he found out how poor the conditions for the German crews were. It was a rare case of compassion between seafarers who should naturally have been closer in spirit.

Even when the German ships first arrived at Scapa, it was clear that their crews were hungry. As each ship pulled into its designated spot, the bulwarks were soon crowded with men fishing. 'It was very comical,' remarked the British observer, 'but they might have been hungry.'[256] Ruge described there being 'swarms of small fish like sprats'.[257] The fish would be 'smoked or fried up in torpedo oil'.[258] Supplementing their diet with fish was the obvious first recourse. Later, fishing became more sophisticated. On *B.110* a net was rigged and was lowered into the Flow from the stern at night. The two stern lights attracted the fish. It was a very successful zero-calorie method of gathering what they needed but did not occupy the men as the old method had.*

Meat, by contrast, was very scarce and 'in awful condition'. 'To supplement their meat rations, they carried out a few raids ashore and slaughtered a few sheep, much to the crofters' concern.'[259] A local paper reported on the highly dangerous attempts to forage on the islands:

> Parties of seamen attempted to land on one of the islands, but were turned back by a picket boat. Under cover of darkness, however, a raid seems to have been made on a flock of sheep. Boat crews of Germans came alongside some of our cruisers, pleading for food. To ensure their strict confinement to their vessels, all boats were removed from the German ships.†

Under the defiant – and slightly ridiculous – headline, 'How British Tars stopped sheep stealing', *The Sunday Post*, carried a detailed story of one such early raid on Flotta.[260] The raid had been organised 'because Tirpitz & Co failed to see the use of throwing good food after a bad fleet'. It meant that the sailors 'would get meat by fair means or foul, preferably foul'.

The endeavour succeeded in bagging a couple of sheep, but although it was reported that the small boats were removed from the ships, later events would show that this was not accurate.

Not long after the incident, a patrolling destroyer's searchlight caught some shadowy figures on a beach. As soon as they were caught in the brilliant white glare, the perpetrators disappeared into the heather. An armed party was put ashore and came to a croft, where they asked the resident if they'd seen any German sailors. 'Eh certes,' explained the old lady, 'I'm thinkin it wadna be Germans ye saw.' Out she dragged her two boys by their ears, guilty only of having slipped out of the house to watch the destroyers.

Even killing seagulls – an act normally held to be anathema by sailors – was good for the pot but their taste left much to be desired. Flare pistols were some of the weapons of choice. Bread would be dropped overboard from

---

* The net had been made using the steel rail netting by the guns, there to prevent the loss overboard of the expensive brass cartridge cases ejected on to the deck after the guns had been fired. On 'good days' they were able to catch 'several hundred fish', which were then pickled in vinegar and fried (Ruge, p. 86).
† This was clearly not the case. When the scuttle came, the ships still had ample cutters and motor launches available. Reuter's barge from the *Emden* is thought to have been one of the few that survived the war and eventually became a sea ambulance service for the people of Longhope. Miller, p. 59 quoting *John o'Groats Journal*, 6 December 1918.

the deck while a colleague would take aim from a porthole to claim the prize. Not ssurprisingly, it was not that successful a method. In one case, the bird in question managed to get away, 'letting off green sparks, the star whizzed on in a great arc until it was extinguished in the water'.[261] The British guards were not amused but could not find the source of the explosion.

Eggs – let alone fresh eggs – were unheard of, and a genuine luxury. A package arrived in the spring of 1919 from a relative in Mecklenburg for B.110's commander. Miraculously, they arrived unbroken. These were the first eggs anyone on board had eaten since they had arrived in November. One egg was even ceremoniously presented by Ruge's commander to Cordes, the Torpedo Boat Flotilla Commander.

Even if the exact numbers of men left on the ships is unclear, the amount of supply needed to maintain even the reduced complement was simply gargantuan.* Ten days' supply meant '10,000 loaves, 250kg yeast and 2,500 litres of rum'.[262] While alcohol was never a problem, cigarettes occasionally were. One of Reuter's signals included a request for one million. Normally the monthly supply would mean around 300 for each man, or seventy-five cigars.

The routine for supply distribution was to first offload in bulk to the flagship, *Friedrich der Große,* and thence, by drifter, distribute to the individual ships around the Flow. Fleet stores were stowed in the *Seydlitz's* large holds. It was time consuming. One shipment that arrived on the *Königsberg* on 21 December took two days to unload and then another eight days to distribute. The operation was not well-managed. On 9 January, again the *Königsberg,* this time accompanied by the new 15in gunned battle-cruiser *Baden,* came back with more supplies.† Again, unloading was a shambles. In the new year, supply improved dramatically with the arrival, in late January, of two purpose-built ships, the SS *Dollart* and the SS *Reiher.*

Two of the biggest supply headaches – coal and water – were taken on by the British, the costs of which were charged to the German government. Bunkering coal was never an easy task but in the waters of the Flow it could become appalling if the weather wasn't kind. The British put severe time constraints on coaling but would still invoice the full *intended* cost even if the amount was not taken on board. At 80 marks a ton, it became a focus of considerable correspondence and angry

* Reuter's own figures in his report put the figures at 5,600 men and petty officers, 142 warrant officers and 175 officers (See van der Vat, p. 135).
† SMS *Baden* had not been on the original list of German ships to be interned. She was included after SMS *Mackensen* was unable to sail with the rest of the fleet in November as she had still not completed construction.

complaints.* As a consequence, energy rationing on German ships was strict. Destroyers enforced 'lights out' at 2330 to conserve diesel oil and, as they were berthed in pairs (and occasionally in threes), all the crews of both ships would retire on to one hull to try to maintain as much warmth within the icy steel walls of their accommodation.† However, leaving one hull uncrewed led to property being stolen. For example, 'when souvenir-hunters on the drifters discovered that the group…was empty every evening and night', the unmanned *B.109* and *B.111* were easy targets. The Germans mounted guards to protect their property and Ruge would spend 'every fourth night there with three of my [his] men'.[263] Amongst other things, the drifter men had taken some of the ship's valves.

Water was a curiosity in its own right. The peat-brown (*gelbbrüner Farbe*) water of Scapa was first met with considerable suspicion by the Germans. They were more dependent on outside supply as German ships did not have any desalination equipment like British ships.

The health and well-being of the interned German sailors was of little concern to the British. Only if they could see an imminent security threat would they become at all interested. The British provided for almost no medical needs at all. Only a very seriously ill sailor would be helped, otherwise the preferred response was to ship the poor soul back to Germany to get another sailor off their hands. There was not a single dentist, even though, with the poor rations, 'toothache and nutritional deficiency diseases' were frequent. Hard tack proved disastrous to loose teeth.[264] On board the interned ships, cases of scurvy were reported, something that had not been seen in the Royal Navy since the early eighteenth century.‡ It was supremely ironic that when Reuter's request for a dentist from Germany was finally met, the man who volunteered, Grote, did so on the 20 June and then only agreed to make the journey on 23 June, two days after the fleet had gone down.

Even Reuter was not immune. He was diagnosed with 'chronic intestinal catarrh arising from the unbalanced nature of his diet, which was low in vegetables and brown bread while containing plenty of meat and too much white bread and cakes'.[265] His reasonable request was met with

---

* Krause (p. 218) noted that around 70 tons of coal per hour was needed for a battle-cruiser like *Seydlitz*, while on the Light cruisers, around 20.

† Cox, Thomas Lowe Gray Lecture, p. 330, commented that sometimes they would find three destroyers sunk together (as they had been 'fastened three to a buoy'), 'resting on top of each other'. It made the task of raising them even more difficult as the individual wrecks had first to be disentangled.

‡ Scurvy is caused by vitamin deficiency and one of its effects is loosening of the teeth.

ridicule in the press: it was 'not clear whether he meant to convey the idea that he was literally sick or sick of his surroundings' quipped *The Courier*.[266] Vegetables were almost non-existent on the German ships. Having fresh produce would have been a luxury. Ever resourceful, sailors started to grow vegetables in their quarters. A paymaster wrote: 'I recently received a white cabbage from Germany, and I tend it like a flower in my cabin.'[267]

Even if the feelings against the Germans were deep-seated, it also seems that there were far too many liberties taken against the spirit of the Hague Conventions.

It was inevitable that a black market would develop. Ruge talked of the 'lively barter trade' that went on all around.[268] De Courcy-Ireland, who was on board one of the guard destroyers, *Westcott*, elaborated, saying that 'it was almost impossible to stop'.[269] Sometimes the bartering within the interned fleet bordered on the comic. The *Hindenburg* once advertised that it had 150 rolls of toilet paper on offer, while the *König* had 195,000 cigarettes it could exchange. However, he also says that it was indirect and that the only contact the Germans had in this trade was usually with the crews of the drifters because 'they did not belong to the Navy and were not against establishing somewhat closer contacts'.[270] Miller confirmed that 'the men of the drifters cheerfully took part in the clandestine trading between ships'.[271] Ruge commented: 'Unfortunately, we had no contact with the islanders at all…but we had quite good contact with the crews of the guard drifters, water boats, oilers and so on.' He went on, chuckling in an interview as he recounted the memory, '…and I remember one of the guard boats was sent back to Scotland and before they left the captain invited me to a good cup of tea and some cakes.'[272]

A newspaper report in *The Courier* quoted a local saying that 'there were always boats out at the ships for one reason or another. I think most of the soap trade was done by the boats that took out water to them.'[273]

Derek Colville's great uncle was going out to a Royal Navy ship in the hope of selling farm produce.* His dog fell out of the boat and he jumped into the water to save it. He got into trouble and one of the crewmen from the ship saw what had happened and jumped in to try and save the lad – both were lost. The boy was only twelve years old.[274]

The new conditions created a new currency. A bottle of schnapps could buy some old newspapers. It was just as well that alcohol was never

---

* Tom Muir, who contributed to the book, can trace his lineage through the Drevers of Westray. His mother was a Drever. Derek Colville's mother was a rever from South Ronaldsay. His great uncle is buried in St Peter's Church, South Ronaldsay.

an issue of supply.* Medals, buttons, postcards with ship photos and even uniforms were exchanged for soap and other necessities such as tobacco, reading materials and tea.

Much of this was 'frowned upon by the senior German officers – disciplinarians who could not countenance slack behaviour among their ratings'.[275] Cordes, for example, was one who strenuously opposed this kind of trade. He appealed to the British to put a stop to it, seeing it as a source for further fracturing the already lax discipline in his ships:

> During the last few days it has been observed from here and has also been reported to me by separate groups that the picket *Pendoran* remains alongside certain groups for hours on end during the day, without having been detailed to do so.... During the whole time that she lay alongside, no work on the buoys or the chains was observed. On the other hand, reports have reached me that she was spending her time there to exploit to her advantage the torpedo boat crew's lack of smoking requisites.... I ask you, for your part, to take steps, by giving suitable directions to the picket, which would help to back up my authority.[276]

It was clear that Cordes pushed for some of the restrictions for his own purposes. Restricting travel between the German ships also meant that the spread of revolutionary ideas was cut down.

Orcadians had been blessed with the economic boom that came with the Grand Fleet being based in its sheltering harbours. This was now a new opportunity to trade. Indeed, the sailors 'invented most wonderful new orders and so on and everyone was happy about it'.[277] But mostly it was not so jolly. Lieutenant Brian de Courcy-Ireland, who had been at Jutland in HMS *Bellerophon*, now serving on HMS *Westcott*, remembered seeing 'a German sailor go up to an officer and pluck the Iron Cross off his coat and offer it to us for some cigarettes. The officer could do nothing.'[278] An Iron Cross would buy chocolate, two bars, if you wanted. As the brisk barter went on through the months the crews started to invent new decorations that were fabricated in the ships' workshops. And the designs could be hilariously inventive. A stoker from the *Seydlitz* when back in Germany was asked by an officer what his medal was as he couldn't recognise it. 'That's the order of Transfer into Internment.'[279]

---

* It seems that this was different depending on the type of ship. Ruge commented that: 'In the destroyers we hadn't much alcohol. The big ships did a roaring trade in alcohol as far as I know.' (Kennedy, *Scapa Flow* UBHG pp. 12–13).

6

DIVIDING THE SPOILS
AT VERSAILLES

O N A COLD January day in 1919, a Saturday, politicians from the Allied powers gathered in Versailles. They were there to end the war that had devastated Europe, brought three empires to an end and caused the deaths of millions.* The peace conference opened in the very same room where, to the day, forty-eight years before, the first Kaiser Wilhelm of Prussia had been named the emperor of a newly united Germany in the famous Hall of Mirrors.

Countries far and wide sent large delegations to hammer out the agreements that would shape Europe's future, although the focus would always be on what the principal nations, France, Britain and America, wanted. Germany was represented by the Foreign Minister, SPD politician Hermann Müller, and Centre Party member, Transport Minister Johannes Bell.†

The day after the meeting started, Germany elected a coalition headed by the Social Democrat Friedrich Ebert.‡ His claim, that 'no enemy has defeated you' as he welcomed back returning soldiers to Berlin, set in motion the long but sure construction of the 'Stab in the Back' narrative. Men such as Scheer fully subscribed: 'Our downfall could

---

* The conference formally opened 18 January 1919 and effectively ended on 28 June 1919 when Germany finally signed the terms. The very next day after its opening, 19 January, saw Germany's political evolution into a coalition Government made up of Social Democrats, the Centre and Liberal Parties.
† Today, the contributions of many other countries, for example China, have been largely forgotten. 100,000 Chinese labourers came to Europe to dig trenches on the Western Front, freeing up the same number of Allied soldiers to fight their war. China had hoped to regain Shantung province from Germany but would find that another Asian ally, Japan, was able to override its own claims. Voting power or representation had little to do with contribution: Portugal's 60,000 soldiers was rewarded with one delegate's seat. Brazil only gave medical help and supplies. It received three seats.
‡ The 19 January elections moved Germany's political structure from revolutionary government into a coalition government made up of Social Democrats, the Centre and Liberal Parties.

only be accomplished by extraordinary means: we had to inflict defeat upon ourselves.'[280]

Lloyd George arrived on 11 January 'in a buoyant mood, having won a landslide victory in the 14 December elections'.[281] His 400-strong delegation was not only made up of fellow countrymen, but also representatives from Canada, South Africa, Australia and New Zealand. America's delegation, composed of 'mainly young and idealistic scholars', had sailed across the Atlantic to the French port of Brest on the *George Washington*.[282] Its ranks would swell to 1,300 over the course of the conference.

The core, the group that ran the overall conference, was the Council of Ten, better known as the Supreme Council, underneath which worked the fifty-eight specialist committees that honed the details of the policy. In the council were the great names, the leaders of Britain, France, America and Italy: Lloyd George, Wilson, Clemenceau, Orlando, their secretaries and two Japanese representatives (By April, it was reduced to a council of four. The Japanese 'had contributed little'). Even the Italian premier, Orlando, 'generally participated only when Italian matters came up'.[283]

When it came to dividing the spoils, the spirit changed. The war had transformed nations – 'France and Italy were exhausted, Austria was dismembered, Russia had collapsed… .'[284] – the politicians' lofty ideals of crafting a worthy and moral peace disintegrated into haggling among themselves for a bigger slice of the pie, and to hammering home Germany's humiliation. Few politicians spoke against the increasingly dangerous clauses that would eventually feed the flames of German resentment and, under Hitler's leadership, eventual retaliation. Lloyd George was one of the few who tried.

In the background, the Royal Navy schemed in a bid to save what it needed and build where it could. 'Only the United States and Japan remained serious naval powers': they might not have tradition or the hulls in the water, but their economies were still powerful.[285] The Royal Navy had initiated 'the ongoing and heated discussion…with the United States about the legitimacy of naval belligerent action to control neutral trade, a discussion made all the more acerbic because the experience of the Great War appeared to show that naval trade control was a strategy of such power that it could bring a great continental power to defeat'.[286] What the British regarded as a quasi-existential necessity, 'a proven means of national survival', the Americans looked at as 'a means of threatening their own economic potential'.[287]

Britain's pre-eminent position in the world had been made possible by sea power. Everything her armies needed was only possible because of the power she could harness and wield over the world's oceans. She fought with the strength of resources of her empire. Sea power also gave her the added military edge of being able to switch theatres of operations and focus. While land powers exercised their strength through territorial acquisition, a sea power such as Great Britain manifested hers through her control of those who had access to and plied the oceans. Britain's war would be about maritime sovereignty. Fighting the war with her empire's support would give Britain access to manpower, raw materials, coaling and supply stations and, often overlooked, intelligence.

America was starting to appear to the British strongly like Germany in the 1890s and early 1900s: as a challenger to its hard-earned maritime rights. Woodrow Wilson wanted to see British dominance ended: either by maintaining the power of others or by directly reducing its components.

Emotions ran high. After all, the Royal Navy had been on the front line, whether in the trenches (as part of the Naval Division), in the air (as pilots in the RNAS) or at sea, facing death every day. When it presented its terms for surrender, its position was very different from Lloyd George's and even Marshal Foch who was not in favour of the harshness of the naval terms. Both worried that if terms were too onerous, national pride would kill any compromise or agreement. Beatty argued that there was no reason – even if the victory was in Wemyss's mind 'no less real because it was not spectacular' – that 'the nation should give up the object [objective] with which it had entered the war, namely, the destruction of German militarism'.[288] Foch would have been content to have seen the German fleet confined to the Baltic.

Even if America had not suffered any level of destruction near that of a country such as Britain (and that was nothing compared to what the French had endured), her commerce had been significantly impacted. And, on the seas, her sailors and citizens fell like any other neutral to the mines and submarines of the belligerent European navies. For them, the naval war 'either ignored international law governing trade by neutral nations or interpreted it to their own advantage'.[289] That meant her position was not at all friendly to, or understanding of, Britain's. That was reasonable: exports of American cotton and copper had very frequently been interdicted and seized by the British. America's reaction was to steadily increase its war preparedness, particularly, its naval forces. Already in 1916, Woodrow Wilson's administration put proposals before Congress to launch a major shipbuilding programme to increase its capital ship strength to thirty-five ships of the latest design, some with 16in guns, taking all the lessons they could from Jutland's less than spectacular result.

The war at sea had left the Americans determined to address the issue of the 'freedom of the seas'. The intentions with which they came to Versailles had been public and stated. Wilson had made the right of free navigation one of his Fourteen Points, stressing that belligerent nations must continue to observe international law even in war. In fact, their delegation arrived in Versailles demanding that it be a basis for the talks. To the British, this was an attack on an article of faith. Lloyd George refused American demands, delivered by Wilson's trusted Colonel House, instead calling the president's bluff that America should seek a separate peace. The British disregard for Wilson's position was inevitable. Sea power was Britain's most formidable weapon. Admiral Sir Charles Madden, Beatty's successor as Commander-in-Chief of the Grand Fleet and Jellicoe's brother-in-law and Chief of Staff at Jutland, wrote that he saw 'freedom of the seas', '... as freedom to prolong the war and amass wealth at the expense of the belligerents who, when exhausted by war, may be at the mercy of the power which has been allowed this Freedom'.[290]

The initial negotiations were probably the easiest. The major issues were the assignment of guilt and its punishment, the reparations that should be paid and ensuring Germany would be prevented from waging future wars. France, which had suffered its second encounter with German militarism in fifty years, naturally took the lead.

Negotiating positions on the most important naval issues were written by Sir Julian Corbett, though the authorship remained largely unknown. His thinking was used extensively by the Prime Minister, Sir Maurice Hankey, Sir David Beatty and Sir Rosslyn Wemyss.

Wilson wanted to push the British. Knowing how stretched the British were financially, he thought that any economic threats would get him what he wanted: his vision of the League of Nations, British acceptance of the Monroe Doctrine and a back down by the Royal Navy on the issue of the freedom of the seas. He sent Benson, Daniels and his trusted Colonel House over to Europe to start softening them up. The British guessed what he was up to and concludd that his talk of a naval arms race was just an empty threat.

It was the second and third issues that led to the thorny question of Germany's navy: with what sort of navy should she be left and what was to be done with the remaining ships? The question led directly to the potential distribution of the German fleet among the victorious navies and was all about 'who was to get what, and how many, what was to happen to it while they made up their minds'.[291]

These were the decisions about surrender or internment, the ships that would remain in German hands and the shape of the German fleet after the war. The consensus was to allow her a fleet that would, in essence, be limited to an all-voluntary force of 15,000 sailors manning six battleships, six light cruisers, twelve destroyers and twelve torpedo boats. What became Article 181 of the treaty was approved by the Council of Ten on 6 March 1919.

The other difficult question – what to do with the ships that the Allies intended to take *away* from Germany – also saw different proposals borne as much out of mutual suspicion as anything else. Each of the Allied negotiating groups had very different views. The positions they took were coloured not by notions of fairness but by their assessment of how their own country would or would not benefit from the various alternatives. And that entailed a view of whom they saw as their likely future adversary or adversaries and the role maritime power would play in furthering their national interests.

Great Britain

Britain had committed huge amounts to the war. The country emerged in 1919 with a crippling financial burden: it owed the US Government $4.7 billion and US banks a further $2 billion.[*] The money owed by Russia had been defaulted upon while France, already badly mauled by the war and equally unlikely to pay, owed Britain another $4 billion.

Britain started the peace talks preferring to see German's ships destroyed to avoid any allocation to her former Allies as this would gradually chip away at her own naval advantage.[†]

Lloyd George seemed to like the idea of towing the German fleet out to the middle of the Atlantic where, to the tune of the Allied nations' national anthems, it might be sunk. It seemed to appeal to his sense of what would be of media interest. Wilson was highly critical of the British

---

[*] See Tampke p. 123.
[†] The Supreme Council eventually announced that the partition of German fleet would be based on the British getting the 'lion's share' (70 per cent) and the balance being apportioned out to the other allies – 10 per cent to France, 10 per cent to Italy, 8 per cent to Japan and 2 per cent to the USA. France and Italy would also receive five light cruisers and ten destroyers in good condition because it was recognised that their shipbuilding industry was unable to produce new ships (*The Sunday Post*, 30 November 1919).

prime minister's love of theatre, saying that the idea 'strikes me as the advice of people who do not know what else to do'.[292] In sum, he 'thought it foolish to destroy perfectly good ships'.[293] It was exactly what his Secretary of the Navy, Daniels, also believed.[*] These ships had cost billions to build, had used capital that could have helped people's welfare instead and now they were being treated as good for nothing. Given the battle Lloyd George had faced with the Admiralty over the 1909 Naval Estimates, particularly with Jacky Fisher and John Jellicoe, it was all the more surprising that he even contemplated something as provocative, even if it were to civilians of a defeated nation.[†] The French compromise, only wanting to see a minimal number destroyed to act as a salutary lesson, was probably the most reasonable.

It was on questions in the maritime sphere that British and the American positions divided. Wilson saw the issue of 'freedom of the seas' as essential. He was adamant: 'I cannot consent to take part in the negotiation of a peace which does not include Freedom of the Seas.'[294]

It was the sinking of the *Lusitania* that had, after all, rocked American public opinion out of isolationism. Among the 1,198 drowned passengers were 128 Americans. It would become the source from which the eventual descent into bickering and disagreement would come as the Allied differences were exposed. It was not just naval rivalry, it was maritime rivalry. America was emerging as Germany's successor to Britain as her new commercial rival on the seas. Sir William Weisman, head of British Intelligence in the United States, foresaw much of what the war's end would bring: 'I think trade rivalry after the war and freedom of the seas are going to be the two dangerous rocks for Anglo–American relations.'[295]

The next two decades started with the question of how a common enemy, the German Navy, should be disposed of. It gradually, but surely evolved into increasing rivalry between former allies. The correspondence between the two powers around Versailles highlights the depth of disagreement.

Geddes referred to conversations he had undertaken with Wilson while he was in Washington. Whether the president was right or not, it

---

[*] Josephus Daniels (1862–1948), a newspaperman and Democrat, was Woodrow Wilson's Secretary of the Navy for the war years. He worked closely with Franklin Delano Roosevelt (1882–1945), the future US president, when the latter became his assistant secretary of state.
[†] In 1909, Lloyd George and Winston Churchill fought side by side against the Admiralty, the politicians wishing to preserve their welfare programme and the navy its dreadnought construction programme in the face of mounting German pressure. The navy won but Lloyd George never forgave John Jellicoe.

was clear that: '…many nations, great and small, chafed under the feeling that their sea-borne trade and maritime development proceeded only with the permission and under the shadow of the British Navy.'[296]

America's position was borne from her dislike of continued British naval supremacy. 'The sailors were as suspicious of one another's intentions as were the diplomats and the politicians,' says Simpson.[297] Some, even more. There was also a certain degree of arrogance and self-righteousness. Wemyss dismissed Wilson's fears, saying that the British had maintained freedom of the seas 'for centuries' and so, consequently, 'Nothing further need therefore be said on this point.'[298] The US Navy went as far as being very nervous that the destruction of the German Navy would 'leave Great Britain the absolute naval master of Europe, without a single threat from any European Navy whatsoever', and that the continued existence of the German Navy would, in fact, constitute 'a balance wheel governing any undue or arbitrary ambition on the part of those who may temporarily be in power in Great Britain'.[299]

Both the Americans and British agreed on one thing, however: the character and fate of Germany's submarines. To their way of thinking the weapon had been used to illegal ends, and had been 'the sole naval weapon that has influenced the conduct of the allies' land campaign during the latter years of the war'.[300] Unrestricted submarine warfare had led to large-scale loss of civilian life from both belligerent as well as neutral countries.

Their position was focused on whether or not the destruction of the German *surface* Navy would be to their advantage or disadvantage. They felt that the continued existence of a German Navy would keep the British in check. And in the same line of thinking, they were equally prepared to accept giving ships to both the French and Italian navies as this would 'hurt' the British. But even if German Navy ships were not destroyed, its division amongst the Allied navies would still only increase British power. The British would, as the power that lost the most naval assets in the war at sea, get the lion's share of compensation.

At its worst, 'a Royal Navy with no European rival would be an instrument of global dictatorship'.[301] A US Naval Advisory Staff memorandum concluded that:

> The German Fleet has ceased to exist, with the result that we suddenly find the British Navy in a position of unparalleled strength. No Navy is left in Europe capable of offering any real resistance to the British Navy… . We do not consider this a

condition calculated to advance either our own interests or the welfare of the world. A power so absolute that it may disregard other powers with impunity is less apt to act with justice than if there be a balancing influence of force as well as world opinion to oppose it.[302]

Almost as bad, the British were extremely 'reluctant' to codify international maritime Law. By April 1919 both Beatty and Madden were arguing for the 'biggest politically possible share' of the German fleet.[303] Beatty wrote to the Admiralty on 4 April explaining his position:

If we, therefore, in the immediate future are to avoid a large building programme, and at the same time counter the American effort, it is necessary to press for the division of German vessels on the basis of Naval losses sustained by the Allies. Such a division should enable us to tide over the next few years, whilst concentrating thought on training of personnel and the development of new types.[304]

Would this have even been practicable? The French certainly thought so. But taking on a German ship would have meant taking on German ship design, armaments and propulsion technology and either integrating it or keeping it and managing it. Both were seriously difficult propositions. One only has to contemplate the implications for training or look at the different approaches to, and the systems in place for, propulsion, ordnance, fire control, turret operations, etc. However, in the circumstances of heavily decreased military and naval budgets with little possibility for new building programmes, this might have been the only way to counter the American threat.

By May, however, Churchill was suggesting to Lloyd George that the Americans should take the German ships. The Americans wanted to be on a numerical par with the British, and Churchill suggested that this might be a way out of a new arms race:

If he wants to increase the American Navy, let him take some of the best German ships and fit them up...on the other hand, if he starts building vessels of a superior type, we cannot fall behind in quality, and though we might wait for a year or two to see how things went on we should soon have to start designing superior craft to match the Americans.[305]

It was not a bad idea. It would have held off huge additional expenditure for the Americans and, even if not incorporating new post-Jutland technology *en masse* into a new navy, would give them ships demonstrably able to challenge the Royal Navy.

A third possibility that has since been lost from much of the discussion was the idea of incorporating the German ships into a new navy, that of the League of Nations. The last of the Fourteen Points held that: 'A general association of nations must be formed under specific covenants for the purpose of affording mutual guarantees of political independence and territorial integrity to great and small states alike.' Acting independently, this idea might have rid itself of some of the glaring issues of integration but the Americans always argued that such a 'heterogeneous combination of naval craft' would need the resources and power of a 'single nationality that is equal in strength to the strongest Navy', i.e. in their mind, American ships to challenge the Royal Navy.[306] This has become the NATO model.

Churchill talked to Lloyd George about Wilson's ideas with a deep-seated caution: '…no arguments, however specious, no appeals, however seductive, must lead you to abandon that naval supremacy on which the life of our country depends.'[307]

There was conviction within Wilson's vision that implicitly recognised what the US Naval Advisory Staff had concluded:

> With two navies of equal strength, the world would breathe free from the fear of naval domination that has the power at any moment of threatening the economic life of any nation. The resulting mutual respect of Great Britain and the United States would go further than anything else towards the establishment of just maritime law upon the high seas both in peace and in war.[308]

Managing the post-war naval balance of power was one consideration. Finding the right balance for punishing Germany was the other. Too lenient, the fear of renewed German aggression would not be dealt with. Too harsh, the spark for a new rivalry would be kindled. Four years of war and the loss of friends had, understandably, hardened the British, while the Americans were deeply distrustful of their new allies.

France

The most vehement, and arguably the most justified, in wanting to get their fair share of the interned German fleet's ships were the French. Because of the sheer scale of destruction and the huge death toll the country had endured, France had borne the brunt of the war. It had been devastated in ways neither the British nor the Americans had.

The country had lost one and a half million men, 'half its male population under thirty'.[309] Twice that number had been wounded. The impact on France's 40 million population was much higher than Germany's two million dead with her population of 75 million. In the ten French departments where the heaviest fighting had occurred, the losses had been staggering – '600,000 houses, 20,000 factories and 6,500 schools had been destroyed'.[310]

France had not been able to rebuild any of her own fleet during the war. Her efforts, like Italy's, were focused on the land war and now they faced a considerable challenge in catching up lost ground. They felt that their losses justified the balance to be redressed. Already by December 1918, the French had supposedly asked for a quarter of the interned ships. The rest they wanted to have broken up.

One indicator of how deeply the war had impacted France was in the value of its currency. By 1921, the French Franc 'had fallen to one fifth of its pre-World War 1 value'.[311]

The United States

The Australian Prime Minister, William Hughes, 'dismissed the American rejection of high reparations as unprincipled and self-serving'.[312] They had seized German property worth $425 billion, had suffered no material domestic damage and had confiscated a large number of merchant ships, twice the number they had lost.

Serious American naval expansion was signalled by Woodrow Wilson's 1916 Naval Act. It was reminiscent of Tirpitz's 1897 Naval Bill in seeking a huge shipbuilding programme to not only catch up with, but to overtake the British, still the world's naval leader. America now planned to leapfrog Japan and what would remain of Germany's navy to directly challenge Britain's continued naval supremacy.

The 15 July 1915 Navy General Board objective was that 'the Navy of the United States should ultimately be equal to the most powerful [Navy] maintained by any other nation in the world'. Wilson went further: he wanted to have 'incomparably the greatest Navy in the world'.[313] The 1916

Naval Act authorised the building of 156 ships including ten battleships, six heavy battle cruisers, ten light cruisers, fifty destroyers and thirty submarines.

In June, immediately after Jutland, Congress debated the programme. The Chief of the US Navy's Bureau of Ordnance, Rear Admiral Joseph Strauss, dealt with Congress' concerns over the safety of the battle-cruiser following Jutland. It still remains unclear whether Strauss was really knowledgeable about what Friedman called the 'suicidally dangerous magazine practices' employed in that battle but the programme was voted into law in August.[*]

Nevertheless, the US Navy was lacking in a 'mature' naval officer corps and the immediate requirements of convoy protection when America entered the war in April 1917. This meant that the emphasis was placed on smaller, rather than battleship, construction.

Tensions with the United States ran high throughout the war: 'The British saw the United States both as an essential supplier of funds and crucial goods, including munitions, as well as a potential rival. And US supplies were certainly helping keep Germany afloat.'[314]

The Americans, more specifically their naval representative Admiral William Benson, had deep fears of the British taking advantage of the moment to incorporate more German ships in a bid to maintain their lead over the American Navy.[†] His reflections on Britain's historical supremacy at sea were a clear warning to the president. Britain, '…has ever maintained her commercial supremacy by superior naval strength. In turn she has crushed Spain, Holland and Germany because they threatened her supremacy at sea.'

For some reason, he omitted France, Britain's traditional and most recent maritime foe before Germany. Benson continued, 'Her objection to our building program[me], both commercial and naval, is because of a belief that we are now probably threatening that supremacy.'[315]

Benson was no Anglophile. He could be riled easily and very often reacted to the moment rather than with diplomatic finesse. Just as often,

---

[*] Magazines on British battleships and battle-cruisers had been designed with fire-proof scuttles that had been built in to protect the magazines from flash from any turret fire. In order to fire more quickly, cordite bags had been stacked outside of the magazines at Jutland to speed up the handling. This was the 'suicidal' practice to which Friedman was referring.

[†] Admiral William Shepherd Benson (1855–1932) was the United States Navy's first Chief of Naval Operations (CNO). He took a major role in the expansion of the navy in 1916 and after America's entry into the war, where he additionally held responsibility for the safe arrival of US troops in Europe. He held extremely strong points of view on the negotiations of the naval clauses as well as naval aviation. The US Navy's air capability, nearly destroyed under his tutelage, was revived by Roosevelt.

View of the German fleet at anchor seen from the Houton Seaplane terminal with Reuter's future, second flagship, SMS *Emden,* centre front. November 1918. (Kirkwall Library & Archives)

SMS *Bayern* coming into Scapa Flow, passing through the anti-submarine barrier at Hoxa, 27 November 1918. (Kirkwall Library & Archives)

ABOVE: The Admiralty tug and former fleet water tender, *Flying Kestrel*, took over 300 Stromness public school children on a day trip around the Flow, 21 June 1919. (Unknown)

RIGHT: Amateur theatrics on a German torpedo boat. (Deutsche Marine Bund)

BELOW: Sailors on the former flagship, SMS *Friedrich der Große*. (Unknown)

The battle-cruiser SMS *Seydlitz* finally sank at 13:50. (Blohm und Voss, Hamburg)

SMS *Seydlitz* lying on her starboard side after sinking. In 1926, during the General Strike, her valuable coal bunkers would be accessed in order to continue salvage operations. (Kirkwall Library & Archives)

ABOVE: A British destroyer, identified by her bow pennant sign F 09 as HMS *Vega,* photographed attempting to beach a German torpedo boat in a desperate attempt to restore order. (Alamy)

RIGHT: MS *Karlsruhe.* A series of time-lapse photographs taken by C W Burrows. (Kirkwall Library & Archives)

BELOW: SMS *Bayern* sinking by the stern. Part of a series of photographs taken by C W Burrows. (SeaWar Museum, Denmark)

ABOVE: SMS *Hindenburg* sinking by the bow. (Alamy)

RIGHT: By 17:00 all that was visible of the most recently built battle-cruiser were her funnels and, at low tide, her main 15in batteries. (Kirkwall Library & Archives)

BELOW: Armed British marines pull alongside a German destroyer. The closest marine is carrying a Japanese Arisaka rifle. (Kirkwall Library & Archives)

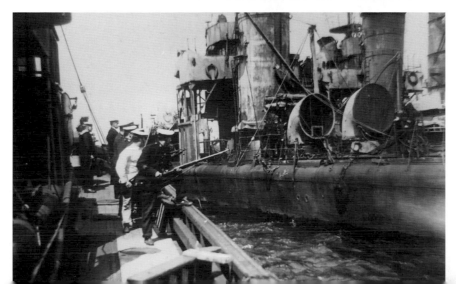

A British officer climbs on to the *G.102* to hoist a British Ensign. She finally came to rest in Mill Bay. (Kirkwall Library & Archives)

Admiral von Trotha meeting the returning interned sailors at the docks,
21 January 1920. (Wilhelmshavener Zeitungs FotoBild Sammlung)

A different kind of tourism. Aboard the salvaged battleship, SMS *Hindenburg*.
(Kirkwall Library & Archives)

The air-lock towers were used by the salvers to enter different submerged compartments from the surface. They were constructed from cut-up boiler sections welded together. (McCrone family)

SMS *Derfflinger*, nicknamed the 'Iron Dog' by British sailors because of her resilience, being taken on a dry dock to the breakers at Faslane on the Clyde river. (Kirkwall Library & Archives)

The battle-cruiser SMS *Moltke* under tow. (Kirkwall Library & Archives)

however, the CNO's thinking was well thought out. He had few friends among the British. Long, the First Lord, quipped that he was 'a man of mulish character and not very quick at grasping any ideas other than his own'.[316] Lloyd George, a politician whose silvery tongue more often than not found ways to belittle his opponents, summed up Benson as a person who possessed a 'double dose of Anglophobia'.[317] But it was obvious, as van der Vat put it, that the Americans would 'not have minded if other navies had been expanded at the expense of the British'.[318] William Sims recalled that, as he was about to leave for London in spring 1917, Benson pulled him aside to give him some last-minute advice: 'Don't let the British pull the wool over your eyes.... We would as soon fight the British as the Germans.'[319]

Given the amount of coastline it had to protect, the US Navy was already very stretched, so its expansion was inevitable. Wilson himself had declared: 'There is no other Navy in the world that has to cover so great an area of defence as the American Navy, and it ought, in my judgement to be incomparable to the greatest in the world.'[320]

Like the Kiel Kaiser-Kanal, the Panama Canal also signalled America's intentions and stature. It was clear that America wanted to build a first-rate navy, one that was capable of fighting in two oceans, the Atlantic and the Pacific. This may be part of the reason why there was so much Anglophobia in the American Navy. Anglophiles such as Sims were the exception, the broader rule were sailors like Benson.

In speaking to Congress, Wilson declared: 'Let us build a bigger Navy than hers and do what we please.'[321] It sounded like the Kaiser's own irritation when, twenty years previously, he had openly declared his support for Krüger and the Boers. Only weeks after the war ended, Wilson was prepared to 'up the ante' and ask Congress to go even further than the 1916 Act. Now, he wanted forty-four battleships and sixteen battle-cruisers.

His threat was simply to use American economic power to massively out-gun his country's rivals. The notion has remained core to American military spending strategy. 'Any nation which sought to equal this new American Navy would have to spend billions of dollars for an indefinite length of time to do so.'[322] It was only after Wilson suffered a stroke that the American naval initiative started to lose steam. 'Without Wilson at the helm, Congressional support for his "Navy second to none" eroded.'[323]

During the war, the antagonisms had been there but had been kept, for the most part, hidden. Britain's requests for help in small craft and commercial vessels frustrated American aims on two fronts: not only, of course, did it mean that America's commercial threat would be delayed but it more concretely took shipbuilding capacity away from dreadnought construction. By the start of 1918, Captain Pratt, Benson's assistant CNO, was pushing Admiral Sims for an answer on when America could relaunch its own dreadnought programme.

When Geddes, the new First Lord of the Admiralty, went to Washington in October 1918 to meet with Secretary of the Navy Daniels, he was in a difficult position. He had taken over Sir Edward Carson's duties when, with Lloyd George, he had engineered the careful ousting of Jellicoe as First Sea Lord. He did what he could to slow the advent of America's inevitable maritime supremacy. While he felt that 'the United States will continue to be a naval liability' (and, undiplomatically, made his views known), he needed American shipbuilding resources.[324] He wanted 128 destroyers. It was made more difficult for him as he did not have the trust of the Americans in the same ways Jellicoe had enjoyed it with Sims.

But the request for destroyers amply demonstrates the surprise with which the collapse of Germany came: 'The sudden, unexpected and total collapse of the Central Powers in the autumn of 1918 caught the coalition unprepared for either an armistice or a peace treaty and the subsequent post-war world.'[325]

It was only a question of time before the disquiet in the two rival navies would rear its ugly head again. In Paris, Wilson and Lloyd George confronted each other. Lloyd George refused to give up the British power of strategic blockade. Great Britain 'would spend her last guinea to keep a Navy superior to that of the United States or any other power'.[326] He would brook no opposition within his own party. But it was not an issue on which to go to war.

Daniels described the moment in March 1919 as the 'Naval Battle of Paris' when the talks between British and US counterparts – Benson and Wemyss – became so heated they actually came close to a physical confrontation. Daniels was labelled 'a resurrected Tirpitz' by the British. He described one of the initial meetings:

> They exchanged such bitter comments that at one time I feared they would pass the bounds and have an altercation... . The British Admiral thought that his country ought to have the right to build the biggest Navy in the world and we ought to agree to it. To Benson that would have been treason to his own country. So, you can see how far apart they were.[327]

The British were furious at the renewed American naval efforts but they were not on very solid ground: 'It was one thing to react in that way, and another to make good the reaction. The treasury was empty: the war had transformed Britain into a debtor country, and a nation that lost thirty-five million working days to strikes in 1919 was not going to welcome an increase in taxes for a new naval race.'[328]

Japan

For the Americans, it was equally disturbing that Lloyd George 'suggested that Britain might rely upon its alliance with Japan for security' in the event of a strong naval threat from the Americans.[329] Churchill again, maybe in part because of his mother, Jennie Jerome's American heritage, argued against such an approach, saying that there could be 'no more fatal policy than that of basing our naval policy on a possible combination with Japan against the United States'.[330]

Japan was in a strong position. She had profited from the European war without materially suffering from any involvement.

> Without mounting major operations, she had gained Germany's Pacific island possessions in the Marshall, Mariana and Caroline groups and taken over German concessions on the Shantung peninsular of mainland China opposite Korea. Meanwhile her exports, particularly textiles, had penetrated eastern markets that western powers could no longer supply, her munitions industries had been boosted by Allied orders, her merchant Fleet had doubled in response to the increase in trade and her shipbuilding capacity had increased sevenfold.[331]

The Europeans and, later the Americans, had their full attention on Europe and the funnelling of resources to the European war meant that 'they were in no position to challenge Japan's expansion in East Asia'.[332]

Although the Americans had naval war plans against Japan in readiness since 1907,* '…most American naval planners at this time did not regard the Japanese Fleet as an independent threat. Rather, it was the possibility of the co-operation of the Japanese and the British Fleets that they felt they had to bear in mind.'[333]

While the Anglo–Japanese alliance was not popular in the United

---

* Plan Orange (Padfield, *Maritime Dominion*, p. 205).

States, Britain's position was not an easy one. Admiral de Chair understood that it was this issue – the Japanese threat – that was driving American shipbuilding.* The US Navy had not dropped the feeling of urgency in the programme 'as they fear the supremacy of the Japanese Navy after the war'.[334]

With Japan's advancing economic growth, the role of her navy was emerging as critical to maintaining the island nation's oil and natural resource imports. In 1920, Japan announced a seven-year building programme to add sixteen 16in-gunned battleships to her fleet.

The power of the military in Japanese politics was particularly strong. It sprung from the changes brought about by the Mejii Constitution. The army and the navy were represented in cabinet by their own appointed ministers. Civilian prime ministers had to pay attention to their demands as each could force an election merely by their ministers resigning.

Japan relied on the alliance with Britain to maintain her position in the Far East. It was a quandary for the British. Non-renewal would be an outright insult to Japan, while its continued existence might threaten the basis on which Britain and America could share naval supremacy. Britain's colonies were also divided on the issue: while Canada worried about its southern neighbour and therefore wished for an end to the Anglo–Japanese alliance, New Zealand and Australia wanted the alliance to be continued. In trying to identify a bigger reason to support Anglo–American unity Churchill argued, 'A giant and a boy may fight a bigger giant, but if the two giants get together the boy has got to be content with innocent pleasures'.[335]

Eventually the solution was found in the Four-Power Treaty between Britain, the United States, Japan and France pledging to respect each other's 'insular possessions and insular dominions' in return for Britain abandoning the 1902 alliance with Japan. Counterbalancing this was the Nine-Power Treaty to preserve the integrity and independence of China and to maintain open trading rights in China for all nations.†

★   ★   ★

* Admiral Sir Dudley de Chair (1864–1958) had been a close friend of Sir John Jellicoe and had been shocked by the manner of his sacking. His naval career rapidly deteriorated after he had spoken too openly with Wemyss of these feelings. In spring 1917, he was part of the Balfour Mission to explore ways in improving Anglo–American relations.
† The powers were Italy, Holland, Belgium, Portugal.

Lloyd George would have liked to have been rid of the battleship as a weapons platform altogether. He considered its continued existence a budgetary black hole. He hoped that a lower-cost solution might be found in airpower or the submarine but the 1920 capital ship subcommittee was adamant that the battleship was not obsolete. The question was how long Britain could delay a new building programme as an inferiority in post-Jutland ships would seriously jeopardise the Royal Navy's power against nations with newly constructed ships.

As Fisher had previously demonstrated, ratios were one thing, construction quality an entirely different issue. Balfour, reported Alfred Chatfield, Beatty's flag captain at Jutland who was asked to lead the Washington conference, naively commented, 'Surely if we all have the same size it does not matter.' Chatfield continued, 'after our lessons of Jutland' that Britain must 'not build ships that were unsuitable'.[336]

There were voices of moderation in the background. Jellicoe, for example, talked of the potential future threat of Japan and of naval co-operation with America. 'The King, Grey, Bonar Law and other British and Canadian statesmen urged that Britain should not respond aggressively.'[337] On the other side of the Atlantic, Wilson faced heavy opposition from many Republicans, who attacked what the US Naval Advisory Staff had recognised as Wilson's hypocrisy: on the one hand, preaching the virtues of disarmament and his vision of the League of Nations and, on the other, backing a programme of huge naval expansion for America.

The political naval leaders – Long and Daniels – sought to calm the situation. Under pressure from Colonel House, Wilson retreated and a compromise was sought. 'The naval officers were quietly shunted aside from the negotiations.'[338]

House and Benson threatened continued American naval building unless the British destroyed their allocation while, conversely, Lloyd George threatened that unless the Americans reduced their naval building programme, Britain would keep her allocation, which was expected to be calculated based on war losses incurred and, therefore, to be massive.

Daniels visited the interned fleet in the spring of 1919 and came away with no doubt in his mind that the US Navy would not benefit from a ship allocation. Beatty, whose 'first hope was that Germany's superior battleships would be added to the Royal Navy as the fruits of victory', saw taking them as the only way to match America's new ships with 'no money down'.[339] Whether or not the difficulties of taking them on had been deeply looked at is not known.

Daniels broke the deadlock. He was 'sure that none of these German ships would fall into the organisation of our Navy'. Furthermore, it was not a question 'of generosity but a recognition of the situation'.[340] Putting the case forward that America would not take its allocation of ships, Daniels refined his position. Rather than saying that he did not want any American allocation, he now said that all the ships should be sunk and that there should be *no allocation whatsoever*. In one way, it made perfect sense. The Allied nations had all been trapped inside an expensive naval arms race for two decades. This was a chance to finally break the cycle. It would also be 'a moral lesson…of tremendous significance to the whole world'.[341]

The British and Americans – the world's two leading naval powers – had formed a club, an arrangement, to dictate terms to France, Italy and Japan. The British stance with the Americans was directed against the French, who were inflexible on the point of naval reparations. The 25 April meeting could not reach a conclusion on this point and even when the conference came to an end in June, the point had not been decided or agreed upon.

Britain agreed to join the League of Nations, respect the Monroe doctrine and agree to the destruction of the German fleet.* A few days after, writing to Lloyd George, Churchill pointed out that agreeing to the disposal of the German fleet was not desirable: 'What spectacle could be more foolish than for Britain and America to begin by sinking all those fine German ships and then starting to waste material and money on building new ones? It is fit for a madhouse.'[342]

Britain came away retaining its control over what America had come to Versailles to challenge, 'freedom of the seas', 'the very principle on which they had gone to war'.[343] The Americans left Versailles with a bitter taste in their mouths.

> President Wilson went home…a sadder, wiser and, if anything, a
> more determined man than he had been when he arrived. He had
> for the first time experienced Old World politicians at their best
> and worst, and he had not enjoyed the lesson. They had rejected
> his ideas about colonies, they rejected his ideas about freedom of
> the seas, they owed the United States money, but they acted as if
> they still owned the world. In 1919, when the Navy came forward

---

* The Monroe doctrine, coined after President James Monroe, was America's declaration against further European colonial expansion in South or North America by viewing such as a 'manifestation of an unfriendly disposition toward the United States'.

with the request for appropriations from Congress, Wilson not only supported its desire to dust off the 1916 program[me], he also agreed to the idea that it should be doubled.[344]

Germany

Very quickly the German population, which had already suffered the privations of war through blockade, now felt renewed pain. Temporarily, conditions improved as large supplies of meat from the horses slaughtered after the war's end alleviated the situation. That did not last long.

Allied planning allowed increased German food imports as long as the Germans used their own shipping to collect supplies in Allied ports. Fearing confiscation, German ship owners baulked. From the other side, the question of how goods would be paid for went unsolved. A loan from America was politically impossible to sell to Congress, while for the Germans using gold reserves turned out to be equally unrealistic given that the French felt that this should be used to help pay reparations.

7

PLANNING 'DER TAG'. SAVING THE NAVY'S HONOUR

O N 13 December, Reuter left Scapa Flow on the SS *Bremen*. He was going back to Germany to visit his family in Wilhelmshaven. He handed over the command of the interned fleet to the captain of the *Bayern*, Kapitän zur See Hugo Dominik. The trip was not going to be an easy one. He was not in good health and the tensions running though the fleet did not help. His ship actually ran aground for a full half-day off the East Frisian Islands of Wangerooge, just off Germany's northern coastline.

Reuter would be away from Scapa for almost six weeks. Back in Germany, he probably started to think about the practical issues involved in scuttling the fleet. At the end of January, he briefly discussed the possibility with his Chief of Staff, Oldekop, after he returned on the *Regensburg* on 25 January. It is more than likely that this was a follow-up to conversations while in Germany with Admiral von Trotha. Trotha had been one of the officers, along with Scheer and Hipper, who had strenuously fought for Plan 19, the ill-fated, and in the end, failed final sortie, saying that it was 'better to go down with honour' than cave in.

Erich Raeder always maintained that both Oldekop and another naval officer, Commander Quaet-Faslam, had carried verbal orders to Reuter. At the extremes, there were those, like Commander Kenworthy, who maintained that the British were in complete connivance with known orders to scuttle the fleet.[*]

Later, at the end of March, after Reuter had moved his flag from *Friedrich der Große*, I would imagine the subject once again came to the fore. While he was always to deny receiving direct orders from Germany, it was at best 'intriguing' and, frankly, 'inconceivable that in the staff

---

[*] Notwithstanding the fact that Lord Strabolgi (as he preferred to be known) had failed his naval examinations on multiple occasions: those to be sub lieutenant, a signalling course and a course on torpedoes. Somehow, he obtained a command but was dismissed from HMS *Bullfinch* for unsatisfactory conduct (he had rammed another ship, HMS *Leopard*) and was seen as a person unfit to command a destroyer. After serving for a short time on the Naval Staff (five months), he resigned from the navy in 1920 to enter politics.

meetings to which he so briefly refers there was no discussion about the ultimate fate of the bulk of Germany's surface Fleet'.[345]

On 7 May, a week after the German delegation arrived at Versailles, they were presented the terms of the 'Carthaginian peace' in the Trianon Palace Hotel, all fifteen sections covering 404 articles.[346]. It was obvious from the moment that Georges Clemenceau started to address them that the price of peace was going to be high. He wanted Germany to be faced with nothing less than total humiliation. 'This is neither the time nor the place for superfluous words… The time has come for a heavy reckoning of accounts.'[347]

The naval terms were, indeed, hard. It was proposed that the German Navy be reduced to a maximum size of six battleships, no larger than 10,000 tons displacement, six light cruisers displacing under 6,000 tons and a dozen torpedo boats and destroyers. In terms of manpower, the full naval force would be capped at no more than 15,000 volunteers and 1,500 officers. She would not be allowed to possess any submarines or aircraft in the future.*

No battleship then in Scapa Flow would be allowed a continued role in Germany's new navy, a force that would merely be a ghost of its former self. And, on top of this, the Allies announced that Helgoland was to stop functioning as a base. All defences and facilities were to be dismantled.

The Treaty's Article 184 was the key:

> From the date of the coming into force of this present Treaty, all German surface warships which are not located in German ports cease to belong to Germany, which renounces all rights over them. Vessels which, in compliance with the Armistice of 11th November, 1918 are now interned in the ports of Allied and Associated Powers are declared to be finally surrendered. Vessels which are now interned in neutral ports will be there surrendered to the Governments of the Principal and Associated Powers. The German Government must address a notification to that effect to the neutral Powers on the coming into force of the present Treaty.[348]

The Germans were given two weeks to respond. Count Ulrich von Brockdorff-Rantzau, 'the physical epitome of the stereotypical Prussian

---

* Hence the future Luftwaffe, Hitler's air force, was trained with gliders in units under the guise of sports clubs.

aristocrat, and just as arrogant' replied for his country.[349] There would be no possibility, he said, of Germany admitting guilt for what he called a defensive war. Instead, he called for an independent commission and blamed the blockade for the continued death-toll. Clemenceau was apoplectic. Wilson commented that it was 'the most tactless speech he had ever heard' and that the response proved that 'the Germans really are a stupid people'.[350] The only real admission of guilt by Germany was that invading France through Belgium had broken international law.

In Germany, the reaction to the treaty was consternation. The government resigned as Phillip Scheidemann summed up: 'The hand that signed the Treaty must wither.' The War Guilt Paragraph was singled out as being the *Schandparagraf* (the Disgrace Paragraph). The consequences of signing or not signing would be huge: it was assumed, and threatened, that hostilities would be resumed on 22 June if the German negotiators did not sign by the deadline of the day before. But, after months of bickering among themselves, the Germans were given minimal time.

It was on 11 May, as always, four days after the event, that Reuter learned a little about the harshness of what had been presented four days earlier and, more importantly, what affected the navy. He read of the naval terms with growing alarm and also read the accompanying correspondence from von Trotha.*

When the news spread, the effect was immediate: it 'lay like lead on the minds of the men'.[351] What made it worse for Reuter himself was that he was getting information from British newspapers and not from official channels. In his letter, Trotha referred to the terms but Reuter probably did not have a copy of the German text. Trotha had written, on 9 May, that given the size restrictions set on the new navy:

> ...it appears that our opponents are considering the idea of depriving us of the interned ships on the conclusion of peace; they waver between destruction or the distribution among themselves of these ships... . In this connection, the first condition will be that the ships remain German...their surrender to the enemy remains out of the question.

---

* Van der Vat (p. 166) says that von Trotha's letter and commentary were only given to Reuter on 18 May. This seems to be too long a delay for such an important communication. Likewise, it seems that 11 May was too early for von Trotha's letter to have made it into Reuter's hands. 16 May is the more likely date. Reuter's papers show that mail was delivered four times in May, on the 6th, 16th and 24th by *B.97* and *B.98* (24 May). See Reuter papers, Freiburg RM8/1311 p. 146.

Trotha's words were suggestive but not conclusive. The British were later to try and make out that what Trotha had written, effectively, constituted his orders for Reuter to scuttle. Trotha maintained, however, that he was merely trying to give Reuter some encouragement, knowing how demoralised he must have become. Reuter would always deny that he had acted on von Trotha's orders:

> In this connection, the first condition will be that the ships remain German, and that their fate, whatever turn it may take under pressure of the political situation, will not be decided without our co-operation, and will not be consummated by ourselves, and that their surrender to the enemy remains out of the question.[352]

Reuter maintained that no one else could take a decision of this importance. He was the man on the spot, the only man who could judge the situation: 'It was quite clear to me that I should be left alone entirely to my own devices. I had refused orders and instructions because I alone and nobody at home could assess and appreciate the situation in the Internment Formation.'[353]

He was in a very challenging position, having to play his game with one hand tied behind his back, and completely in the dark about the real state of the negotiations in Versailles. His only sources of information were old newspapers and gossip. It was bound to increase his agitated state. His health was deteriorating badly at this point and, two days after he had received the devastating news about the naval terms, on the 13 May, he officially requested a transfer back to Germany on the grounds of ill health, enclosing a medical certificate with the request saying that he, 'had been suffering from severe digestive troubles which gave rise to the surmise that an internal complaint is developing, pains in the bowels, almost entire sleeplessness, severe headaches and daily attacks of giddiness, nerves strongly affected'.[354]

It was hardly surprising. On Reuter's shoulders lay a massive burden of responsibility. He tried to think out what the alternatives for the politicians might be: accept, negotiate or reject the terms. Accepting the terms would be abhorrent, rejecting them dangerous in Germany's weakened state. Negotiation would mean treating 'his' fleet as a bargaining tool. It would have been an act below his dignity as a German naval officer.*

---

* Reuter referred to the 16 June edition of *The Times* where the newspaper cited the Allied position as one of refusal to regard the interned fleet as an object of barter and was altogether negative in regard to the German counter-proposals.

Kaiser Wilhelm's standing orders were that no German ship should ever fall into enemy hands.* Even if he were no longer the Kaiser, that duty remained. No new written orders were needed for this. It was more an article of faith among his naval officers. As far as Reuter was concerned, Germany would either have to accept the humiliating terms of the 7 May declaration or refuse to sign altogether. Which would mean resuming hostilities. The former would mean the disgrace of the navy. The latter the certain seizure of the interned ships by the British.

Reuter discounted the idea of resistance. His men lacked the means. They had no weapons and no ammunition. There was no means to fire any of the guns as the breech mechanisms had been removed. To try to resist British attempts to seize their ships might have sounded heroic, but it could only have had one outcome: slaughter. So, his only reasonable option was to scuttle.

If Germany could not keep her fleet, then neither should her enemies be allowed to take it. It was Reuter's only way out. The only way to preserve the honour of the service; to make sure that whatever happened in Scapa, the actions of that day would not remain an indelible stain on the German Navy's record. Whatever that future might be.

Marder called Trotha's letter 'a veiled invitation to scuttle'. And, according to Admiral Raeder, Trotha, an enthusiastic advocate for the fleet's last sortie had,

> privately impressed upon Junior Captain (Commander) Oldekop, Admiral von Reuter's Chief of Staff, that the ships must be scuttled at all costs. This important message was sent through Junior Captain Quaet-Faslem, the commander of the dispatch boat which maintained communications between Admiral von Reuter and Germany.[355]

For Reuter, however, Trotha's letter was important enough to keep in his safe on the *Emden II*. That act does not constitute conclusive evidence against either Reuter or Trotha. Indeed, if the correspondence was important enough to be in his safe, why on earth would he leave it there? Why would he not destroy the documents rather than risk their retrieval by the enemy?

It comes down to supposition and perspective. Ruge, for example, was

---

* 'All ships put out of action must never fall into enemy hands' (Brown and Meehan, p. 131).

adamant that the letter was not what the British thought: 'It is grotesque that anyone should read out of this [an] order to scuttle the ships.'[356]

Fremantle might have been rather naïve in assuming that Reuter could only anticipate a favourable outcome in Versailles. It was likely that he simply did not really get to know what made Reuter 'tick'. He wasn't able to 'get inside his head'. He'd had no time to be able to. If he'd given it the time, the Defence Ministry signal should have given the British admiral pause for thought; however, he was clearly distracted when he received it. His ships were just weighing anchor. Fremantle's own words were very suggestive of his own idea of 'fair play': 'Presumably, some days will elapse after the treaty has been signed, and before transports arrive to remove the German officers and men. It is during this interval that damage to the ships is to be apprehended.'[357]

As a consequence, Fremantle proposed to Madden that he inform Reuter that his ships would be inspected after the Armistice had been signed and that the men would only be allowed to return to Germany once this had been carried out to British satisfaction. He thought this might be a sufficient threat. Clause XXXI had always referred to damage *prior to*, rather than *after* the ships had been handed over to the Allies. Reuter's tendency might be seen as to look at many of these issues from an extremely legalistic perspective but he was a man of strong principle and was thoroughly correct in his dealings with people. And, understandably, he was the same in how his fleet was being treated. In later correspondence to his superiors in July, he noted that 'in consequence of this omission, a loophole was created which in itself justified the scuttling, particularly since it was a question of German and not foreign property'.[358]

An important day was fast approaching. The 31st of May, Skagerrakstag, was only two weeks away. To this day, there is little agreement about who actually won the much-awaited *Entscheidungsschlacht* at Jutland.* For the British it led to disappointment, finger-pointing and, later, vitriol. The continuation of the status quo ante was in British interests and Jellicoe was right to play his cards prudently. He had everything to lose on the day, and very little to gain. What the unforeseen consequences of Jutland were, however, is a different thing. The overwhelmingly obvious power of the Royal Navy convinced Scheer that he should push the Kaiser and the cabinet for an aggressive resumption of unrestricted submarine warfare and risk the consequences of an American entry into the war by aiming

---

* The meaning of *Entscheidungsschlacht* is a literal translation of Mahan's decisive battle: the deciding battle.

for fast success in the undersea war. In the resumption of that approach, he very nearly succeeded.

So, it was natural that there would be many on the German ships who would want to celebrate the battle's anniversary to rub their jailor's nose in the mud. Reuter, however, wanted to make sure that the anniversary would be low key. He had already issued orders on 30 April to that effect, paraphrased by van der Vat as saying that 'these days in particular could bring us in particular a[n] [e]specially bitter decision' as peace terms were expected to be announced.[359] Most ships respected that wish, although some crews ignored him and strung out brightly coloured buntings and lights. They shot off red and white Very signals (probably from the battle-cruisers) while the destroyers along with *Seydlitz* and *Moltke* decorated their ships with the Imperial ensign and the red flag.* It was the kind of provocation that made Reuter nervous. 'Needless to say, peremptory orders in effect to "take down that washing" were issued by the British Admiral on the base.'[360] The Germans, Fremantle concluded, had 'celebrated with a little too much exuberance'.[361]

The sailors' council shared Reuter's concerns. They'd issued orders that important papers should be destroyed if the British used the anniversary as the day to board their ships. Van der Vat even maintains that Reuter told his captains 'to be prepared to sink the ships if the attempt was made'.[362]

The destroyer crews, generally, were the crews that retained the most discipline. A young RN sub lieutenant, Andrew Yates, in the accepted language of the day, compared the morale of the different crews: 'They are the most beaten lot I ever saw and I don't think will do anything. The destroyers are however quite aggressive still and the officers very Prussian.'[363]

Jutland Day went by without serious incident. Two weeks later, on 15 June, Reuter's request for a medical transfer was passed on to Madden by SNOAS, Sydney Fremantle, with a note saying that he concurred and the request was sent to Germany.

Two days later, on 17 June, Reuter read an article in *The Times*. This was to be, he later said, the final source of information on which he based his decision to go ahead with the scuttle. His written orders, below, went out to the ships of the interned fleet that day.†

All that now remained was to act.

* It's not clear to me whether the reference to 'red flags' were not the *Stander-Z* attack flag that had been used at Jutland rather than the communist flag.
† English translations are given in van der, pp. 229–231, and Ruge, pp. 161–162. I have chosen versions from each to help the readability of Reuter's critical order. One copy of his orders was found in the water after the scuttle and translated by a Lieutenant Colonel Dibblee.

INTERNMENT ZONE COMMAND
Order No.39   June 17th, 1919

FOR OFFICERS ONLY
Personal

To all commanding officers and Destroyer Captains.

(1) The necessary preparations for scuttling the ships are to be made immediately, in such a manner that each ship can be sunk as quickly as possible on receipt of the order.

(2) Final preparations are to be made only after the crews, who are currently being repatriated, have been taken off. Commanding officers must use their own discretion in deciding whether individual ratings may take part in these preparations, and be informed of the intention without there having any risk of endangering the success of the plan, as for example, by treacherous disclosures to the British.

(3) The following preliminary measures are to be taken. All inner doors and hatches are to be permanently left open, e.g. doors to the side of the ship, bunker doors, longitudinal and transversal bulkheads, gangway hatches, ventilators, portholes etc. Depending on the views of the commanding officers, the following further steps may be taken: measures needed for the speedy opening of torpedo tubes, opening of condensers, opening of sea cocks and sluice valves not used for flooding purposes.

(4) Boats. Where possible, no more than one boat should be made ready for the evacuation of the crew. A flag of truce should be readily available in the boat. When lowered, all boats should make for the nearest land with their crews. They will remain under orders from their officers.

(5) Scuttling is to take place:
    a. In case the British occupy the ship by force.
    b. On receipt of a specific order from me.

(6) With reference to 5a., commanding officers are to carefully consider what steps should be taken to guarantee the success of the scuttling should the British try to seize the ships by surprise. A demand by the British for the surrender of the ships, if not approved by me, is to be regarded as a forcible attempt at seizure and is, therefore, to be answered with scuttling.

(7)   With reference to 5b., orders may be issued to either (a) scuttle the ships at once or, (b) to scuttle the ships at a certain time.

(8)   Signals. For immediate scuttling, as in 7a., the following signal will be given: TO ALL COs AND LEADER OF TORPEDO BOATS. CONFIRM PARAGRAPH ELEVEN. COMMANDER OF THE INTERNMENT FORCE. The signal is to be passed by every possible means. The scuttling of ships must begin immediately. For scuttling ships at a certain time, as in 7b., the following signal will be given: TO ALL COs AND LEADER OF TORPEDO BOATS. CONFIRM PARAGRAPH ELEVEN.0913. COMMANDER OF THE INTERNMENT FORCE. In this signal, the first two numbers refer to the date, i.e. the 9th, and the last two to the time when the scuttling is to begin. The time will be reckoned from noon to noon (astronomically).

(9)   Confirmation. The receipt of the signal is to be confirmed in the following manner: TO THE COMMANDER OF THE INTERNMENT FORCE. PARAGRAPH…IS CONFIRMED.

(10) Since the acceptance or rejection of the peace conditions and the resumption of hostilities is about to be decided, the next few days will be particularly critical. From Wednesday, June 8th increased vigilance will be needed day and night, not only as regards and unusual behaviour by the British but also to pay attention to any signals from the *Emden*. As absolute reliance cannot be placed upon the men, the officers must take over the required look-out duties.

(11) It is my intention to scuttle the ships only if the enemy should try to take possession of them without the consent of our Government. Should our Government agree to the surrender of our ships in the peace negotiations, the ships will then be handed over to the lasting shame of those who put us in this position.

(12) Commanding officers are to keep this document locked up. It must not fall into the hands of the enemy.

Reuter stressed that these last few days would be 'particularly critical'. For the senior British officers at Scapa – Fremantle and Prendergast – it was the same (although, for Fremantle it was that the days *following* the signing that were critical). So too did Madden. But the Admiralty in London appeared almost purposefully disinterested.

    That a handover would bring 'lasting shame' left Reuter's officers little choice in the matter. A scuttle would, under almost any circumstances, be inevitable. It highlighted the problematic relationship between the military and democratic power in Germany. Rarely would the military feel it their obligation to bow to the decisions of political institutions. Taking the lead from a single, autocratic force – the Kaiser – was different.

Reuter's orders were passed to the officers around the fleet from the *Emden*, ironically, by British guard tenders. These vessels had served to advance the very purpose against which they were to defend – suspicious activity signalling any move by the Germans to interfere with the terms of internment.

In the same way Reuter distrusted the politicians back in Germany, he also understood that he had to keep the plans secret until the very last moment as he could not place 'absolute reliance' on the men.

The last, large repatriation of crews to Germany took place the next day, 18 June, on two ships that had arrived separately, on 15 and 17 June. Around 2,700 men left Scapa Flow, leaving Reuter with around 1,700 men manning the seventy-four ships under his command.*

RETURNING TO GERMANY – SHIPS' COMPANY REDUCTIONS

Date	Number	Ships	Comments
3–4 Dec 1918	3,975	SS *Sierra Ventana*, SS *Graf Waldersee*	Twenty-five officers and 1,000 men (*Ventana*), 150 officers and 2,200 men (*Graf Waldersee*). 600 additional men are evacuated
7 Dec 1918	6,000	SS *Pretoria*, SS *Bürgermeister*	250 officers. 4,000 (SS *Pretoria*), 1,500 (*Bürgermeister*)
13 Dec 1918	5,000	SS *Batavia*, SS *Bremen*	200 officers and 2,800 men (SS *Batavia*) to Kiel, 500 officers and 1,500 men (SS *Bremen*) to Wilhelmshaven
18 June 1919	2,700	SS *Bedima*, SS *Schleswig*	
TOTAL	17,375		

* The men were distributed seventy-five to a battle cruiser, sixty to a battleship, thirty to a cruiser and a small crew for the destroyers.

Among those to be repatriated, Reuter and his officers had planned to include as many of the remaining troublemakers as they could. Their departure on two transport ships, the SS *Bedima* and the SS *Schleswig*, made all the plotters feel instantly more at ease to start preparations within the rusting but still impenetrable ships' hulls.*

It was not as though the British did not expect that something might happen. Fremantle was jumpy and later wrote in his memoirs that the Germans were suspected of being up to something:

> Certain minor occurrences and movements had been observed on board the German ships which led me to suspect that some momentous action was contemplated by them. I had, accordingly, arranged, with Admiralty approval, that at midnight on the 21st we should board and take possession of all ships, confining the officers and men under close confinement and using any force which might be necessary.[364]

Fremantle added that 'secret orders and preparations' were in place to seize the German ships. He was not alone in worrying about a 'momentous action' by the enemy. He was just unfortunate enough to be in command of the Scapa Flow guard force on 21 June. He was in the wrong place at the wrong time. Oliver, before him, had shared his conclusions and was concerned enough to similarly develop detailed plans for the seizure of the ships, by force, if necessary. Admiral Sir Henry Oliver's thoughts on the restrictions and limitations placed upon him make interesting – if not rather chilling – reading. They underline the ambiguity of the interned fleet's status:

> Suppose the crews are detained in the transports and told they will be punished if the ships are found, on inspection, to be damaged. Damage is discovered and the question of punishment arises. What is it going to be? If a percentage are picked out and shot summarily, it is extremely doubtful if our ministers would support the action of the Admiral. The Germans are not prisoners of war and cannot legally be tried as such, and they are not subject to our Naval Discipline Act. If they are not summarily imprisoned, the legality

---

* This reduction brought the crew levels down to Royal Navy caretaker levels, seventy per battle-cruiser, sixty per battleship, thirty per light cruiser and whatever was necessary for the destroyers, a total of about 1,700.

might not be questioned, but it should place the cost of keeping them in prison on the taxpayer. In the event of a disturbance, no one is likely to question what is done in hot blood to quell it, but I think we shall have to be extremely careful about what we do in cold blood.[365]

When Madden took over command of the Grand Fleet, he forwarded Oliver's ideas but the Admiralty did not seem to share his concerns: 'the Admiralty evinced no interest', was how he put it. Both Keyes and Leveson had also worked out plans, although the latter with the idea of seizing the ships *before* the delivery of the final peace treaty and holding the German sailors as prisoners at Nigg, on the north shore of the Cromarty Firth. Their fears had been well-founded.

The fact is that Madden had given the Admiralty timely warning of what he thought might happen, explicitly stating that he should receive 'early intimation' of any deadline changes at Versailles as these would clearly influence Reuter on the timing of any scuttle. Madden had detailed plans for a seizure of the ships. On the hoisting of the letters 'M.Y.' German ships were to be boarded by as many as sixty for a battleship or battle-cruiser and twenty-nine for a cruiser whose task it would be to *prevent* scuttle. A number of German sailors would be kept aboard to assist – a petty officer and four ratings (of which one was to be a signaller). Reuter would be picked up by one of eight destroyers moving through and around the Flow.

On 16 June, Fremantle told Madden of his plan to seize the German ships, saying that he would do so at midnight the night of 21–22 June.[*] Three days later, on 19 June, Madden approved. You can argue that Reuter had done well to not wait until the deadline. Rather, he had assumed that the British would 'play the game' with double standards.

In the materials that Madden sent to the Admiralty the day after the scuttle were his earlier telegrams and memoranda. They covered the possibility of a German attempt to pre-emptively scuttle their ships:

> In the event of the Germans refusing to sign the Peace terms, it will be necessary to seize the German ships at Scapa before the operation ordered in admiralty letter M 01677 of 20th April 1919, is undertaken. Should the crews of German ships receive information of a proposed German refusal before they are seized, they may be sunk or damaged.

---

[*] The plans were organised for the event of peaceful surrender of the ships (Plan SA) or for the forceful seizure (Plan SB).

He went on to say:

> Request therefore that I receive early intimation of the date on
> which the German reply to peace terms is to be given and any
> information in the possession of Their Lordships which may help
> to forecast the nature of that reply in order that a sufficient force
> can be concentrated at Scapa. Can the German crews be accom-
> modated in internment camps?[366]

According to Arthur Marder, the Admiralty 'paid no heed' to either
Madden's or Fremantle's concerns and requests for direction.[367] This might
have been true in practice. It was not the spirit of the Admiralty response
given the same day. The reply said that they were looking into internment
and that Madden would be kept 'fully informed' regarding 'progress of
events at the Peace Conference'.

What changed everything was that the deadline for the signing of the
Peace Treaty to end the war, originally scheduled for midday, 21 June, was
extended.

All that Reuter knew from newspapers was that the German
government had to give its new reply within five days of the Allied reply
to its own counter-proposals: 'Since this reply [the Allied reply rejecting
the German counter-proposal] was made on June 16th, I had to conclude
that if the peace was not signed on Saturday, June 21st, a state of hostilities
would be resumed' since 'during the last three days of this five-day respite
the Armistice would automatically expire.'

What happened in Paris did so without formal communication
reaching the key players in Orkney. It was a critical oversight. A sensitivity
to timing should have been understood. It was crucial. Fremantle (and his
predecessors) had always felt that the Germans might attempt a scuttle at
the last minute, so these last-minute changes were of vital importance: 'I
had no anxiety that any gross breach of the armistice would be committed
until possibly the last moments before the German representatives were
required to sign the Treaty.'[368]

What had happened? In Berlin, Phillip Scheidemann's government had
resigned the day before the deadline, on 20 June. It was monumentous.
The man who had declared the republic and announced the death of the
Hohenzollern monarchy was gone. He could not bring himself to sign a
treaty that in so many Germans' eyes humiliated their country, not just
because of the severity of the Allied retribution, but as much because of

the inclusion of the so-called *Schandparagraf* (the Disgrace Paragraph) that assigned Germany the ultimate responsibility for the war. Reuter could not imagine that such terms would be accepted by Germany and, therefore, was starting to feel that the renewal of hostilities was an inevitability.

Who knew what in those last days? As the clock ticked away, nearing what Reuter thought was the final day, he was demonstrably out of touch with what had been going on in Paris. On 17 June he had seen an old copy of *The Times*. It was dated 16 June and contained the text of the German counter-proposals. Reuter was becoming increasingly nervous and said that he 'dispatched a wireless message to the German government requesting that the officers should be relieved of their duties before the handing over of the ships'.[369]

Madden had been informed but, apparently, had failed to pass the information in a timely manner to Fremantle, even though he had approved of Fremantle's 21 June plans for seizure on 19 June. The fact was, that late the next day, 20 June, at 1700, the authorisation to seize of the German fleet had been moved by the Council of Four in Paris to a new timetable, 23 June at 1900, the new signing extension.

Fremantle, however, did know about the extension when he took the 1st BS out of the Flow on the morning of 21 June. He had supposedly seen it announced in a press statement on the evening of 19 June. (although elsewhere it states that he 'only learned of this two-day extension from the newspapers').[370]

It is well known that he had grave misgivings about Madden's insistence that the exercises be carried out despite the timing. Even if he qualified what he'd said, making a distinction between 'scuttling' and 'damage' to the ships, he still maintained that:

> I had, however, considerable anxiety as to the possibility of damage being done to the German ships either (1) in the event of the Treaty being signed, during the interval between the signing of the Treaty and the repatriation of German officers and men or; (2) in the event of the Treaty not being signed, before I was able to assure the surrender of the ships.[371]

Who knew what in those last days was, therefore, of fundamental importance. As the clock ticked away, nearing what Reuter thought was the final day, he was demonstrably out of touch with what had been going on in Paris. All he had in his mind was what he'd seen from The Times' 16 June report which gave no indication of the extension, and only referred to the German counter-proposals. Reuter was becoming increasingly nervous and said that he 'dispatched a wireless message to the German government requesting that the officers should be relieved of their duties before the handing over of the ships'.[372]

THE COUNTDOWN – CRITICAL DATES AND ACTORS

Date	Scapa – German	Scapa – British	Other
22/4		Madden's requests to be 'fully informed'. His request is ignored.	
29/5			Germany: In the Reichstag, Chancellor Scheidemann rejects the proposed terms of the treaty.
16/6 Mon		Fremantle informs Madden of plan to seize ships on 21/6 at 2400. Writes to Madden about fears of damage.	
17/6 Tue	The Times 16 June report on final peace treaty terms seen by Reuter. (Hewison p. 128). Issues scuttle order.		
18/6 Wed	2,700 men leave Scapa in the morning. Scuttle order of 17 June distributed by British drifter.		

19/6 Thu	Stormy weather.	Madden approves of Fremantle's 16/6 plan for seizure. Hears of signing extension to 23/6 at 1000 in a press statement on the afternoon of 19/6.	
20/6 Fri	Stormy weather. Reuter request composes signal to permission to resign commissions.		Germany: Phillip Scheide-mann's government resigns. Paris: Allied agreement given to the seizure of German ships at the expiration (23/6 at 1900).
21/6 Sat	Blue sky weather. On *Revenge*, Reuter denies knowledge of the signing delay until 23/6.	0900 (approx.) Fremantle receives Reuter's Defence Minister signal (request for officers to resign commissions). 2100 original orders for seizure to be opened, but, with the new signing extension, switched to 1900 on 23/6. 2400 planned forced seizure of the interned fleet (approved by Admiralty).	Reuters carries a report of the rumoured Allied plans to seize the ships on 23/6.

The German government had to give its new reply within five days of the reply to its counter-proposals. 'Since this reply [the Allied reply rejecting the German counter-proposal] was made on June 16th, I had to conclude that if the peace was not signed on Saturday, June 21st, a state of hostilities would be resumed' since 'during the last three days of this five-day respite the Armistice would automatically expire'. That same day – 16 June – it was reported that the German government of Prime Minister Phillip Scheidemann had resigned in protest at the harshness of the terms. Reuter could not imagine that such terms would be accepted by Germany and, therefore, was starting to feel that the renewal of the war was an inevitability.

The fact that the ultimate deadline had now been extended in Paris with the agreement of the Allied powers to 1900, 23 June, was unknown to Reuter and never seems to have been officially communicated to Fremantle. Fremantle wrote to Madden on 16 June about the legal inter-pretation of damage but, in the note, he made it clear that he had not seen any of the treaty details:

> ...have not seen the full text of the draft Peace Treaty and am therefore not aware whether any stipulations are made as to the condition in which the ships are to be surrendered. There is no condition in the Armistice which stipulates that no damage is to be done to the ships, while interned... .[373]

But even if the signing deadline had been moved from 21 June to 23 June, the British still planned to seize the German fleet. Fremantle's sealed orders were distributed and were to be opened at 2100, 23 June, to coincide with the new deadline.

For his part, Reuter always assumed that the British would seize the ships by daylight, which, for the summer solstice, would be at 2121.* Fremantle only switched the intended date of seizure to 23 June when he finally agreed to Madden's orders to take the Battle Squadron out (which he did after learning of the signing extension, although, to be honest he could not easily refuse the order).

Reuter always maintained that Fremantle never told him about any extension to the Paris signing deadline and that he had 'not received this news until the evening of the 21st'. Marder wrote – because he did not believe Reuter's account – that 'before sailing, Fremantle informed Reuter unofficially of the extension of the armistice' [374] Fremantle later wrote that he told Reuter 'in an official note'.[375] Being 'official', there should have been a record but no copy of the 'note' has ever been found. Reuter always

---

* Given the time of year, darkness does not come to the Flow till around 2300. First light comes back around 0230.

maintained that it was only in the afternoon, while on board *Revenge*, that he learned about the two-day extension of the Armistice when he was told about it through Fremantle's interpreter.

Reuter maintained that to regard his actions as an act of treachery was unfair as 'the Armistice was at an end when he had done so'. Even Fremantle, in his own report of 24 June seemed to contradict what he had said, and would later continue to say.[*]

What complicates Reuter's denial is that the information seems to have been known by others in the fleet. Oldekop, for example, said he had known. If this were true, it's almost preposterous to suggest that Reuter, sharing the same bridge on the day, did not. He knew that some newspaper articles had been strongly against the idea of the fleet being used to negotiate for financial concessions.[†] Ruge, on *B.110,* said that a British officer told him about the extension until 23 June that morning, even showing him the newspaper's headline.[376] It is more than surprising to hear this from Ruge: that, on the very same day as the scuttle, his C in C maintained that he had been told nothing while a junior torpedo boat lieutenant was instead shown the headlines. Ruge also pointed out that the sailors weren't that tense as '…until now every date had, in the end, been extended'.[377] Is it believable that he had more insight than Reuter?

> Moreover, on the *Köln*, Kapitänleutnant Johann Heinemann later wrote that one of the sailors had managed to rig up a clandestine radio set on which the announcements of the extension had been picked up, even if in fairly garbled form.[‡] Extraordinarily, he then wrote that, 'I considered whether or not I should tell the Admiral this (the news about the extension). In the end I let the idea drop. After all, on the *Emden* too they would have knocked a receiver together… .'[378]

It does seem odd that with all the planning and ingenuity shown, there was no system in place for getting this kind of intelligence back to Reuter as a normal procedure.

---

[*] In the report, he maintained that: 'Admiral von Reuter had never received any communication from me regarding the date of the termination of the Armistice, or with any reference to the terms of the Peace Treaty generally.'
[†] See van der Vat, p. 170.
[‡] Ruge stated (Ferguson, p. 7) that the ship's radio wireless receiver was only taken away by the British in spring 1919.

As if the situation was not tense enough by the looming deadline and the lack of officially communicated information, in the background Madden had been planning to take the Atlantic Fleet to sea for a cruise and wanted the fleet elements based in Scapa sharpened up. Fremantle had completed most of the required exercises except for one: manoeuvres to defend against a massed torpedo attack against the battle squadron in daylight. The exercise had twice been delayed because of bad weather but, on the evening of 20 June, the conditions were good.

Initially, Fremantle had not wanted to carry out these exercises on Madden's timetable. He preferred to wait until the Armistice was settled, asking that the exercises be delayed 'until the Germans were off our hands'. 'He [Madden] did not like this' so Fremantle was left little choice but to obey his commander-in-chief.[379] Madden's order was odd, even, many would argue, rash. The danger of scuttling was always going to be a risk. For him to have insisted on this particular day, out of the 209 days that the fleet would have been in Scapa, was astonishing.*

With the news of the deferment of the signing, the situation changed. Fremantle, who did at least have some inkling of the goings-on in Paris, now concluded the 1st BS 'could now safely proceed to sea'.[380] It was at this point that he said that he talked to Reuter to communicate his new understanding of the extended deadline: that the Armistice was still 'in operation'.[381] Reuter denied that conversation ever took place.

While the talks in Paris were coming to a head, in the 19 June edition of *The Orcadian* there was a column-long story about Haig and Beatty being honoured with the Freedom of the City of London. By contrast, there was scant attention paid to the treaty that was about to alter the course of the twentieth century and have a profound effect on the islands.

Once Madden's ships had left the Flow, the die was cast.

---

* Conspiracy theories abound but there is not one single piece of written documentation to support them. Would there had been? I seriously doubt that such an order would ever have gone down on paper should it have been the case.

8

MIDSUMMER MADNESS

SATURDAY, 21 JUNE was the summer solstice, the longest day of the summer. As forecast, it was a perfect Orkney day. Blue skies, light breeze, 'warm and sunny'.[382] The way German sailors might have described it was rather more prosaic: *'Zur Sommenwende herrscht Kaiserwetter'*.[383] Blue skies were always associated with the Kaiser, hence *'Kaiserwetter'*.* Heinrich Burmeister, a machinist mate on *Brummer*, had a picture of how the day started: *'Die Sonne scheinte warm und silbergrau glitzerte die Wasserfläche des ganzen Beckens.'* ('The sun was warm and, across the waters of the Flow, there was a silver-grey sparkle.')[384]

It would become, arguably, the second most important date in Germany's naval history. As important, maybe more so, than the one and only great meeting of two fleets at the Skagerrakschlacht.

Around 0900 the ships of the 1st Battle Squadron received the orders to weigh anchor. Three quarters of an hour later, at 0945, the battleships – Fremantle's flagship *Revenge*, followed by *Ramillies*, *Royal Oak*, *Renown* and *Royal Sovereign* – accompanied by two light cruisers and nine destroyers – majestically steamed out of the Flow, leaving it eerily quiet.

While *Revenge* had been weighing anchor, Fremantle was handed a copy of the signal that Reuter had written a few days earlier, after he had seen *The Times'* 16 June report. He had sent it to Fremantle for transmission to the Admiralty in Germany. The text of his signal read:

> To the Imperial Defence Minister, Chief of Admiralty, Chief of Baltic Station, Chief of the North Sea Station, 21st June.
>
> In the English papers, I have today perceived that in the German counter-proposal the Government intends to use the interned ships

---

* In the 1930s, the association changed to *'Führerswetter'*.

as an object of trade. Even if economical, distress is so great at this, my feelings of patriotism and honour cannot accommodate themselves to such treatment of the interned German Fleet. In this view of the matter I am assured of the support of all the officers of the Squadron. Accordingly, I request that a new adjustment of the Peace Terms may be caused, or, if this is not attainable, that we, officers and officials, may be definitely relieved before the surrender. (Sgd.h) Rear Admiral von Reuter.[385]

This could have been a moment in which Fremantle, had he not been distracted by having to satisfy Madden, might have 'read between the lines' or thought more about the implications of what Reuter was saying. Although Madden said that he doubted that Reuter's signal 'need have aroused any suspicion' in Fremantle's mind, the text quite clearly implied that the obligation to hand over ships was below the honour of any serving German naval officer.[386] The fact that Reuter said his sentiments 'cannot accommodate themselves to such treatment of the interned German Fleet' should have been a red flag.

Fremantle did not send the signal. He decided to attend to it when he was back and that the squadron continue the exercise. Nor was Reuter aware that the message had not been sent to Germany. Was this Reuter's way of leaving a paper trail for posterity? A future justification of his actions?

In the Flow, only a few ships were left behind: a depot ship *Sandhurst* and an old, stripped out battleship, *Victorious,* plus three destroyers.* *Victorious* was a dockyard ship and workshop even though she was also the flagship of Rear Admiral RJ Prendergast, senior officer commanding Orkney and Shetlands. One of the three destroyers, HMS *Vega,* was alongside *Sandhurst,* having her boilers cleaned. The other two guard destroyers, HMS *Walpole* (F.15) and HMS *Westcott,* normally lay at their buoys amidst the German destroyers in Gutter Sound, with 'steam up', *Walpole* at D.7 and *Westcott* at J.4. 'Steam up' would mean that they 'kept steam at five minutes' notice'.[387] On 21 June, *Westcott* was refuelling at Lyness.†

---

* HMS *Sandhurst* was originally the SS *Manipur,* which had been a 7,654-ton cargo ship built by the Belfast yard of Harland and Wolff in 1905. The larger, 14,890-ton HMS *Victorious,* was an old *Majestic*-class pre-dreadnought armed with 12in guns. It had already served as a guard ship on the Humber before coming to Scapa Flow.

† On the day, the crew on *Walpole,* it seems, only 'managed to get steam up after fierce work in the engine room' (Bowman, p. 33).

Moving among the German ships were a number of guard trawlers: *Cabalsin, Cudwosin, Ramna, Caersin and Clonsin.* There would also have been two communications drifters, *C.D.1* and *C.D.2* as well as *Trust-On*†and a flag dispatch drifter, *Recluse*, plus the two Admiralty tugs, *Flying Breeze* and the water tender, *Flying Kestrel*. On this Saturday, *Flying Kestrel* was picking up a group of Stromness public school schoolchildren for an outing on the Flow.

At around 1000 Reuter appeared on the quarter deck of the *Emden*. Unusually, he was wearing his dress uniform with all his medals. Deep in thought, he walked up and down the deck, occasionally stopping to look closely at his own ships through his telescope.

His Chief of Staff, Iwan Oldekop, approached and told the news that the British had just left harbour. It must have been just after 0945. It seemed to be both an opportunity to act as well as a possible signal that the British might be up to something. The sortie was easy to misinterpret. It might be connected to the resumption of hostilities: the squadron going to sea to do battle. Reuter's mind must have been racing. Maybe the discussions in Paris had finally broken down, his country finally, in his mind, doing the right thing and refusing to be pushed? Maybe, this *was* a sign that the British were going back out to sea on active war duty? Later, Ruge rhetorically asked, rather disingenuously, 'Why was the Fleet scuttled?' His answer: 'The Fleet was scuttled,' he continued, 'because the English gave us the possibility to do so.'[388] Reuter himself later said that he would have scuttled the fleet even if Fremantle's squadron had remained in Scapa. The fact is that it is very difficult to prevent a ship sinking from a well-planned scuttle. The absence of the bulk of the British guard forces did not act as an encouragement, it merely might have made his task easier.

It seems that at this late hour, Reuter's Chief of Staff had more information than his commanding officer. Oldekop had seen a copy of *The Times* (although maybe not the news about the treaty signing extension) and also knew that *B.98* would arrive the following day with news from Germany. Might he not have argued for Reuter to delay for twenty-four hours? Apparently not. A seemingly innocuous signal – the international code flags D.G. – was hoisted to warn the fleet that an important signal would be imminent and that *Emden*'s bridge and,

---

* *Ramna* was skippered by George E. Lambert, *Caersin* by Charles Yorstin.
† See ADM 116/2074 Fremantle to Admiralty, 24 June 1919.

especially, her flag hoist should be kept under constant watch. It was a little after 1000.*

After a short delay, giving the British ships time to travel further before committing his officers and men to the next, irretrievable steps, the final signal was hoisted on *Emden*.

To all Commanding officers and the Leader of Torpedo Boats. Paragraph eleven. Confirm. (*Paragraf elf. Bestätigen*).

The hoist looked innocent enough. 'The upper flag was a white ball on a blue pennant, the lower one a yellow and blue pennant.'[389] But behind the signal lay its meaning, the signal to execute the scuttle.† The British, of course, had no idea.

The timing of Reuter's signal was significant but it is difficult to be precise about it. Some say 1030, others around 1100.‡ While *Emden*'s outgoing signal timing was not completely clear, the initial confirmation signals back to her from ships receiving the instructions are a little easier to establish. The last newspaper reports he had seen was the 17 June copy of *The Times* where the deadline of 21 June was highlighted. Reuter's own conclusion was that the most likely hour for the deadline was midday and that, if he had been in Fremantle's shoes, he would have organised a seizure of his ships in daylight and as close to that deadline as possible. He had to pre-empt the possible (and, indeed, planned) seizure of his ships.

As Reuter had outlined in the smuggled written orders, *Emden*'s hoist was repeated by the ships closest by semaphore and searchlight until all ships around the Flow and down to Gutter Sound had received it. Since there were many ships that were out of the visual line of sight with Reuter's flagship, it took about an hour for the furthermost ships, the destroyers, lying in Gutter Sound west of Faro Island, to also get the message.

* 'Kurz nach zehn' (Krause, p. 296). Ruge (p. 110) maintained that a semaphore signal ordering that the red pennant, *Stander-Z*, should be prepared. The symbolic flag usually signalled the attack but it is unlikely that von Reuter did anything of the sort. This is not to say that the pennant was not raised once the scuttle was under way. This was certainly the case on the *S.138*, Cordes' command torpedo boat.
† Paragraf Elf refers to a nineteenth-century German students' tradition to 'keep on drinking'. Aping all things military, they would exhort each other with the phrase.
‡ Estimates for the time of the second signal, the actual scuttle signal, vary significantly: Woodward p. 183 (1020), van der Vat (1030), Hewison (1030), Hewison 1030, Brown and Meehan, p. 132 (1040), Krause (around 1100 'etwa elf gewesen' p. 296), Ruge confirms the receipt time at the end of the torpedo boat line (1130).

The destroyers were the last group to hear of Reuter's initial signal. The men on *B.110*, lying east of Rysa and west of Fara, knew something was up when there was a message from *Seydlitz* and men were seen hurrying about: 'We had never seen anyone running on a big ship in Scapa. Something must be wrong,' concluded Ruge.[390] The signal was Reuter's second, executive signal: *'Paragraf elf. Bestätigen'*. They could also see the red pennant, *Stander-Z*, being hoisted on *S.138*, Cordes' boat, which was lying directly to their east, close to Fara. The scuttle was on.

The commander of Ruge's boat, Mensche, might have been musing about some past memories: when ships of the 4th Squadron had sortied out from the Schillig Roads in the early hours of 6 November, *B.110* had collided with *Friedrich der Große*, damaging her bow. Meurer, who'd been standing on the quarter deck, merely 'smiled and expressed his regret'.[391]

Slowly other ships also started to signal back, confirming that they had received the orders: 'Paragraph eleven is confirmed' was signed off by the captain of each ship. It would be the one of the supreme ironies of the day that Reuter himself could not give the order to scuttle his own ship, *Emden*, until 1210 when, with the British drifters finally gone, he gave Kapitänleutnant Ehlers the 'go-ahead'.

Ruge said that the order was received around 1130. It is more likely that he was confusing signals and never mentioned the first D.G. signal at all. *Markgraf* received *Emden's* second signal around 1130, *Kaiser* around ten minutes later.[392] Both ships were well to the north, *Markgraf* east of Cava, *Kaiser* slightly further south, on the other side of Cava. Both were in sight line of *Friedrich der Große*. The torpedo boats were not.

With Fremantle out at sea and with the first steps to initiate this extraordinary act taken by Reuter, the Liverpool-based fleet water tender, the *Flying Kestrel*, was about to set off for a tour among the interned ships.*

---

* The *Flying Kestrel* was a large tug that later, in 1934, was engaged in the launch of the RMS *Queen Mary*. The two-masted ships was of considerable size. Few now would associate the *Flying Kestrel* with the important role that she played in the early days of the Grand Fleet. Her name is now mostly only remembered and linked to that one day: 21 June, 1919. In 1914, when the Grand Fleet was first at Scapa, *Flying Kestrel* was the ship that carried the most important supplies – water and mail. At the start of the war, there was not enough water on Orkney and, before the reservoirs were built above Stromness, she would bring supplies over from Scrabster. Over the five years, she had delivered more than a quarter of a million tons of water. But she had also ferried 25,000 men to and from Scrabster as well as 60,000 bags of mail and 2,000 tons of ammunition and supplies. When HMS *Vanguard* exploded, she was the one that carried the two survivors back on shore and she had gone out to find HMS *Hampshire's* survivors when the seas were judged too rough for the lifeboats. In the words of her Captain, Edward Davies, she did everything in the war 'except fire a gun'. She was a well-known ship with a very proud record.

That fateful day, Captain Davies, *Flying Kestrel*'s skipper for the previous four years, had slowly left Stromness harbour around 0930 to tour the lines of rusting hulls with around 400 schoolchildren from the Stromness public school.* This group of lucky students had been allowed to go on a special day outing to see the guardians, the British *Revenge* class ships of the Atlantic Fleet's 1st Battle Squadron and their prisoners, the interned German fleet.

As they set off, the schoolchildren learned that the British ships had already left the Flow at 0945. Naturally, there was disappointment but it did not last long. It was a day out of the classroom, a rare luxury, and there was a tremendous sense of adventure in the air, even if they were accompanied by 'the capable, if much feared schoolmaster, Colonel Hepburn'.[393] He was the school's headmaster and had just been demobbed. The children 'sailed away very triumphantly and feeling very important'.[394] And important they would certainly become: the trip – with its 'youthful, effervescent cargo of schoolchildren' – became one of the scuttle's most important primary sources of witness accounts.[395]

They were in the Flow where the lines of German battleships and battle-cruisers were lying at anchor. To see these ships close up must have delighted them despite Freemantle's ships having left. 'We were a bit put out but once we went down the Flow and began to see the German destroyers looming up we forgot all about that. They were absolutely massive alongside us.'[396]

Some of her crew, Captain Edwards for example, were curious about the total lack of British ships in Scapa: 'We thought it strange, because it had never happened before, even during the Battle of Jutland.'[397]

As they passed the ships, the children waved to both the German sailors on the interned ships as well as, when they got to the southern end of the Flow, to the base flagship, *Victorious* and the RN hospital ship, moored near Flotta. They had been 'warned by the teachers that (we) hadn't to make any noise or cheer'.[398] 'I thought it was rather hard. And not to wave to the men.'[399] Kitty Tait was a little nervous, 'dubious' as she put it, 'because I had a great fear of them [Germans]'.[400] James Robertson said that they were told 'not to jeer or gloat over a beaten enemy'.[401]

In some cases, the Germans were the culprits: 'The sailors thumbed their noses. Our teacher tried to anxiously explain that perhaps we would

---

* Ferguson, who wrote his account of the scuttle in 1985, says the number was closer to 150, not 400.

do the same if we were prisoners of war being stared at by a crowd of gaping school-children.'*

As *Flying Kestrel* passed each of the larger interned ships, their names were announced by an older boy. George Mainland had been given the duty by the headmaster. He was 'an excellent guide, shouting in a loud voice the name, tonnage and gun power of each ship'.[402] There was going to be a competition to see how many ships and what their names were so the children were very attentive, scribbling down information as fast as they could.

Some of the German crews were wearing freshly laundered uniforms. Their whites were a contrast with the ships – dirty grey and rusting. It was 'an odd sight, the algae hanging from the anchor chains and growing like a beard on the hulls just under the waterlines'. ('*ein seltsamer Kontrast an den mitgenommen Schiffen, den Tang und Algen hängen von den Ankeketten herab und wuchern wie lange Bärte am Rumpf unterhalb der Wasserlinie*'.)[403]

Katie Watt remarked that there was nothing obviously out of the ordinary: 'I don't think anybody noticed anything peculiar on the outward journey at all. Some of the big ships were taking on supplies from boats alongside, and we did see one or two flags going up on the destroyers.'

Her comment could have put the time – very roughly – around 1130 and the position around Gutter Sound. That would have been two hours after they had started off that morning (normally, a straight run would take around ninety minutes). Under Davies' experienced helmsmanship, *Flying Kestrel* had probably reached the southern end of the area in which the interned ships were anchored just above Lyness. Now she was heading back up Gutter Sound on her return journey.

On the German ships, well-prepared planning was put into almost faultless execution. Everything that could be was thought through, all the actions designed to make it almost impossible to reverse the decision once initiated. 'Everybody knew what they had to do. It had been prepared very well.'[404]

On most ships, the officers gave a quick pep talk, explaining what was planned and why what they were about to do would benefit Germany. In what they said there was a strong flavour of nationalism ('*eine kleine Vaterländische Anspräche*', a small patriotic speech).

---

* James Taylor, 'The Strangest school journey ever made', *Teacher's World*, June 1940. Quoted in van der Vat, p. 172. At the time, Taylor was fifteen (Booth, pp. 11–12). One of the other children, Rognvald St Clair, said that he was just 'sorry he hadn't brought his catapult' when the teacher said that he should feel sorry for the sailors who could not help being German, as much as they couldn't help being Orcadians.

After the talk, the men went to work. There was a real sense of purpose, of giving the British a taste of their own. Well-oiled sea-cocks, carefully prepared for this moment, were opened. They had been 'set on a hair turning and lubricated very thoroughly'.[405] On many of the ships, hammers had been distributed and were lying next to valves that could be smashed to accelerate the spread of water.

On the destroyers, rods would be used to open the main valves from deck level. The valves had been designed this way so that the compartments could be flooded easily if fire-fighting support was needed.* Each water-tight compartment had a water-valve for fire-fighting purposes that could be operated from above deck as well as below. The connecting rods that enabled the flood valves to be operated from above were therefore removed so that a boarding party would be unable to turn them off.[406]

Without Reuter knowing, Cordes had been working in parallel – and in total secrecy – for the very same purpose. On 13 May he and his officers had held a secret meeting on S.138 and 'drew up [his own] plans to scuttle'.[407] Not only is the technical detail in Cordes' planning of interest, it was also the fact that Reuter had not been working alone and that the discussions had been so secret that Reuter himself did not find out about the talks until early June.

Once opened, the rods were thrown overboard. Since some of the sea-cocks might have become inoperable as the boats had been at anchor for six months and a good deal of barnacles and seaweed would have accumulated, there was a genuine concern that they would not operate and that a scuttle might be thwarted. Ruge said it was because they had been there several months that he 'didn't trust the sea valves' alone, which after months in the Flow, would be covered in seaweed, and so they opened up everything they could think of.[408] Additional internal holes were bored through bulkheads, internal doors left open and portholes opened.

Keys and handles for any other valves and sea-cocks were thrown over the side immediately after they had been used. All scuttles and ventilators

---

* George (p. 28) states that this practice was one adopted on German ships in general, not just torpedo boats: 'They could drain every compartment of their battleships by means of two 24in pipes, one along each side of the double bottom. A valve enabled each compartment to be flooded or emptied, and this valve had a control rod which passed to the armoured deck and worked through a universal joint situated at the bottom. When the ships were scuttled, the universal joints were disconnected so that it became impossible to pump compartments dry separately. When salvage work was finally started, it was therefore impossible to stabilise a ship by isolating its various compartments' (Bowman, p. 124 refers to these pipes as being 12in)

were loosened or opened. 'Spindles [had been] bent', 'actuating spanners thrown overboard' and 'the anchor chain shackle-pin ends had been hammered over so that they could not be unscrewed'.[409] On some ships, it was later discovered, 'the sea-cocks appeared to have been treated with acid to prevent their being closed'.[410]

Additional holes were bored into bulwarks to speed the spread of water, torpedo tubes were opened and watertight doors were bored with holes, rendering them useless to anyone coming aboard to prevent successful scuttling. Deck-level steam condenser covers were removed, adding a massive addition to water intake when the level of seawater finally reached the decks. When Cox's men later examined four destroyers during one of the salvage operations they found that 'condenser doors had been removed and that all auxiliary valves, sea connections in boiler rooms and magazine valves had been opened'.[411] Removing the condenser covers would have been left to the last possible moment as it meant losing power. Even toilet plumbing was tampered with.[412]

When Wessex's boarding party got aboard the Frankfurt to prevent her sinking, they were able to see just how meticulous the Germans had been in their preparations. Even the rubber gaskets had been removed from the scuttles and water-tight doors and, like other ships, wherever they could, the cables had been interfered with: 'Owing to the cables of the destroyers having been secured with several turns to the bollards and wire lashed overall whilst the pins of shackles were hammered down so that they could not be removed, their cables could not easily be freed.'[413]

The comments mirrored other reports stating that 'mooring cables were wired down to bollards, while the shackle-pin ends on anchor chains were hammered over so they could not be unscrewed'.[414] If possible, the anchor capstans would be demobilised. Anything that could make uncoupling a ship from its anchor more difficult was done.

Years later, when work started on the salvage with the destroyers, Cox found that 'with typical Teutonic efficiency', as Hewison described it, 'all the instrument panels and especially the instruction plates in the ships, particularly those referring to the operation of valves, had been removed'.[415]

The scene on the Kaiser was the same on all the big ships. As the pump master (Pumpenmeister), Otto Bries' responsibility was the sea-cocks. He was told to accompany his commander on Kaiser's bridge while they waited for Reuter's orders. Promptly, at 1130 the signalman, Heinrich Fuchs, alerted them: 'Paragraph eleven, Confirmed.' The signal was hoisted immediately and Bries given his orders. After half an hour's work, he reported back at 1200 to Kapitänleutnant von Wippern, saying that the cocks were open and the screws destroyed with a sledgehammer.

Generally, once the valves were confirmed open, the men collected their bags and went up on deck to await their turn to board the cutters. Around 1145, crews from the *Friedrich der Große* and the cruiser *Frankfurt* could be seen throwing belongings and luggage over the side into boats. The crew from *Kaiser* would have followed suit.

Aside from the children on the *Flying Kestrel*, there were a few other witnesses in the flow that morning. One was the marine artist Bernard F Gribble.[*] He was on board an Admiralty trawler *Sochosin*, and 'at noon she was lying off the *Baden*' just south of *Friedrich der Große*. He had been asked by Fremantle to join the sortie on a destroyer but had decided to stay behind and had spent much of the morning finishing off some sketches of *Friedrich der Große*. He had noticed flags flying on a number of ships and talked about it to the *Sochosin*'s lieutenant, but it had not gone any further.[†] But then he saw boats being lowered into the water. One of the *Sochosin*'s officers, Sub Lieutenant Leeth, confirmed what Gribble had seen: 'I see them. I think they're sinking their ships.'[416]

After Gribble's warning, Leeth ordered the *Sochosin* to go in closer to take a look at the nearest ship, the *Frankfurt*. When he'd confirmed the worst, an urgent message was flashed at 1205 to Rear Admiral Fremantle. From another drifter, Charles Yorstin's *Caersin*, the crew opened up on *Frankfurt*'s sailors with rifle fire. They were close by the *König Albert*, which would go under an hour later but, as she was already going down by the stern, they boarded some of her sailors.

Sochosin's skipper now warned his men to be ready with rifles and cutlasses. Try as he might, Leeth was unable to persuade the Germans to comply with their orders. The Germans simply refused to turn their boats around to return to their own ships. When hailed, the sailors shouted back: 'We have no oars.' They had, of course, thrown their oars overboard. Leeth had a fruitless exchange, warning them: 'Return to your ships at once. If you do not do so I will fire on you.' Only after fire had been opened was there a reply: 'You have killed four of my men and we have no arms. I want

---

[†] Bernard Gribble R.A. (1872–1962) was a prolific maritime artist. His paintings are in galleries in the United Kingdom and the United States (and on the jacket of this book). I have seen another of his paintings in the galleries of the Washington Navy Yard. It depicts the scuttling of the German fleet from the perspective of one of the American ships of the 6th Battle Squadron.

[†] Eventually, the trawler would prevent both the crew from *Baden* and *Bayern* from disembarking.

to look after the men.' When further ordered to go back, the officer said it was impossible: 'We can't go back, they are sinking.'[417] They wanted to come aboard the British trawler but were pushed away.

From *Sandhurst*, boats of every type were immediately sent out. Her captain, Sellis, gave orders that the Germans were to be turned back to reboard their ships. The men were to open fire upon them if necessary.

The calm of the Flow had, all of a sudden, been transformed beyond all recognition. As cold water came into contact with the hot steam pipes, all hell broke loose. Sizzling and hissing could be heard, clouds of steam rose anywhere close to the super-heated pipes. All around became a cacophony of whistles, high-pitched howling and hissing as air was expelled under the huge pressure of surging water. Whip-like, staccato cracks signalled steam pipes rupturing. Groaning bulkheads started to give in and as the ships rolled, heavy machinery screeched across steel plating. As the ships' hulls creaked and groaned under intolerable stresses and strains, the telltale sounds of the wretched wail of a fleet in the last pangs of a death struggle carried across the waters. As ships listed, their bells tolled, calling out their final moments in an almost funereal way.

One story has it that when the *Seydlitz* keeled over on to her side, pigs could be heard, squealing hysterically. 'The Germans must have had pigs aboard as one swam away squealing in terror until it eventually cut its own throat with its front hooves.'[418]

Katie Watt captured these strange new sounds:

> Out of the vents rushed steam and oil and air with a dreadful roaring hiss, and vast clouds of white vapour rolled up from the sides of the ships. Sullen rumblings and crashing of chains increase the uproar as the great hulls slant giddily over and slide with horrible sucking and gurgling noises under the water.

Flying Kestrel had by this point already passed by some of the major battleships, the *Baden*, *König Albert*, *Kaiserin* and *Kaiser*, and also the battle-cruisers, *Derfflinger*, *Hindenburg* and *Seydlitz*. On one of *Baden*'s turrets, a lone sailor, dressed in summer whites, danced the hornpipe on the armoured steel roof.*

---

* The hornpipe was a traditional dance dating from the sixteenth century. One of the key gestures involves the dancer cupping his eyes, like that of a sailor shielding his eyes against the sun to scour the ocean's horizon.

From *Victorious*, CF McMenemy:

I noticed a number of small boats pushing off from the German ships. In minutes the German flags were hoisted on the ships, and then as in a dream of fantasy I saw them moving. Some wobbled, some rolled over on their sides, many sank stern or bows first, the lighter craft sank squarely; many were enveloped in clouds of steam.

Soon, every type of vessel was out there, trying to round up the German sailors and bring them back: 'Most of the Germans were cheerful, some boats came alongside cheering and singing a national song, even top brass did not mind lugging their kit-bags or cases on deck.'[419]

At sea, off Duncansby Head on the north-east tip of Scotland's mainland, *Sochosin*'s message was received on Fremantle's flagship at 1207.[*] They were some distance from the Flow. In the report, '… the 1st division of the First Battle Squadron (*Revenge, Ramillies* and *Royal Sovereign*) were in a position 58° 33½' N., 2° 29' W., 25 miles from the entrance to Scapa Flow, the 2nd Division (*Resolution* and *Royal Oak*) were 10 miles to the southward… .'[420]

Fremantle signalled *Westcott*, demanding to know why he had not received his report 'until ten minutes after it had been observed by the skipper of some fishing boat or other' (*Sochosin*).[421] There was no love lost between *Westcott*'s captain and Fremantle (he had 'no great regard', de Courcy-Ireland wrote) so his reply was frosty, saying that, '…if the C in C preferred to accept the unsupported statement and time-keeping of the skipper of a fishing boat over that of one of his commanding officers who was on the spot, he had no explanation to offer'.[422]

At 1235 the signal cancelling the torpedo exercise went out. The squadron was ordered to return to the Flow as fast as possible and ahead of the battleships, her destroyers, HMS *Spenser* and six others, were sent ahead at high speed. Two other destroyers stayed behind to pick up the practice torpedoes and 'for eventualities'.

The six destroyers headed directly to Gutter Sound and arrived there around 1400.[†] Fremantle sent out additional orders once they were en route:

---

[*] The timing of the signal is not absolutely clear from the various reports following the scuttling. See ADM.116/2074 VADM 1BS Report, 24 June 1919, p. 1. The message did not get into Vice Admiral Fremantle's hands till 1220.

[†] Rather conceitedly, the western entrance through Gutter Sound was referred to as 'the tradesman's entrance' while the battleships would head to the right, the eastern side, of Hoxa point.

One hundred Royal Marines were to be landed on each side of the harbor in proximity to anchorages of the German Fleet, to arrest any man attempting to land. On no account were any German seamen who succeeded in getting away in their own boats, or were swimming, to be fired upon, but they were to be taken prisoners.[423]

The Squadron's 1st division – *Revenge, Ramillies* and *Royal Sovereign* – did not make it back and anchor till around 1430; the 2nd Division – *Resolution* and *Royal Oak* – even later, at 1600.* Each of the five battleships had two German ships assigned.

As *Revenge* rounded Flotta, the 'sight that met our gaze…is absolutely indescribable', ships going down all around them, *Bayern* listing heavily over, her bow rising sharply.[424]

1216

SMS *Friedrich der Große*

At 1216, Scheer's former flagship led the way, sliding beneath the dark waters to the bottom of the Flow, before any other.[†] That the Jutland veteran should take the lead was fitting. It was also ironic. Her crew had been among the most mutinous and had forced Reuter to leave the former flagship and instead hoist his flag on the *Emden*. If any crew was going to hinder a scuttle it would have been on 'the big Fritz'.

As the huge ship started to roll, the 'loud and vigorous tones of single strokes of the ship's bell sounded across the water, the signal for "Abandon Ship!"':[425]

Friedrich der Große started to settle, water poured into her through open portholes. After a few minutes, she keeled over and went

---

* The destroyer screen included *Spenser, Shakespeare, Vidette, Westminster, Winchelsea, Vectis, Vesper, Venetia* and *Wessex* (see ADM 116/2074 p. 2). Hugh David's account misstates the time of getting back to Scapa as 1530 rather than 1430. Divisional allocation see ADM 116/2074 Fremantle report 24 June 1919. He talked about the arriving back to see *Bayern*, 'her bow reared vertically out of the water', being in 'the act of crashing finally bottomwards'. *Bayern* sank around 1450, so this would tie in with an earlier arrival time.
† A young girl had seen a ship going down 'between 1215 and 1230'. *The Orcadian* said she saw her starting to take 'a sudden list' and went on to say that: 'She called her father's attention to this, but even as she spoke, masts and funnels disappeared, the hull bottom up, lay exposed for a matter of seconds, and then went out of sight' (*Orcadian*, 26 June 1919). This could have been the SMS *Friedrich der Große*.

down. Air escaping from her funnels caused the water to swirl and eddy in two huge patches. Then everything went silent. There was only floating debris left where she once stood. The clock stood at sixteen minutes after twelve.*

Friedrich der Große was the first ship to go down. The preparations had been carried out so well that she sank in little over forty-five minutes, 'in fact', in Ruge's opinion 'too quickly, because, as a result, the British received an early warning'.[426] The ship's bell warned the British.†

Eventually, she would be followed by every ship in her class of five battleships – *König Albert*, *Kaiser*, *Prinzregent Luitpold* and, finally, *Kaiserin*. All were turbine powered, all had 30.5cm guns mounted with super-firing fore turret, two midship turrets mounted '*en echelon*' and one aft turret. And all fought on the North Sea during the war.

A nine-year-old boy, John Tulloch, had just been helping take the cattle out to the 'calf of Cava'. His description of the setting is beautiful. The 'calf' itself was,

> a small diamond of land that jutted out from the north end of the island connected to it by a narrow causeway of shingle that had washed up there on the tides of a thousand years. Primroses filled the depressions amongst the heather and spread their exotic perfumes on the fairy breeze. The grass was a deep, healthy green and the heather was about to burst into a purple carpet intermixed with a wealth of beautiful flowers that the Orkney Island has been gifted with.[427]

That morning he watched as the Imperial flag was hoisted up the halyards on the *Friedrich der Große*. It was the nearest ship to where he was sitting.

---

* '*Friedrich der Große, legt sich weiter über, in die offenstehenden Seitenfenster ergießen sich Ströme von Wasser ins Innere — noch einige Minuten, er kentert und sinkt in die Tiefe. Die aus den Schornsteinen austretende Luft wirft noch zwei große Wasserstrudel auf — dann ist alles still. Einige Trümmer treiben auf dem verlassenen Legeplatz. Die Uhr zeigt 16 Minuten nach 12'.* (Gerd Fesser 'Sinnlose Selbstver-nichtung der wilhelminischen Armada / 66 Kriegsschiffe wurden im Juni 1919 versenkt Scapa Flow – das Grab der deutschen Flotte'. Berliner Zeitung, 18 June 18 1994).
† You can still see one of her bells, albeit badly damaged in the sinking (or maybe, later, in the salvage) in the Stromness museum on the floor beside the bell from the *Dresden* among a collection of pinnace propellers. Some of the Scapa Flow bells have been returned to Germany. This was the case for one of *Friedrich der Große*'s. Also, for *Derfflinger*, where one of the bells was returned to the FGN on 30 August 1965, as was *Hindenburg*'s on 28 May 1959. Bells from *Bayern* and *Kaiser* are in German museums.

'When the flag reached its highest point, a light breeze caught it for a moment and it fluttered out, the Iron Cross and the double Eagle of Germany, and then right behind it another red flag climbed but no breeze stirred it like a piece of old rag [it] hung in shame.'

He went on: 'Then across the water a bell began to ring, clang, clang, clang, clang, at first, I thought it was the church bell in the Auld Kirk of Orphir, but listening keenly, I could hear that it came from one of the ships, either the *Baden* or the *Bayern*.'[428]

In fact, what he most probably heard were the first tolls from the *Friedrich der Große*, which had been anchored between the two but whose bell had 'announced' the scuttle, 'to wake up all the remaining ships at one stroke'.[429] On the water near her was a British drifter. Its siren sounded a warning wail across the Flow.*

There was little need for further pretence. But on the *Emden*, however, Reuter had only been finally able to give the order to scuttle his own ship six minutes before, at 1210. Immediately, his own crew had sprung into action. They too opened everything they could – all the sea-cocks, valves and underwater torpedo tubes.

Soon, Reuter had to move his staff off his foundering ship to the remaining 'dispatch boat', on which he was taken to the shore. There he was met by a young officer, dressed as if he were ready for tennis, claiming to be Prendergast's equivalent: the Senior Officer on Land. He was, in fact, the RFC commander. When he and Reuter met, the British officer was 'exceedingly angry, hardly listened and really didn't understand a word [he] said'.[430] Reuter was asking him to put an end to the indiscriminate firing in the Flow. Without considering the request, the officer disappeared back into his car. Putting aside any concern for men getting killed, he'd instead gone to find his camera as he wanted to 'get some snaps'.

Reuter was then to be taken back to the *Emden* but the drifter on which he was embarked did not get far. The tide was ebbing and it stuck 'hard and fast on a shoal'.[431] If that was not galling enough, all Reuter could see from the small bay where he'd been taken was *Emden*'s flag, the only thing visible over the low hills, feebly flapping over the ship that refused to go down.

From the depot ship *Victorious*, two young officers were ordered by Rear Admiral Prendergast to take a boat out and document as much as they could.[432] Leaving the *Victorious* at 1220, they passed through

---

* Hermann Cordes (Reuter, p. 118) maintained that the drifters' sirens actually spelt out in Morse: 'German ships are sinking'. More likely that they were only to use their sirens if there was an attempt to damage or scuttle their ships.

Gutter Sound to head north to where the big ships lay. When they left Fara behind them, they started to pass ships in the throes of death. Where and when they could, they stopped to document what they were seeing and take photographs. Many of the photos taken by one of the officers, CW Burrows, would eventually be regarded as iconic.* His were the memorable images that come to mind when we now talk of the Scuttle: *Seydlitz*'s hull stretched out helplessly on her side, the only visible signs of *Hindenburg* – her turret, masts and funnels – or *Bayern*'s final listing plunge.†

On the *Flying Kestrel*, meanwhile, around the time they re-entered Gutter Sound from the south after having passed by the Flotta hospital ship, the schoolmaster Hepburn shouted out in a disgusted voice, 'What a damned cheek!' as he saw some Germans hauling down the British flag and run up the Imperial Flag in its place.[433]

It's not quite clear when the *Flying Kestrel* was really alerted. Either at Lyness, from one of the drifters or from their own observations.‡ Given that they had left that morning at 0930, it was most likely to have been on the way back.

Supposedly, a drifter came by and a sailor shouted the news of the sinking ships. Peggy Gibson remembers a man using a megaphone to shout the news across, telling them 'Turn back. The German ships are sinking.'[434] A *Kestrel* crew member, Edwards, was more exact: 'We were about a third of the way through the Fleet when all the ships began to sink simultaneously, as if at a pre-arranged signal.'[435]

Which was, of course, precisely the case. But it was also the case that the children did not need to be told, it was fairly obvious. Ivy Scott said that the chaos was immediate, some ships sinking 'on an even keel and some upended and plunged down quickly and only a wash of waves to show where they had been'.[436] They remembered the scenes: 'We were looking at them and I saw what I would say would be one of the biggest

---

* Burrows' companion was Lieutenant Roderick Grant, RNR. Locals also profited from the fleet's presence. Orcadian postcard publishers such as Thomas Kent and J. Omond sold collections of cards with photographs of the now rapidly deteriorating German ships rusting in the Flow. Burrows eventually published his photos in *Scapa in Camera*.

† The photographer who 'came away with the goods' was also the ship's cashier. Burrows happened to be an 'expert photographer' and so in demand became his photos that Prendergast even tried to claim copyright (for himself!).

‡ James Robertson said it was approaching Lyness, on the downward leg of the journey. At that point, he said 'a rumour somehow hit the ship that something odd was happening…We saw that some of the ships were adopting an odd attitude, mastheads leaning over and that sort of thing'.

ships – suddenly it shuddered and shuddered and shuddered and then suddenly it toppled over and I can remember seeing Germans coming off on rafts.'[437]

1254

SMS *König Albert*

Forty-five minutes after *Friedrich der Große* had disappeared, the *König Albert* followed. It was 1254, The *König Albert* was the closest battleship to *B.110*, which might have been why the torpedo boat crews felt 'particularly attached' to her.[438] As each ship went down, cheers went up from the sailors. It was described by John Tulloch as being a German cheer, "hooch, hooch, hooch"'.[439]

The ship listed heavily over on to her starboard, dramatically accelerating the intake of water as it poured through the open hatches on her upper decks: '*wild stürzte das Wasser durch die Seitenfenster in die oberen Räume*' ('the water came pouring in through the portholes on the upper spaces'.)[440] Böhmer, her commander, had waited to the last before joining his men. When she finally went, it was fast. As her upside-down hull slid below the water, her keel pointed skyward.

Later Burrows and Grant passed up the line in between *Kaiserin* and *Karlsruhe* and came to where *König Albert* should have been. Here the two of them were hailed from the deck of the trawler on which Reuter was being taken around.

Two drifters were sent on to the *Bayern*, lying between where they were and where Reuter had been on the *Emden*. The admiral had told Burrows and Grant that many of *Bayern*'s crew were struggling in the water. The time would probably have been just after two o'clock as *Bayern* went down at 1430.

1315

SMS *Moltke*

Moltke – the first of the battle-cruisers – now also started to go down. Behind her was *Seydlitz* which had been anchored off the south-western tip of Cava. *Seydlitz*'s crew were lined up against the rails and were watching intently. As the vessel slipped below the surface, turning over as she went, *Seydlitz*'s crew sang the national anthem. It was a solemn moment. Many, despite their weariness with the war, must have been in tears, tears of pride, tinged with a heavy sense of sadness. The sort of sadness any seafaring man would feel at the moment of death of a great ship. It was what she represented; the *Moltke* bore a proud name, it had fought with honour and was now disappearing in ignominy.

Kapitänleutnant Crelinger had only given his men fifteen minutes' warning as the news spread over the ship at 1145: *'Leute, in einer viertel Stunde müssen wir das Schiff verlassen.'* ('Men, we will need to leave the ship in a quarer of an hour.')[441] Years later, when Cox's men had brought her back to the surface, the evidence pointed to how little warning was given: 'In the crew accommodation, personal effects still lay scattered amid the debris. Clothing, photographs, books, and even money was still in drawers and lockers…many bottles of good quality wine were also found.'[442]

On *Derfflinger*'s deck, a hastily convened ship's band played an old hunting song, *'Wohl auf Kameraden, aufs Pferd, aufs Pferd!'* its aggressive, militaristic thump hammering across the waters. At around 1315, *Moltke* too started her final descent. *'Wie zu einem letzten Kampfe gegen die Gewalt, die ihn herabzog, erhob er sich hochaufbäumend, den Bug um dann mit einer gewaltigen Schwenkung über dem Heck nach der B. Seite zu kenntern.'* (roughly, but not literally, 'It was as though the ship was finally giving up the fight against mightier odds, her bow lifting up and her hull falling over on to her port side.')[443]

Above the singing, Orcadians who were close enough could hear *Moltke*'s 'masts and superstructure crunching as it broke with her weight bearing down upon them into the sea bed'. Gradually the ship settled in the water so that 'only her keel showed at low tide'.[444] Almost as soon as her crew had cheered their last 'Hurrah', they were picked up and joined crews from *Kaiserin*, *König Albert* and *Frankfurt* in a long line of dinghies, towed behind a British steamer.

The pace was picking up. Around the same time as *Moltke* was sinking, four other battleships joined: *Kronprinz Wilhelm*, *Kaiser*, *Große Kurfürst* and *Prinzregent Luitpold*, as well as one of the first light cruisers, *Dresden*.

The British were panicking. For many on the *Flying Kestrel* it was the same. Kitty Tait and Willie Marwick were 'terrified'. 'It was very, very frightening,' Tait later said.[445]

Ships were, in fact, starting to go down all around them: 'Some were upending, some were settling in the water, some were turning over. And the sea itself was boiling and swirling…The men were scrambling in boats and on rafts and some were swept overboard by the pressure of the water from the ships.'

James Taylor's strongly visual memories recalled the scene:

...without any warning and almost simultaneously these huge vessels began to list over to port or to starboard; some heeled over and plunged headlong, their sterns lifted high out of the water...out of the vents rushed steam, and oil and air with a dreadful roaring hiss. And as we watched, awestruck and silent, the sea became littered for miles around with boats, hammocks, lifebelts and chests... . And among it all hundreds of men struggling for their lives. And as we drew away from this nightmare scene we watched the last great battleship slide down with keel upturned, like some monstrous whale.[446]

Katie Watt, eighteen at the time, remembered the chaos: 'The ships were lying at all sorts of crazy angles. Some rolled on to their sides, others went down stern first or by the bow.'[447] Amidst this chaos, Peggy Gibson was absolutely clear that there was one thing they all had in common: 'Every one of them had a flag on top of the mast.'[448]

Some of the children – the ones who weren't traumatised, dumb-struck or crying, the ones who treated the scuttle as though it were tailor-made for their entertainment – started to play a game: how many ships could they count going down. More specifically, 'The competition on the boat, among the pupils, was to see how many of the names of the ships we could get.'[449] It soon became impossible. Too many ships were going down around them too fast. Peggie Gibson got as far as twelve before she gave up.

The *Flying Kestrel* was ordered to return to Stromness as fast as she could: 'Proceed port, land children and report back.' Maybe the captain misunderstood his explicit orders as it seems that the *Kestrel* initially went about, back to the German ships, not land. Or, maybe, it was because Davies decided that he also had a higher duty: to save men from drowning in the churning waters.* Ivy Scott, eighteen years old at the time, thought that they had been 'rudely told to clear out quick'.[450]

The *Kestrel* had gone back to pick up sailors struggling in the cold waters of the Flow. For the children, it wasn't turning out to be the adventure that all were expecting. All around were small boats full of

---

* There is some disagreement here. Cousins maintains that Davies's 'instinct was to go in among these sinking ships and join in the fight to save them. But that was impossible with four hundred children on board so he ordered full speed ahead...to the little town of Stromness... . Once in Stromness Captain Davies disembarked his young passengers and within a few minutes was at sea again... .' Cousins, p. 2).

German sailors, 'every boat had a white sheet fastened to the mast or an oar held vertically'.[451] Despite these acts of surrender, the young children witnessed at least one man open fire, sniping away 'to his heart's content'.

An eleven-year-old, Len Sutherland, recalled: 'I saw at least one sailor shot on the deck of one vessel, but whether by a German officer or a British officer I could not say. There was chaos aboard the ship. Sailors were making rafts and jumping into the water.'[452]

The sight of hundreds of struggling sailors, many in the water, deeply affected some and 'in many cases [the children] were reduced to tears'.[453] But others, like nine-year-old John Knarston, were able to 'thoroughly enjoy' themselves.[454]

One thing was sure: any child who saw these scenes would never forget that day. They would remain vivid memories for the rest of their lives.

As ships started to go down, dangerous whirlpools appeared, threatening to suck anything or anyone near down into the depths. All around, you could see the detritus of defeat – from personal possessions and clothes to furniture and even small boats.

On his ship, Davies had his work cut out. 'They were really afraid for the safety of the boat, that the suction of the German ships going down would pull the boat we were on down.'[455] The sea was 'just churning all the time. Men were being swept off the rafts and off the boats.'[456]

Bubbles exploded from their confined underwater spaces and erupted on the surface in loud thunderclaps, like loud, flatulent burps. The surface boiled as the water was pulled downwards in great torrents by the sinking ships. Kitty Tate talked about the water 'cascading up all around us'.[457] Oil, calming the waters, spread thick slicks across the Flow and but also brought beauty: large patches of iridescent water, in the ever-changing and shimmering colours of the rainbow.

1315

SMS *Kronprinz Wilhelm*

Almost to the hour after *Friedrich der Große*'s end, *Kronprinz Wilhelm* joined her.

To scuttle a ship, as much water as can be properly managed is let into the hull. The obvious inlets are the main seawater pumps, which bring seawater into the ship for many different tasks: cooling engines, providing water for fire management or trimming the ship, always making sure that weight is evenly distributed to keep her decks level. Other ways to bring water into the ship include opening up outlets that are only used in combat, including torpedo

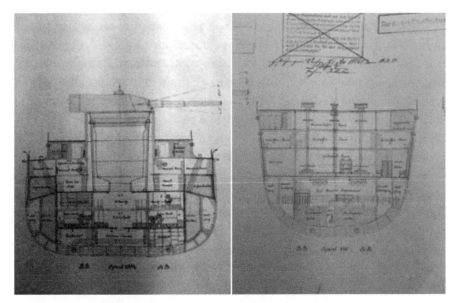

Kronprinz Wilhelm showing torpedo tubes and main seawater pumps.

tubes. Apertures such as portholes, normally way above the water line, only become useful during the later stages to add more volume. When scuttling, the Germans thought that rolling their ships would make it more difficult for later salvage operations. Hence, water was purposefully pumped to one side to create a list that eventually would roll the ship over on to her back.

Once water is in the ship, then the question becomes how to distribute it as fast and efficiently as possible throughout the ship. That means compromising bulkheads so that water will flow through, under or around any obstacle.

★   ★   ★

A small 'puffer', the *Nellie Laud* (sometimes referred to as *Nelly-Land* in the German reports) had acted with great initiative and commanded the captain of the *Kronprinz Wilhelm* to order his men back. It had not made any difference. Her fate was sealed. Later, *Nellie Laud* would take a hundred German crew captive, the captain putting them in her hold until he was able to transfer them to a battleship. For one of the *Kronprinz Wilhelm*'s crew, a stoker named Karl Bauer, his luck ran out. He'd already been wounded once in his leg but as he lay in the dinghy he was hit two more times, once in his chest, the other in his stomach. His shooting was witnessed by a fellow sailor, Obermachinistmaat Bausch.[458]

Like the fleet's former flagship, the *Kronprinz* would be the first of her own class of four battleships. The three other ships followed, after fifteen minutes, *Große Kurfürst,* half an hour after that, *König,* and, finally, at 1645, the *Markgraf. König*'s last moments were caught on film and she is seen rolling, like an inflated, beached whale, on to her port side. In the distance some of Fremantle's squadron can just be made out.

Like the *Kaiser*-class ships, all four battleships had been engaged in North Sea operations during the war and had all been at Jutland. They represented the very latest in naval technology: each was turbine powered, also all had 30.5cm guns mounted with a second super-firing fore turret, but instead of the two mid-ship turrets mounted '*en echelon*', there was only one centre-line turret (like the British *Iron Duke*-class) and two aft turrets, one of which was also a super-firing turret.

Dreadnought Deck and Turret Layout

Both the *Kaiser* and *König* classes of battleships had super-firing turrets. This layout allowed for two turrets to be mounted along the same centre-line, one behind the other, with the front turret at a much lower level and the turret behind on a raised column-like barbette, which allowed its guns to rotate and swivel over the fore turret.

The *Baden*, which was Germany's answer to Britain's *Queen Elizabeth* class, only mounted four turrets along the centre-line, two super firing turrets fore and aft.

Turrets were usually either mounted along the centre-line or with a midship combination "*en echelon*", one being mounted further forward than the other.

Five-turret centre-line layout: *Große Kurfürst*
Source: Jane's Fighting Ships 1919

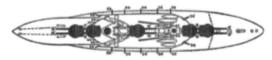

Four-turret centre-line layout: Baden & Bayern

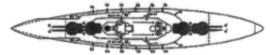

Midships '*en echelon*' layout: *Kaiser*

1325

SMS Kaiser

Kaiser's crew were only informed of Reuter's plans to scuttle minutes after her commander, Kapitänleutnant Wippern, had received the executive signal at around 1140. Orders were immediately issued, three cheers ('drei brausende Hurras') were made for the unfurling and raising of the ship's battle flag and then the crew went to work around the ship.

Forty minutes after orders had been received, the crew – only sixty-two of them were left aboard now – got into their cutters and made off for the closest shores, those of Cava island. Like crews from other ships taking to the waters (Seydlitz's crews lowered their boats five minutes later), they did not get far before being warned that the British were firing on anyone who landed ashore (According to Obermaschinenmaat Schäffer, the warning had come from some of Nürnberg's men, anchored to her west, a little closer to Cava). So, they stayed on the Flow and watched the ships around them going down.

The orders given to all crews, from the destroyers to the battleships, made it very clear what needed to be done after they had left their ships in boats. The scuttle would obviously provoke a strong British reaction and so they were told to disembark, '…with the prescribed gear which they have had ready for days, in order to row to the land in accordance with their orders, where they would assemble and sit down to await the further sequence of events.'[459]

In other words, do as little as possible to warrant any British overre-action. Westcott's commanding officer, however, came in for criticism in the official reporting three days later in that he, '…did not take similar action to that taken in Gutter Sound, drive the Germans back to their ships by small arms fire, and remove or sink boats alongside'.[460]

Eventually, Kaiser rolled over on to a starboard list and went down. As the other crews had done, those on Kaiser cheered their own ship's last minutes. It was 1330, two hours after Reuter's initial signal. They watched as not only their own ship went down but others added to the scenes of pandemonium playing out around them: bows reaching up, clouds of hissing steam, the howling of air escaping under pressure, shouts, hurrahs, grinding, screeching and crashing machinery, shouts, barked warnings, ships' sirens, rifle and machine-gun fire, band music, struggling livestock. The memories of the children from the Flying Kestrel share this extraordinary commonality of the mad visual and acoustic chaos of the scuttle. It had the insanity of a scene from a Hieronymus Bosch.

As the German sailors were being towed behind one of the drifters, Fremantle's Battle Squadron came back into the Flow. *Kaiser's* tiny cutters were brought alongside HMS *Ramillies*, one of the five huge *Revenge*-class battleships.*

'*Kaiser's* end had been sudden, she turned over at great speed,' John Tulloch said:

> I was watching her turn over and saw a steam pinnace that was in the davits on her off-side soar into the air; the fastening ropes broke and it somersaulted over and over slowly in the air before it dropped down into the sea right side uppermost and floated away to drift in below my home... .'[461]

1330

SMS *Große Kurfürst*

When the *Große Kurfürst* finally sank she did so in spectacular fashion. She 'reared herself steeply into the air. Both cables parted with a large clinking; she fell heavily to port and capsized. The red coating of her bottom shone wide over the blue sea.'[462]

A British vessel close by very nearly got caught: 'As she went she rose steeply into the air and then crashed downwards onto her port side. Her two towering masts hit the water only a matter of yards away from the onlooking British vessel...she then turned turtle and went under.'[463]

A mile and a half above Orphir, right down the coast road from the Houton Naval air base, a five-year-old girl shared her parents' opera glasses with her elder brother. She wanted to get a closer look at what she instinctively knew to be a unique event. The telescope was already being used and these ornate glasses were the best solution available.

Candy Nancy watched in awe as 'a two-masted ship rolled slowly over' looking at its 'rusty bottom coming out of the bottom'.[464] She was probably looking at *Große Kurfürst*, which would have laid almost directly in front of her childhood house. On film, Jane Dunn later recounted the event, sitting on her lawn looking over the same view, ninety-four years later, aged ninety, her memory still as crisp and detailed as it had ever been.

---

* The *Revenge*-class, confusingly, are sometimes also referred to as the *Royal Sovereign*-class. Even Sir John Jellicoe referred to them with both classifications.

1330

SMS *Dresden*

Near *König* was the *Dresden*, just a little distance south of the Barrel of Butter, marking the old Carlin skerry.* It had become known by its later name because of the annual rent, a barrel of butter, that Orphir seal hunters paid to be able to hunt on the small, rocky outcrop.

Dresden nearly did not sink.† A drifter, the *Clonsin*, had started to tow her to the Cava, where it was hoped she would have been beached on the eastern side of the island. But on the way, the German ship sank 'so quickly that there was no time to cast off the tow rope',[465]

1345

SMS *Brummer*

The men on *Brummer*, as on *Bremse*, had been warned the day before that the English would probably try to seize the German ships sometime on Saturday.‡ Their commanding officer, Kapitänleutnant Prahl, had read out a short statement to the men as they gathered around him on the ship's stern. What he said made it clear that Reuter's orders were that all ships were to be scuttled rather than allow the British to board: '*Unser Schiff gesenkt werden, sobald der Befehl dazu vom Admiral gegeben würde.*' (Our ships were to be sunk as soon as the order from the Admiral was given.')[466]

Most of the men were happy. After months on the Flow, feeling forgotten and helpless, they now felt that they could finally strike a blow for their country: '*Alle strahlen nun vor Vergnügen, dem Engländer diesem Streich spielen zu dürfen.*' (roughly, 'Everyone was smiling at the thought of the pleasure involved in playing such a trick on the English.').[467]

When the order came, 'just before twelve', the sailors had already

---

* *Dresden* was lying to the south-east of *König* and a little to the south-west of the Barrel of Butter.

† There are some large discrepancies regarding *Dresden*'s time of sinking. Van der Vat's 1130 must have been a typo. George's 1530 sounds far too late given that attempts to rescue her were made but that 'she sank so quickly that there was no time to cast off the rope'. *Bremse*, the next ship to the north, got the scuttle signal '*kurz vor 12*' and sank around 1345 (Gondermann, *Selbsversenkingsbericht Bremse*). *Dresden* was a heavier ship. Even *König* went down at 1400. A 1330 time ties in with the probability that *Clonsin* was right in the middle of multiple tasks around the Flow.

‡ On the other minelayer, *Bremse*, the commanding officer, Oberleutnant zur See Schacke, had called his men together on 20 June for a meeting in the mine storage (*Minenzentrale*). This was regarded as so odd that the men knew something was up ('*Das musste etwas besonders sein, denn der Zeitpunkt unsere Zusammenkommens war ungewöhnlich*'). At the meeting the crew were informed, according to the report by Obermachinistmaat Grullys, of what might occur the next day (Scuttle Reports, p. 397).

packed their kit and it was piled on the light cruiser's deck. It was odd that Prahl had allowed these preparations to be made. It would have only taken a routine drifter visit to let the cat out of the bag. It would have been difficult to explain. One questions whether Burmeister's memory really served him well. There would have been time to bring the bags up on deck after the order to open valves had been given.

As soon as the order was given, the work started, both below and on deck: Two dinghies and the motorboat were lowered into the water ('zwei Jollen und Motorboot'), the men climbed down and soon set off to the shore. Almost as soon as they pulled off, the motorboat gave up and had to be towed. Around 1220, the small group of boats was approached by an English drifter, from which an English officer shouted furiously at them, waving his pistol. Nobody understood what he was talking about, and he wouldn't have understood their efforts to communicate either. Without warning, and despite the white flags they carried, he and his men opened fire. The Germans had almost reached the shore and only had another 120m to row. Luckily no one was hurt and he soon sped off, no doubt to do the same elsewhere. It was almost exactly what happened the same day to some of the *Bremse* crew. It had been a ruthless, senseless act ('einfach rücksichtslos'). It was then that another boatload group of sailors – they had come from the *Frankfurt* – warned them against continuing to the land, saying that they would be shot there. Reluctantly, they turned back.

They must have still been on the water an hour and a half later as this was when Gondermann, a Machinistmaat, reported that his ship finally went down. At 1345.[*] First of all, she listed heavily over to her starboard, then rolled and went under ('und zwar legt er sich nach Stb. über und kenterte').[468] The crew gave three cheers as she slid below the surface. Unlike most of the other German ships, *Brummer* was not flying her colours. Prahl had ordered the flag burned so that there was no possibility of the English taking it.

1350
SMS *Seydlitz*
Burrows, who had left *Victorious* at 1220, arrived at the *Seydlitz* around

---

[*] There is a large discrepancy between Gondermann's estimate (Bericht Gondermann, Machinistenmaat, p. 411) and the time used in George (p. 143). I considered whether Gondermann had used German time and discounted the idea: *Köln*, to her east, sank around 1350, *Brummer* was in line of sight from *Emden* and getting the signal 'kurz vor 12' sounds right (Bericht Burmeister, *Machinistenmaat*, p. 401).

1305.* When the *Flying Kestrel* passed, some remarked on how much activity was to be seen on board.†

The battle-cruiser was not only still afloat, she was riding high enough that Burrows was able to board her and pull her colours down. He and Grant also tried to release her cable to let her drift ashore but it caught. There was nothing more to it and they left for the *Hindenburg*.

Seydlitz herself would take almost three-quarters of an hour to sink, but when she went down at 1350, only her bilge keel remained visible above the lapping waters. She had been sunk in relatively shallow water so that she remained uncovered. 'There she lay like a monster whale with one half above water.'[469] On the way back, an hour later, around 1500, Burrows would photograph her, lying silently and vulnerable, on her side.

Brauer's crew had been singing as the first waters started to lap into the ship through the airducts: *'Kaum war das Rieterlied verlungen, als auch schon durch di ersten geöffneten Ventils das Wasser gurgelnd in das innere unseres Schiffes eindrang.'* ('The hunting song had barely finished before water started to gurgle into the ship's interior through the first open valve.').[470] Together they solemnly sang their national anthem. It was already 1225 when they started boarding the dinghies.

The *Flying Kestrel* seems to have been in the area, although the accuracy of many of these reports is a little shaky even if the recollections still give vivid impressions of the day's events. One of the students, Henrietta Groundwater, later said: 'We didn't understand that it was a piece of history we were seeing enacted,' that it was 'something extraordinary'.‡ William Groundwater remembered how vivid each passing second was: 'Everything was beginning to get very exciting...like a kind of slow-motion picture'. Henrietta thought that at the point they'd reached *Seydlitz*, they must already have been ordered 'back to the depot ship' (HMS *Victorious*§) as the situation was clearly starting to get

---

* The short journey had still taken around forty-five minutes, they later reported.

† The recounting of the story has them reach the *Seydlitz* around 1100 but this is most likely mistaken. It would more likely have been midday after the '*Paragraf elf*' signal had been sent and after the first acknowledgments had started to come back, between 1130 and 1140. However, the fact that the comment was made that flags were being raised on the destroyers suggests that *Flying Kestrel* was at that point down south at Gutter Sound and so this must have been on the run back to Stromness. *Seydlitz* did not go down until around 1350.

‡ Ferguson (p. 70) refers to Henrietta as Mrs William Groundwater or Rosetta Groundwater. William Groundwater was, later, the Rector of Stromness public school and Rosetta, the provost of the town. There are many of Henrietta's relations still on the island.

§ As is always the case with these accounts there was considerable confusion in years to come about the identity of some of these ships. Ivy Scott thought it was called the *Imperieuse*. (Ferguson, p. 70). She probably meant HMS *Victorious*.

potentially very dangerous. She said she 'definitely saw one man shot and he dropped off the stern of the boat'. The recollections are a little hard to follow. In one interview, she did not go quite so far at first, saying she did: 'remember hearing at least one rifle shot' and then later adds the certainty of seeing the man on the stern shot while others around him were 'standing with their hands up'. Which she 'presume(d) [it] was surrender'.[471] The *Seydlitz* was just 'a few hundred yards away' (and Henrietta said that this was at the moment when the *Flying Kestrel* was going back to the depot and when she vividly recalled that the ship 'turned turtle'. You can feel the sense of bewilderment mixed with the excitement. At the extreme, some of the younger ones came away with the impression that this extraordinary piece had been 'just put on, probably for our benefit as school-children'.[472] Ships were starting to go down on each side. The activity was 'just tremendous'.[473] Eventually *Flying Kestrel* was ordered back by a different route to get her out of the danger zone as fast as possible.

Another girl on board was ten-year-old Peggy Gibson, known at the time as Peggie Matheson. Along with her three sisters, Lillian, Anna and Tina, she had been included in the special school trip. At first, they all thought that the Germans were putting on a show for them, nailing flags up on the masts as if they were decorative bunting. They were quite excited: 'Small boats were seen alongside tied to rope ladders. We were all very interested but nobody guessed what was going on.'[474] As is always the case, perceptions of the same event can be so different even from those who, very often, were standing side by side. When the Germans began jumping from the ships the children were certain something was wrong. Major Hepburn ordered all the pupils below decks but George Mainland and John Knarston – joined by two other girls – hid behind some towing hawser coils so that they could continue to watch.

1340

SMS *Köln*

The *Köln* report is the only one where a precise time was given for Reuter's scuttle order: 1129.[475] This was for the second signal that followed 'D.G.', the international signal used to alert captains that an important signal would be following. Orders immediately flew left and right (*'Befehle flogen hin und her'*) to get preparations under way.[476] After work was completed below decks and the cases prepared, two boats were lowered for the crew – one the motorboat, the other a cutter. Heinemann, her commander, went in the cutter, while a young lieutenant took charge on the heavily laden motorboat. It did not take long before it developed problems. It was leaking badly.

Luckily, one of *Bremse's* motorboats came to the rescue, soon pulling *Köln's* two boats plus three from another ship over to the shore. Around the time that the little group of boats was tied up alongside an English drifter, *Brummer* sank ('*zu dieser Zeit sank Brummer*').[477] It must have been minutes before *Köln*, 1,200 tons heavier, also went down. Around 1330 one of the crew reported that her quarter deck was, for the most part, below the waves and that, ten minutes later, she rolled on to her side and sank.

After witnessing the ship's end, *Köln's* crew drifted around on the water for another hour ('*etwa 1 Stunde umher*'). When an English cutter came close by, on board were a number of officers including Reuter ('*das unseren Admiral mit noch einigen Offizieren und Besatzungsteilen deutscher Schiffe an Bord hatte*'). As it passed by, the cutter took them in tow over to Fremantle's flagship, *Revenge*. Once there, they boarded but were not allowed to take any of their belongings on board.*

Once taken into one of the gun casemates, they were fed. Bread, marmalade and corned beef was on the deck for them. While they were eating, their cases were searched. It was the same story as elsewhere, although Bowman recalled that the British sailors were also partial to collecting militaria: buttons, insignia, even taking the cap tallies off a sailor's cap.

1400
SMS *Prinzregent Luitpold*

The men on *Prinzregent Luitpold* had been preparing for a special feast on 21 June. Max, the pet pig, had been fattened up just for the occasion. The lucky pig would survive and, instead, become a gift given to one of the trawler captains, an American.

Late Friday afternoon, Kapitänleutnant von Reiche, *Prinzregent Luitpold's* commanding officer, talked to his men in one of the forward batteries. It was clear that they should get on with the preparations. One task was to make sure that the engines on the steam pinnace were working properly ('*die Machine der Dampfpinne probeweise in Betrieb gesetzt*'). The crew on the *Brummer* would have done well to have also thought of that.

---

* In the *Köln Selbstversenkungsbericht*, there is a story that shots were fired from one of *Revenge's* portholes at the German sailors as they pulled alongside. Harmlessly, the shot hit the water behind the cutter. This was the only mention of a shooting so close to a British capital ship and is suspect (see p. 359, Report by Oberheizer Peiler).

Around 1245, a British drifter, already towing a whole row of other ships' boats, started over in the direction of the *Prinzregent Luitpold* crews as they made their way slowly across the water. Before she arrived, the sailors were able to catch a view of their ship, with a sudden judder, take a strong list to starboard. The ship looked as if she was winning the battle to stay afloat and then sank back as though she'd lost her strength (*'da sinkt er kraftlos zurück'*) and roll completely on to her side. As she went, the sailors could see her three battle flags waving for the last time. After she'd disappeared, one of her motor launches came bobbing back up briefly to the surface, swivelling around crazily in the eddies left by the suction, only to be pulled back down after a few brief moments.

In most records, the time of her sinking is given as 1330. This is more than likely too early. Obermaschinistmaat Günther who wrote the main report commented that *Prinzregent Luitpold* only followed when most of the battle-cruisers had gone down (*'mußte auch...dem Beispiel der Panz-erkreuzer folgen die großtenteile schon unter Wasser waren'*). At that point, only *Moltke* had gone down and the next battle-cruiser sinking was not till 1350 when *Seydlitz* went under and then 1415 when *von der Tann* followed. *Derfflinger* would hold on till 1445. That would put *Prinzregent Luitpold's* own sinking closer to 1400 than 1330. I have opted for an approximate mid-point between *Seydlitz* and *Derfflinger*.

The drifter was now on station and took the small boats in tow to one of the supply ships (*Stationschiff*) and from there on to the returning battleship, *Royal Oak*. Given that *Royal Oak* was back at Scapa around 1430, this would put *Prinzregent Luitpold's* sinking anywhere between, say 1350 – when *Seydlitz* went down – and 1445, when *Derfflinger* joined her, and not 1330.

Beached
SMS *Emden*
Another of the great ironies of the events of 21 June was the fate of Reuter's second flagship, SMS *Emden*. While his orders were being carried out by the rest of the fleet, Reuter was incapable of immediately following through on them for fear of tipping off the British. Three British ships – a watering tender and two drifters – were tied up alongside, blissfully unaware of the monumental events unfolding around them. Reuter must have been 'champing at the bit' but had to appear calm and quietly professional.

This meant that he could not execute his own orders till a little while after noon, probably around 1210. The tender, *Trust-On,* was still transferring stores over to the light cruiser when a number of her crew rushed up on to the deck and shouted to the British that they wanted to be taken off as their ship was sinking.

Long before the ship's commander, Ehlers, could execute Reuter's orders, the crew had 'twigged' what was happening, even though the information had only been entrusted to his officers. When they finally found out what they had to do, they took the time needed to let their comrades put their few possessions into kit bags and throw them into the waiting life boats. Then the ropes were held tight, allowing them to slide down into the boats.

Reuter tried to 'pull rank' on the skipper of the *Trust-On,* saying that he should be taken to the British flagship. Instead the *Trust-On* turned and sped back to HMS *Victorious,* where Rear Admiral Prendergast was in the middle of reading the signal that had come through from *Westcott's* Lieutenant Charles R Peplow with the news that *Friedrich der Große* was sinking.* It was moments after sailors had been seen jumping from the cruiser *Frankfurt.*† Eventually, Reuter and his staff reached HMS *Revenge.* The second communications drifter, *C.D.1,* took them first to Houton and from there to Fremantle's own flagship.

Reuter had not managed to scuttle *Emden.* HMS *Shakespeare,* 'with the assistance of a tug and trawler', towed the German light cruiser on to the shore, after cutting the sinking cruiser's anchor cable. *Shakespeare* had gone to her directly when she'd arrived back in the Flow with *Spenser* at around 1400. They were optimistic about saving the ship as she was clearly riding 'less low in the water than other ships'. When she was boarded, the water had only just started to reach the level of the engine and boiler room floors.[478] They just had the time needed.

---

* *Westcott's* signal was sent at 1205 and received by the First Battle Squadron at 1215 (Fremantle himself stated in his 24 June report that he received the signal at 1220 – 'German battleships sinking' – shortly after which he then received a signal from Prendergast). Prendergast's signal gave more details, if somewhat confused: 'Battleship Kaiser Friedrich class sunk. All battleships and cruisers hoisting German ensign. Crews of destroyers preparing to abandon ship'. *Westcott's* 1207 signal had been received by HMS *Victorious* (Fremantle report, 24 June 1919) which had 'at the same time' started to see both the ensign and the red burgee, the *Stander-Z,* attack flag raised. This was nine minutes before *Friedrich der Große's* bell was heard to start ringing (ADM. 116/2074). A message was sent out at 1211 for 'all available small craft to assemble at *Victorious'.*

† Because of the connection with the *Frankfurt* sightings, the signal is sometimes attributed to another drifter, the *Sochosin,* which had also sent a signal. *Wescott's* captain was angry at Fremantle for having attributed more credibility in that signal than his own.

1400
SMS *König*
SMS *Kaiserin*

At 1400, when the *Spenser* and the *Shakespeare* arrived back in the Flow, *König* and *Kaiserin* would sink. Ten German capital ships had already gone down and, within the hour, another fifteen more would join.

König's crew left their ship around 1235. They'd been delayed looking for some missing sailors, despite their being so few on board. Even though they were being fired upon, they still managed a last rousing cheer for their ship.

Before she'd even managed to lower some of her boats into the water, *Kaiserin* had started to list badly over to port ('*hatte bereits starke Schlag-Seite*').[479] The problem was that none of the winches – electric or hand-operated – were working.[480] Her complement, after the last repatriation of men on 18 June, was now down to only fifty-three men.[481]

From the *Prinzregent Luitpold*, *Kaiserin*'s sailors could be heard shouting for help. It seemed so dangerous at one point that von Reiche ordered the ship's pinnace to go over and see if they could help take men off. The pinnace never made it. As she got to the distressed ship, she was intercepted and brought back by a drifter. Dreschmann, a machinistmaat on *Kaiserin*, saw how aggressively the British drifter was behaving given the circumstances and that white flags were clearly visible on the ship's mid-deck. '*Doch wie wurden wir enttäusscht, als auch gleichen Zeit die Geschütz-bedienung des Drifters das auf der Back des letzteren stehende Geschötz auf unser Schiff richteten and damit den Rettungsversuch der Pinnaß vereitelte.*' (roughly: 'You can imagine how disappointed we were when we saw that the Drifter's stern gun crew were shooting at our ship, thwarting any attempt by the pinnace to rescue us.')[482]

Reiche then thought that he could get his own men to shore, leave them there and send the empty boats back. As the boats neared the shoreline, they came under strong rifle fire. They turned back on to the Flow, leaving the sailors on *Kaiserin* with little choice but to throw what they could later hold on to into the water, jump from the ship, and kick away from the danger of being sucked under. Viertel, her commander, was last off. They were 3,500m from land and, knowing now that they would probably be shot if they even got there, they waited in the water for rescue by the drifters. It took about an hour before help came.

Some of *Kaiserin*'s sailors were picked up by English drifters, others by boats from *Baden* and *Prinzregent Luitpold*, which is probably why small numbers of her crew ended up on each one of the British battleships, rather than as one group. After two hours, in some cases, in 7 to 8° waters, the sailors were cold and welcomed the warming drinks and dry clothes they received from *Baden*'s sailors. Together, the two ships' sailors were taken in tow over to *Ramillies*.

From the main island, it was an extraordinary sight. From a nearby hill a farmhand, AS Thomson, was grabbed by his brother, who shouted excitedly: 'Look, there's a sub.' 'That's no submarine, it's a German ship going down,' was how he replied.[483] Of course, they had never seen anything like it and drew what they thought was the most obvious conclusion. The form of a sinking ship was so unusual that it seemed to take on the smooth lines of a whale, or in Thomson's brother's case, a submarine.

Elsewhere on the mainland, on a farm at Smoogro overlooking Swanbister Bay, it had already been a long and hard morning's work. Arthur Burnett was used to farm labouring. Before the war, he'd worked on the family's farm of Grievehouse in Stenness. His grand-daughter, Morag Robertson, now working for the Orkney Island Council, recalled the details of the story that her father had told her.*

Arthur had been cycling back to his home at Stenness and was pedalling hard to get back in time for lunch. Just after Ophir, the Scorrodale road cuts inland and heads up over the hills to re-emerge on the other side, behind Houton. He was starting up over the hill. Past what had then been the shop and a pub, neither of them there any longer, he reached the summit needing to stop and rest a few moments. He got off his bike, wiped his brow and glanced casually over to his left, towards the Flow.

He could not believe what he could see, which was ships in the bay, in various stages of sinking and at all manner of angles: down by the bows, sterns jutting skyward, rolling over or just gliding beneath the waves. He watched for some time, thinking that he must be seeing things, and gave himself a 'good talking to', muttering, 'I really have done too much this time.'

When he got home, Arthur sat down quietly at table, not breathing a word of what he had just seen. He honestly thought that it was a case of either being 'too thirsty, too hungry or too tired' and that he must simply be hallucinating. So, the meal went on as though this day was like

---

* Arthur, Morag's grandfather, was a character. He'd been in the war and had lied about his age to join up when he was seventeen. He'd been told he was too young, so following advice, he went around the corner, came back and announced his age as eighteen.

any other. That is, until the postman knocked and asked if they had heard the news. His mother came into the kitchen and said: 'Well, lads', Arthur recalled, 'you'll never believe what the German Fleet have just done. They've scuttled themselves. Would you believe it?' One of his three brothers had been lost in France during the war and, as Morag described it, the family 'did not care much one way or another what the Germans did, they were so saddened by the loss'. All they had to show was 'a large coin', the large death medal, to commemorate the family's loss.[484]

Arthur finally understood the enormity of what he had seen with his own eyes. His mother immediately admonished him, asking why he had not said a word about such an extraordinary thing. 'Simple,' he replied, he had kept quiet as he did not want them to think he had lost his senses.

Back in Orphir, just along the bay, there was a commotion going on in the church. Someone had run in, excitedly urging the hushed congregation to follow him out to see something extraordinary. He was immediately 'shushed' by the priest, who let him know in no uncertain terms that he was in the house of God. However, the same clergyman started to walk slowly down the aisle, quite deliberately quickening his pace and gathering his robes around his waist as he went. 'Right, now I stand a chance.' Out he then raced, intent on securing the best view.[*]

A burial was in progress and its solemn dignity completely shattered. Just as the body of an elderly lady was being lowered into its final resting place, there was a sudden commotion at the graveside. 'I think the German Fleet is sinking,' someone was heard saying. The pallbearers dropped the casket's ropes. Off they went, leaving the minister standing all alone beside the unburied coffin.

1430

SMS *Bayern*

Finally, more 'official' photographers arrived on the scene. One was from *The Orcadian* newspaper. He had gone to Houton as soon as they heard something was happening, around 1300.[†] Burrows, an amateur but very talented photographer, had already been on the Flow for some time.

From the shore above Houton, some of the same encounters could

---

[*] The story was recounted to me by John and Sarah Welburn from Orphir. Hewison quotes Kenneth Flett's memory of the event (Hewison, p. 132).
[†] Both ships had been painted black to commemorate – according to the report in *The Orcadian*, 26 June 1919 – their attack on the Norwegian convoy and the sinking of the destroyer, HMS *Mary Rose*.

be seen. As the British tried to save one of the ships, the newspaperman saw a 'long splash between destroyer and battleship that showed that the towline had parted…and more quickly than a photographer at my side could change a plate, not a vestige of the ship remained'.[485]

Bayern's end came fast. In one of Burrows' photos, taken around 1400, the ship can be seen still settling on a seemingly even keel. Just four minutes later, he took what would become the classic photo of *Bayern* listing dangerously over on her port side. When John Tulloch had seen her listing, he had at first just thought that they were cleaning off her barnacles. As he said later, 'many times I'd see ships listed over so that seaweed and barnacles could be scraped off their bottoms'.

Another photo caught a group of sailors, wildly waving their hats. They are in a cutter, *Bayern* in the background. It was this photo that became the source for a painting of the scuttle in which splashes from rifle fire were added.*

Reuter's journey took him close by the *Bayern*. The 28,600-ton super-dreadnought, now in her final moments, had been moored between his own flagship, *Emden II*, and *Friedrich der Große*. When the admiral saw that other British drifters were tussling with *Emden*'s cables in an effort to take her in for beaching in shallower waters, he headed straight past her to the *Bayern*.

No sooner had his drifter picked up some of *Bayern*'s crew, than the battleship rolled further over, her keel facing up. It was 1409. When *Bayern* did eventually sink, sometime shortly after 1430, she went with 'a cloud of smoke bursting boilers as she went'. She went down 'with the German flag flying'.[486]

John Tulloch saw the whole spectacle unfold. He was terrified: 'Two boats loaded with sailors, they headed straight to the Calf of Cava – the nearest shore – right below where I was standing.' As they approached him, he saw the *Bayern* 'finally drop over on to her side, hesitate before turning bottom up and disappear under the water in a smother of foam and exploding bubbles'.[487] He started to 'high tail it for home', 'terror fill[ing] [his] young heart'.[488]

Just as the pride of the German Navy – one of her latest ships – sank,

---

* Possibly this was the boat on which Hans Hesse had been shot, and that the occupants weren't cheering; they were shouting their surrender. Could it be Hesse that six-former Katie Watts saw shot? In the confusion the *Bayern* signalman had been shot when three rescue boats full of German sailors were being towed back to captivity by the British. He had tried to cut the towing rope and was shot for his efforts.

advance elements of Fremantle's Battle Squadron raced back into the Flow.[489] It might have been *Bayern*'s end that GL Bourdillon, the chaplain of the *Royal Sovereign*, one of the first British ships back at 1430, had witnessed. It's hard to say now. The pastor wrote of the first impressions when his ship came back in the Flow:

> The first sign we saw was the masts of a ship at a sharp angle over Flotta. Half the German ships had disappeared, and several of the remainder were in a sinking condition! One battleship had her quarter-deck awash, and as we watched thro' glasses, we saw her gradually lift her bows out of the water, roll over, and disappear below the surface, leaving nothing but a vast patch of bubbling foam.[490]

1415

SMS *von der Tann*

Right up until the last moments, *von der Tann* was offloading supplies from a steamer that was shuttling stores across from the *Dollart*. She had tied up around 1100 and had only just left when Reuter's signal came across. Immediately, a motor boat and a dinghy were lowered on the ship's starboard side. Her sixty-five-strong crew took to the boats as soon as they could but, after only half an hour or so, were stopped by an English guard drifter. After they had confirmed that they were not armed, they were taken in tow.

Amid the chaos, a few calmer minds prevailed. One was John Hodgson's grandfather who, seeing the flag of the *Von der Tann* was still aloft, quickly went aboard, took it down and secreted it away, along with a ship's clock and some postcards that had been left out on a galley table.

Von der Tann started her port list around 1358. Two minutes later she already lay keel up, ready, but just holding off her final dive into the depths. When she went at 1400, *von der Tann*, once the fastest battle-cruiser on the seas at 27 knots, 'turned completely turtle and disappeared in a smother of foam'.[491] At that moment, the violent death that *Indefatigable* had suffered at her hand at Jutland had finally been avenged, albeit ignominiously.

1430

SMS *Bremse*

Attempts were made by *Venetia* to bring the *Bremse* ashore. The fast, light cruiser that had been built in 1916 as a minelayer was easy to disguise from the British. Her main mast could be lowered to make her look like a Royal Navy *Arethusa*-class cruiser.[492]

Venetia's attempts failed when *Bremse* capsized. Reuter later wrote that 'in spite of the English sailors who had seized the vessel', her 'gallant commander', Oberleutnant zur See Schacke, succeeded in sinking her.[493]

Now the bigger ships of Fremantle's Battle Squadron started to arrive back. At around 1440, at full speed, around 21 knots, they swooped into the Flow. Nine German battleships, three battle-cruisers and four light cruisers had *already* sunk.[494] Some of Germany's finest ships: *Friedrich der Große, König Albert, Kronprinz Wilhelm, Kaiser, Große Kurfürst, Prinzregent Luitpold, Kaiserin, König, Bayern*, as well as the battle-cruisers *Moltke, Seydlitz* and *von der Tann*. Of the light cruisers, *Brummer, Dresden, Köln* and *Bremse* had also all disappeared.

In his report, Fremantle listed as 'obviously sinking but still afloat' *Baden, Markgraf, Hindenburg, Derfflinger, Emden, Nürnburg, Brummer* and *Frankfurt*.[495] The inclusion of *Brummer* was probably mistaken. Most literature reports her sinking at 1305 but the ship's report says that she was the first of the light cruisers to go down, at 1345.[496] He possibly might have meant *Karlsruhe*, which sank around 1550.

It might have been too late to save more of the larger ships but the return seemed to put an end to the free-for-all firing. Reuter's later account says that 'the firing dies away and is gradually silenced'.[497] At least something was achieved.

By that point, even though each of the *Revenge*-class ships were already assigned the German counterparts for which they were responsible, they were clearly too late. Large armed guard groups were immediately sent out from each ship: the group from *Revenge* were assigned to concentrate on the south-west portion of the German lines, from *Ramillies*, the centre and from *Royal Sovereign*, the north-east. When they arrived back, *Resolution* and *Royal Oak* were to assist operations on *Baden* and *Emden*.

The squadron's remaining escorting destroyers raced off in a desperate effort to tow ashore some of the ships remaining afloat. Arriving back half an hour sooner, *Spenser* already had her hands full. Not many of the German ships were still floating – only two battleships, one battle-cruiser and four light cruisers.

As had already been done, the first thing they had needed to do was to cut the anchor chains so that the ships could drift ashore. Sometimes the only way to sever the chain was by gunfire. On *Flying Kestrel*, the headmaster, Mr Hepburn, said that he had seen *Westcott* firing at one ship's anchor chain.[498] The sight was incongruous. Towing their great loads, 'drifters were pulling at huge battleships like ants with large beetles'.[499]

1450

SMS *Derfflinger, The 'Iron Dog'*

After Burrows had photographed *Bayern*'s final plunge, he and Grant continued on their way. At 1415 they headed back to the west, passing *Baden* on their starboard side. They did not stop. The ship seemed to be 'floating well' and a trawler was already alongside. The two then headed slightly back east to *Karlsruhe* on the way back to *Derfflinger*, which was anchored close to the shoreline of Hoy, opposite the northern tip of Cava. *Karlsruhe* would probably have still been riding quite high on the water as well. She would not go down for another hour and a half.

The scene around *Derfflinger* was very different: she had few neighbours left floating. To the east, *Prinzregent Luitpold*, and to her north, *Kaiserin,* had both gone down. Soon *Derfflinger* would join them. She had rolled dramatically on to her port side, half of her 689ft-long hull already under water and only her two rear turrets, *Caesar* and *Dora*, still visible and dry above the waterline.* Aft her rudders were now clearly visible as the ship's stern lifted, her bow pulling her down. In her last photo, the waters around her are clear of boats.

The night before, at 1700, *Korvettenkapitän* Pastusczyck had gathered the skeleton crew in the officers' mess, telling them the same as had other captains: that the enemy was expected to take their ships once the peace terms were signed. For him, the idea that they might sink their ship, the faithful *'Eisernen Hund'* could only be good news. He started his announcement by saying so: *'Ich habe eine freudige Mitteilung zu Machen.'* ('I have a happy message to give you.')[500]

The British came to respectfully call *Derfflinger* the *Iron Dog* (*'Eisernen Hund'*) because of the amount of punishment she had been able to take at Jutland. She was anchored south of the cliffs that locals knew as the 'nose of the Bring'.

Her crew left her quite early on. Around 1150, the first series of boats, five *Flöße* ('rafts') were lowered with thirty men. Forty minutes later, the remaining men, twenty-four of them, were lowered in three more

---

* *Derfflinger* was armed with four 30.5cm (12in) guns, mounted two aft and two forward, and, as was the practice in the German Navy, they were named, from bow to stern, Anna, Bertha, Caesar and Dora.

dinghies. The German supply steamer, *Dollart*, had just ended landing stores and had left the ship's side. She had come alongside about an hour or so before Reuter signalled the scuttle's start, around 1000.

As they left the ship, their floating home, the crews gave a resounding cheer ('*drei donnernde Hurras*'). Five hundred metres or so from the sinking ship, a British destroyer (it was most likely *Westcott*, although one report's author talks about the ship's markings as having been GF03, not F03), was seen emerging from the mass of sinking German torpedo boats and was opening fire, left and right, on the crews from the various battle-cruisers, those from *Seydlitz*, *von der Tann* and on the crew of *Hindenburg*, who were just getting into their boats.

The cutter the children saw when one of the British destroyers – *Westcott* – raced past the *Flying Kestrel*, might have been one of these boats. It is difficult to be certain. *Westcott* had been 'cleared for action and the guns manned'. Most found the gunfire and the confusion terrifying, although some did brag that it was a 'thrill'. *Westcott* was opening fire at the German ship's mooring cables. Men were jumping into the water, others taking to the boats. It was chaos. 'We saw them landing on the island of Cava, and running up from the shore.'[501] On Cava, they got an unwelcome reception, a 'group of women wielding pitchforks and other farm tools managed to scare off a party of Germans who were trying to land on the beach'.[502]

Around the same time (it must have been around 1310), *Moltke* rolled on to her side. An eyewitness recalled what he'd seen:

> She made a great fuss about sinking. After listing over and over until she lay on her side then she turned turtle and her stern shot up into the air until she appeared to be standing up on her bows, then she dived into the depth below, something aboard her exploded and fountains of water shot into the air, after a little way a second explosion sent more water rocketing out of the sea above her. The water around where she had vanished seethed and boiled for a long time after she had gone.[503]

1550

SMS *Karlsruhe*

The chaos provided huge opportunity to the islanders. The pickings would have been rich. Nobody hesitated; everyone got to work. John Tulloch talks of how he and his uncle immediately started retrieving as much as they could:[*]

> I was in my glory dragging suitcases, kitbags and boxes out of the sea.... My uncle Harry had yoked one of our horses in a cart and he appeared on the scene, we all threw our findings until the cart was piled high...when we had time to look over our treasures some of them proved to be treasures indeed, there were binoculars, typewriters, bottle(s) of whisky, uniforms with gold braid, flags, chocolate, in fact thousands of things that were priceless. I had found a beautiful officer's dress sword in its scabbard and belt but my uncle spoke me out of it. For weeks afterwards, I wore an officer's full-dress cap that sat on top of my ears but it had all the gold and trimmings that befitted a high-ranking officer.[504]

When Tulloch's uncle, Bill, saw the Germans coming ashore on Cava (something that Peggie Gibson also talked about), he went to get a gun. Armed with a Very pistol, he:

> ...spotted this boat and hastened over to order them off.[505] Most of the men were sitting on the rocks and refused to move. Bill asked them if they were all there and one officer who could speak English told him that there was one man who had gone into a peat bank to ease himself at the call of nature. Bill searched and found the sailor squatting in the peat bank. Pointing the Very light pistol at him, he told him to get moving. The sailor grinned so Bill pressed the trigger. Fortunately for him and the sailor the gun misfired but nevertheless the sailor pulled up his pants and high-tailed it for the boat, then they all climbed aboard and headed out to sea again.

Whether true or not, it makes a wonderful story. It would be wrong, however, if this gave the impression of being a single incident. In fact, 'the island – Cava – seemed to be covered with men' and encounters like this probably weren't isolated incidents.[506]

---

[*] Tom Muir later said that Tulloch had a reputation for telling rather tall stories. But his stories of what happened on the day seem to ring true and are, in any case, wonderful visual patchworks of memories.

SMS *Baden*

After the second group of Fremantle's ships got back at 1600, *Baden* was also boarded. She had been seen earlier to be riding high on the water and, seemingly, not under immediate threat. Her commander, Kapitänleutnant Zirzow, had received Reuter's message right at the outset, at 1137, and immediately ordered fires extinguished and his twenty-eight-man crew to start the scuttle preparations.[507]

HMS *Ramillies* sent some men over to her. They found that many of her sailors 'had been away from the ship drawing stores when the order to scuttle was given, so she was not in such an advanced state of sinking'. Nevertheless, they now found that the ship was 'rapidly making water, all W.T. doors and scuttles open, but lights still on allowing for the ship to be 'thoroughly searched'.[508]

A British officer, Lieutenant EJ Gowdy, remembered the way in which the men behaved:

> Water was almost up to the floor plates and I could get no life in the diesel so told the [German] lieutenant to start it and he looked blank and said, 'No Inglis'. So, I said, 'Right – up on deck.' I shouted to Cartwright I'd found two Huns below and this one pretended not to understand I wanted him to start the diesel. Cartwright replied, 'Take him below and shoot him if he won't do it.' Down we went again, by this time the water was over the floor plates. I took my revolver out of the holster and pointed it to his head and said, 'Go on, start up.' He replied, in perfect English, 'I'm not going to start it for you, you can shoot me.' I said, 'So you do speak English,' and he replied, 'Yes, perfectly.' I couldn't help admiring the man and I remember thinking, 'What would I do if I was in his position.' The water was rising and it was too late to start the engine, and I did not do my duty – I had an admiration for the man.*

Was Gowdy's behaviour any different than many of the other men trying to find some way to save the ships that the Germans had so successfully

---

* Hugh David had been on the boarding party and had gone below, managing to close some of the sea-cocks, though it didn't seem, at the time, to be working. A German sub lieutenant had been threatened by his flag captain with being shot if he did not help, a threat to which he bravely replied: 'You can shoot me now, I do not mind.' This is likely the same story (Source: Phipps Hornby correspondence to Prof Arthur Marder, UCI, 24 October 1966 and 16 September 1968).

prepared for scuttling? Gowdy's sympathy with this German officer's own sense of duty probably reflected the feelings of quite a few officers at Scapa, including Fremantle's. It took courage for an unarmed German to disobey British orders. That had been amply demonstrated during the day. Many of those in the boarding parties were already angry and frustrated at having been shown up by the Germans and it clearly did not help matters when, in some instances, the British were being goaded by German sailors.

The captain of HMS *Revenge*, G T Swabey, expressed the fear that any one of us would invariably have had of going down into the bowels of a sinking ship:

> I went aboard (the *Baden*), a few of the *Baden*'s men with us. We could get nothing out of them as to the position of the seacocks which had been opened to cause the flooding. It is not difficult to imagine what it was like down in the bowels of a strange ship, minutely sub-divided, as all German ships invariably are, with no lights barring a hand torch, and knowing that she was sinking and that an any moment she might heel over and go to the bottom.[509]

The British did manage to get *Baden*'s generators running and this helped them carry on working below decks to get her pumps running and restoring her seaworthiness. The diesel dynamo 'kept going. This work was effected with great ability and promptness and had the effect of saving the ship.'[510]

Baden was eventually saved. *Flying Kestrel*'s Captain Davies, whose 'knowledge of the Flow and its current and shallows was profound' now figured prominently in a completely new story: he 'cleverly manoeuvred [the *Baden*] into shallow water' where she was beached in Swanbister Bay after a 4-mile haul through the Flow.[511]

1645

SMS *Markgraf*

Markgraf was boarded by men from the drifter *Cabalsin*, which had also fired on her but had not been able to get the desired effect from gunfire alone.[*] The battleship's captain. Korvettenkapitän Walter Schumann, was

---

[*] See ADM 116/2074, p. 4, Fremantle to Admiralty, 24 June 1919. Cabalsin's CO said that the fire 'produced no effect' on their attempts to lower a steamboat.

coming up from below decks and was carrying a white flag. From the water, British marines on a drifter shouted at him to order his crew below to close the sea-cocks. He refused to do so and was shot in the head by a young British officer, Lieutenant JPFG Turner, when he 'started to argue the point…'.

As Phipps Hornby coldly put it, 'the bullet entered through the luckless German's upper lip'. It was, in his words, 'a very good shot too'.[*] He died immediately while another two officers, one his engineering officer, were severely wounded. As soon as the British drifter had pulled away, a gunner, Günther Soormann, had gone to see whether his commander was still alive after the shooting, only to find him dead.[†]

His body was brought back on the same drifter that carried Reuter back to the *Revenge*. One of the officers there, according to Hugh David's account that only emerged in 2015, painted an extraordinary and upsetting picture. 'A group of ragged desperadoes were clustered together in the bow, a little further aft sat the German Admiral von Reuter and at his feet lay a German commander with a bullet through his head.'[517]

That man 'with a bullet through his head' must have been Schumann. His grave on Lyness betrays nothing of the unjust violence of his death or his rank. The gravestone simply reads 'W. Schumann'.[‡] Herman Dittmann was an Oberheizer, a leading stoker, but has been variously described as Schumann's 'first officer', an 'engineering officer' and a 'petty officer'. His body now lies on the other side of the two rows of headstones in the cemetery at Lyness, near three of the four sailors from the *V.126* and *V.127* who were killed. It is a pity he is not lying beside his captain. His grave simply reads 'Dittmann'.[§] While Dittmann had been topside, the work below decks was completed by the fleet engineer, Faustmann.

Schumann's body was laid out in the German motor boat, where it stayed through the night tied to the stern of another battleship, *Ramillies*. This was supposedly so that it could await burial, or as Phipps Hornby put it until 'our "chippy chaps" had had time to make a coffin for it'. The next

---

[*] Source: Phipps Hornby correspondence to Prof Arthur Marder, UCI, 24 October 1966 and 16 September 1968.

[†] Soorman is described by Booth (p. 15) as a 'Chief Gunner'.

[‡] Schumann's wife had earlier written to Wilhelm asking him to come home. She was facing severe difficulties raising their four children ('I have four children and am alone, you know what this means in these times,' Reuter, p. 114). Reuter had tried to persuade him to go home but, to Reuter's admiration, he elected to stay.

[§] Who is lying next to Walter Schuman is, strangely enough, Wilhelm Markgraf. He had nothing to do with the SMS *Markgraf*. He had served on the torpedo boat *V.126*.

morning, a British Sub Lieutenant Horne had woken up at 0530, looked out of the scuttle from his cabin right aft in the middle deck to see what the weather was doing, and found himself staring directly into the face of the dead German officer.[*]

The British boarding party from *Vectis* could not find a way to cut *Markgraf*'s cables. Nor could sailors from *Revenge*. The ship spent a full half an hour under tow and only sank around 1645 when a way to slip the cables, cutting them on board and letting them run over the side, could not be found in time.[†]

A TALE OF TWO SHIPS – *MARKGRAF* AND *IRON DUKE*

Markgraf was launched in Bremen on 4 June 1913. Work on her in the AG Weser shipyard (on the banks of the Weser river) took nineteen months after her keel was laid down in November 1911 as a replacement for another ship, the *Weissenburg* (hence her dock name was *Ersatz Weissenburg*). The ship was christened by the Grand Duke of Baden, Friedrich II, in honour of the Kaiser since the latter was also the Margrave of Baden.[‡] It took another fifteen months to complete her fitting-out and she was ready for service two months after the outbreak of war, on 1 October 1914. By contrast, HMS *Iron Duke,* started two months later, was ready for service six months earlier. It's quite telling.

Markgraf was a large battleship – 25,390 tons, 28,600 fully loaded with ammunition, fuel and stores. At 575ft, she was somewhat shorter than many of her British counterparts but with a much wider beam, just under 97ft. *Iron Duke* was almost 50ft longer but 7ft narrower in the beam. Generally, this additional deck area made German ships slightly more stable as gun platforms. The draft of both ships was roughly the same: *Iron Duke*'s was only 6in less than *Markgraf*'s 30ft, the height of a three-storey house.

The almost identical armouring of the two ships is interesting. This was unusual. German ships normally had a higher armour to weight ratio, meaning thicker armour plating. *Iron Duke*'s belt armour, the

---

[*] Correspondence Phipps Hornby to Arthur J Marder 24 October 1966.
[†] ADM 116/2074 1BS Report 24 June 1919 reports the sinking time at 1630.
[‡] Her name was probably a reference to the military exploits of Markgraf Ludwig Wilhelm (1655–1707) known as Turk-Ludwig because of his role in Austria's campaigns against the armies of the Ottoman Turks, which he decisively defeated on 19 August 1691 at Slankamen (Serbia). He was also present in the Wars of the Spanish Succession, helping win the victory at Schellenberg against the French and Bavaria (2 Jul 1704). Source: Shipbucket site.

armour that runs along the hull sides, was only slightly less than her German opponent – 12in versus 13.8in. Turret armour was, again, almost the same: 11in versus 11.8in. But *Iron Duke* actually had thicker deck armouring – 2.5in as opposed to 1.2in. One also needs to be aware of the quality of the German ship's armoured steel. Her deck armour was a steel hardened with nickel (*'Das horizontale panzerdeck würde ein neu verfügbarer Nickel-Stahl verwendet'*).[513]

Both ships could steam at roughly 21 knots, though *Iron Duke* probably had a minimal half-knot advantage, putting out 29,000 shaft horse power (shp) from her four Parsons turbines while *Markgraf*'s rating was considerably higher, 40,850shp, from three Parsons/AEG Vulcan/Bergmann turbines, the equivalent of 30,450 kilowatts (kW). Normally she would have carried around 3,000 tonnes of coal plus another 600 tonnes of oil. She had three oil-fired Marine-type boilers and twelve Marine-type boilers heated by twenty-seven fireboxes, each of which was pressure-fed to sixteen atmospheres.[514]

The biggest difference lay in armament.[*] Both had two super-firing turrets and a single midship's turret in a single centre-line configuration. But *Iron Duke*'s ten main guns were Vickers 13.5in 45-calibre Mark vs. *Markgraf*'s were 30.5cm (12in) SK L/50s.[†] The difference in 'hitting-power' really becomes clearer when the shell weight of a 13.5in projectile is compared with that of a typical 12in shell. A British 13.5in projectile would weight 1,266.5lb (574.6kg) while a British 12in shell 850lb (385.7kg). The additional 1.5in in calibre (that is only a 13 per cent increase) adds *49 per cent* in shell weight. The German 12in shell was heavier. It was 892.8lb (405kg).[515] The guns' muzzle velocity, maybe a more accurate measure of its shells' hitting power, was 855m/sec.

In terms of performance it is generally accepted that the German guns were superior to British guns – the 30.5cm SK L/50 could outperform the British 12in guns in terms of penetration power and performed only slightly less than the 13.5in guns (as were on *Iron Duke*,

---

[*] For an excellent technical presentation of the 30.5cm SK L/50 see www.navweaps.com.
[†] A few words about 'calibre' and gun barrel measurement. A gun's 'calibre' will refer to the metric or non-metric diameter of the shell size; British capital ship weaponry ranged from 12in to 15in calibre for the primary armament. A gun on HMS *Iron Duke* could be described as being 13.5in L/45 ('L/45' refers to the barrel length – it is 45 x 13.5in shell calibres in length, i.e. 607.5in). German guns were classified in metric measurements, so that the main eight guns on SMS *Lützow* might be referred to as 30.5cm SK L/50 ('SK' referring to '*Schnellfeuerkanone*' or fast-fire artillery); 'L/50' is comparable to the British barrel length.

for example). With an elevation of 13.5° the guns could throw their shells 17,700yds (16,200m). Just over 10 miles.*

Secondary armament was pretty similar, *Iron Duke* had BL 6in Mk VIIs, *Markgraf* 15cm (5.9in) SK L/45 QF guns.† In this case, *Iron Duke* had one fewer pair than *Markgraf*'s seven (i.e. twelve versus fourteen guns). One substantial point of difference could have been that *Iron Duke* also had two torpedo tubes on the broadside. These would fire the standard Whitehead 21in torpedo.

Markgraf was manned by a slightly larger crew. There is quite a large variance in estimates on her crew size. Gröner's profile lists forty-one officers and 1,095 ratings (Another eighty-two men would have been on board if *Markgraf* had been the fleet flagship. Normally, a flagship would be expected to have a slightly larger crew complement because of the additional staff positions needed for fleet management). *Iron Duke's* complement was approximately 1,022. *Markgraf* cost around 45 million marks, *Iron Duke*, about £1.8 million.

In the archives at Kirkwall, there is a series of photos taken on the afternoon that record the last moments of the 25,000-ton battleship. In one, she is clearly settling deep in the water, but still appears comfortably on an even keel. In the next three, however, she takes a pronounced 10° list to port, then 45° and finally is lying on her side, her starboard hull almost evenly visibly above the water. Sadly, the precise timing of each photograph was not recorded by the photographer, a publisher in Kirkwall, J. Omond. A different series of photographs looks out over Cava island and in the last, thankfully noted at 1625, catches *Markgraf* noting that she 'turns turtle' before she sinks twenty minutes later, lying with her hull facing upwards.‡

* *Prinzregent Luitpold's* guns were changed just before Jutland (others after) to increase the elevation to 16°. This increased the range to around 22,300yds (22,400m).
† Some explanations: 'BL' refers to breech-loading rather than muzzle-loading. In today's age it's almost trite to talk about this but these were the decades in which the changeover was made from muzzle-loaders. 'QF' refers to quick-firing guns.
‡ I've seen *Markgraf* close up when she was dived on in April 2018 as part of a *National Geographic* television series. The captain of the MV *Karin*, Yorkshireman John Thornton, took us out on a typical Orkney day that started calm but soon turned sour. The divers did not have great visibility but were able to capture detail that was revealing. All the portholes were open. Most looked as though the portholes had been lifted off. Importantly, of the ones that remained, the fact that they were open showed the careful preparation for the scuttle. On her hull side, where a pinnace would come to drop off officers, it looked as though the hatchway was completely open. As soon as the water level reached its level it would have added a huge intake of additional water. Try as I might, I could not find detailed ship's drawings to confirm that.

1700

SMS *Hindenburg*

Heyden, *Hindenburg's* commanding officer, had warned the crew about the scuttle and when the order came their preparations were immediate and the diesel dynamos were started up so that the boats could be lowered with their mechanical winches at 1215. The men got in but had to wait. Two men were still missing.

After the *Seydlitz*, Burrows went on to the *Hindenburg*. He arrived around 1320. He and Grant only remained for around five minutes, again hauling down the colours. Given the importance of their documentary work, it was extraordinary that they would even waste the time for a purely symbolic gesture that could have been just as easily carried out by other British sailors not under specific orders to keep a photographic record of this extraordinary day. After five minutes, they set off again. It was 1325. They passed a number of ships that had already sunk (*Kaiserin* at 1400 and *Friedrich der Größe* earlier at 1216). The *Karlsruhe* would have still been afloat as it sank at 1550.

Derfflinger was starting to roll over as the two continued back south towards *Victorious*. The only remaining visible signs of *Hindenburg* were her distinct funnels and masts. They would stay there, lapping the water, for eleven years, like a cross marking a gravesite.

Moltke and *Seydlitz* had also gone, the latter lay on her starboard side, her port propeller clear above the waterline. Behind her outline, which many people would later mistake for the shape of a low-lying island, were silhouetted *Hindenburg's* masts and funnels. It was just 1500, just over three hours since Reuter's signal had been hauled up. Burrow's photos would become iconic, an extraordinary visual recording of the greatest loss of shipping. It was his lucky day.

One of the ships *Westcott* visited was *Hindenburg*. As she pulled alongside, men were clattering down *Hindenburg's* ladders and clambering into the waiting, bobbing cutters. The British officer tried to get his German counterparts to order their men back on board but were told 'No understand English'. So, two midshipmen who had a 'smattering of German' carried out the task. Still no reaction: 'they paid not an iota of attention'.

Arms shot up in surrender, shouting '*Kamerad*'. With no hold on the lines, the boats drifted off. 'We looked pretty silly,' was how Henry McCall summed it up.[516]

Through his megaphone, a British officer shouted in German for the sailors to go back to the sinking ship and close the sea-cocks 'or else they would be shot. They got in an awful flap and said that they had thrown all the valves overboard.'[517] Despite machine-gun fire and a salvo being fired, it was a quasi-theatrical exchange:

British officer:	Why are you sinking your ships?
German officer:	We got order by our admiral.
British officer:	Go back on board or I fire.
German officer:	We can't. The rooms are already flooded.

The British opened up with a Lewis machine gun. The bullets clanged and zinged against the great steel hull with loud, whining ricochets. They 'spattered the ship's side…just before the gangway, exactly as the last man tumbled into the boats'. Newspaper reports from the time say that the 'rat-a-tat-tat of a machine gun – however directed against the men – was heard'.[518]

Westcott's men boarded. Water was already slopping over most of her deck. One of the officers recalled the moment:

> I went on board the *Hindenburg* when she was sinking to shut down all the doors we could find. It was awful on board, you could hear the swishing of the water in the boiler-rooms and see the oily surface of the water getting gradually higher and higher. We closed as many doors as we could, but it was no use and eventually she sank. One diesel engine was still running, making the electric light, so we could still see a bit, but it stopped suddenly when the water came upon it, and we were plung[ed] into absolute darkness on board the sinking ship… . When we had closed as many doors as possible, we had to come away as there was a great danger of one of the boilers bursting. The ship was also beginning to heal dangerously.[519]

Under extremely dangerous conditions, explosives were successfully placed on *Hindenburg*'s anchor chains.[*] From their small boats, her crew heard, then saw what was going on. A cloud of smoke rose up after the explosion: '*Eine Explosion in Richtung* Hindenburg *ließ uns aufhorchen, im gleichem Augenblick sahen wir am Bug unseres Schiffes eine Rauchwolke*

---

[*] Two 2½lb primer charges were placed 'on each cable just above the water line' (ADM. 116/2074 VADM Report, 24 June 1919, p. 4).

aufsteigen – die Engländer hatten die Ankerkette gesprengt.' ('An explosion in the direction of Hindenburg got our attention. At that moment, we saw a cloud of smoke rising up from the ship's bow – the English had blown her anchor chain.')[520]

She was in the middle of being towed into shallower water near Cava but foundered. By now the water came up to just under the forward super-turret, *Bertha*. She was in just 70ft of water, 'easily recognizable by her massive funnels'.[521]

De Courcy-Ireland had been among a party of twenty-five men with two officers to board her before she finally settled in the shallow waters around 1700. 'The ship by now was already in a bad state and all the power had been disconnected so we had to work in the dark to try and close the hatches.'[522]

As the came into the shallows, they worked below deck. It was difficult work as 'many of the clips were rusty and stiff' but de Courcy-Ireland thought that they must have closed 'about two hundred'.[523]

They started to get increasingly nervous, especially when the water reached the upper deck. Hatches were literally being blown open under the mounting pressure. If they didn't get off soon they would go down with her. Eventually, they were picked up off the almost wholly submerged ship by a small whaler.

A last effort by some destroyers and tugs was made to try and shift her but she rolled. Hugh David, who had been on the *Revenge* when Reuter was brought aboard, arrived just as she went 'very nearly taking [him] with her'.[524] Seeing there was little more to accomplish there, he went 'with an armed guard to save the *Hindenburg*', saw that she was already well on her way to going down and went straight on to see what he could do with the *Baden*.

The 'fog of war', as is always the case, shrouded much in ambiguity. Eyewitness accounts – from people who were almost in exactly the same place at the same time – are often contradictory. In an article on the 17 July, *The Orcadian* wrote that men had gone back to get dynamite to blow the ship's cables but that she had foundered and sunk before they were able to do so. The unreliability of many of these comments makes one pause: the same witness said that he had gone through the wardroom and 'bashed in' a portrait of *Hindenburg* but that he had not taken any of the ship's silver as 'there was too much hurry'.[525]

Hindenburg now rested, her 700ft hull on the floor of the Flow. Her commanding officer, Korvettenkapitän Heyden, told Reuter that he wanted 'to sink her on an even keel to make the disembarkation of the crew more certain'.[526] Above the ship's Imperial ensign, a white ensign had been hoisted and was fluttering in the calm breeze.

Beached
SMS *Nürnberg*

According to the Scuttle reports, on the light cruiser, *Nürnberg*, Kapitän-leutnant Georgi's men had been notified of the possibility of a scuttle the day before it took place. The ship's report recounts Reuter's orders being received around 1150. It is not only highly doubtful that it was so late but it was more likely to have been on the same day, 21 June. *Friedrich der Große* was *Nürnberg*'s next ship in line, so she must have received the orders around the same time.

After *Westcott*'s men had tried – unsuccessfully – to save the *Hindenburg*, they went on to tackle the *Nürnberg*. The first thing they did was to tear down the Imperial ensign. The men had already left her. Two cutters had been lowered and they were on their way over to Cava island. However, en route, gunfire from the drifter *Clonsin* successfully held them at bay while HMS *Walpole*'s crew cut the light cruiser's anchor cable. Once *Walpole* (F.15) joined the 'fray', she forced the crew back on to their ship after, following orders from her commander, Lt Commander Charles Naylor, she had fired on deserting crews and sank their boats. The enemy ship was then left. The British 'allowed her to drift on shore', on to the shingle beaches 'directly below' Tulloch's family on the island of Cava's western shoreline.[527]

Beached
SMS *Frankfurt*

The boarding parties from *Royal Sovereign* and *Wessex* (F.32) found fourteen German officers and men still on board the light cruiser *Frankfurt*.

From *Wessex*, a boarding party, including a repair specialist (Leckbe-dienungsmaat, or leak management mate), armed with all the equipment they needed went aboard. With them, they had hammers, crowbars, saws, planks (*'hämmern, brechstange, sägen, bohlen'*).[528] They were able to see first-hand how much thought had obviously gone into the planning but also to take anything they wanted. Neitzlel, the Obermachinistmaat who wrote the scuttle report, said that anything that wasn't nailed down (*'nagelfest'*) was stolen: ships' clocks, oil skins, weather gear, spanners, signal flags. You only have to look on the shelves of the Stromness museum to get the idea.

Frankfurt lay deep in the water. The water came right up to within two hands' width of the portholes (*'etwa noch 2 Handbreit unterkannte der Seitefenster im Wasser'*).[529] Despite these precautions, she was successfully towed to Smoogro Bay by the *Wessex*. It did not start out well. The first steel line snapped and it was only on the second attempt that the ship started to inch forward off the bottom (*'Langsam kam die 'Frankfurt' in Bewegung'*). There she was 'grounded in 3½ fathoms of water amidships before sinking' with help from two trawlers, one of which was the *Clonsin*.[530]

The German crew of fourteen were taken off by men from the *Royal Sovereign*, who were manning a small cargo ship (*'ein kleiner Frachtdampfer von ca. 80–100t. Ladenfahigkeit'*). A large number of British sailors came with them, armed with all sorts of tools to strip off whatever else they could – empty bags, wire pliers, tin snips and crowbars. (*'leeren Beuteln, Drahtzang, Blechscheren und Brecheisen'*).[531]

Neitzlel said that he and his men did a lot of standing about as the English tried to organise themselves. At one point, he'd asked for something to drink and was given a mug of coffee by one of the drifter skippers. No sooner had he started to warm up, than a rather less well-meaning sergeant ripped the mug from his hands and tossed the contents over the side.

★   ★   ★

In Gutter Sound, out of sight from Reuter's initial signal from *Emden*, the German destroyers carried out Reuter's orders as soon as received.

Before the *Flying Kestrel* came by, 'we had been quiet, cleaning ship on Saturday morning', said Ruge.[532] He'd been below decks repacking his kit bag (*Gefechtskoffer*) and came up on deck just as a British drifter came by dropping off newspapers. It seems that Reuter's critical signal was not actually seen from the *S.65*. Ruge commented that it was roughly when *the Flying Kestrel* passed by that, '... a few minutes later we saw men in one of the battle-cruisers running – it had never happened before – and so we looked at the flagship and she flew the signal for scuttling the Fleet.'[533]

It is odd he said this; the ships had been specifically warned to keep a sharp lookout for signals coming from the *Emden*.

One of the guard ships, the *Westcott*, was ideally placed alongside the German destroyer, B.109, on a buoy in Gutter Sound. Her boilers were already ready for full steam. A German sailor was spotted going up the mast of a destroyer in the sound and hooking up the Imperial flag. 'There was some dubiety as to the identity of the flag, as some thought it was only a certain signal flag.'[534] Almost the same moment a drifter came past telling them to go back as German ships were starting to sink. One ship 'beyond the north point' of Cava could be seen sinking.

On board, a sub lieutenant thought he saw a German destroyer sinking and immediately shouted a warning through the hatch into the wardroom. It was crowded with officers drinking their pre-lunch Pink Gins. They promptly told him to shut up: 'Don't talk such tripe,' shouted the skipper, Lieutenant Charles R Peplow.[535] The self-assured smirks and guffaws quickly disappeared when they saw the sheer scale of what was going on outside and what they now faced. It was immediately obvious: all German ships were flying their colours. An urgent message was immediately signalled to Vice Admiral Fremantle.

Peplow's crew set out to try and prevent the larger ships going down while 'an excellent and bellicose Petty Officer with orders to beach as many destroyers as possible by parting their cables and allowing the wind to drift them ashore' was left in the ship's skiff. He succeeded in getting eight ashore.*

Peggy Gibson remembered the *Flying Kestrel* passing between two lines of German destroyers in the Gutter Sound, 'an avenue' she called it, and that the German ships 'lay in pairs'. They passed 'so near that we could read their names and see the men on them'.[536] It continued on, remembered Gibson, when a message came saying that the British ships had left and that they would 'only see HMS *Victoria* (sic) which was the hospital ship at that time and that they would go alongside her but they would only see the German Fleet'.[537] It was well after they had passed all the paired-up destroyers that a trawler came up and a man shouted across using a megaphone that the German fleet was sinking. They were told to 'Make for the *Victorious*' (her memory was failing a little and she mistakenly called the ship the *Victoria*).[538]

Captain Davies decided to go on and, as a result, they had 'the most spectacular view of the Fleet sinking'.[539]

One of the first destroyers to go down – Ruge stated it was 'the first of the 50 destroyers' – was *B.112*, the destroyer to which the young officer's own *B.110* was moored.[540] He stayed aboard as long as he could, making sure everyone was off. Breakfast was still on the stove, 'meatballs sizzling in the big pan' and 'as he passed, each man took some'.[541]

---

* *The Sinking of the German Fleet in Scapa Flow 1919*. Admiral Sir Henry McCall correspondence to Arthur J Marder, UCI.

Forty-five minutes after starting the scuttle, that is around 1215, the torpedo boat was down so far that the men 'could comfortably step into the cutter from the port side of the stern upper deck'.[542] Normally, the stern upper deck would have been 2m above the water. Fifty-eight men crammed into four cutters with all their belongings. It was a tight fit.

B.112 gave 'a brief lurch to port' dragging a seemingly reluctant B.110, tied up to her port side, with her. 'Masts, funnels and superstructure were torn off' as B.112 went down.[543] B.110 followed, capsizing to starboard, but would not sink immediately. She had come to a rest on her 'mooring partner', B.112. As a result, she rested on an even keel while the captain, Mensche, was standing at her stern till the last moment. Before leaving B.110, he gave a small speech to his men telling them what they had done that day was for their country's good. Eventually B.110 slipped off, metal groaning and screeching, and disappeared. It was as though she finally accepted her fate and just gave up clinging to life. Mensche, Ruge and the men rowed their way towards Fara island. With Ruge was his beloved guitar.

On the way, they went close by S.138, Cordes' flotilla leader boat. The staff surgeon (stabarzt) was getting into a cutter, and like him taking the guitar, was clutching 'his trumpet under his arm'.[544]

As soon as he was able, Rear Admiral Prendergast – along with the German torpedo boat commander of S.54, Kapitänleutnant Steiner – boarded some of the destroyers to evaluate the situation for himself.* Steiner's statement that he told Prendergast that they had been 'ready for the last month' was probably true as Cordes had taken it upon himself to start planning the torpedo boats' scuttling without knowing what Reuter was working on, or even telling him what he was doing.

Prendergast made a point of saying that he had ordered the colours struck on any German boat that was flying them. As a result, he reported, 'very few German ships went down with their colours flying'. It was a pretty small victory compared to the successful sinking and an odd prioritisation of tasks.[545]

S.65 and S.138 were going down. The drifter Ramna tried frantically to intervene to prevent the collection of small cutters in which Ruge's group rowed nearby from getting to Fara. The firing was haphazard. ('...unter Feuer genommen, aber...glücklicherweiser was der Blutdurst größer als der

---

* Steiner is described as the German Flotilla Maintenance Commander in Bowman (p. 19). Prendergast's report (ADM 116/2074) merely said that he was 'the German officer in command of the division of destroyers'.

Schießkunst').[546] Roughly translated, 'though the British might have been pretty bloodthirsty, luckily they couldn't shoot worth a damn'. It looked as though there were civilians on board shooting but this may have easily been officers who had rushed on board without having had time to change. *Ramna* headed back to the *S.138*. Cordes was unimpressed and waved them off, despite the British officer bellowing insults across the water:

> There was no question of anyone being in charge. They shot wildly all around, aimed at one lifeboat, then left off the next minute in order to haul down and trample the war ensign of a boat sinking in the vicinity, or indiscriminately to collect 'souvenirs' from the cabins and below decks, to steal and to pillage.[547]

The destroyers more often than not went down by the stern and 'as the after-part of the ship disappeared, the bows and a hundred feet or more of the hull, projected sheer from the sea, looking like some huge whale leaping through space'.[548] This is certainly what the farmhand, Thomson, had thought. And, from where he was working on Lyness, William Spence could see into Gutter Sound. Listening to the gunfire, he watched as many went down.

Then *B.109* followed, although another 2nd Flotilla boat, *B.111*, did not. Her bilges had probably blocked. She floated off her mooring buoy (J.3) and drifted a little south. She could be identified easily as 'half her side had been freshly painted'.[549] The newest boat, the *H.145* (actually, technically under the command of the 7th Flotilla) sank and then came back up again to show her masts.

There were other violent confrontations with the British. The British destroyer *Spenser* (F.90) pulled in beside *S.132* and *V.43*. Both were sinking fast.

On *S.132* the British officer commanding the destroyer group, Captain McLean, was threatening the German flotilla commander, Kapitänleutnant Oskar Wehr. The British officer said that he would shoot any or all Germans should they refuse his orders to stop the boat from sinking. The German sailors were lined up and a Royal Marine firing squad faced them but then – miraculously – nothing came off it after he gave 'devilishly sounding, earnestly meant, and unmistakable orders to his officers'.[550] It turned out to be a bluff.

Another British officer, however, then unholstered his pistol and put it to the German officer's head. 'He pulled the trigger...and missed. In the heat of the moment the barrel had slipped and the officer survived with a bad cut, muzzle-blast burns and a loud ringing in his ears.'[551] Sub Lieutenant Lampe had been an extremely lucky man.

The threats by the British on *S.132* had the desired effect 'of his ordering the inlets to be shut, and steam to be raised on *S.132*. *S.132* was saved but *V.43* had later to be beached'.[552]

A petty officer in a lifeboat belonging to *V.127* was shot and severely wounded as he and his crewmates tried to row ashore. Another man, a warrant officer, had received a grazing wound on his leg.* The whole cutter crew had been forced back on to one of the other sinking destroyers and ordered to close up her valves. There was not that much they could do but the petty officer eventually died from his stomach wounds. The commander of the *Sandhurst* (C.9) only sent help two hours after it had initially been requested. This might sound callous but then one has to imagine the sheer panic and pandemonium that must have been taking place.

Some of the most violent confrontations were in Gutter Sound, where *Vega* and *Vesper* (F.39) attempted to restore order among the south-ernmost torpedo boats, those of the 6th Flotilla. 'Exactly half the casualties, four dead and eight wounded, incurred during the scuttling' were among this flotilla's crews.[553] Thirteen men from *V.126* were in a cutter with Leutnant Zaeschmar. Three were killed: Friedrich Beike, Wilhelm Markgraf and Gustav Pankrath. Three more were wounded. The fourth to be killed was Karl Funk, a stoker from *V.127*. He was severely wounded in the stomach and is probably the sailor that Ruge referred to as being left out to die by the crew on *Victorious* after they had been told about his condition.

It was not clear where some of the schoolchildren had seen men being shot. It was most likely here: Rosetta Groundwater said she 'definitely' saw 'one man shot.† He dropped right out of the stern of the boat.' Kitty Watt also saw one of the sailors killed.[554]

Prendergast soon took the decision that the ships should be beached rather than an attempt made to close sea-cocks. Furthermore he 'had rightly decided that it was useless to waste the services of his small craft on the large German ships and concentrated his efforts on the destroyers'.[555] Between his own efforts – and those of Captain Salls from the *Sandhurst* – a significant number of German destroyers were successfully beached.

* Ruge, p. 116.
† Miss Rosetta Groundwater was a former provost of Stromness. She appeared in *Yesterday's Witness* on BBC 2 along with Friedrich Ruge and two other witnesses, Captain RCV Scott and WG Waterson. The former had been a midshipman, the latter a boy seaman, during the scuttle (*The Press and Journal*, 1 June 1970).

BEACHING GERMAN DESTROYERS

On Fara: *S.31. S.54, V.82, S.60, V.80, S.137, V.81, V.73,* and *G.89. V.44* on south-west corner following *Sandhurst's* orders.[556]

On Hoy: *V.128, V.127, V.125, V.46* and *V.126* following *Sandhurst's* orders. Prendergast's report also mentions the *V.43.*

In Mill Bay: *V.100. G.102* was 'towed to anchorage in Mill Bay. Tug tried to keep her afloat with two 6" pumps. Being unable to prevent the water from rising, she was beached at 11 p.m.'

On Rysa island: *V.83* and *G.92,* the latter after being towed in by one of the early arriving destroyers sent ahead of the 1st Battle Squadron, the *Winchelsea.*

Sources: Much of the detail comes from Rear Admiral Prendergast's report to Fremantle (see ADM 116/2074 p. 3).

★   ★   ★

The scuttle 'was the greatest act of naval self-immolation ever known, truly Wagnerian in its magnitude'. It was also supremely ironic that 'the problem of what to do with the German fleet had now been solved by the Germans themselves'.[557] Bill Hewison, concluded that: 'In all its colourful history, and it's had plenty, Scapa Flow had never seen anything that could equal this cataclysmic event. And it never has since, not even in World War Two.'[558]

The British did manage to save a few ships by beaching them. *Baden, Frankfurt, Emden, Nürnberg* and nineteen torpedo boats were saved from effectively participating in the last wartime act of the High Seas Fleet.[*] The light cruisers *Frankfurt* and *Emden* were beached in Swanbister Bay along with *Baden.* The other LC – *Nürnberg* – on Cava. Like the *Emden,* she was the second ship bearing a name from an earlier ancestor.[†]

---

[*] *Frankfurt* was saved perhaps by the actions of *Sachosin,* which took four boats in tow (ADM. 116/2074 VADM 1BS 24 June 1919, p. 5).
[†] The first *Nürnberg* had been sunk in the Battle of the Falklands. This 496ft version had only been completed two years earlier in 1916.

It is extremely ironic that two of the last ships with which Reuter was so closely associated, *Baden* and *Emden*, were among those that could not be sunk. It was in his cabin on *Baden* that Reuter had agreed to accept the task of taking Germany's ships into internment and from the bridge of *Emden* that he raised the signal for its destruction.

The British ships that remained with the interned German vessels did what they could. Destroyers, trawlers, drifters and the depot ship *Sandhurst* all joined the effort. *Sandhurst* herself managed to keep four destroyers afloat and beach seven others.[559] She had been right at the very centre of the action. Her Chaplain, the Reverend WB Matthews, later wrote of the 'thrilling experience' of witnessing the scuttle.[560] These two years had been particularly eventful for the cleric.* Not everyone felt that way: 'Ti' David saw the futility and sadness in the whole affair. He knew 'the Huns hadn't got a weapon between them' and that 'the whole thing is a colossal disaster' and that 'we all await the criticism of the public on the British Navy with some misgiving'.[561]

In all, fifty-four ships had gone down, 'under the very eyes of the British Fleet'. *The Orcadian* did not mince words. Only twenty to twenty-five torpedo boats, one battleship and four light cruisers had been beached or remained afloat.[†] In a few hours 'approximately 500,000 tons of warship tonnage with an estimated value of 856 million Marks disappeared into the sea'.[562] The cost – not only for the fleet's construction but also its maintenance – had been staggering.

On the Flow, the contrast from one day to the next was extraordinary. Once packed with ships lined up all around, the Flow now felt empty and silent. Upturned hulls, beached ships and half-sunken wrecks all around. The hulls of three battleship could be easily made out. *Hindenburg* lay silently, instantly recognisable by her funnels.[563] As Ludovic Kennedy, who had spent many years in Scapa, so poetically put it, again it was just 'a place for the wind and the birds'.[564]

---

* Matthews had also witnessed a huge munitions explosion the year before. On the morning of 6 December 1917, a Norwegian vessel, SS *Imo*, was involved in a collision with a French ship, the SS *Mont Blanc*, which had been carrying a cargo of high explosives. A whole district of Halifax, Richmond, was badly damaged by the explosion and 9,000 people were said to have been injured.
† The term 'beached' has an underlying meaning to it that can make the count difficult. Sometimes, it is used by contemporary commentators to signify a ship that the Germans did not succeed in sinking. Any boat that had to be salvaged later is not really considered 'beached'. For this reason, Reuter's own count puts the *S.60*, *V.80* (both beached at Fara), *S.132* (floating) and *G.102* (beached but damaged under water) in a separate category from 'sunk at anchor'. The beached light cruisers were *Frankfurt*, *Nürnberg* and *Bremse*. *Emden* was still afloat but I have counted her as 'beached' for this exercise.

The silence was only broken, apparently, by a sudden, shattering explosion from one of the sunken battleships. An eyewitness said it was accompanied by 'a pillar of water a large quantity of debris several hundred feet'.[565]

Scapa had become the very centre of the world's attention as tense negotiations carried on in Paris.

The fear for the children that had been on the *Flying Kestrel* must have been palpable. Being ashore, not being able to do anything, hearing the mix of rattling machine-gun fire and single rifle shots echo across the Flow must have been terrifying for any parent stuck on the jetty. The piers were packed solid – 'every pier' said Peggie Gibson – when the *Flying Kestrel* made it back.[566]

There was genuine cause for concern. Any sailor knew the dangers of being sucked under by a sinking ship. Kitty Tait's brother was in the navy and visiting. 'He was lying in bed and of course they were all up the wall about us down there – frightened we were going to be pulled under with the suction of the ships going down.'[567] Despite the sheer pandemonium of the experience, some – like Rosetta Groundwater – continued to put on a brave face, 'No, I don't think anybody was afraid, just wide-eyed wonder. That about explains it.'[568]

There were other eyewitnesses on the waters that day. One was a small fishing boat, *Betty*, based out of Wick that had been 2 miles off the Pentland Skerries. She'd seen Fremantle's squadron heading south earlier in the morning and now they decided not to go back to Wick with their catch. Instead, they'd headed towards Scapa. They arrived right in the middle of many of the ships going down and passed close by the upturned hull of at least one destroyer.

Like Fremantle, who privately, shared that admiration, Gibson could not help herself:

> They had all raised their flags to top mast. Every ship had its flag flying when they were scuttled. I think that was a wonderful action for them. After all it was their Fleet. And although they had been defeated, they were to go down with flags flying.[569]

9

CAPTIVITY
AND REPATRIATION

T HE SCENE ON the Flow had been one of utter chaos. Some of that
chaos could have been avoided. Little thought had been put into how
a scuttle would have been dealt with, *in practical terms*. Even mooring the
larger ships in shallower water would have been sensible. Maybe saving
the ships might always have been impossible, but the round-up of German
sailors seemed completely haphazard and chaotic.

Boats, brimming with sailors, were stopped, fired upon and then left
to fend for themselves. All commands were spoken in English and there
was little or no thought given, for example, to what the most important
commands might have been on such an occasion. *Brummer's* sailors were
eventually picked up by a second drifter, hauled aboard and placed in the
hold. Slowly, boats from other ships were consolidated: those from
Friedrich der Große, *Köln* and *Markgraf* all now lay alongside an individual
drifter. Leaving their luggage in the boats, the men came aboard in groups
of twenty and, after an hour or so, they were then taken over to *Revenge*.

As soon as they could, the British started rounding up the German
crews. Around 1330 boatloads started to be assembled by the *Victorious*
and *Sandhurst*, where armed guards kept watch over them on the quarter
deck. Prendergast 'personally concerned himself with the welfare of the
Germans'.[570] They ran out of space almost immediately and boats were
then ordered to be moored up alongside instead. The children from the
Flying Kestrel also made it back to the *Victorious*. There they saw that 'they
were collecting the captains and the officers of the German ships and we
could see them all in a boat with sailors with guns trained on them'.

Many of the officers were 'dressed in their best uniforms', while
'personal belongings did not show indications of being packed in a hurry'.[571]
To Prendergast, in *Victorious*, it seemed that much preparation had gone
into the planning. He had heard this from one of the torpedo boat officers.
Fremantle, however, writing a day later, came to the opposite conclusion:

The view that the order was entirely unexpected is borne out by the facts of no sabotage having taken place in the ships, other than that required to ensure their rapid sinking, the condition of officers' cabins and men's living spaces which showed that trunks and bags had been packed in a great hurry, and that in some ships the mid-day meal was found untouched on the tables.[572]

It is not surprising that the two explanations were at odds. Reuter had told his officers to keep the scuttling planning limited to only those men they trusted. The actual scuttling was well-planned and executed even if the evacuation of some individual ships had been extremely hurried.

On the islands of Cava and Little Rysa, the British tried to organise the exhausted but jubilant sailors. Many were taken straight to the battleships when they arrived back at Scapa. Slowly the sailors were rounded up and small boat convoys snaked back and forth out to the huge ships.

In Orkney newspaper reports it was usually stated that the Germans had been called upon to surrender and had refused: 'they would not surrender when called upon to do so' or that they had been 'trying to effect their escape seaward'.[573] The *Orkney Herald* did add in the same article, significantly, that 'the naval authorities in Longhope are very reticent in giving any details for publication'.

Reuter went looking for a British officer with whom he could try to negotiate a ceasefire. He wasn't able to find anyone senior enough as the ranking British officer was out trying to bring some order to the chaos. After a junior officer was not able to help, he got back on the drifter intending to go back to the *Emden*. Instead, he was run aground off the Cava shoreline and when he finally managed to refloat – around 1330 – the drifter he was on was nearly hit by the collapsing masts of the *Große Kurfürst* as they went close by the ship after it rose sharply before falling back on to her port side.

On Fara, Ruge and some of his men sat on the warm rocks eating corned beef from a 5kg tin they had found on one of the cutters. Corned beef 'had never been seen before in Scapa Flow' and it was enjoyed to the fullest.[574] They had not been ashore for 230 days.* One of his men came up to him holding an old atlas that Ruge had lent him. Despite the scuttle, he

* That being the case, Ruge must have been aboard *B.110* for twenty-one days prior to arriving in Scapa Flow.

brought it with him to fulfil the simple duty of returning Ruge's property. Ruge left the small red-leather-bound *Meyer's* pocket atlas on a rock.

Ruge's men reboarded their boats and rowed over to the *Sandhurst*. As they rowed back, they passed *B.111*, still very much afloat, and *G.102* moored to the north-west on the Q-series buoys. By 1630 they were back on the cutters a third time, this time to be taken over the British battleships where all the German sailors were being consolidated. On the way, they passed back through the torpedo boat lines and, finally by now, *B.111* had sunk. They also saw *Hindenburg*, lying at a list of 25 to 30°, surrounded by British destroyers and drifters trying to pull her ashore. And *Baden*, resting on her hull, her funnels and bridge clear of the water. When they finally arrived at *Resolution*, they would then join other sailors from *Kaiser*, *Nürnberg* and *von der Tann*.

At first, the prisoners were treated as any shipwrecked sailors would have expected. It was clear that the 'usual formalities' were not going to be employed but the atmosphere was 'not unfriendly'. The searches were not aggressive and 'articles were expressly recognised as our private property'.[575] Everyone was given 'tea and white bread and jam'. The sailors came aboard the British ships from their own grey, rusting hulks. The contrast could not have been stronger. Here 'the deck surfaces were scrubbed snow-white, the brass shone and the paint was in perfect condition'.[576] But, 'loaded with extraordinary baggage, such as puppies, musical instruments, kitbags and home-made boxes' the groups of German sailors were a rag-tag affair.[577]

That there was also tension was inevitable. Reading through the German reports from each of the ships, one is struck by the descriptions of the heavy-handedness of the guards and the widespread pilfering of personal possessions.[*] Ruge had put down his coat and beloved guitar on a 'low ventilation head' and had been told sharply to remove it, a British officer 'putting his foot on the guitar and [throwing] the coat on the deck'.[578] When a chief petty officer from the 4th Torpedo Flotilla confronted the man, he had his ankles kicked hard. Ruge listened while Mensche translated what was being said and then defended their actions. *Kaiserin's* Möckel, an Obermachinistmaat, mentioned a similar event on

---

[*] In the *Bundesarchiv* are the reports collected under the title of *Serlbsversenkungsberichte*, scuttling reports. They are from almost all the ships – the capital ships including *Derfflinger*, *König* and *Seydlitz*, each of the light cruisers and then grouped together by flotilla for the torpedo boats. I was struck by how few people seemed to have read the reports. Among four of five names, I recognised two. Those of Daniel Krause and of Friedrich Ruge. Nobody else seemed to have touched them.

Royal Oak where a junior officer – he mentioned he had two stripes, so it would have been a lieutenant – struck one of *Kaiserin*'s men on the back, seemingly without any reason (*'auf nichtssagenden Gründen'*).[579]

The atmosphere started to deteriorate. What had at first been the exception now became the norm. In fact, Fremantle gave express orders to the effect that customary formalities were to be dropped immediately and the Germans henceforth to be treated as prisoners of war. The German scuttle reports (*Selbstversenkungsberichte*) that were prepared by each ship share too many similarities for them not to have been prepared without some sort of outline or briefing: The structure of each is almost identical, some of the wording the same, the reporting of petty theft ridiculously legalistic and the tone strongly nationalistic. But they also give an idea of how the day deteriorated through many small anecdotes.

Brummer's report talked of the pilfering: an officer came over to collect things, a bag in hand (*'mit einem Beutel in der Hand'*). All the men's knives and razors were bagged. That was completely understandable. What was not were the personal objects. Obermatrose Kurt Lesne had all his photographs stolen.[580] Others, binoculars, scissors, watches, pocketknives. Even in the sickbay, the German sailors' property was not safe. It was no longer surprising to open your case and find nothing inside. A senior machinist, Obermachinistmaat Peinemann, went too close to the rail and was clubbed over the head with a rifle butt (*'kam der Persinnig zu nahe und wurde mit den Gewehr kolben an den Kopf geschlagen'*. The prisoners were prodded with bayoneted rifles.

Just after 1600, Reuter finally gave himself up and was taken aboard Fremantle's flagship, *Revenge*. As he 'climbed wearily over the side there was a deadly hush aboard'. One can imagine the scene. The meeting of the two admirals – Fremantle in all his trappings, greeted Reuter 'dishevelled, wet and white as a sheet' with dripping sarcasm: 'I presume you have come to surrender.'[581] Nothing more was said except for Reuter's request that he be accompanied by his flag lieutenant to be accepted. The meeting was over in seconds. Fremantle had been 'hissing' the words as he spoke said a young officer, Hugh David, who was a 'few feet behind Reuter and heard every word'.*

It was not until the evening that the men were even given water, let alone food. Nothing warm, just white bread and cold corned beef. Most

---

* Hugh David (Edward Hugh Markham David, known familiarly as 'Ti', 1901–57) joined the Royal Navy in 1916 and served as a sub lieutenant in HMS *Revenge*. Some of Hugh's letters were kindly provided by his daughter, Hillary Chiswell Jones.

did not even get corned beef. Just a mug of cocoa (described as a very weak, watery cocoa: *Wassercacao*).[582] That night was hard. Officers slept on cocoa matting in some of the 6in gun casemates. At around 0500 Ruge and his men were woken up. They had to transfer off *Resolution* on to the *Royal Oak*. *Resolution* was to stay up in Scapa 'to direct the salvage work on the *Baden* and the cruisers which had not been sunk', while the others were to make their way south to Rosyth.[583]

The next day, 22 June, at 0600, after a meagre breakfast of 'thin cocoa and hard tack', the British ships weighed anchor and set sail for Cromarty Firth. After the months of perpetual sameness in the Flow, it was exhilarating to be at sea again, feeling the freshness of the wind and salt air. Among the Germans there was a sense of duty accomplished: denying the British their fleet. However, even if 'morale was excellent', the German crews who arrived around midday were exhausted and cold.[584] The adrenalin that got them through the previous day had long worn off. Ruge only remembered the restless night spent on the hard, cold steel of a British ship. Fleeting sleep was interrupted by their own dog, Tommy, which kept them awake until 0200.

Before they landed, British naval officers went through their belongings. It was just another opportunity to pilfer: books, photos, letters. Some personal belongings were simply thrown overboard. Today, we have little left of these gems that could have been the source of so many rich and varied stories. Once the ships were at anchor off Invergordon, the men were allowed to get their belongings. If they had not already been prepared for it, they were in for a rude shock. Almost everything had been pilfered and valued mementoes stolen. Ruge lost his old box but managed to keep his kitbag. He got the box back later and even found some of his photos from Scapa, including the one that showed him playing his guitar on the deck of *B.110*, his commander sitting beside him, the men sitting around, listening intently, but without many smiles. He had hidden them behind a rather dour-looking family portrait. Even Reuter's admiral's greatcoat had gone missing. One of his staff officers had brought it over to the *Royal Oak* for him. After vigorous complaints, the ship was searched and some items returned but most remained hidden safely stowed away in the hands of new owners.

As they came into the Firth, Cromarty was passed to the south. To the north of the enclosing pincer of land lay their first new home – although they did not know it yet – Nigg.

Fremantle assembled Reuter with his officers on the deck of the

Revenge, surrounded by a marine guard. Ruge and his group could see them from one of *Royal Oak*'s drifters as it passed close by *Revenge,* transferring prisoners to land. Fremantle was holding something in his hands and addressing the two lines of assembled German officers, held back by sentries with fixed bayonets that 'glistened' in the harsh sunlight. A few yards from the stern flag, Reuter stood 'bolt upright' with his chief of staff, Fregattenkapitän Oldekop, and his flag lieutenant, Oberleutnant zur See Schilling, standing behind him.[585]

Fremantle accused the Germans of a breach 'in faith and honour' in what Ludovic Kennedy later generously described as a 'pompous speech'.[586] It was a speech written for the press (a correspondent from *The Times* was present) and reeked of hypocrisy given Fremantle's own intentions to seize the ships that same night – with full knowledge of the extension of the peace signing deadline.

Admiral von Reuter: I cannot permit you and your officers to leave naval custody without expressing to you my sense of the manner in which you have violated common honour and the honourable traditions of seamen of all nations. With an armistice in full operation you recommenced hostilities without notice by hoisting the German flag in the interned ships and proceeding to sink and destroy them. You have informed my interpreter that you considered the Armistice had terminated. You had no justification whatever for that assumption. You would have been informed by me of the termination of the Armistice and whether the representatives of your nation had or had not signed the Treaty of Peace. Indeed, letters in readiness to send to you to that effect as soon as I had received official intimation from my Government were written and signed. Further, can you possibly suppose that my squadron would have been out of harbour at the moment of the termination of the Armistice? By your conduct you have added one more to the breaches of faith and honour of which Germany has been guilty in this war. Begun with a breach of military honour in the invasion of Belgium, it bids fair to terminate with a breach of naval honour. You have proved to the few who doubted it that the word of the New Germany is no more to be trusted than that of the old. What opinion your country will form of your action I do not know. I can only express what I believe to be the opinion of the British

Navy, and indeed of all seamen except those of your nation. I now transfer you to the custody of the British military authorities as prisoners of war guilty of a flagrant violation of Armistice.[587]

'Tell your Admiral', Reuter replied, 'that I cannot accept the purport of his words and that my views do not accord with his.' He ended by saying something with which almost all silently empathised: that 'any English naval officer placed as I was would have acted in the same way' and that it should be understood that he 'alone carried the responsibility'. But he also added that he had not acted on orders from Germany, a claim that looks increasingly less likely with time.*

He specifically addressed the issue of his being kept in the dark about the Armistice negotiations. Ruge paraphrased his reply:

The extension of the Armistice had not been communicated to him. According to the official reports in the British press, the German Government had been given an ultimatum which expired at midday on 21 June. The Government had clearly stated that it could not sign. With that, the state of war again existed. As Senior Naval Officer, he was obliged not to let the ships fall into enemy hands. Scuttling was the only way left open to him.[588]

Reuter had worked under the assumption that no government in Germany could accept the humiliatingly aggressive terms made public by the Allies on 7 May. For him, it meant that renewed hostilities were inevitable.

Fremantle was constrained in what he said publicly. Privately his feelings were very different: 'I could not resist feeling some sympathy for Reuter, who had preserved his dignity when placed against his will in a highly unpleasant and invidious position.'[589] Fremantle had held the German admiral in high esteem, saying that he 'was a man who kept his word and never knowingly infringed the conditions of internment except in the single significant case'.[590] In his report of 24 June, he said that British orders had always been carried out 'punctually' by Reuter and that his own 'requirements had been fully complied with'.[591]

Back up in Scapa, a further lone German destroyer came into the Flow during the day. It was *B.98*, the proud 2nd Flotilla leader at Jutland,

---

* Kitty Tait's sailor brother echoed the point. He turned to his mother, saying 'Yes mother, if that had been the British you would have said – "What brave men!".' (Ferguson, p. 75).

now reduced to the menial task of delivering the fleet's mail.* When they had set out from Wilhelmshaven, they had known nothing about the scuttle. They were met by *Westcott* out at sea and were taken by a 'roundabout route' avoiding the main anchorage.[592] The reason was straightforward: *Westcott*'s orders, de Courcy-Ireland explained, were to make sure she did not scuttle like the rest of the fleet: 'It was felt that as soon as she grasped what had happened, she would scuttle herself in an awkward spot.'[593]

They were further taken by surprise when the British aggressively boarded and took them prisoner. Heugstenberg, her commanding officer, protested that they had entered the Flow 'under the white flag and had not committed a breach of the conditions appertaining to the bearing of the white flag'.[†] The British counter was rather extraordinary. They maintained that 'a state of war existed' since the scuttle but then limited that condition to only apply 'in the Flow'.

At least sixteen or so unarmed German sailors were shot and wounded in the struggle to get away from the sinking ships.[‡] Eight died of wounds received on the day of the scuttle. Their bodies lie in a corner of the Lyness naval cemetery on Hoy, overlooking the Flow. It is a desolate place but beautifully cared for by the Commonwealth War Graves Commission.

Each grave is marked by a simple gravestone, in the German military style.[§] They only record the name and date of death, 21·6.16. W. Schumann,

* Mail and supplies were delivered by SMS *Regensberg* and SMS *Konigsberg* in addition to two torpedo boats, *B.97* and *B.98*. In Reuter's Freiburg documentation he detailed the frequency and dates of the visits.
† Heugstenberg's protest against seizure and imprisonment seemed to have been supported by the fleet's own legal department saying: 'there would not be any justification for the detention of the crew or the ship in retaliation for the act of the Germans in sinking their Fleet'. In addition to *B.98*, the British also seized the German transport steamer *Dollart*.
‡ A German report in Germany (*Nordwoche*, 20 June 1969, Arnim von Manikowksy) put the number as high as twenty-one wounded.
§ The Fleet pastor, Ronnenberger, had wanted to erect a memorial stone to other sailors who had died while in Scapa Flow. A total of 1,500 marks was raised among the crews and Ronnenberger bought a headstone on a trip back to Germany. It was lost when the ships went down in the Flow. Maybe, one day, it will be found again.
¶ The spelling of the name of the sailor shot aboard HMS *Resolution* is not clear. It was 'Evertsberg' in Krause (p. 310), Ruge (p. 163) as well as in the German War Graves documentation. The British death certificate spells it differently, as 'Eversberg'. The recommendation of the *Volksbund Deutsche Kriegsgräberfürsorge e.V.* was originally to follow the spelling in the official Lyness German Graves list and not the death certificate but the overwhelming evidence seems to be that the German literature had it wrong and that his name was Eversberg. Kevin Heath's local research concluded that if the sailor's service number was correct (363/18 IWD), so too would more than likely be his name.

Wilhelm Markgraf, Friedrich Beike, Gustav Pankrath, Karl Funk, Hans Hesse, Kuno Eversberg and Hermann Dittmann all lie together.¶ Dittmann's headstone already stands out as there is neither a first name nor even an initial. The ninth grave, where Karl Bauer, a stoker on the *Kronprinz Wilhelm*, was laid to rest, is not to be found with his comrades.

Schumann and Wilhelm Markgraf were most likely placed side by side by a simple mistake. Schumann was commander of the battleship, SMS *Markgraf*, and so someone must have thought that anyone also called Markgraf should lie beside him. Hermann Dittmann should have been there instead of Wilhelm Markgraf. Dittmann was by Schumann's side, supposedly, when his commander was shot. Wilhelm Markgraf was not even on a battleship. He was an engineer on a torpedo boat, *V.126*.

Other graves, some from the fleet at the time of the internment are also here – a stoker from SMS *Moltke*, Johannes Thill, Max Aumueller, an engineer from SMS *Nürnberg*, two sailors, Albert Haushälter and Friedrich Bonneder, from the battleship *Prinzregent Luitpold*, and Otto Hinte from SMS *Kaiser*. There are also some German graves from the Second World War of the airmen shot down.

There were reports that some of the German officers had been threatening their own men and that some deaths had resulted. *The Orcadian* wrote that: 'Germans were seen in small boats stabbing each other, and the German officers were frequently observed to be using their revolvers against their men.' It is highly unlikely that anything of the sort actually happened but it certainly might have been the case in an isolated incident if any crews had resisted their officers' orders to scuttle. One witness supposedly 'found a German surgeon lying dead, with three stabs in the back'.⁵⁹⁴ There was no later evidence of that and there is absolutely no evidence that any of the deaths were as a result of German actions.

On one of the eight Scuttle headstones at Lyness is engraved the name of nineteen-year-old Kuno Eversburg. He was an engineering apprentice aboard the light cruiser, SMS *Frankfurt*. His date of death was mistakenly – and in his case, shamefully, given the circumstances and later treatment – engraved on the stone as 21 June.

On the night of 23 June, Eversburg had been aboard HMS *Resolution* as she lay at anchor on the Flow. The ship had stayed behind to co-ordinate the immediate salvage operations on the *Baden*, beached in Swanbister Bay. Kuno Eversburg was killed in cold blood by a twenty-year-old British seaman, James Wooley, who shot him in the back from where he had waited on the boat deck.*

Wooley had been heard by another seaman, Able Seaman John Copeland, to say that he wanted revenge, as 'he'd lost two brothers in the war and was going to have his own back'.[595] The bullet passed right through and was later found lodged in the deck planking.

The way in which Eversberg's death was recalled by a close friend adds to the sense of outrage we can feel today:

> *Ich schaffte meinen Kameraden mit größte Mühe, ohne Hilfe zu erhalten, ins Schiffslazarett. Hier mußte Ich die Beobachtung mache, wie gleichgültig und langsam sich das Lazarett des schwerverwundeten annahm. Mein Kamerad bat mich, sein Bahrgeld in Bewahrung zu nehemen, als er mich das Geld zureichte, faßte mich der Posten ins Genick und schob mich zur Tür hinaus. Einige Stunden später wurde der schwerverletze auf ein englisches Lazarettschiff geschaft.* (Roughly translated: Only with great difficulty, and without any assistance, did I manage to get my comrade to the ship's hospital. There I watched how slowly and indifferently medical treatment was rendered. My friend asked me to look after his money while a guard took me by the scruff of my neck and pushed me out the door. A few hours later the severely injured man was transferred to an English hospital ship.)[596]

According to Dr Bolton, the critically wounded Eversberg only arrived on the hospital ship HMS *Agadir* at 0300 the morning of the 24th. The wound had perforated his bowel in two places and the danger from sepsis was acute: 'the patient's recovery was very doubtful owing to the extensive infection'. However, Eversberg seemed to be on the mend despite the doctor's pessimism:

> For a time he did far better than I expected. He was perfectly conscious and at one time was bright. He asked for food. Vomiting was a troublesome symptom. On the evening of 26

---

* See newspaper reports, *Aberdeen Daily Journal* (10 February 1920) and *The Manchester Guardian* (10 February 1920). Documentation from Leader of Torpedo Boats 7534/V cited by Ruge. The report in *The Western Times* (10 February 1920) said that Wooley was not on one of the turrets, rather he had been on the boat deck. Fremantle contradicted this saying Wooley had been 'behind one of the forward turrets' (*Sinkings*, p. 12).

June a faecal-smelling discharge from the sacral wound was noticed. Eventually a faecal fistula formed. The abdominal wound remained perfectly clean and there was no discharge from it. The fistula was treated in the usual way. Peritonitis supervened. The patient took a turn for the worse and died on 29th June 1919 at 9.40am.[597]

Part of the story of what happened came out in the newspapers in 1920 and was included in Friedrich Ruge's book, *Scapa Flow 1919*.[*]

Bolton recalled his conversations with the wounded sailor: 'He told me that while going to the heads on board the 'Resolution' he had been shot in the back. He told me that he had a sentry on each side of him. He did not say whether one of them fired the shot or not, but I gathered from him that it was not one of the Sentries.'[598]

It is fitting that the erroneous date on his tombstone should have been corrected on the scuttle's centenary.[†]

These nine German sailors were the last fatalities of the First World War. Reuter was not bitter about their deaths. He realised that it was mostly a question of the confusion of the day, 'most of it was prompted by a feeling of panic, anger and impotence'.[599]

Immediate press reports in British newspapers condemned the scuttle in no uncertain terms. *The Times* called it a 'gross act of perfidy' that was a 'breach of a solemn international agreement' as it had been intended to divide up the interned ships among the Allies. The *Glasgow Herald* used the same tone, describing the action as a 'uniquely Teutonic blend of perfidy, cowardice and rank stupidity'. *The Scotsman*, that the act of scuttling such a fleet, worth, according to *The Times*, an 'estimated £60,000,000' 'casts a slur on German faith'. *The Daily Record and Sketch* said that it was nothing short of 'a reminder of the folly of trusting Germans'.

In one report, *The Sunday Post*, wrote off the deaths, saying that 'some

---

[*] See Ruge, pp. 121–122.
[†] Although I am writing this before the centenary, the plans have been agreed. A concerted effort was made by a number of people, myself included, to have the gravestone corrected. In the end, it was through the personal intercession of the president of the Commonwealth Graves Commission, Victoria Wallace, that the corrections were made. Kevin Heath, a local diver, was able to find the actual death certificate that the CWGC had needed. This was despite years of documentation attesting to Eversberg's murder (For example, Ruge, 1969; Krause, 1999; Miller, 2001). Ruge wrote quite extensively about the incident (p. 121) and quoted both the 20 February 1920 reports from *The Manchester Guardian* and *The Daily Telegraph*. There is no reason, in my mind, why it should have taken another fifty years to correct his misdated headstone in Lyness.

of the boats which refused to stop when ordered to so, were fired on, and a small number of Germans were killed and wounded'. Sir Percy Scott, the man who revolutionised gunnery in the Royal Navy, was quoted: 'It serves us right...they have shown that they are not a civilized race, and they never ought to have been treated as such. They are barbarians.'[600]

On the same page, it carried the navy's spin, saying that arrangements were said to have been made to board the German ships, but only on the following Monday after the peace signing at which point they would have passed into Allied control.

The Scotsman was baying for blood. It might have even been aimed at Madden. 'It was well-nigh incredible that care and surveillance should have been interpreted as permitting the leaving of the German ships and crews, at the most critical juncture, entirely to the freedom of their own will... .'[601]

It stood very strongly behind the need for an enquiry: 'How could so astonishing, one is almost tempted to say, ridiculous, a finale to a world-famous transaction have been allowed to come about?'

In Germany, predictably, the reactions depended on which side of the political spectrum you stood:

It was typical that this manly act – the first sign of light on a dark cloud-covered horizon – was enthusiastically received...only by small minority groups, by the Free Corps and the Naval brigades of the Ehrhardt and Loewenfeldt. The great mass of the people was led to condemn the act. Even the majority of the right-wing, middle-class press could only see its consequences from the point of view of foreign policy, which were painted in the darkest colours.[602]

Media reaction was split: liberal and socialist papers condemned the act, conservative papers praised it. To the *Lokalanzeiger*, it was: '...an act of courageous men which is like a refreshing breeze in the sultriness of these oppressive days. However angry the enemies may be at the loss of their booty, we think in their inner hearts the will not be able to deny respect to the brave men who preferred death to disgrace.'

For the *Tageszeitung*: 'Whatever damage the act may inflict on us, the German Navy has again made good to Germany's honour much of that in which it has sinned against it.'[603]

Reinhard Scheer, the commander-in-chief of the German High Seas Fleet at Jutland, told *The New York Times* journalist Cyril Brown that he 'rejoiced' at the news, while Alfred von Tirpitz, the creator of the German

Navy, lamented the service's failure to have played a more important role after 1916: 'The German people do not understand the sea…in the hour of our destiny we did not use our Fleet. Whether our grandsons will be able to take up the task again lies hidden in the darkness of the future.'[604]

On Orkney life went on. The two main newspapers carried on reporting the day-to-day life of the island community with an almost startling sense of distance from the great fleet that had been interned in its waters for seven months. Or, indeed, the tense negotiations that were coming to a head in Versailles. The first edition of the *Orkney Herald* on 25 June did not run with the extraordinary story on its front page. One of the most extraordinary stories in its history was relegated to the second column on page two.

It was the same in *The Orcadian* edition of Thursday, 26 June; the story ran on page four. Hewison rather misleadingly described it as having been 'splashed across four columns of the paper's centre-spread'.[605] The story might have been written that same afternoon but it was hardly breaking news by the time it got to print, five days later. The front page gives no clue of the seismic change that had just occurred. It is the same presentation of summer bargains and sales. On page two, William le Queux's serialised weekly shortened story, *The Riddle of the Ring*, continued. Joan Grey's column on wartime cooking hints was also there. Finally, one column on page four announced 'German Fleet scuttled'.

Days after the scuttle, on 28 June, the First World War officially came to an end. The Treaty of Versailles was signed. A few months later, on 15 September, the navy closed its headquarters in Kirkwall. A new word had entered the English lexicon tied to Scapa Flow: being 'scuppered' became a byword for any ship scuttling.

*   *   *

It was only when Ruge and his fellow sailors arrived at the dockside that they were able to take in the beauty all around them. Finally, they were ashore, among 'real houses and human beings, green trees and shrubs'.[606]

After a short wait, they started on their way. The 3km march should have been almost a stroll, easily within their ability, but many found it tough after having been confined for so long in the Flow. Despite best efforts, physically their condition had deteriorated. Along the way, even though it was forbidden, they chatted with their guards. The war was over, the peace treaty ready to be signed.

The camp was a pretty spartan affair but at least it was on land. Even the empty barracks 'for lack of decoration, exceeded anything we had known in Germany'.[607] The evening meal was hard tack and corned beef, so red that they curiously nicknamed the concoction 'minced policeman'. There were no beds. Two blankets were provided for the men to sleep on the wooden floor. The morning arrived with intense cold but they had all slept well.

Soon Reuter joined the rest of his men in captivity, though there were still a few left up in Scapa, on *Resolution*. A total of 1,744 officers and men made the journey, now as prisoners of war.[608] Reuter was finally able to talk to them more openly, something he had never been able to do in Scapa because of the risk of leaks. The scuttle had been successful but now they had to wait out the return to Germany.

Their stay in Nigg was only overnight. That evening, they marched back to the town, direct to the railway station from where they would catch the train south. There were some ugly scenes with locals,

> ...as hostile crowds of off-duty soldiers, women and children spat and jeered at the prisoners. Punches were aimed at them and stones were thrown. Reuter himself was taken under a British military escort to a bank to change money. A boisterous crowd of around 1,000 people quickly formed about him shouting abuse. Reuter was struck on the shoulder by a woman, and a lump of coal thrown from the crowd hit him in the face.[609]

Tommy, the torpedomen's dog, did not come with them this time. The need to avoid the risk of rabies saw him passed into the care of one of the British sergeants. Passing by Loch Ness, Ben Nevis and along the Caledonian Canal, the homesick sailors stared out into the freedom and beauty of Scotland, yearning to be back home. Past Edinburgh, Perth on to Chester and Gobowen. After a journey of more than seventeen hours they finally arrived, exhausted, at 0900 on 24 June. Twenty minutes later they were behind locked gates and barbed wire.

They stayed for another seven months at Parkhall. Had the German sailors realised just how long they would be there, Ruge commented, they 'probably would not have found the new world, which opened up (for us), so varied and interesting'.[610] It started badly. Another baggage inspection ended with Ruge losing most of the few films and photos he had so carefully and, until that point, successfully secreted out of Scapa. Few photos have survived from this time. Ruge's photographic memories, the experiences of a young sub lieutenant on an interned torpedo boat, would have been a priceless heritage.

In fact, German stories have been very difficult to find. Much of the written documentation disappeared at the time of the scuttle itself. There was a story of a 'large bundle' of letters belonging to an officer on the *Dresden* to his sweetheart in Germany to whom he was engaged and another lady, a British woman, in Newton Mearns. They were found on the shoreline off the Banffshire coast in a chest of postcards and photos. The postcards from Germany had been addressed to this officer in 'Scapa Flow, England'.

That night Reuter felt that he was finally able to get a good night's rest. But he had few illusions as he was still under threat. The British did not believe he acted alone and he felt vulnerable to prosecution.

The sailors had to hand in their German money, which was exchanged at new inflationary rates with sterling for which they received a special coinage only valid in the camp. While they were surprised by how much their own currency had devalued, it became even more worrying when they now saw how its value was plummeting as hyper-inflation took hold in Germany, making life for those that they had left behind a daily nightmare. One can only imagine the stress that this caused these men and how helpless they must have felt in fending for their families.

Oswestry was, in fact, a collection of five individual camps housing thousands of prisoners, many of them German Army. They did not have names, merely labels. E1 and E2 were for the NCOs and men, E3, E4 and E5 for officers. The men were in tents, the officers such as Ruge in barracks. These were large, well-ventilated rooms with more than twenty beds, the two rows separated by long wooden tables and the room warmed by a 'midget iron stove'.[611] There was no privacy and so added interior decoration between the beds, using glued-together newspapers, provided a much-needed screen.

Days and evenings started to drag. There was not much to do but play endless card games such as *Doppelkopf* or *Knochen*. But isolation is the mother of invention. Like all prisoner of war camps, the inmates' creativity was phenomenal. Clearly, there were the usual educational courses in mathematics, languages and sciences.* Football went down very well. Ruge played as a half-back, while the commander of the *von der Tann*,

---

* Ruge's commander, Mensche, gave Spanish lessons, for example, and since his mother came from Scotland could also teach English.

Kapitänleutnant Wollanke, and Hermann Cordes' flag lieutenant, Kapitän-leutnant Schniewind, were both forwards. Both would reach flag rank, Wollanke, a rear admiral and Schniewind, a full admiral. Camp E.5 also had another great footballer asset: Ritter von Halt would become head of the German Sports Authority.

One enterprising officer, Karl Käse, organised 'Käse's Tour of Berlin'. The barrack hut's tables and benches would be pulled together to resemble the top deck of an open-air bus. Käse would then conduct an imaginary guided tour of the great city. 'It was part of the game to look precisely in the direction where Karl pointed with his arm', men cupping their eyes against the equally imaginary glare of the sun as they 'ooghed' and 'aaghed' at the sights.

Despite all these efforts, tension and frustration was high. *The Western Times* reported at the end of November that a strike – reported elsewhere as having lasted three days – was quelled only when 'troops with fixed bayonets' were called in.[612] A note was left by one of the sailors saying that 'Britanny' (sic) should let them go home.*

Towards the end of October, plans to move the prisoners again were put in place, one group at a time. The next destination would be Donnington Hall near Doncaster, west of Nottingham. On 7 November, Ruge's group left for their new 'home'. Arriving late at night, they set off, accompanied by a group of taunting children, around 2100. This time they were not in yet another gloomy barracks; Donnington Hall was an old family home taken over for the war years. Along with six other 'subs', junior lieutenants, Ruge went into a large south-facing room where each bed had its own washstand.

Reuter, the fleet commander, had already been at Donnington for some time, since the summer. In July, he sent back a verbal report to the Admiralty in Berlin through an Oberleutnant zur See Lobsien (which he then followed up in writing a few weeks later). Reuter was building a jus-tification for the actions taken at Scapa: 'The Senior Naval Officer in command in foreign waters, who is without contact with home, has to act in accordance with his own judgement of the best interests of the Reich and the honour of the Navy.'

Furthermore, he insisted, he was acting under the overall understand-ing that: 'German warships must on no account fall into the hands of the enemy in time of war... .' He found himself in an increasingly difficult position. There were those who wanted him tried as a war criminal for

---

* See *The Sunday Post*, 30 November 1919.

his part in the scuttle. Reuter later wrote personally to the prime minister, David Lloyd George, to plead his case when he felt repatriation to Germany was being unfairly delayed.*

In his mind, a resumption of war had seemed inevitable as the terms were so onerous to Germany that there was almost no chance of them being accepted. Indeed, Reuter had even heard that 'the Chancellor had even declared in the National Assembly that he would rather his hand wither than sign the Peace Treaty,' while he himself, as an officer 'was unable to think it was possible that such a Treaty could be signed'.[613] He knew that he was obliged to act with independence and that his duty was to not allow his ships to fall into enemy hands. The only way he could do that – being completely unarmed – was to scuttle the fleet.

He had to be a little wary of what he said openly but, more so, of what he put to paper. 'I gave no more information on my motives. I did not want to be committed to anything in writing.'[614] The situation took an ominous turn when the British were able to open the safe from *Emden* where he had left von Trotha's letter. On 3 December, the Director of Naval Intelligence, Commodore Hugh Sinclair, called a press conference. Based on this letter alone, the British tried to establish a hard case against Reuter; they did not have anything else. Reuter fully expected to be tried, either for a beach of the Armistice, the offence of 'barratry' – a kind of maritime deceit against a ship's owner or master – or even, under direct Allied pressure, by his own countrymen for destroying state property.

It was getting near Christmas and so preparations were made to bring some Yuletide spirit into the rooms. They even made an *Adventskranz*, a Christmas wreath, for the admiral out of holly, sneaking into his rooms when he was out. The day before Christmas, carols were sung while Reuter recited the Christmas story. Even their British guards could not have failed to have been moved by the hushed but evocative strains of '*Stille Nacht*' and '*Oh, du Fröhliche*' drifting through the great house. The few gifts that had made it through the precariousness of the post-war postal system were handed out.

It was not from the guards that the prisoners felt hostility or anger. The Seaforth Highlanders had actually established a good reputation for how they treated the Germans; the bad feeling was more from the civilian population.

With the New Year 1920, good news finally arrived. The Paris Peace Treaty had been ratified on 10 January and Germany had signed her

---

* Letter Rear Admiral von Reuter to David Lloyd George, 23 October 1919.

agreement to the reparations' bill. The last obstacles to their homecoming were gone; they had been away for almost fourteen months. On 19 January, the news finally broke that they would soon be going home. The reaction was thunderous, even if ten more nail-biting days went by before they heard that they had received their final marching orders: to be ready to leave at 0400 on 29 January.

Soon, they were off to Hull, where a 'dirty, run-down transport' ship, the *Lisboa*, was waiting to pick up the roughly eighteen hundred 'forgotten mariners'.[615] The men were restless; they just wanted to be done with the loneliness.

At midday they weighed anchor. The trip over the North Sea was swift, strong currents pulling them back to Germany as if even nature felt their *Heimweh*, their longing for home. So fast was the crossing that their ship had to stand offshore in the Schillig Roads so as to be able to co-ordinate their arrival with the welcome reception that was awaiting.

A German destroyer flotilla had come out to meet them halfway out into the North Sea and they were now escorted back into harbour to an emotional welcome. Every man sailor looked as good as they could. They were greeted with pride and warmth by Admiral von Trotha as the band struck up. He stood, surrounded, in the crowd of sailors and civilians under fluttering pennants. That evening, 31 January, there was a last, large reception for all the men. They had become a brotherhood. From Wilhelmshaven they went on to Kiel.

Some other sailors who had gone to Scapa weren't with them. There were fatalities outside of the scuttle, totally unrelated to war. One of these was probably an Oberheizer from the *Kronprinz Wilhelm*, Jadbusch. A 20 December 1918 a report on his absence noted that he 'fell overboard unnoticed during the night' of 6 December. His body was never found.[616] Another five died during the winter months. At the end of November and early December, two sailors died of influenza (engineer Amueller from *Nürnberg* and stoker Thill from *Moltke*). Their deaths worried the British. Spanish flu was wreaking havoc and there was genuine fear that these two deaths might be the tip of the iceberg.

The March 1920 Kapp putsch, a right-wing attempt to throw back the revolution, put paid to any thoughts of a nice, long leave.* Some of the

---

* It was named the 'Kapp' putsch after one of its two leaders, Wolfgang Kapp. It is also known as the Kapp- Lüttwitz putsch after Walter von Lüttwitz. The abortive Berlin-based coup was supported by some elements of the *Reichswehr* and other right-wing units including the Munsterlager *Friekorps*.

men went into the new, armed units, although Mensche's efforts to form a Scapa Flow section in the Munsterlager Friekorps did not amount to anything.

Reuter had also been allowed to re-join his men after the Allies had unsuccessfully tried to prove that he had acted in full complicity with his senior officers in Germany. The case was never proven. A Naval Section memorandum dated 26 August 1919 and entitled 'Status of Scapa Flow Crews' gave an early warning of the difficulty: 'The Law Officers of the Crown are being consulted as to prosecuting Admiral von Reuter on a criminal charge... . An alternative to a criminal charge is not at once apparent. It would presumably be for a breach of the spirit of the Armistice, and would be full of difficulties.'[617]

He received a hero's welcome and was promoted to vice admiral by the Reich president, Friedrich Ebert.* Instead of being able to enjoy that new seniority, Reuter immediately set to work writing his *Memorandum on British Breaches of International Law Committed Against the Crews of the German Fleet Scuttled in Scapa Flow.*

By the time it was published in February 1921, Reuter was no longer in the navy as there had been nothing for him to do in the new, smaller-sized, force. The defence minister, Geißler, wrote to him in June 1920. It was a sad end to what had been, in many ways, a brilliant career:

> The events which have occurred and the measures thereby made necessary, make it no longer possible, to my regret, to employ the services of Your excellency in the Navy in a position appropriate to your rank. You are therefore respectfully requested to hand in your resignation. I should not like to allow this occasion to pass without expressing thanks to you for the outstanding services you rendered the Fatherland in the Navy. History will record your name as that of a man who contrived to make many German hearts beat faster in the dark days of 1919.[618]

Reuter duly handed in his resignation and went to live initially near Dresden at the Schloß Gauerwitz to write his memories of what had

---

* There is a touching photo, taken on the deck of the *Lisboa* after it had docked in Bremerhaven, of Reuter seen reunited with his wife and two of his three children (*The Graphic*, 28 February 1920). As a sign of the times, opposite the welcoming return of the sailors were photos of German soldiers pulling up Spartakist rifles from a river where they had been hidden. This was just a month after Luxemburg and Leibknecht had been assassinated.

happened on the Flow, *Das Grab des Deutschen Flotte*. The family moved again, in 1923, to Potsdam, where he went into local politics. He died in 1943. He had been on his way to work when he collapsed from a heart attack. He was buried next to one of his sons killed in the early days of the second world war.

★ ★ ★

Back in Scotland, the Royal Navy was obliged to put James Wooley on trial. On 30 January 1920, he was remanded in custody for murder in Edinburgh after a police sergeant had been sent south to escort him north from Chatham. On 9 February – after a twenty- or thirty-minute 'trial', he was acquitted in the packed courtroom. In a contemporary newspaper report he was photographed sitting in the dock. The verdict, in an outcome that was peculiar to Scottish law was unanimous,* 'unproven'.[619]

It was a strange outcome. An amount of £300 was agreed to by the Admiralty as a payment to Eversberg's next of kin 'in consideration of the fact that the man was murdered'.[620]

The courtroom, apparently, broke out in unseemly cheering and clapping. Wooley walked out, being clapped on the back by his friends. 'There was considerable applause in court, and accused was heartily congratulated by his naval friends.' Wooley had had no idea whom he was going to shoot. He had been celebrating the Paris peace signing and was drunk. In short, the hearing had been a travesty and till today, a question mark hangs over its verdict.

---

* See Ruge, p. 121. He explains that in English law a jury is required to come to a verdict of either 'guilty' or 'not guilty' while under Scottish law, if a jury decides that the evidence is not compelling one way or the other, a verdict of 'unproven' may be the outcome. Some recent speculation has fallen on another sailor, Able Seaman Berry, who was on deck at the time and whose evidence brought Wooley to trial. He apparently changed his story to implicate Wooley.

10

SCAPA – AT THE CENTRE OF WORLD ATTENTION

IN A WONDERFULLY succinct written summation of the immediate reactions of the main players, Dutch historian van der Vat wrote: 'The British were publicly indignant and privately relieved; the Germans officially regretful while protesting their innocence, but unofficially proud. The French were furious and vengeful, while the Americans shrugged their shoulders.'[621]

In Paris, the news of the scuttle hit like a thunderclap. The question of how to deal with the defeated German Navy had occupied a disproportionate amount of time and had revealed deep cracks of mistrust between the alliance partners. Now it was all for nought.

Public reaction called for Germany to pay for this act. But before they could talk about how, the Naval Council needed to work on formulating its recommendations. The task was tackled immediately. On 23 June, a group of Allied admirals met at the Ministère de la Marine in Paris to prepare a report for the talks on what additional ships or equipment should be surrendered as compensation.

The next day, the Council of Four were officially informed of the scuttling by Lloyd George. He reminded them that Admiral Benson, supported by Marshal Foch, had strongly argued against demanding the surrender of the German Fleet in favour of internment. They had both feared that the demand would delay an eventual agreement on the Armistice. They may have been right but Lloyd George, nevertheless, took the opportunity to rub their noses in it.

The prime minister defended the British Admiralty's decision not to place guards on German ships and added that this would have been impossible under international law, even in neutral ports. Admiral Knapp thought that the Americans, in the position that the British found themselves, would have.*

---

* Vice Admiral Knapp, USN (1856–1923) was not present at the 24 June discussion but was when the naval terms were finalised. After the Armistice, he was appointed naval attaché in London.

The discussion turned to the question of German government responsibility and whether they could be made to pay more reparations. The importance of establishing national responsibility now became clear. Most of what the Naval Council had looked at it dismissed as being of 'small military value' but it was soon able to identify suitable replacements: five light cruisers (*Graudenz, Königsberg, Pillau, Regensburg* and *Strasburg*), fourteen destroyers from the 1908–09 *Bauprogram* and eight torpedo boats.

Wilson then tried to pacify those countries with weaker navies by suggesting that there were still enough ships to be allocated to them, 'to compensate' them.[622] Clearly, the French were not impressed, even though the British prime minister in the 25 June session supported Wilson's suggestions, saying that there still remained the battleship *Baden*, some light cruisers and a number of destroyers. Clemenceau, however, smelled blood and a chance to turn the screw further. Maybe it is easier to understand his attitude when one realises that he had just received the news that French flags surrendered to the Germans earlier in the war that should have been returned to his nation had, instead, been burned by them. It was now a matter of profound national honour and was felt to have been a 'wanton insult'.[623] At the same time, it seemed that the Germans intended to provoke an insurrection in Upper Silesia, although the orders would be denied.

The French prime minister demanded that Essen, a centre of arms production, be occupied. Lloyd George was inclined to support him but felt that it could not be done before ratification without putting the German signature at risk. And he felt that doing this afterwards would inflame moral opposition. It was out of the same concern that the demand for the German fleet's surrender before the final peace signing was dropped.

In the end, they agreed a common statement be issued to the Germans: 'The destruction of these ships, instead of their preservation, constituted at once a violation of the Armistice, the destruction of the pledge handed over, and an act of gross breach of faith towards the allied and Associated Powers.'*

The scuttle's success had left the British with a very bad taste in their mouth. Some officers took the news almost personally, seeing it both as some kind of act of treachery and as a personal affront. Sir

---

* The changes in the wording are rather fascinating: (1) 'Gross breach of faith' was originally 'insubordination'. Article 31 was also specifically cited. Clemenceau wanted to refer to the flag burning and Wilson to a possible prolongation of the Allied occupation of German territory.

Herbert Richmond wrote that 'the Germans have made the British Navy ridiculous'.

But others in the Royal Navy had a distinctly different take. Although they howled for blood, some were actually relieved. The scuttle had dealt with the thorny issue that had divided the Allies. It got rid of the extremely undesirable repartition of the German fleet with other Allied powers, particularly with the French or the Americans. Rosslyn Wemyss put his feelings this way: 'I look upon the sinking of the German Fleet as a real blessing. It disposes, once and for all, the thorny question of the redistribution of the German ships. When the facts become known, everybody will probably think, like me, "Thank the Lord".'[624]

The convenience of the event had some predictable reactions. In France, some went so far as to accuse the British of having connived with the Germans to avoid their benefiting. In particular, and with justification, they felt aggrieved after the suffering that the war had brought upon their country and after they had forfeited the naval race to the British to take the brunt of the land campaign.

While there seems to be no physical evidence that the British were either in connivance with the Germans in actively planning the scuttle or that they might have encouraged it, what happened on Orkney can only be described as extremely convenient. There is a solid argument that the British had motive and the circumstantial context of the day only added to these suspicions.

The motives were simple: the British wanted to maintain relative numerical supremacy over their allies in naval strength. To neither the French nor American fleet did the British wish to give a leg up and decrease their own ratio of superiority in ships. America might have been less outspoken than the French but some still felt as strongly about the issue. From Wilson down to his Secretary of the Navy and to Benson, the Anglophobic Chief of Naval Operations, the feeling was that this was now America's time.

The timing of the British Battle Squadron's torpedo practice was nothing short of extraordinary. Madden had insisted on Fremantle – despite the latter's protest, albeit rather weak – leaving the Flow on what was agreed by all to be the most sensitive day of the entire seven months of internment. Of all the 220 or so days to choose from, 21 June was not a good date to pick.

The American historian Arthur Marder was even told that one ship's captain, John Luce of HMS *Ramillies*, went as far as warning Fremantle that if they went out on exercise 'he would be likely to find no German ships afloat when he got back'.*

There is substantial documentation to suggest that this was a completely avoidable situation. Fremantle – and before him all the previous naval officers who held his position at Scapa, Leveson, Keyes and Oliver – had all said that the only way they could avoid an inevitable German scuttle was to seize the German ships as soon as was practicable. Madden not only signed off on their plans of seizure, he also specifically asked the Admiralty for guidance. None was forthcoming. It seemed that, without Wemyss physically in London (he was in Versailles for the negotiations), the great apparatus of naval administration was incapable of any decision-making. Or did it just wish to avoid accountability?

In 1938, Lloyd George, in a book called *The Truth About the Peace Treaties*, distanced himself from the document that bore his signature. Lloyd George – rather later than he should have – joined Ferdinand Foch in the sentiment that Versailles had been a blunder: Foch predicted that the peace would not last, saying that it was merely 'an armistice for twenty years'.

---

* This is what Phipps Hornby (on HMS *Chester* at Jutland and then on HMS *Ramillies* in Scapa during the scuttle) wrote to Arthur J Marder on 20 October 1966, although he qualifies it saying 'this is only what I heard'. Phipps Hornby did not have a high opinion of Fremantle and his own father had said that 'twice, in his younger days, Fremantle had committed blunders that would have "put paid" to the promotion prospects of most men' (UCI Arthur J Marder Papers).

11

REBALANCING SEA POWER – FROM SCAPA TO WASHINGTON

GREAT BRITAIN ENDED the First World War with a huge naval arsenal. It had 'sixty-one battleships, 129 cruisers, 443 destroyers and 147 submarines; there were 37,000 officers and 400,000 men'.[625] The Royal Navy also possessed four aircraft carriers, 3,000 aircraft with the staff, crews and pilots to man them. It was a gargantuan machine but one that, after years of war, Britain could ill-afford to maintain. America had entered the war late but ramped up its military machine at a witheringly high speed. Naval manpower exploded, from 65,000 to 497,000 in the two short years of its engagement.

With the war decided, budgets were knifed. Churchill argued for a new approach to military expenditure in order to meet these severe budgetary pressures. Britain's August 1919 Defence Expenditure forecast was for £500 million for all the services. The navy had planned to build another twenty-one ships but the Treasury wanted a cap at fifteen.* The cabinet accepted that drastic cuts were needed and the decision was taken to cap the new budget *for all forces* at £135 million. This was £35 million below the 1919 budget for the navy *alone*. Its own new share of total defence spending was reduced to almost of a third – £60 million. Cuts had been started – in new ship orders and recruitment – but nothing as drastic as what was foreseen.† Two years later, in 1922, the ex-businessman First Lord, Sir Eric Geddes, took an even more drastic approach, cutting the service so deep that his reforms and cutbacks would be remembered as the 'Geddes Axe'.

---

* This was at a moment when America had eighteen dreadnoughts and a further eleven pre-dreadnoughts at sea.
† Already in 1918–19 'one of the three E class light cruisers was cancelled, as were 38 modified V and W class destroyers, two S class destroyers and 33 submarines'. Three of the four new, Super-*Hood* battle-cruisers were scrapped, although the need for the service to modernise was not entirely overlooked. The new D and E class cruisers and the four new battleships proposed in 1920 were kept. For the moment. The ranks were thinned. Voluntary redundancy was offered though not taken up as much as had been hoped: Only 407 out of 650 lieutenant commanders took advantage of the 1920 scheme.

FLEET SIZES POST-FIRST WORLD WAR

	Great Britain	United States	France	Germany	Japan	Italy	Britain vs. USA	Britain vs. France	Britain vs. USA and France	USA vs. Britain and Japan
Battleships	61	39	20	40	13	14	1.6	3.1	1.0	0.5
Battle-cruisers	9			5	7					
Cruisers	30	16	21	3	10	7	1.9	1.4	0.8	0.4
Light Cruisers	90	19	8	32	16	10	4.7	11.3	3.3	0.2
Flotilla Leaders	23					8				
Destroyers	443	131	91	200	67	44	3.4	4.9	2.0	0.3
Submarines	147	86	63	162	67	78	1.7	2.3	1.0	0.4
Aircraft carriers/seaplane tenders	4									

Source: Roskill, *Naval Policy Between the Wars*, Vol. 1, p. 71. The 'most accurate estimate available'. The size of the navies at the cessation of hostilities.

The Search for a New Power Standard

Britain came out of Versailles with, for the politicians at least, greatly reduced naval ambitions. The navy would eventually agree to drop the ruling metric of fleet strength, the 'two-power standard', and replace it with a new definition in which Britain's naval strength should not be inferior to any other single nation, a 'one-power standard'.* The nation in mind was the United States.

With peace came the budgetarily convenient assumption that another war would not be fought for at least ten years. During that time the politicians felt that a reduction in building was called for. The problem for the Royal Navy, however, was likely more acute than for the other services. The navy relied heavily on a diverse and substantial industrial infrastructure for shipbuilding, weapons development and turbine building, and a drastic cutback in orders would threaten all that.

At the time of the Armistice, Great Britain had been building the first of what were planned to be four *Admiral*-class ships, HMS *Hood*, *Anson*, *Rodney* and *Howe*. Originally *Hood* was to be an improved *Queen Elizabeth*-class battleship but Jellicoe noted that while Britain's lead in battleships

---

* The two-power standard held that Britain should maintain a significant margin to the combined strengths of the next two lesser naval powers. Van der Vat (p. 54) illustrates the issues as it was seen in 1909: 'By this time, the Royal Navy's lead over Germany and America combined in terms of capital ships amounted to 13%, but the margin had fallen by 25% in three years and the lead in completed dreadnoughts was just 4%. Allowing for the German and American building programmes but also for the retirement of old ships, Britain would have to lay down seven dreadnoughts in 1912 to achieve a 10% margin in 1915. The Admiralty made it clearer than ever that Germany was its overriding concern by redefining the essential superiority as Germany-plus-60 per cent in dreadnoughts, a ratio of five to three.'

was secure, there was a shortage in battle-cruisers that could outperform Germany's planned (but never-to-be-finished) *Mackensen* class.* *Hood's* design was inevitably heavily influenced by Jutland, where Sir David Beatty had lost three battle-cruisers in the first hours of engagement.

Hood was laid down in September 1916 and commissioned in May 1920. Work on the other three battle-cruisers, *Anson*, *Rodney* and *Howe*, was stopped in March 1917 and all three were eventually scrapped in 1919 but only after an estimated expenditure of £860,000 on their hulls and turbines. While *Hood* was already too advanced, it was thought better to completely rethink the battle-cruiser design for the other three.

The four Super-*Hood*s, the result of the rethink, would not be ordered until October 1921. The G3 design concept bordered on a fast-battleship design with the planned 16in armament but it was the higher planned speed of 32 knots that really epitomised its battle-cruiser designation. Alongside the construction of the G3 battle-cruisers, the British also planned an improved battleship, the *N3*. Neither would see the light of day. The G3s were immediately put on hold in November 1921.[†]

In August 1916, the US Congressional Naval Construction Act gave approval for ten more battleships, six battle-cruisers, submarines and a host of support vessels to be built.[‡] Wilson's actions sent a clear signal of American naval intent and spurred on both the British and the Japanese. It was ironic: the Anglo–Japanese alliance had been the impetus behind the push for a 'navy second to none'. If America's naval strength was compared to the combined power of both the Royal and the Imperial Japanese navies, then American concerns were warranted. The US fleet would have been at a decisive numerical inferiority.

While Britain hesitated, building programmes in both Japan and the United States advanced. The Americans had completed the USS *Maryland* while the *West Virginia*, *Colorado* and *Washington* were 'well-advanced, and

---

* SMS *Mackensen* was thought to have a speed of 30 knots and to be armed with 15.2in guns. The *Renown*-class battle-cruisers and the *Courageous*-class 'large light cruisers' were as fast but considered very lightly armoured.

† The G3 Battle-cruiser design would be cancelled in February 1922. The Admiralty was on the cusp of launching an accelerated programme of naval construction – four G3 battle-cruisers followed by four N3 battleships. The intention had initially been to concentrate first on the N3s, with four planned for the 1921–22 Fiscal Year alongside one battle-cruiser. The final N3 design was approved in November 1921, just as the Washington Naval Conference was about to sit. Much of the thinking that went into the N3 design eventually ended up on the new *Nelson*-class.

‡ In September 1918 the US Navy Department recommended going considerably further, to add another twelve battleships and sixteen battle-cruisers.

the other six were about 25 per cent complete'.[626] These last, the *South Dakota*-class ships, planned as 23-knot, 16in-gunned battleships, would have been the heaviest-gunned ships in the United States Navy. In Japan, the 16in battleships *Nagato* and *Mutsu* had already been commissioned and work had been started on the battleships *Kaga* and *Tosa* and the battle-cruisers *Amagi* and *Akagi*.

The British concern was not so much the potential numeric disparity; it was their potential inferiority in modern, *post-Jutland* ships. During the war the British had successfully tied up American capital shipbuilding by the wartime construction needs being met by US yards. With the war ended, British orders fell off and the path for America's own capital ship-building programme finally made feasible.

But there were also those in America who wanted to avert a new naval arms race, this time between America, Britain and Japan. One such person was Idaho Republican Senator William E. Borah, an isolationist and a fierce opponent of the ideals of Wilson's League of Nations. In December 1920, he successfully introduced a bill to launch an arms limitation conference with Japan and Great Britain. With the European war over, America's interests now focused more closely on Asia and the enormous market in China. Japan's acquisitive territorial ambitions directly threatened that commercial opportunity, while the Anglo–Japanese alliance put a strong question mark over America's Pacific naval strength.

Wilson's successor, Warren Harding, was looking for ways to reduce not only the financial burden of new naval construction and the obvious risks of a renewed naval arms race but it was he who enlarged the proposed agenda to cover wider issues of peace in the Pacific.[*] Borah's ideas were of little interest initially, but Harding soon saw the potential to hijack the platform and present what he was doing as the Republican alternative to Wilson's League of Nations. In July 1921, the call went out from Washington for an international naval arms limitation conference.

On 12 November 1921, the International Conference on Naval Limitation was opened in the US capital.[†] Rivalry between the great powers was almost tangible. Britain's request to hold a separate session to jointly formulate a common position was swept brusquely aside by the

[*] Warren Gamaliel Harding (1865–1923), a Republican, was the twenty-ninth president from 1921–23.
[†] The conference would be in session until 6 February 1921. Like the Versailles Peace Conference, Russia was not invited. The attendees included the United States, Great Britain, France, Japan, Italy, China, the Netherlands, Portugal and Belgium.

Americans, who were not at all disposed to give the British any favour. At the same time, Britain's relations with France were strained and had been so bad that the 1920 Anglo–French security agreement was never concluded when the American Senate failed to ratify the Treaty of Versailles in March:

> Great Britain and France from 1919 through 1922 respected each other's colonial spheres of influence but divided on the issue of stability with(in) continental Europe. France wanted Germany to remain weak and economically crippled while by 1922 Great Britain desired Germany to begin to regain some of its former position with European affairs.[627]

The opening of the conference by American Secretary of State, Charles Hughes, was like a thunderclap, announcing, as he did, that America proposed not only that all capital shipbuilding programmes be abandoned but that some of the older ships also be scrapped. It might have been welcome news for the politicians, fighting to balance budgets, but the enormity of Hughes' proposal came as a complete surprise. The former British prime minister and serving foreign secretary, Arthur Balfour, was, it was reported, 'stunned', obliged 'to define his country's policy literally as he sat waiting to reply'.[628] Ernle Chatfield, now an admiral and given the responsibility of safeguarding Great Britain's key naval interests at the talks, must have been equally taken aback.

The conference, whose original intention was conceived of as an arms limitation forum, evolved into a much more comprehensive discussion about the balance of power in the Pacific and, as part of that, the balance of power between the navies whose national interests were often at odds in that theatre. The original aims were necessarily expanded into territorial agreements once the negotiations started.

Washington would result in a number of agreements, two of which were the most significant: a Four-Power Treaty between the United States, Britain, Japan and France in December 1921 and – with the addition of Italy – a Five-Power Treaty in February 1922. The first guaranteed that all four countries would be consulted on 'any Pacific question' should there be disagreements. The second focused on the naval balance of power but, as a means of achieving agreement, necessarily included questions of regional presence and the Anglo–Japanese alliance. Including Belgium, Portugal, the Netherlands and – most importantly – China, an accompanying Nine-Power Treaty was signed in February 1923. Its purpose was to guarantee the territorial integrity of China against Japanese expansionism. Two days before it was signed, a separate agreement, the Shantung Treaty, returned Shantung (a German colonial possession since 1898 that had been handed to Japan at Versailles) to China.

The proposals aimed at dramatically cutting world naval tonnage, starting with an immediate ten-year building holiday. For Britain, this meant a cut of around 580,000 tons (this would involve cancelling the four newly proposed 45,000-ton Super-*Hood*s, only just ordered as they exceeded the proposed 35,000-ton capital ship limit, and scrapping nineteen older ships); for Japan, 450,000 tons (cancelling the seven proposed battleships, scrapping ten older ships and seven under construction).* This would allow Great Britain to retain twenty-two capital ships (600,000 tons), the USA eighteen (500,000 tons) and Japan ten (300,000 tons).

Going forward, Hughes proposed that the existing relative strengths between navies should be used as the basis for the future and, importantly, that tonnage, affecting more the design of individual ships, not the number of ships, be used as the measure of strength.† *In total* Hughes' proposal amounted to 1,878,000 tons, was nothing short of a gigantic cut. With the proposals, he had created a unique role for himself. He had, '…sunk sixty-six capital ships, more ships in fifteen minutes than any of all the admirals of the world in a cycle of centuries'.[629]

Beatty responded to Hughes the very next day. He accepted the proposed 5:5:3 ratio but remained uncomfortable about the 'naval holiday', worried about the quality of the ships the Royal Navy would retain and, like Chatfield, the basis of measurement. Among these, he pointed out, only the '*Hood*, five *Royal Sovereign*'s and five *Queen Mary*'s' were modern.[630] The only great addition, *Hood*, had been laid down at the end of 1916 so that, in his mind, Britain had already had a 'Five Year Holiday' while, he added, the ships the navy possessed were 'tired' after four years of war. Britain's counterproposal was to suggest that both she and America would be able to build four capital ships in 1922–32 given that they would, in any case, be obliged to pay subsidies to maintain

---

* Britain's contribution was 583,375 tons while Japan's total amounted to 448,928 tons.
† Chatfield felt the approach based on tonnage would risk a reduction in the size, and therefore, the power of Britain's battleship fleet. The Americans, who like the British regarded the battleship as the backbone of the fleet, preferred to look at the relative strengths by the tonnage within that type of ship.

industrial skills. Balfour agreed with the Admiralty position but found himself overruled by Lloyd George, who cabled back on 10 December that 'the Ten-Year naval holiday…should be agreed to'.[631] Roskill laid the blame solidly at the prime minister's feet.

Because of the British focus on the numerical advantage in *post-Jutland* ships, they accepted a tonnage equality with the United States. The treaty killed sixteen of the latter's planned heavy capital ships, including all the powerful new *South Dakota*-class.[*] The fact that many of the new ships had been shelved should not necessarily force one to conclude, as Friedman does, that the 1916 Naval Act was 'nothing more than a mirage' Rather, the '…planned and unfinished ships of the Naval Act of 1916 won a kind of silent naval war'. It had achieved American naval parity with Great Britain and decidedly limited Japan's naval growth.[†] And, with the agreement on a 5:5:3 capital ship ratio, assigned Japan the inferior outcome.[632]

The idea that another war was unlikely in the immediate aftermath of the whirlwind that had just devastated Europe led to formalisation of the 'Ten Year Rule' idea. In Britain, the services had already been asked to cut their budgets based on the assumption that: '…the British Empire will not be engaged in any great war during the next ten years, and that no expeditionary Force is required for this purpose.'[633]

The rule asked of each service to plan to be able to rearm over a period of ten years if the risks of war were, at some point, deemed valid. Some say it was Churchill who came up with this sensible construction delay in the light of rapid innovation. As early as June 1919, he argued that: 'The longer you can delay building new ships without letting your margin fall too low, the better and more powerful is the ship you can build when the time comes.'[634]

Normally, it would also mean that 'at the end of the ten-year period,

---

[*] Two had been launched and several almost fully completed. Hughes also proposed to scrap fifteen pre-dreadnoughts.

[†] While Great Britain, the United States and Japan agreed on the 5:5:3 ratio (525,000 tons each, Japan 315,000 tons), France and Italy were held back to 175,000 tons each. The figures were guidelines. Britain ended up with closer to 600,000 tons. The United States had been able to read Japanese diplomatic code and was aware that 315,000 tons was the lowest level of tonnage the Japanese delegation would be willing to accept (see Roger Dingman. *Power in the Pacific: The Origins of Naval Arms Limitation, 1914–1922*, (1976) p. 217). The day before the conference convened, there had been a right-wing coup in Tokyo and the prime minister, Hara Kei, assassinated. ONI concluded that this would leave the Japanese delegate, Baron Katō (Tōmosaburo), 'essentially operating without significant oversight from Tokyo' (Setzkorn, Eric. *Open Source Information and the Office of Naval Intelligence in Japan 1905–1920* in International Journal of Intelligence and Counter Intelligence 27, 2014).

the armed services should be ready to fight a major war'. [635] Ironically, however, it would also be Churchill who in some way contributed to the rule being used as a means of avoiding rearmament. In 1925 it was used to block the expansion of British naval forces in the Far East to counter Japan while, three years later, in 1928, Churchill again proposed that the clock should be reset each year for another ten years.

Beatty himself had not been against the *idea* of a 'naval holiday' but he pointed out that the holiday that had been enjoyed since the war had already almost broken the arms industry.* What he worried about was that this approach 'would result in the decay of naval ship construction and armament industries, unless firms were heavily subsidised'.[636] Not surprisingly, when he heard what Hughes had proposed, Beatty was astonished: it was quipped that he sat up sharply, 'in the manner of a bulldog, sleeping on a Sunday doorstep, who had been poked in the stomach…', while Arthur Lee, who had become the new First Lord of the Admiralty the previous February, supposedly turned 'several colours of the rainbow'.[637]

Of course, the British admirals would have preferred to have retained *supremacy* but *parity* was acceptable. In 1920, the British First Lord of the Admiralty spoke of the spirit of this eventual agreement before Parliament: 'We are very fortunate in the fact that the only Navy approximating in strength to our own is that of the United States of America, with whom we are associated in such a way that the idea of competition in armaments between us is, to put it mildly, repugnant to us all.'[638]

Given what Benson had earlier advised Admiral Sims when he came over with much-needed American naval resources in May 1917, such a statement, even after the two years of war, seemed surprisingly naïve.†

What about non-capital ships? Parity might have been achieved in capital ships and carriers but it soon became clear that, because of the fierce rivalry, an acceleration in building vessels of other classes – cruisers, destroyers and, even, submarines – would now take place. While Washington had succeeded in halting the naval arms race so far as capital ships were concerned, it had, arguably, merely moved the race elsewhere.

---

* While he was travelling in the US, prior to the conference start, Beatty wrote to the King that 'it almost broke the armament firms of the country' and that any holiday would be followed naturally by a 'hectic period of feverish building'. (Ranft, TBP, vol. 2, p. 190. Letter to King George V, 12 November 1921).

† Benson, the American CNO, had left William S. Sims in no doubt where his feelings lay. He told Sims, an Anglophile, to make sure he didn't let the British 'pull the wool over his eyes' as he would 'just as much fight the British' [as the Germans].

While saying that he thought the proposal to extend the 5:5:3 ratio from capital ships to cruisers, destroyers and submarines fine in principle, it raised 'questions in detail' for Beatty. The submarine was one of the weapons discussed. Some wanted it classed a forbidden, 'criminal' weapon, but that idea was rejected by the Americans and the Japanese and most forcefully by the French near the end of the conference on 28 December. Their position – that they wanted to retain 90,000 tons in the class – gave Balfour what he needed to argue for the maintenance of the cruiser and destroyer numbers. However, the French defence of Germany's unrestricted submarine war was badly presented and caused exceptionally bad feelings among the delegates.

The conference did try to address the worst characteristics of submarine warfare. Delegates agreed on the principle that unrestricted submarine warfare would be banned in the future. This would have been difficult to enforce but: '...what was revolutionary though about this treaty was that it held submarine crews and their captains personally responsible for any violations of the treaty terms, irrespective of whether their government or military command ordered the submarines' officers and crew to violate the treaty terms.'[639]

Next, the cruiser: while there was no limit on the number of ships, there was on calibre and tonnage. The new 10,000-ton, 8in-gunned 'Treaty Cruiser' became 'the source of a new international arms race'.* With no room left to expand in capital shipbuilding, cruiser (and carrier) expansion took up the slack. In time it generated the need for the second naval arms limitation conference, which would take place in Geneva in 1927.[640]

The restrictions on the traditional battle-cruiser lent more weight to the development of the aircraft carrier. It is ironic that the key development that would be the key to America winning the Pacific War twenty years later was decried by none other than the CNO, Benson, who said (in 1919) that he 'could not conceive of any use the fleet will ever have for aviation'.[641] The British made the development of their own carrier strategy that much more difficult by the endless haggling that started in April 1918 over who would control the fleet-based aircraft.

---

* Roskill argued that the British proposal was made on the basis of wanting to retain their *Hawkins* class, which was 10,000 tons with 7½in armament. Heavy cruisers were allowed to mount 8in guns, light cruisers 6in. A submarine was not allowed cruiser-sized guns. Britain, with the largest imperial policing role, was allocated the highest tonnage for the type (192,000 tons). The USA was allowed 143,000 tons, Japan 100,000 tons.

It was the neglected child with two squabbling parents. It was underfunded, underdeveloped and directionless. The Royal Navy's aircraft carriers were stuck in the past, its planes were inadequate and it had too few pilots. Finally, there was no strategy for an offensive carrier Force.[642]

How did the conference succeed in getting the Japanese on board? It was clear that they were not happy (nor were the French, for that matter, as they had also wanted parity with the British and, at the very least, come out with a higher ratio than the Japanese). Japan's naval building programme was forging ahead and the proportion of the national budget devoted to the military a massive 49 per cent. Japan had 'tripled its naval budget' from 1917 to 1921.[643] The Japanese representative, Baron Katō Tōmosaburo, demanded a higher tonnage allowance than the 250,000 tons proposed.[*]

Japan managed to gain 81,000 tons in three new aircraft carriers and, when compared to either Britain or the United States (which were each allowed 135,000 tons), had maintained 'almost twice the number of modern, post-Jutland capital ships allowed'.[644] Katō was also able to keep the last *Nagato*-class battleship, the *Mutsu*.[†] The USA would retain two completed battleships, while Britain would be allowed to build two new capital ships within the 35,000-ton limit.[‡]

Replacing the previous treaty with the Four-Power and Nine-Power treaties was a mistake. They were 'ambiguously worded and unenforceable'.[§] Additionally, that the new arrangements 'turned a potential ally into a potential rival in the Far East'.[645] With the signing of the Four-Power Treaty on 13 December 1921, the Anglo–Japanese Alliance was effectively at an end. One great thorn in Anglo–American naval relations might have been removed, another deeper threat emerged. Roskill concluded that the Washington talks had merely put off the day: 'What the Washington Conference did accomplish was to impose a check, albeit a temporary one, on Anglo–American naval rivalry.'[646]

Eventually, Japan's agreement to accept lower tonnage was reached on condition that the other powers maintain the status quo in the Pacific.

---

[*] Admiral Baron Katō Tōmosaburo (1861–1923) was Japan's naval minister.
[†] *Mutsu* was 98 per cent complete at this point (Roskill, *Naval Policy*, p. 316).
[‡] The USA would keep the USS *Colorado* and the USS *Washington*.
[§] It meant that, even if there was strong reaction against the 60 per cent ratio (by people like Katō, the vice chair of the Naval General Staff, who argued for 70 per cent), Japan could barely afford a larger building programme (see Lisio, pp. 31–34).

The advantages she received from the 'fortification clauses' offset the Anglo–American strength in ship tonnage. Japan was placated by assurances that neither the Americans nor the British would fortify their bases, for the former in the western Pacific, the latter east of Singapore. 'Essentially, they said that the North Pacific area from Hawaii to Malaya could be regarded as a Japanese preserve. That seemed a better idea in 1922 than it did in 1942.'[647]

Balfour tried to intervene by saying that while Guam and Manila were understandable, Hawaii was so far from Japan that he could not support its inclusion.

Katō's negotiating tactic was well-thought through. Even if the Japanese had to accept the 6:10 ratio (rather than 7:10 that he had been instructed as being the minimum acceptable ration between Japan and the United States), Katō assumed that the United States would not build to the treaty limits. 'As it turned out, this is exactly what happened.'[648] Furthermore, the actual strength of a fleet diminishes markedly the further from home it has to fight, because of questions such as supply and materiel fatigue. American naval officers recognised this. One of the long-term effects of the Japanese bringing the bases into the negotiation was on American naval design. American naval planning started to focus on the logistics of force projection. Necessity strengthened the independence of the task force concept: 'After the Washington Conference, Navy officers were forced to think in terms of fighting a distant naval war in the absence of any significant bases in the projected theatre of operations.'[649]

What had been a two-power standard for the British now became a one-power focus: America. Now started the next leg of the deterioration of British sea power: Naval parity with America coupled with continued superiority over the next two minor powers – France and Japan.* 'By the Washington Naval Treaty of December 1921, the two nations agreed, rather gracelessly on the part of their professional advisors, to share the Trident of naval supremacy.'[650]

Britain's acceptance of the 'one-power standard' had given the Royal Navy the best it could hope for in the days of heavy cost-cutting and saved the country from another very expensive arms race. One of the reasons is that America never took advantage of the building capacity that had been agreed to in Washington. The ratio that was effectively achieved

---

* The final ratios agreed in Washington (signed 6 February 1922) were 5:5:3:1.75:1.75, i.e. that Japan's navy could not be more than 60 per cent of either Britain or America's, while Italy and France could only amount to 35 per cent.

ended up 'closer to 5-4-3 between the wars', with Britain still in first position.[651]

The Americans had, with the stroke of a pen, succeeded in one month in reversing centuries of British sea power dominance. In Britain, the politicians were happy. The financially draining impact of a renewed naval arms race had been averted but at a huge, long-term strategic cost. The Admiralty, however, 'took the unusual step of protesting publicly against the strictures of the Washington Treaty, but it did them little good'.[652]

Ernle Chatfield, Assistant Chief of Naval Staff, pointed out that the proposed remaining British ships would be seriously outdated ('distinctly inferior') by the termination date, 1932.[653]

The Washington treaty remained in force from August 1923 to December 1936. A further conference in Geneva in 1927 tried, unsuccessfully, to extend the Washington provisions to other vessels, notably cruisers. The discussions on the limitation and reduction of naval armament continued three years later in London and ended with the April 1930 agreement between Britain, the USA and Japan that specified displacement tonnage, replacement rules and limitations or cruisers, destroyers and submarines.

The British Royal Navy budget was £52 million in 1923, ten years later it had only grown by another £1 million. In the twenty-three years between 1913 and 1936, only two battleships – HMS *Rodney* and HMS *Nelson* – had been built. They bore an uncanny resemblance to the N3 *Admiral*-class designs scrapped in 1921. The men were no better off. By 1932 the navy's manpower was 90,000 men, only marginally higher than America's navy before she entered the war in 1917. Discontent was high. Ratings who joined after 1925 received less pay than ratings who had signed on before. In 1931 the dissatisfaction with pay boiled over when public service workers' pay was reduced by 10 per cent and effectively cut some sailor's pay by 25 per cent by resetting them to the 1925 rates. On 11 September, ships of the Atlantic Fleet went on strike at Invergordon. Two hundred sailors were discharged in the so-called 'mutiny' and the leaders jailed.

In 1933, Chatfield became First Sea Lord. He immediately set to work. To start with, the 'Ten Year Rule' was dropped. Naval budgets started to rise, even if only slowly at first, from £53 million in 1933 to £81 million three years later and £127 million in 1938. In ships, the Royal Navy was able to expand its aircraft carrier strength. Work started on HMS *Ark Royal* in 1934 and by 1937 four additional carriers were laid down.* He also

---

* HMS *Illustrious, Victorious, Formidable* and *Indomitable*.

started to try and untangle the mess that had been created with the navy winning back total control of the Fleet Air Arm in 1939. Chatfield recognised the importance of carriers (and noted the suitability of the *Lexington* and the *Akagi* for carrier conversion):[*] 'The number of aircraft carriers in a Fleet action will decide who is to command the air, and command of the air is likely to be vital in the next naval battle... .'[654]

After the only two battleship deliveries in the twenty or so year gap, Chatfield succeeded in getting five new *George V*-class battleships in 1936–37.[†]

Midway through the 1930s cracks started to appear in the ten years of stability that Washington had successfully brought to relations between the great powers. In December 1934, Japan denounced the 1922 and 1930 treaties, while in March 1935 Germany reintroduced military conscription (which had been forbidden by Article 194) and also initiated air rearmament.

Britain quickly concluded a new treaty with Germany, agreeing to a new German naval strength that would be 35 per cent of her own worldwide strength. It made little sense: Germany was already building ships that were inconsistent with the treaty's obligations and four years later, on 28 April 1939, Germany threw aside even these provisions.[‡]

The New German Fleet

After Versailles, Germany was left with a fleet that lagged fifteen years behind the former Allied navies in technology and design. The limitation to 10,000-ton displacement on battleships meant that the only type of ship that Germany could now put to sea were pre-dreadnoughts.

Other restrictions had the same crippling effect. Limitations were set at 6,000 tons for light cruisers, 800 tons for destroyers and 200 tons for torpedo boats.[§] No submarines were permitted. Battleships and cruisers could not be replaced for a further twenty years. It bound Germany to the prospect of an antique navy, one that would consist of six battleships (of the *Deutschland* or *Lothringen* class), six light cruisers and a dozen each of destroyers and torpedo boats.

---

[*] The USA also converted the USS *Saratoga* as a carrier. Tonnage allowances were proposed at 80,000 for the USA and Great Britain, 48,000 for Japan. Britain did not want to increases maximum carrier tonnage to 40,000 tons as it could only have used one of the Super-*Hood*s for that purpose. They remained at 27,000 tons while an increase in total class tonnage was made to 135,000 tons for the USA and Great Britain, 81,000 tons for Japan and 60,000 tons for Italy and France.

[†] The first, HMS *George V*, was commissioned in December 1940. The last, HMS *Howe*, was completed in August 1942. HMS *Illustrious* was finally completed in May 1940.

[‡] Submarines were not to exceed 45 per cent of naval strength.

[§] Article 190 displacement limitations, Article 191 submarine clause.

Ships that had survived the scuttle now, as further compensation, had to be surrendered to the Allies. They amounted to eight battleships and eight light cruisers, forty-two destroyers and fifty torpedo boats.* A number of floating docks, cranes and tugs totalling 400,000 tons were also included in the penalties.† Most of the ships were regarded as of 'small military value and are only suitable for breaking up purposes' such as the fourteen pre-dreadnought battleships of the *Deutschland*, *Lothringen* and *Wittelsbach* classes, or the seven battleships of the *Kaiser Friedrich* and *Brandenburg* classes. In any case, what was left hardly covered the loss of high quality ships in the scuttle.

Britain took five battleships, six light cruisers, thirty-nine leaders and destroyers and thirty-eight torpedo boats; France one battleship, five light cruisers and twelve leaders and destroyers;‡ Italy three light cruisers and three leaders and destroyers;§ Japan two battleships, one light cruiser and four leaders and destroyers. Finally, the United States one battleship and one leader or destroyer.[655]

Scapa Flow became the cornerstone in the creation of the new German Navy: 'In its suicide, the Fleet redeemed itself in the eyes of the nation. The mutinies were soon forgotten. The scuttling provided a new narrative and a fledgling start for the new Reichsmarine, limited by treaty to 1,500 officers and 13,500 men.'[656]

Six years after war's end, a new *Emden* – the third ship to bear that name – was launched in Kiel. A sleek, 6,000-ton phoenix symbolically named after Reuter's flagship, kept alive the humiliation of Rosyth and the brotherly bonds created at Scapa. Tirpitz praised Reuter's actions and saw the hope that it had given Germany: 'That Admiral Reuter and our officers have saved somewhat the honour of our flag has deeply touched all of us here and quietly re-awakens our hope for the future.'[657]

In the von Reuter family, the deeds of 21 June 1919 were commemorated for years among family, friends and German naval officers. In one gathering, Yorck von Reuter, Ludwig's son, raised his glass to the memory: 'I give you a toast to the events of Scapa Flow. May the same spirit that prevailed there, also prevail for the future.'[658]

---

* Battleships included *Oldenburg, Thüringen, Ostfreisland, Helgoland, Posen, Westfalen, Rheinland* and *Nassau*. Light cruisers included *Stettin, Danzig, München, Lübeck, Stralsund, Augsburg, Kolberg* and the *Stuttgart*.
† The additional light cruisers included *Königsberg, Pillau, Graudenz, Regensberg* and *Strasburg*.
‡ France renamed the light cruisers it received the *Metz, Strasbourg, Mulhouse (Mülhaus)* and *Colmar*.
§ Italy took the *Pillau, Strasburg* and the *Kolberg*, which was renamed *Ancona*.

Hitler embellished the story of Scapa Flow. He used the naval mutinies to breathe life to the 'stab in the back' myth. Less than ten years after the German Navy's 'self-immolation' at Scapa Flow, the keel of the pocket-battleship *Deutschland* was laid down in Kiel. This new *Panzerschiff* was designed as the answer to the 10,000-ton displacement rule. Partly because of new design technologies such as electrically welded hulls, it was able to achieve as much broadside weight and armour protection as the older heavier tonnage battleships although, in fact, the real displacement was still 11,500 tons. In February 1929 the heavy cruiser *Lützow*, named after her Jutland ancestor, was also launched. The man who would drive German naval rearmament would be Vice Admiral Hans Zenker, the former captain of the battle-cruiser SMS *von der Tann*. He had served as Inspekteur der Marineartillerie for the previous three years, now he became the navy's commander in chief.

In 1935, Germany still possessed no submarines. However, by war's outbreak she would again have an impressive fleet and would once again launch a destructive undersea war.

It is one of history's ironies that it is highly likely that the same German steel that built the Kaiser's fleet also built at least part of Hitler's new fleet after it was salvaged. And, in the case of the *Graf Spee*, suffered a similar fate, not once, but twice when her captain scuttled the pocket battleship in the River Plate in the opening months of the Second World War.

The New Japanese Fleet

As early as 1919 – after he had completed a naval inspection of the major colonial navies – Jellicoe recommended the stationing of a large fleet in the Far East to counter the emerging threat from Japan. His ideas were not taken on board. Roger Keyes argued that the presence of a fleet was unnecessary, more important was the ability to quickly transfer naval resources to the region should such a move be necessary.

This led to an extended debate about how a fleet would be regionally supported and supplied. Churchill wanted the establishment of a strong Far Eastern base in Singapore with an equally large oil storage infrastructure and, in 1922, prophetically argued: 'If Singapore fell in the first two or three months of a war, the whole of the Pacific would fall under the complete supremacy of Japan, and many years might elapse before either Britain or the United States could re-enter that ocean in effective strength.'[659]

In January 1924, Ramsay MacDonald's new government put an end to the Singapore lobby. For Churchill, it sent a profoundly worrying signal to New Zealand and Australia: '...the stubborn, brutal fact remains that the decision to abandon the Singapore base leaves Australia and New Zealand to whatever fate an anxious and inscrutable future may have in store.'[660]

Britain did not face up to the growth of these three militaristic powers. When Japan invaded Manchuria in 1931 the Royal Navy stood by. When Italy moved troops for the invasion of Abyssinia in 1935, Britain did not close the Suez Canal. The British government signed its approval of Germany's naval rearmament and in 1939 Neville Chamberlain signed away Czechoslovakia.

In 1937, Japan started construction of three battleships, the *Yamato*-class. The monster battleship displaced 70,000 tons and carried nine 18.1in guns. Nothing like these monsters had been seen on any ocean.

12

THE GREATEST SALVAGE
OF ALL TIME

IT DID NOT take long for people to realise that something would have to be done with the sunken ships. Two days after the scuttle, the whaler *Ramna* ran 'aground' on the upturned hull of *Moltke*. It would not be the last time this would happen to the island's seagoing fishing boats. The talk quickly turned to how dangerous the wrecks might become for the seafaring life of Orkney.

The Admiralty did not do much more than issue orders that no press was allowed further access to the Flow.* The naval salvage experts that came to the Flow left Scapa all convinced that the big ships would be impossible to lift off the floor. The Admiralty report said: 'There can be no question of salving the ships. And, as they offer no hindrance to navigation, they need not be blown up. Where they were sunk, there they will rest and rust.'[661]

The ships offered immediate benefits to the islanders, who often worked at night to pull off anything of value that could be prised loose. The repurposing was inventive. Boiler tubes became curtain rails, while other valuable scrap was 'shipped from Orkney in herring barrels to markets in the south'.[662] Torpedo tubes, for example, contained very high quantities of extremely valuable metals and were of a manageable size.

Nevertheless, some early talk about what to do with the shipwrecks involved floating and then resinking the wrecks after filling with concrete to act as a protective breakwater for fishing boats in the Bay of Skaill. This was a precursor of what would later constitute the Churchill barriers, which took the same idea into military application. Ships that had not been sunk were towed away for breaking up. Sixteen of the destroyers had been run aground on the various islands of Cava, Rysa and on Hoy by Lyness.†

---

* Chris Irvine kindly supplied a copy of the Admiralty signal to the *Daily Mail*, one of the newspapers specifically forbidden further access.
† Aside from one battleship (*Baden*) and three light cruisers (*Emden, Frankfurt and Nürnberg*).

In February 1920, ten British destroyers tried to tow seven destroyers to Rosyth but were caught in storms off the Pentland Firth. One of the German ships ran aground, one sank when it got back to the Flow and the others were lost. The Admiralty kept a tight lid on the embarrassing story even though eight had been taken successfully south just the week before.

The first real talk of commercial salvage took two years to come to fruition. In June 1923, the Scapa Flow Salvage and Shipbreaking Company was formed with the limited objective of raising four sunken German torpedo boats. Each had been bought, it was said, for a price in the '£200–250 region, perhaps equal to somewhere around £20,000 in today's prices'.[663]

JW Robertson, the former convener of the Shetland County Council, set up the company and based it out of Lerwick. Its capitalisation was modest by later standards, £7,000. At the end of August 1924, the first, the *S.131*, was raised with additional help of the United Kingdom Salvage Company.[*]

Before work even began, a new man arrived on the scene, Ernest Frank Guelph Cox, an electrical engineer from Dudley, near Wolverhampton.[†] Cox's company had seen the demand for scrap and had purchased some old battleships from the Admiralty in 1921 to break up in his new Queensborough yard on the north-west corner of the Isle of Sheppey.

He had been visiting Denmark and meeting with a Danish company, Peterson and Allbeck, when the subject of the price of scrap metal came up in conversation. It was then that the idea that would make him world famous was born. The suggestion was made that he should think of salvaging the German fleet. Cox modestly said that as he 'had never lifted a ship before, the project was somewhat ambitious'.[664]

Nevertheless, Cox went to the Admiralty showing some interest in the remaining destroyers. On their suggestion, he then went to Scapa to have a look for himself but did not bother to read the old Admiralty salvage report. He was an engineer by training and demeanour and wanted to form his own opinion. It only took a single day at Scapa and he was hooked. He went back to London to see the Admiralty again.

[*] The *S.131* was part of *Kapitänleutnant* Wehr's VI Torpedo Boat Flotilla.
[†] Ernest Frank Guelph Cox (1883-1959). Despite having left school early (at thirteen), Cox was able to advance himself in engineering largely because of strength of character and persistence. He went to work at his wife's father's steel works (the Overton Steel Works) after he married her in 1907. He was financed by his wife's cousin, Tommy Danks, in setting up his own business.

His company, Cox and Danks,* purchased twenty-six torpedo boats that lay between Lyness and Cava but also the salvage rights to raise two large battleships, the 24,980-ton SMS *Seydlitz* and the 26,180-ton SMS *Hindenburg*. *Seydlitz* was a mythical ship that had fought under Hipper's command at Jutland with distinction. The Admiralty also sold Cox two old Admiralty seagoing tugs, the *Sidonian* and the *Ferrodanks*. Initially, they had been blocked by storms at the Pentland Firth but had been brought through the Switha Sound by the coxswain of the Longhope lifeboat, Bill Mowat. He also bought a German floating dock with a lifting capacity of 3,000 tons for another £20,000. It had, ironically, been handed over as part of the revisited reparations agreement after Germany had scuttled its main assets, the interned fleet. Cox actually had little interest in the structure that would later, after extensive reconfiguration, turn out to be the cornerstone of his future operation. All he had really wanted was the 400ft-long, 40ft-diameter steel pressure cylinder that came as part of the package. It had previously been used as a pressure testing chamber for U-boats but he wanted it solely for its scrap value.

The purchase price was £24,000 but he was forbidden from disclosing the details and it was only fifteen years later that this was revealed.[665]

Cox brought with him two men, known as 'the two Macs'. They would play a vital role in the success of his salvage operations: one was a former naval engine room artificer (ERA), Ernest McKeowan, the other a former diver and naval salvage expert, Thomas McKenzie.

Cox was a confident man. He took the time to study problems, work out solutions and then see them through. He knew his own capabilities and, to a large extent, his weaknesses. Certainly, when he made mistakes, he was big enough to admit to them and then try and learn from them:

> Without boasting, I do not think there is another man in the world who could have tackled the same job. Before I undertook this formidable task, I had never raised a ship in my life. Quite frankly, experts thought me crazy, but to me these vessels represented nothing more than so much scrap of brass, gunmetal, bronze, steel, etc., and I was determined to recover this at all costs.[666]

Cox was also persistent, dogged even. He would not let go until he found the solution he needed. After the first successful raise, one of the men

---

* Cox's partner, Danks, had been bought out in 1918.

commented about this side of Cox's character: 'If he hadn't been a mixture of a genius and a mule, he'd never have *started* a job that size, let alone finished it,' adding, 'Apart from McKeowan and McKenzie, there wasn't any one of us who knew the first thing about salvage, and *they* didn't know that much ... .'[667]

Cox's company raised its first boat, the 924-ton *V.70* lying a half mile off Lyness, just east of Rysa Bay.* She was only lying in around 50ft of water and close to Lyness, where Cox had bought an old abandoned air force base and naval station. It was an ideal ship on which to start operations.

He thought – against strong advice from McKenzie who wanted to use more expensive steel wire – that he could use thick chain to form a cradle under the destroyer and raise her that way.† First wires had to pull the chains under the wreck. Before that, 'prickers' (long steel rods) were pushed from one side of the wreck to the other in the soft mud. On their ends was attached wire, and to the wire, finally, chains.‡ Twenty-four two-man teams manned the winches and started the turns. For a while the 3in, No. 10 chain worked. Then suddenly one snapped: 'There was an explosive crack like a gun going off and one of the chains parted, its massive links flailing through the air in a deadly whiplash.'[668]

It was, frankly, a miracle that not one of the fifty men who were working there, half on each of the floating platforms, was injured. The chain had taken so much strain that the hooks had ripped through the ship's steelwork. The noise was deafening, like 'an artillery bombardment' commented one of the salvers afterwards.[669] The problem was that the upward lift could have worked but could not take the additional strain when 'bent over the small pulley winches' on the two floating docks.[670]

In July, Cox used thick, 9in wire cable and that worked. The cables were massive: each loop that was passed under the German destroyer to form the cradle weighed 250 tons. Ninety-six men working on the twenty-four pulley-blocks, each with a 100-ton lift capacity that had been purpose-built for the floating dock, got the *V.70* going on her ascent to the surface. Cox reckoned that four men to a winch was 'safe', but six men – an indication of the strain on the tackle – was 'asking for trouble'.[671] Before anything was brought up, Cox was already £40,000 in the red. He knew right from the start that the financial challenge was going to be a steep one. Cox was nothing if not a risk-taker.

---

* Hall states her displacement as 750 tons, Reuter 905 tons. Rysa is also spelled Risa.
† The chain was from the scrapped HMS *Orion*.
‡ See Booth, pp. 30–31.

Getting the dock positioned correctly was also a challenge. It was 240ft long while most of the destroyers were at least 320ft long. The lifting cables had to be very precisely placed otherwise not only would the load tilt, the docks would also take unequal strain at each end.

As the spring tidal difference was between 10 and 12ft, Cox's men could take up the slack, take their load into shallower waters and there repeat the entire process. They finally performed the operation four times before being able to beach their prize at Mill Bay on a sandbank. The depth of the water was roughly 10ft. It was a Saturday, 1 August 1924. A decade after the start of the Great War.

The second lift had started the same day, in the early morning of 1 August. At 0400. From start to finish the operation would take six weeks, although the actual lift time was, as George pointed out, 'little more than seven hours'. A good sign when starting out was that the cables were not 'necking'. This happens when cables are about to snap and they quiver, moving rapidly from side to side in the water.

V.70 was not scrapped, however, as the price of scrap metal had fallen.* She would have only fetched around £1,500.[672] Scrap prices had plunged 'unexpectedly from £5 to about £1 15s per ton'.[673] Instead, V.70 was patched up and, once watertight, became known as *Salvage Unit No. 3,* a 'sort of floating carpenter's shop' was how Hewison described her.[674]

Cox was severely disappointed, however, with the islanders who made off in the night with anything that could be removed. Bill Peterson, one of Cox's early divers who often would dive with Herbert Hall, said that Cox should inquire about the missing items from 'the quiet boys ashore'.[675]

The next destroyer that Cox raised was easier. He applied the lessons from the *V.70* operation and learned new ones. As the ship had come up on her side in the cradle, she was too large to fit through the gap between the floating docks and had to be taken back out again to be righted in the cable sling in deeper water. This was quite easily accomplished; simply pulling one side up righted the ship. On 29 August 1924, the same day that *S.131* was raised by Robertson, Cox had already raised his third destroyer, *S.55.*†

---

* The price of coal had, in fact, plummeted from £5 to around £1 15s a ton.
† The second destroyer, *S.53,* was raised two weeks after *V.70,* on 14 August.

A FEW WORDS ABOUT GERMAN DESTROYERS

It is a little intimidating reading an endless list of numbers following what seems like meaningless letters – *V.70*, *S.55*, etc.

The combinations quite simply show the yards in which the torpedo boat was built and the maturity within the series. The following table highlights the typical armament and tonnage for each class.

S series – Schichau, Elbing and Danzig (Dansk)
V series – Vulkan, Hamburg
B series – Blohm und Voss, Hamburg
G series – Germaniawerft, Kiel
H series – Howaldswerke, Kiel

Builder	Class		tonnage	Speed (kts)	Length (ft)	Beam (ft)	Draught (ft)	Guns	Torpedoes	Mines
Schichau	S.31	S.32, S.36	802	33-36	261	27.5	11	3 x 3.4-inch	6 x 20-inch	24
	S.49	S.49, S.50, S.51, S.52	802	34-36.5	261	27.5	11	3 x 3.4-inch	6 x 20-inch	24
	S.53	S.53, S.54, S.55, S.56,	919	35-36	272.5	27.5	11.5	3 x 3.4-inch	6 x 20-inch	24
		S.60, S.52	919	35-36	272.5	27.5	11.5	3 x 4.1-inch	6 x 20-inch	24
	S.131	S.131, S.132, S.136,S.137, S.138	919	33-34	273	27.5	12.5	3 x 4.1-inch	6 x 20-inch	24
Germanienwerft	G.37	G.37, G.38, G.39, G.40	822	34	261	27.5	11	3 x 3.4-inch	6 x 20-inch	24
	G.85	G.85, G.86, G.89, G.91, G92	960	34	272.5	27.5	11.5	3 x 4.1-inch	6 x 20-inch	24
	G.101	G.101, G.102, G.103, G.104	1,116	33.5	313	30.5	12	3 x 4.1-inch	6 x 20-inch	24
Vulkan	V.43	V.43, V.44, V.45, V.46	852	34	261	27.5	11	3 x 3.4-inch	6 x 20-inch	24
	V.67	V.67, V.70, V.73, V.78, V.80, V.81, V.82, V.83	924	34-36.5	269	27.5	11.5	3 x 3.4-inch	6 x 20-inch	24
	V.125	V.125, V.126, V.127, V.128, V.129	924	34-34.5	321.5	30.5	12.5	3 x 4.1-inch	6 x 20-inch	24
Blohm und Voss	B.109	B.109, B.110, B.111, B.112	1,374	36-37.5	321.5	30.5	12.5	3 x 4.1-inch	6 x 20-inch	24
Howaldswerke	H.145	H.145	990	33.5-34	277	27.5	12.5	3 x 4.1-inch	6 x 20-inch	24

Source: van der Vat. pp. 224–255.

The methods that Robertson had used on *S.131* were quite innovative. Air balloons (called 'camels') were used either side of the sunken wreck with heavy chains attached to them. In Robertson's case, 10in steel belts were slung under the hull to lift the wreck and, once it moved free of the silt, the 'camels' were inflated underwater to lift the prize to the surface. Once on the surface, one of Robertson's ships, the *Trustee*, towed the destroyer ashore.

The practice for the interned destroyers had been to moor them in pairs in a 'great avenue' (as one Stromness schoolchild later described it).[676] This was done to reduce the heating needs as crews would transfer to one at night. Cutting the ties could be dangerous work. At first hacksaws were used, then a French flame-cutter. For each, the sudden release of tension could be extremely dangerous for the diver as cables could whiplash dangerously, even under water. In the end, gelignite was the preferred solution. The days needed for the lift halved each time with new learning being incorporated immediately into a fast-evolving technique manual. Most of the problems that were encountered came about more as a result of labour shortages than technical challenges. At least at this point. As an example, during the lifting of the fifth destroyer, many of Cox's men had to return home to help with the harvest and it was the Longhope lifeboat crew who took up the call and helped out.

With the sixth destroyer raised came an odd find – a petty officer's cat o'nine tails with his name engraved.* There is a photograph of the diver and his find in the Orkney archives. It is curious – and disturbing – to engrave an instrument of punishment with your name.

Robertson finished off the year buying G.89 from the Stromness Salvage Syndicate after the successful raising of the 280ft-long boat in mid-December. She was towed to Stromness on a Sunday with Captain George Porteous directing the operation from her bridge. *The Orcadian* reported (on 14 December 1922) in a wonderfully reserved manner: 'A certain amount of excitement was manifested on Sunday when an operation unique in the annals of the little town took place.' G.89 had served as a minelayer: on her deck were the rail lines designed to run the mines along down her deck to be dropped off the stern. After she had been raised, she was towed to Stromness for breaking up. In the end, her life was extended when her hull was sold for £50 to Cox and Danks 'to be employed as a counter weight to balance the list' of the *Seydlitz* as she was being lifted.[677]

Robertson gave up salvage after the winter of 1924. By then he had raised the four destroyers he had bought, but in the process had damaged one of his concrete barges. Cox stopped salvage work for the winter after 20 November and prepared shore equipment and facilities. He had added G.91 and G.38 to his list, having raised them both in September, respectively, on the 12th and the 27th.

* This was S.52, raised on 13 October 1924. Booth (p. 88) says reassuringly that they 'were only used to beat officers' uniforms clean'.

By 1925, the process of raising the smaller destroyers had been mastered. They were able to pull them up a rate of one a month. As much as anything else, it was the salvage expertise of the Glaswegian engineer, Tom McKenzie, that had made the difference. The Admiralty's overly pessimistic report about the prospects of salvage could not have been more off the mark. When it came to the overturned destroyers, especially the ones lying on their backs with the hulls upturned, McKenzie had perfected the process. It became so easy for a guide rope to be put under the ships to pull a cable through that the entire cabling process, 'setting an entire string of cables' by 'reeving' the lifting wires, could be completed 'in the incredible time of forty minutes'. [678]

The start of the year did not pass, however, without event. On 25 January, there was a severe gale that ran Cox's floating docks aground and on 22 April, there was a fire on the old German dock. Enough explosive had been stored there to have caused a very large explosion and, again, it was only because of McKenzie's quick-witted action that it was saved. Accidents continued into the year. A later explosion occurred when a fireman threw out some hot ashes on to the water by the dock. The dock was holding a newly raised destroyer in her cradle and, as was always the case, a large amount of surplus oil covered the surrounding water. McKenzie recalled how lucky they had been: 'Had the fire reached the store, there was enough explosive to blow the whole dock into the air.'[679]

Once again, McKenzie came to the rescue and damage to the workshops and lifting gear was slight. On another occasion, an electric crane collapsed and a dock worker, Donald Henderson, was killed. It was the first fatal accident of the whole operation. While Cox's company was acquitted of any liability in his death, it must have shaken him. He was that sort of man, ready to do anything he could for his men's safety. He would not ask them to do anything he would not do himself.

There were also lighter moments. A locked safe was found inside one destroyer and, with much anticipation, was opened in front of a crowd of the dock workers. There must have been a roar of laughter when it was finally prized open. The only thing found inside was a chamber pot. It was later ceremonially presented to Mrs McKenzie.

The first ship of the year, *H.145* – Cox's seventh destroyer – was raised on 19 March, and the day before another large German floating dock had arrived. It would help speed up the already well-practised operations. From August 1924 to April 1926 twenty-eight torpedo boats were raised and broken up for scrap. One, *S.65*, which was raised on Saturday 16 May, was

achieved in a record time: four days. Two weeks later, on 2 May, the flotilla leader *S.138* was raised. Six years after she had gone down, the fifty or so copies of the *Daily Mirror* found on board were still, astonishingly, 'easily readable'.

On 7 September, a milestone of sorts was reached; *V.78* was raised. It was the last of the smaller, 750-ton destroyers. The last of the low-hanging fruit, so to speak. Cox was ready for a bigger challenge after these early successes. Revenue from destroyer scrap sold to the Alloa Shipbreaking Company amounted to £32,000.

The new dry dock made light work of the heavier destroyers such as *G.103* or the flotilla leader, *B.110*, raised just before Christmas.[*] Sometimes, however, as was the case with *S.55*, Cox found his efforts frustrated. The torpedo boat been lying in around 40ft of water but somehow the precious, non-ferrous metals from inside her torpedo tubes had already been taken.[†] Propellers, in particular, were highly valued for their phosphor bronze alloy. He had also had problems with the heavier 1,116-ton *G.103*. She broke free 20 miles off Rattray Head on the Aberdeenshire coast and drifted ashore, where she broke up. *G.103* had given Cox problems early on. She had been too wide for the normal floating dock inverted 'double-L' approach and so one side of the dock was removed. That proved too unstable, and it sank with *G.103* attached. Raising the two again caused so many technical issues that the floating dock was only used from then on as a workshop.

On 1 May 1926, Cox raised the equally large *G.104* and with that finished the initial round of salvage.[‡] All twenty-six of the destroyers he had purchased were now off the floor of the flow. In twenty months, he had brought up 23,000 tons of shipping with what was calculated at a market value almost ninety years later of around £31 million.[§] Now he could turn his full attention to the ultimate challenge: the battleships.

The huge vessels were not the easy pickings the destroyers had been. Early on, Cox took a close look at the 26,180-ton *Hindenburg* to see how

---

[*] The 1,215-ton *G.103* was raised between 29 September and 4 October 1925, *B.110* on 16 December.

[†] It was reckoned that each torpedo tube (because of the phosphor bronze used) would fetch around £100 (Booth p. 37 in reference to the *V.70* tubes).

[‡] Alloa had purchased three destroyers at the end of June 1926 – *G.104*, *G.101* and *B.109*. The purchase price was £1,800 but the value of the 360 tons of salvaged metals was around £20,000 (Buxton, p. 12).

[§] Hewison, p. 185 says that the contemporary market value was around £50,000, which he stated was worth between '£31/32 million' when he wrote his account (1999).

she could be salvaged. He was thinking that he might be able to use the ship as a platform from which to raise the heavy guns off of the *Seydlitz*. Her internal divisions and armour plating were 'greater than any warship then in German service, which contributed greatly to the…salvage value'.[680] At the time, she cost £2 million to build, equivalent to £75 million in 2003.*

As always, Cox and McKenzie were the first into a wreck. Neither would ask of their men something they themselves had not done or would not undertake. They had 'no submersible lighting, for it would not have penetrated the inky blackness caused by mud and particles stirred up when they moved. It must have taken courage and a lot of nerve to be first. Everything had, therefore, to be done by touch.'[681] To give its readers a sense of the conditions inside these massive ships, *The Times* commissioned a local photographer, William Hourston, to take photographs. It was a hazardous, some would be tempted to say an almost irresponsible, assignment. Hourston nearly lost his way in the pitch darkness. His candle started to flicker and went out. Luckily, he was able to get close enough to the hull to see a glimmer of light above. The next time he was more careful; he unwound a ball of string.

More divers were sent down into the ship. Once back up, they said it was like walking through a 'vast submarine forest', marine growth was everywhere, hiding most recognisable objects.[682] When it was fresh, it was full of a wonderful array of colours. It soon turned brown and started to stink. As they went through the sunken ship, they found telltale signs of the last moments before she had been abandoned. What they saw in the wardroom gave them an idea of the mood in the officers' quarters as they waited for the final, irreversible orders to scuttle. Empty champagne bottles and glasses were littered all around. As she had gone down without rolling, some semblance of where things had been positioned was still discernible.

Bringing her up represented an entirely new challenge; 9in cable was certainly not going to work. *Hindenburg* was heavier than the entire collective weight of the twenty-six destroyers already raised. She was 700ft long and had a very wide 96ft beam. So, instead of *lifting* the ship, Cox would try to *float* her back up. It would mean resealing the ship's hull, closing all the openings that had been used to scuttle her, pumping the water out to give her buoyancy and then controlling her ascent as she

---

* Booth's estimate was made in 2003 (p. 71).

lifted. Lying flat on her hull, however, meant that divers could not easily access the valves on the hull's keel and so they would have to patch them from the inside.

Cox was greatly helped by one of his team of sixteen divers who found something in the control room that even the Royal Navy had not found – complete ship's plans including most importantly, the pumping layout etched on metal. They found the plans at the very same moment that Cox had, after considerable difficulty, tracked some down in Germany, excitedly telexing 'Have found plans.' 'So have we,' was the immediate reply. McKenzie called the plans 'a gift from the Gods' as they 'not only showed the ship's piping arrangement, [they] also showed the control points for each valve'.[683]

The task was gigantic. To anyone else but a man of Ernest Cox's conviction and strength, it would have been overwhelming. Nothing would happen until he went down along with McKenzie in full dive rig to see for himself. More than 800 patches had to be built and secured to *Hindenburg*'s hull. How they did it was to construct a wooden template frame on land, test it and make a metal version in Lyness. They then took that out to the wreck, where divers would bolt it on to the hull, sealing the hole with quick-drying cement and patching material soaked in tallow.* This was when they discovered a problem with the eating habits of a local fish. It turned out that a fish called a saithe (or saithey), developed an unhealthy taste for the tallow and gradually undid all the patient work that had gone into the first attempt at patching *Hindenburg*. At first, Cox was furious when a diver mentioned that a fish was the culprit but was disarmed when the reply was, 'But we thought ye'd know.' He realised that it was the awe in which his men held him that was the problem. They just assumed he knew everything there was to know.

A 10 per cent Portland cement mix was added to the tallow and between the actual patch and the ship's hull a so-called 'pudding joint', a sacking bag full of oakum, was added. This was nailed to the outside of the joint, which gradually compressed as the patch was bolted into place, reducing its thickness from around 3in to around a quarter of an inch. Despite the significant amount of additional work this created, McKenzie found that the new mix had 'better sealing properties than the original tallow alone'.[684]

* The divers used a special gun that could fire self-threading bolts into the ship's metal hull at pressures of 1,000in². The gun was called a 'Cox gun' but had nothing to do with Ernst Cox. It weighed 36lb and so would be suspended on steel cables to allow the diver to work with it more easily underwater.

Of course, some of the holes that needed to be patched were extremely large and complex. When one of *Hindenburg's* funnels had to be removed as it was badly corroded, it left a 21ft wide, 40ft long gap that had to be covered up. The patch that was built was mounted on a trestle of 3in timbers supported on 6in steel H beams. What usually made these tasks even more difficult was measuring the ship's surface in the dark murkiness of the deep where obstructions and contours were impossible to see. Touch was often the only way.

On 6 August, Cox started pumping out the ship and by the end of the month, she was finally off the bottom. The only problem was that after five days of pumping, and as soon as she started to rise – with buoyancy achieved by taking the water out at a rate of around 3,600 tons an hour – she also began to list badly. He found that the more water he pumped out, the more the ship took on a list. The situation was doubly precarious because, as Cox admitted, he had assumed the 3ft-wide stern section of the keel would sink in and hold while she was raised. But, rather than resting in the soft cradle of shingle, the stern was balancing on solid rock. As he put it, 'we were trying to balance the battleship of about 100ft width on a stern 3ft wide!'[685]

On 2 September, late in the afternoon, she finally – unexpectedly – came up. After only an hour, one of Cox's men, diver Harry Hall, jumped across and fixed a red ensign to her stern. 'Within fifteen minutes,' however, 'a strong wind began blowing down from the north-west.'[686] It quickly became a gale.

Double-strung cables were attached from her masts to a destroyer still sunk off Cava – three-quarters of a mile away – to hold her neutral. These soon proved inadequate.

The ship had been afforded some initial protection by the two destroyers lying alongside, previously attached to her side in an attempt to neutralise her list, but 'she was now rolling so violently that one of her derricks, some 2ft in diameter and 30ft high, snapped off and crashed on to her decks'.[687]

That night one of the destroyers, *G.38,* smashed against the floating dock, once again flooding the battleship. Worse yet, the pumps failed on one of the docks. It was the dock that powered half the pumps keeping the monstrous ship afloat and the tugs were not able to compensate for the lost power. Sixteen of Cox's divers – always in teams of two – worked in the depths trying to keep the pumps going but to little avail. It was perilous work; she was listing dangerously at 25° as 55-knot winds howled across the boiling waters of the Flow. She rolled and sank again. The pumping gear was taken off just in time. It had been an expensive and frustrating time. It was a miracle that no one was sliced in half as the cut cable lashed dangerously across the water like a whip.

With little to show for all his effort, Cox was £30,000 the poorer. His men had fought valiantly – but unsuccessfully – to save *Hindenburg*. Some were said to have cried, even if Cox himself was quiet, resolute. Turning to Ernest McKeown, he promised: 'We'll fetch her up next spring. I've been thinking it out, and I see the idea now.'[688] After halting any continued work on the *Hindenburg*, Cox was now going to try a new approach on the *Moltke*

The Germans had very deliberately tried to roll their ships as they scuttled them, thinking that this would make salvage more difficult. In fact, it made it easier. The 23,000-ton *Moltke* was in around 70ft of water, lying at a slight list of 16.5° 'bottom up near the island of Rysa' but because she had turned on her back she might offer another, a different solution.[689] *Moltke* had only been commissioned in 1912 so she, also, was still a young ship.

What Cox now contemplated was to add an Italian innovation already tried out on smaller ships to his own hull-sealing technique. It meant not only pumping the water out of the hull, it also meant pumping air back in under high pressure. *Moltke*'s hull valves and torpedo tubes were relatively easy to find and sealed with quick-drying cement, *Ciment fondu*.* In August 1916 the 24,000-ton *Leonardo da Vinci* had sunk in Taranto harbour and the Italians had managed a successful salvage using this approach. One of their team, a Major Gianelli, came to Scapa to share these experiences with Cox. However, at first he was not impressed with what he heard. '...it misled me, not because it was inferior work, but because the circumstances were essentially different. The Italian ship in Taranto harbour had a list of only 8°, whereas the *Moltke* was lying at the bottom with a 17° list.'[690]

In his mind, compressed air could not correct such a heavy list.

Any remaining holes in the 610ft-long *Moltke*'s hull were sealed with quick-setting cement sent down to the divers in jute bags.† In places, her

---

* The cement dries with a chemical reaction rather than from water evaporation: 'After twenty-four hours, the substance is as hard as normal cement is after twenty-eight days.' (Booth, p. 74)

† Although *Moltke* displaced considerably less and was almost 90ft shorter than *Hindenburg*, she actually lay on a wider beam, 96ft 3in.

side armour was a good 12in thick. After bulkheads had been strengthened, air was pumped in through the very valves that the Germans had used to flood her. 'Air pipes were embedded into the bottom valve openings with *ciment fondu*,' and then the pipes connected to three compressors on the surface on the *Sidonian*.[691] Air, at a rate of 300,000ft³ a day, was now pumped in.

Because her hull was upturned and in relatively shallow water, Cox came up with an ingenious solution that would add more working hours and better conditions for his gargantuan task. Cutting up old boilers into 12ft lengths, 6ft in diameter, and joining them together, his men built a long entry tube that would allow someone to go from water level down to the submerged hull's surface. Cutting a hole in the hull and adding hatches at the entry and the exit points then allowed workmen to enter the space that had been pumped free of water without being encumbered in diving suits. The airlock tower would be like an air-tight tube with hatches at each end. After entering through the top hatch and closing it, the internal air pressure was raised to equal that of the ship. In early 1927, the first of these new tube-like entry tunnels were attached on to the *Moltke*. That was the theory. The practice was a little more uncomfortable. As they cut through the hull, the smell was horrendous, 'a choice mixture of burnt red lead, oil, paint and boiled bilge water'.[692] It was not only the smell. The smoke was so intense that McKenzie and Cox could hardly see what they were doing. In fact, it was so bad that they had to jump out of the shaft to get fresh air and medical attention. They came 'tumbling up out of the air-lock like a couple of pantomime demons in a burst of dramatically coloured smoke'.[693]

The other innovation was establishing a safety valve on the bow. Letting air out could hold back the kind of uncontrolled ascent that would spell disaster. The ship's buoyancy was more controlled. A state of 'neutral buoyancy' in the wreck was what Cox was after: just enough air to allow the divers to work, but not enough to cause a sudden ascent. Between 15 and 22psi of pressure was needed to give her buoyancy.[694] Air management was a constant challenge. If there was an air leak, the tell-tale signs could sometimes be seen. A 'fog-like effect meant that compressed air was starting to expand and vaporize'.[695] McKenzie was working below once when this happened:

We shouted for the men to make for the airlock…we had to pass through doors little bigger than manholes, which we had cut in each of the bulkheads between us and the airlock. The air was rushing through these holes with the force of a hurricane. Our hats were blown off. Our jackets were blown over our heads and flapped wildly around us. Pieces of rust and coal stung our faces as we forced our way forward.[696]

After ten days of pumping, the water at last began to be forced out and by the eleventh day her hull was 7ft above the waterline.[697] In December 1926, *Moltke* was raised gently, the hull still upturned. Unlike *Hindenburg*, Cox had no ship's plans on which to base his calculations. He had used a pre-war copy of *Jane's Fighting Ships*.

Most of the work was done at 60 to 70ft, in the cold darkness of the Flow, the divers' only contact with the surface the microphone built into their heavy brass and copper dive helmets. The helmets were fitted with a 4.5in diameter face glass, half an inch thick. The diver breathed air pumped in through a pipe at the back where a non-return valve was fitted. It meant that, if the valve was turned off, the diver's suit would fill with air, giving him lift. It was a heavy and cumbersome outfit in which to work the usual two three-hour daily shifts. The boots weighed 16lb each and a further two lead weights – each weighing 40lb – were tied across the diver's chest and back.* The diver's suit was a rubberised twill under which was worn underwear, a shirt, trousers, a sweater, a scarf and two pairs of socks. The physical exertion of the work in these conditions and with this kind of kit must have been extreme.

Despite the cold, a diver did not wear any gloves so his hands 'often became swollen and numb'.[698] Below, there was the added danger from conger eels hiding in the wrecks and at least one diver, Harry Grosset, was badly bitten by one.

Inside the hull, the high-pressure working environment was dank, cold, stank of decay and contained a lethal explosive atmosphere in which operating blow torches was extremely hazardous. A blow torch, in any case, would not work below 15ft and so wreckage would only be cleared by using a time-consuming hacksaw. Cox started to use gelignite when a cable under high tension had nearly killed a diver by whipping him to the surface. It took divers a few days to get used to the cracking in their ears from the pressure, but it did mean that whatever the conditions might be on the surface, work could continue below. John

* See Booth p. 43.

Tulloch who, as a child, had witnessed the scuttle, worked on *Moltke*. He recalled the world of a salver:

> Inside the wreck there was a wilderness of oil-covered machinery, pipes, companionways and other obstructions all topsy-turvy as, of course, the ship was bottom side up. This wilderness became worse as we cut our way through bulkheads and made paths to get where we wanted to go. Day by day we burned, cut and patched, all the time getting further into the bowels of the ship. Electric lights were strung across the wreck above our heads and as we cleared our way, these were extended from compartment to compartment but they never really gave out much light. Outside the radius of the lights the interior was dark and gloomy, full of traps and hidden openings, hatches, ventilator shafts and other holes that had to be carefully watched (out) for all the time. The realization that the sea was being held back all around us by the hull of the ship only made things very eerie at times.[699]

Fitting the airlocks on the ships whose hulls still rested above water presented no special challenges but the deeper ships required total precision. The great towers were welded together on land and towed out to the wrecks.

Despite the rigours of working for hours at depth, the productivity of the divers was 'quite remarkable'. Harry Taylor, an apprentice fitter and turner, who joined Cox and Danks right out of school, talked about how airlocks were fitted as a way of illustrating the speed of the work:

> The day that an airlock was fitted, two divers working together, would drill, tap and bolt sixty bolts down at the base of the airlock and meantime two (other) divers would be passing up the wire ropes used for guys which were very, very necessary as the bolts alone...would have sheared off with the list of the ship and the angle that the airlock was lying at.[700]

One diver would follow another. 'The "safety man" who followed each diver had to guide his leader's air pipe and other lines through the tangle....'[701] A diver's life would depend on the second man, often called the 'linesman'.

Taylor had seen nine German battleships being raised, three by Cox and Danks and six by Metal Industries. His descriptions of the Scapa salvage operations give a real flavour of, and insight to, the daily challenges the men faced.

Entering a ship through an airlock could be an unnerving experience for a novice. The work was not for the faint-hearted. As the air-tight hatch was opened, it would have sounded liked an express train was coming. The compressed air rushed into the airlocks with a howl. The air would have thickened 'like an old-time London fog and one's eardrums [would have] seemed about to burst'.[702] McKenzie would always be right there when the oxy-acetylene torches started to cut through. The stench was overpowering. After a day's work workers would welcome the climb back up into the fresh but biting winds of the Flow. It was tough but satisfying work.

Quoting an *Orcadian* report that he believed was written by JG Marwick, a future convener of Stromness, visiting the *Kaiser*, Hewison wrote about the daily end of work ritual: 'Presently from each of them (author's note: the airlocks), emerged half-a-dozen grimy men in overalls. Some of them stride into the sea up to the waist in order to wash off the greasy slime which covered everything, while others emptied muddy water out of their boots.'[703]

The work was divided into the shore and salvage squads. When the work got tight, the normal shore routine was dropped and the salvage squads were reinforced by shore crews. But there was always a balance: 'Normally we didn't work the weekend,' Taylor recalled.

Pay for a forty-hour work week was around five pence an hour, about 16s. Taylor was paid around 30s a week, which for the time was 'good money', and Cox, with whom his father had arranged an interview, paid him £5 for the expenses in getting to Scapa, where he joined the salvage before he had even finished his schooling. Cox had told his father that the young lad could join in the work at Scapa but that he should 'send him up right away'.

Cox's men were totally committed to the work and clearly deeply respected him. Taylor said they were simply 'too busy looking after the job…our purpose was to lift the ship and that was that', and that they did not bother to look for memorabilia. Not many people would have been able to resist the temptation.

Moltke's list was solved partly by sealing off compartments within the ship to control the buoyancy as she rose and attaching cables to help maintain the correct attitude of the ship under water. Initially, the cables rubbed and would fray as they were sawn through on the sharp edges.

Once that had been sorted out, no more obstacles remained.

On 13 June 1927, *Moltke* finally came up to the surface and stayed there.* It was around lunchtime and many of the workers had taken a break.† She came up with such a sudden rush, like an express train, that: '...set the attendant docks rolling violently and bashing against their anchor-chains and cables. It was surrounded by a spectacular turmoil of compressed air which escaped explosively, sending up 20ft waterspouts and clouds of vapour saturated with oil and coal-dust.'[704]

There were men on the airlocks, placed there to keep an eye on the pressure within each of the compartments under their towering airlocks. As *Moltke* shot up, it must have been like the experience of a circus performer as the human cannonball. One talked about the experience: 'I don't know about lifebelts. It's flaming parachutes we want up here!'[705] One workman had tied up beside the floating ship and was about to enter an airlock when he was startled by the ship rapidly starting to rise.

In typical Cox style, even if he had been unprepared, he took advantage of a group of tourists on a local ferry, the *Countess of Codogan*. They were invited aboard and were able to walk up and down the upturned hull to their heart's content. *The Orcadian* carried a full, illustrated story a few days later.

On 16 June, *Moltke* was towed to Lyness. *G.83* had been used as much as possible to ferry ashore as much that could be immediately taken off. The tow was not without further setbacks. As she was being towed hull-up, one of her gun barrels fell out of its locking mechanism, started to drag below the vast superstructure and then stuck fast in the mud. It was blasted off but it would still take until August to complete the journey. When she did arrive, gangs using cranes took as much equipment off her as they could – around 3,000 tons. A further 250 tons of armour and 312 tons of non-ferrous metals such as manganese, bronze, copper, brass and gun metal.[706] Gun metal was prized because of the high mix of nickel and chromium and cutting through the metal with oxy-acetylene torches could be carried out at a rate of around a foot a minute.‡ Only after the winter storms had calmed was *Moltke*

---

* Booth (p. 91) has the date as 10 June.
† Bowman (p. 160) states that she came up at 1315.
‡ Non-ferrous metals included 'brass, copper, lead, bronze, gunmetal and manganese' (Booth, p. 21). Cox claimed to have become such an expert that he could tell the metal, he claimed, 'simply by shutting his eyes and tapping it with a hammer' (Booth, p. 19).

taken on to Rosyth, where the Alloa Shipbreaking Company would break her up.*

On 8 May 1928, she made way on the perilous open sea journey. Huts had been built on her upturned hull. These would house the crews keeping the pumps going on her last voyage to the breaker's yard. It was almost like a little village – a kitchen, bunkhouse and mess room for the crew, plus, of course, the most important, the compressor powerhouse. During the crossing it was more vital than ever to make sure that there was no danger of the pressure falling and the hull going down.

It was difficult going and in the treacherous waters of the Pentland Firth, in a bad sea, the huts were flooded. Only after the seas had calmed did they make the Firth of Forth. The crossing must have caused Cox quite considerable stress as 'Alloa had insisted on purchasing *Moltke* on a delivered basis', i.e. he took the insurance liability. And that was expensive: £8,000 'for only two-thirds of the risk'.[707] Three German tugs – the *Seefalke*, *Simson* and *Pontos* – took her across the 230-mile sea crossing to Rosyth.† At times they were being towed by the sheer weight of the 22,640-ton *Moltke* rather than towing her.‡ At one point as they were rounding the Moray Firth they found themselves pushed by a very strong wind with 'Dunet Head abeam, around 15 miles in the wrong direction'. Dunet Head was 15 miles west of the isle of Stroma and they were, at this point, drifting past. *Moltke* started rolling so badly that compressed air was continually escaping out from under the hull. For those in the small huts on her back, it must have been a terrifying crossing. It was cold, water was sloshing all over and the fire had gone out, so there was no hot food. Miserable. At any moment the ship could have gone down, taking many of them with her. She was rolling so hard that it was not even possible to get extra pump power from another of the tugs, *Sidonian*.

They struggled for most of the afternoon. At 1600 the tides eased and they started to make headway again and after twilight they were back abeam of the Dunet Point lighthouse.

As they approached the Forth Bridge, the pilots started to argue with

---

* The Alloa Shipbreaking Company would eventually merge with Metal Industries and the two would buy out Cox & Danks.

† Rented from the Hamburg company of Bugsier, Reederei und Bergungs, AG. Booth (p. 93) says the name of the third German ferry was *Posen* not *Pontos*.

‡ Very often Dutch tugs such as *Zwarte See* or *Witte See* were used for this part of the tow. They were considered expensive but also to have the most experience. *Zwarte See* was built in 1933 for L Smit & Son of Kinderdijk NL (Source: Ronald Stewart, 20 June 2006, Kirkwall Library and Archives).

each other. One, the first one aboard, was a Firth of Forth pilot. The German tugboat captain had naturally let him on. The Admiralty pilot, who had been contacted by Cox, came on second. They both argued points of maritime law on who had the right of command. Both were completely unconscious of the fact that they only narrowly missed hitting the structure of the bridge itself. Actually, the upside-down ship went through the bridge without any tugs. They had gone one side of the central pier as *Moltke* glided past the other and the lines had to be cast off. *Moltke* became 'the only battleship ever to pass beneath the Forth Bridge upside down, unattended and out of control'.[708] It took the tugs 'more than half an hour to regain control'.[709] As they approached the breaker's yard at Rosyth, the ship crept in with only one foot to spare underneath and finally got to her assigned place without any mishap. For Cox and his team the relief was palpable. Had the ship gone down he would have lost everything. Months later he received a letter from the Admiralty saying that the cost of damages to the dock were in the enclosed bill. Cox nervously opened the attached envelope. It was a bill for £8.

The *Seydlitz* was an equally difficult and expensive operation, and the battle-cruiser was actually raised twice: the first time while Cox was away on holiday in Switzerland. He immediately ordered her resunk to await his return – and the planned media coverage. He decided to split his workforce between working on her and another battleship, SMS *Kaiser*, which was lying near where *Moltke* had been.

Moltke's 25,000-ton sister ship lay at around the same depth, 12 fathoms down, but on her starboard side.* She was 'an improved version of the *Moltke*',[710] being 46ft longer and 3½ft narrower in the beam at 93ft, and faster. Around 20ft of her 656ft-long hull could be seen above water. 'Strangers entering Scapa Flow sometimes mistook her for a small island'.[711] She was a mere six years old when her end finally came.

Seydlitz would benefit Cox in ways that he could not have predicted even if her lift was going to prove a very difficult one. The price of coal at the start of 1926 had risen sharply, spurred by the lack of supply during the General Strike. *Seydlitz*'s coal bunkers had been full when she went down and as the price of coal soared from £1 a ton to £4 15s a ton, she gave Cox a 'custom-built mine'. All that was needed was to cut out an entry through her hull, which at points, even though she was lying in 70ft of water, was 20ft above the surface of the Flow.[712]

---

* A British fathom is equal to 6ft.

The General Strike could not have been an easy time for Cox but he must have found reassurance in his workforce. Not a single man joined the strikers. That is maybe why that Christmas, as a sign of gratitude, all his men were given three weeks' *paid* holiday. A £3,000 Christmas present.

In June 1927 the work began. Cox started on the armour plating bolted on to the ship's sides in sections that were 14ft long and 1ft thick, held on by thick bolts, 'extremely valuable as scrap metal'.* Cox was also able to strip off just under 1,800 tons of 12in armour plating with equal ease. Both of these significantly helped his operation by supplying much-needed ready cash at a time when he was starting to face severe financial pressure. Considering that his weekly labour costs were running at £1,000 with an equivalent weekly bill for coal, *Seydlitz*'s supply was a heaven-sent gift.

By June 1928 the ship's innards had been sealed off and six separate water- and air-tight compartments built to balance her out.† The huge, gaping 1,300ft² gap left by her two missing funnels had been covered over and sealed. The lift was scheduled for 12 June, when conditions were as good as they could be. Around 1500 she came up, 'amid the din of hissing air and oily exhaust odour'. What seemed like a triumph – he was the first man to 'raise a ship sideways' – now fell apart.[713]

The problem had been caused by the disproportionate loss of weight from the tons of armour that had been stripped off. The men heard a sudden muffled noise, 'followed by a dull explosive concussion'. Two bulkheads had collapsed and the carefully managed air allocation completely thrown out of balance. A whole sequence of events led to her rolling over and sinking back down. The collapse destroyed much of the work that had been accomplished. Patches were ruined, compressors and other equipment lost. As she, her bridge, masts and some superstructure were crushed and the derrick posts placed to hold her in position now smashed through some of the decks as she came back down.

Another lift was tried in October but the buoyancy issue had still not been solved despite an equal amount of weight being added by using sandbags. Numerous test lifts were made: 'Twenty times she was nearly righted, and twenty times we had to begin all over again,' was how Cox summed up the heart-wrenching frustration he must have felt.[714] Whenever Cox had to lay her back down, he felt the pressure. 'It was a heartbreaking procedure as I was getting short of money.'[715] Finally, a

* See Booth, p. 98. I have seen one of these bolts at Scapa. Jonnie Miel was kind enough to show it to me, quizzing me as he handed me the huge nut.
† George (p. 82) maintains there were eight water-tight compartments.

successful lift was made on 1 November and was filmed for posterity by *Pathé* and *Movietone News*. Still, it was filled with drama. As she broke the surface, a series of really loud cracks like a gun firing were heard. It was the cables parting. Ten parted but, thankfully, twelve remained as the ship found her final buoyancy, listing a minimal and easy to correct 8°.

Seydlitz was put in tow by *Ferrodanks*, *Sidonian* and *Lyness*, but then ran aground and it took a week to get loose and, on her way, again to Lyness. Once there her decks were further lightened – machinery, armour and a forward turret were taken off, freeing up 7ft of freeboard. The following year – 29 May 1929 – she was again put under tow, this time for Rosyth. What started out as a 'fine' morning ended with a gale. That evening conditions had become appalling, and after having snagged a barrel at the bottom of the Flow like *Moltke*, she took another week to complete the journey. One man, James Sutherland, was swept overboard but luckily rescued. Barrels of fuel had careened along the keel and fallen into the sea. A tool chest had crashed into the crew quarters, smashing through one of the walls, leaving the crew open to the elements, soaking stores and putting out fires. It was a miserable, frightening journey where everything was on the line, hour after hour. At one point, it took a full twenty-four hours to only progress 17 miles.

Two months before, on 30 March, the 24,380-ton battleship *Kaiser* was also raised. Work had been under way for some time even before *Seydlitz* came up. The lift 'proved to be the easiest of all'.[716] The concrete pillars holding any further list were not needed. After the 200-ton turrets had been removed, the lift went faultlessly. It could have turned out very differently. One man, AS Thomson, had been caught on board and only escaped Cox's fury when he joked that he had been below, giving her an extra push.

Three divers were killed in the course of Cox's salvage. One near accident occurred when *G.91* was being raised and a diver became stuck under a collapsed funnel between her and *S.65*. McKenzie got on a surface phone to the diver to try and talk him through a possible panic but before he could even open his mouth he heard 'a very poorly rendered' version of 'Home, Sweet Home' coming up from the depths. The diver was very calm indeed. You have to admire the kind of men these were.

The first death was of a forty-five-year-old diver from Portsmouth. 'Nobby' Hall had been a petty officer and diver in the navy and had also been one of Tom McKenzie's first divers, with him right from the start along with Bill Peterson, his close friend.* He was 'very capable, willing and always anxious to do his best', in the opinion of his commanding officer at HMS *Vernon*.[717] Hall had written to his 'own darling wife', Alice, in early March 1929 saying that he was in great condition, 'the best that I have felt for a long time' but, ominously, he ended his letter saying that his hands were 'in a shocking state' and that he kept on getting 'the cramp in the fingers'.[718] Hall died on 27 May 1929 while working in the aft section of the *Kaiser*, lying at Lyness Pier. He had refused a life-line being attached. Hall knew that it was against Cox's orders but he felt that it was as likely to snag him. Ironically, he had been in very shallow water and he was a tall man. His body floated out from the compartment in which he had been working and was spotted by his linesman on the day, Magnus Scott. The face plate was speedily unscrewed. His face was swollen and covered in blood, bleeding from his ears. No one at the time understood quite why one of McKenzie's divers had died. The inquest put it down to a weight having caused a traumatic asphyxia but McKenzie said he was convinced that some 'natural cause' had 'accelerated his death'.[719]

Kaiser arrived in Rosyth shortly after *Seydlitz*, in July. There was only one small snag when her conning tower stuck in the mud. It was almost like *Moltke*'s and *Seydlitz*'s barrels snagging. The decision was taken to allow the natural fall of tide to push the tower back into the superstructure and then float her off. There is a photograph of her salved bell, photographed with two of her salvers standing proudly beside it.

The *Bremse*, a light cruiser, was one of the first fast minelaying cruisers in the HSF. She was lying also on her side in Swanbister Bay, her bow still visible, right where she had been towed by the destroyer HMS *Venetia* (F.14) on 21 June. Much of her superstructure was taken off and on 30 November she was taken to Lyness for breaking up. It was decided not to tow her south to Rosyth as she was considered too unsafe for the journey. She had oil-fired engines and the tons of fuel on board had already proved extremely dangerous. McKenzie explained: 'On more than one occasion we had to run for our lives with flames chasing us as far as the airlock, owing to the fuel oil having been ignited.'[720]

In a 2017 expedition the small outboard survey vessel from Gert Normann Andersen's *Viña* found the still-visible imprint of where her 460ft-long hull had rested under what is now a fish farm.

---

* Nobby saved Bill Peterson's life when Peterson had climbed on a heavy wooden ladder, which fell away and then blocked not only his way out but was crushing his air hose. Hall had gone back to find his friend when he heard something unusual.

In January 1930 Cox went back to tackle the *Hindenburg*. Even though it had not been long since his men had first started working on her, only 500 of the 800 filler patches still held. Cox's idea to right her list was to sink a section of a destroyer – a 40ft by 30ft wide section of her heaviest section, the engine room – filled with 600 tons of quick-dry cement next to *Hindenburg* to use as a wedge. Alone, that operation cost £2,000. Anything that was still on the surface was taken off, for example her large forward gun. Again, this was both to lighten the lift as well as free up some additional cash. Cox's team managed to raise her 16ft above water. Then the list came back, this time to starboard. So, another destroyer was used for the other side. Blocks were built under each of the propeller shafts as a secondary means of correcting the list.[721] Two salvaged destroyers were then brought alongside, put there as a breakwater against Orcadian storms.

On 6 August, Cox tried to raise her. Air was being pumped into her and water – at a rate of 3,600 tons an hour – pumped out. As she emptied, the stench of rotting vegetation was overwhelming. It was nauseating, like the cloying smell of death. But Cox could not beat the *Hindenburg* into submission that day. As she rose, she started to list badly. Finally, as her port list reached 40°, he decided to let her fall back in and try a stern lift. The same thing happened. He concluded that 'the damn ship is heavier on the portside' and decided to counterbalance the starboard side with one of the salvaged destroyers filled with water.[722]

At one point as she started to lift there were ominous cracking sounds. The fear was that her back was breaking – either from 'sagging' where the ship's hull is in a trough or 'hogging' where the centre is carrying all the weight. Cox, hardly a strong diver, went down himself to check that the decks were not cracking.

Time and money were running out and Cox decided to take a three-week break while preparations were under way. When he came back everything was ready and in July a successful lift was made. It was, however, very tense. A man had been put aboard her to shout back reports on the list as she rose. The shouted reports came back: 2½°, 3°, 3½°, 4°, 4½°, 5°, 5½° and then it stopped at 6°. After fifteen minutes or so, another ¼° was added but then it settled at 6°. Cox knew it was alright. He had just succeeded in raising 'the biggest ship in the world that had ever been lifted'.[723] In his jubilation, Cox, immaculately dressed as always, jumped across on to her washing deck. One of his workers jumped across to 'give him a hand' and promptly fell into a deck cavity. The two of them 'disappeared in a floundering splash, to rise up gasping, clinging to each other, and laughing like children'.[724]

Hindenburg was first towed to Mill Bay and beached there to lighten her in preparation for her final voyage. After a three-day passage, setting out on 23 August 1930, she finally passed under the Forth Bridge on the way to Rosyth. She was an impressive sight. Two of her guns, one fore and one aft, were still there. Unlike the ignominious end of so many of the other great ships coming in with hulls upturned, *Hindenburg* came in decks clean and manned (*Hindenburg* was even able to supply some workable diesel generators). Looks aside, not being on her back would also mean that she would be easier to break up but the price he got, rumoured to have been around £75,000, was 'as much as Cox had spent raising her'.[725] It meant that at the end of these successive years of operation he had now almost financially broke even. He was only £20,000 out of pocket.

In October, Cox turned his attentions to the 19,400-ton battle-cruiser, SMS *von der Tann*. She was only lying at around a 100ft down but would prove to be Cox's nemesis. She was to be the source of a number of serious accidents.

There was one particular near-fatal accident. Three men had been working together: Bob Kelday, Jim Sutherland and Sinclair 'Sinc' McKenzie, when there was another large explosion. Kelday had been cutting a pipe when Tom McKenzie was climbing down to join him. The cutting set off an explosion and McKenzie was blown back up the ladder with such force that he was knocked unconscious. Kelday had thought his back broken, McKenzie his leg. Neither turned out to be the case, although McKenzie's nose had been smashed to a pulp when he'd been knocked against the steel bulkhead. Attempts to rescue them were foiled by a virulent and impenetrable fire.

Kelday could not immediately be found. Nor McKenzie. Sandy Robertson remembered finding him: 'We saw this man floating in the oil. We grabbed him, hauled him up and turned him over. The oil on his face had to be scraped off and we did not know who it was until we saw his collar and tie. "My God! It's McKenzie", someone said.'[726]

All ended up with bad facial burns. Tom McKenzie's head injuries turned out to be the most serious and he was taken off work to recuperate.

At 1500 on 6 December 1930, 'the tip of the rudder and four propellers burst through the surface'.[727] Men worked through the night and the next day, a Sunday, the bow appeared. She was stabilised. The day after Tom McKenzie came back from hospital, 4 February 1931, the *von der Tann* was towed to Lyness.

Von der Tann changed Cox's life and led to his decision to retire, leave Orkney and move his family south again. He did not take the decision immediately or lightly. He first put his entire workforce on paid leave while the explosion and fire were investigated. *Von der Tann* was towed to be beached on Cava while metal prices improved and work on *Prinzregent Luitpold* started. An immediate breaking up was held off while anticipating a market recovery.

Cox's last lift was the 25,000-ton *Prinzregent Luitpold*, which he raised on 6 July. She had been lying in 18 fathoms of water listing at 18°. The flawless lift was the best testament Ernest Cox could leave on the stage he had just vacated. Single-handedly he had created a whole new industry and so many people had gone through his employment that some credit him as being the creator of the Royal Navy's Second World War salvage operations.[728] It was a terrible blow that the very last lift should involve the death of a young Thurso carpenter, William Tait, who had been knocked unconscious during a gas explosion and drowned. It was suspected that he had lit a cigarette and this had caused the explosion that ended his life. Tait had been studying to become a diver to earn more money.

Cox had taken considerable risks but, sadly, barely managed to break even on the operations. Before he left the Flow, Cox had raised the *Bremse*, six capital ships and twenty-six destroyers. When he retired, Cox had not actually made any profit; his ventures had seen a net loss of around £10,000. Since 1924 he had spent £450,000 on Scapa alone, probably equal to some £30 million at 1999 prices. Raising the *Hindenburg*, for example, cost him around £30,000.* His operations had been a 'very big boost to the Orkney economy, especially at a time of deep recession'.[729] So great was his reputation that he – and his men – had learned that Cox's name was on the list of those who would be arrested and liquidated had Operation *Sea Lion*, Hitler's planned invasion of Britain, succeeded.† That is quite an acclaim.

The man who took on Cox's mantle was Tom McKenzie. He carried on the business and succeeded in managing its financial performance more successfully than his mentor. Metal Industries Ltd took over the work, and McKenzie went to work for it. For £2,000 the firm purchased the salvage rights on *Grosse Kurfürst*, *Bayern* and *Baden*.

---

* Buxton (p. 20) put the estimated cost far higher, closer to the reputed selling price of £75,000 ('Her price was probably around… .').
† *SeeLöwe* never got off the ground. Cox joined august company on the list. Other names included Sigmund Freud, Charles de Gaulle, Aldous Huxley, Winston Churchill, Neville Chamberlain and Lady Violet Bonham-Carter.

For the rest of 1932, little happened. Metal prices had fallen again so the two last great ships, *von der Tann* and *Prinzregent Luitpold*, lay rusting at Lyness. Finally, in May 1933, *Prinzregent Luitpold* was sold for £33,000 and taken to Rosyth with *Seefalke* again out in front towing her on her final voyage. In July, the *von der Tann* followed. *Seefalke* was there again but this time each of the German tugs flew the flag of the new German state, the swastika. It was a premonition of things to come.

Luckily for Orkney, Alloa merged with Metal Industries and a week after the *von der Tann* had been towed from Lyness, the works there were taken over by the new consortium. Continued operations to salvage the last thirty-three ships would continue. Metal Industries managing director Robert Watson McCrone was 'as determined and forceful as Cox, but far better equipped both mentally and technically'.[730]

THE SALVAGE MEN

Frank Ernst Guelph **Cox** (1883–1959) always simply known as Ernst Cox, had very little formal education, probably six years until he was aged thirteen. Trained as an engineer, largely by his own persistence and passion, he eventually made his money during the war manufacturing shell casings. Following the end of the war, in 1921 he went into shipbreaking and purchased HMS *Orion* and *Erin*, both of which had been at Jutland. From shipbreaking, where he learned the value of scrap, it was a short step into salvage, even if he had no prior skills. He had not thought of salvage until a Dane, Petersen, of Petersen and Allbeck, suggested he could do it. The rest is history.

Cox was a strong family man and adored his daughter, Bunty, and wife, Jenny Jack, even though he would get irritated at being over-coddled. They would address him as 'Father', which was what his men started to call him, too. He would inevitably appear on site, impeccably dressed in plus fours and polished shoes but would not hesitate at rolling his sleeves up when needed. He was a very demanding boss and had a meteoric temper. However, just as easily as he got angry, he would forget and act as if nothing had happened. He was also a very generous boss and someone who would never ask his men to do something he would not do himself.

Two men contributed significantly to Cox's enterprise. One was his chief salvage officer, who later worked for Metal Industries and 'had a better technical understanding than Cox'.[731] Commodore Thomas

---

'Tom' **McKenzie** had been on Clydeside in the shipping yards and had also worked for the Admiralty Salvage Department. The thirty-one-year-old was an 'energetic and skilful marine engineer whose good clean looks were marred by a sharp scar across his left cheek'.[732]

The other was his diving officer, Ernst P. **McKeowan**. The young, recently married ex-submariner was hired by Cox in 1922 and was initially not keen on moving to Scapa Flow. 'Apart from McKeowan and McKenzie, there was not one among us who knew the first thing about salvage and they did not know much at the start'. (Booth, p. 35, quoting Sandy Thomson)

McKenzie worked for both companies as the chief salvage officer. When Metal Industries bought out Cox's operations in July 1933 for £3,500, McKenzie, then aged forty-one, who had already persuaded McCrone that continued salvage operations at Scapa were viable, was put in charge. His salary at £450 was 'low' but he negotiated a strong bonus package for each ship raised. Helena Young, McCrone's youngest granddaughter, remembers him as a 'very kind man' and that he would bring her gifts. One toy, a horse and carriage, she lost but remembers clearly even today.

Cox's operations were, in van der Vat's words, 'taken over by its principal customer, Robert McCrone of Alloa Shipbreaking Co.'. This then merged with Metal Industries, usually simply known as 'Metals' and set up in Glasgow in 1922 by Robert **McCrone** (1893–1982). He was a decorated war veteran (he had won the Military Cross in the Royal Engineers), had set up Alloa with Stephen Hardie and Donald Pollock in 1923 and remained its managing director until 1955. At the start of the Second World War, he had served with the 51st Highland Division in France after he had been commissioned in the Royal Engineers.

McCrone was a tough but fair man. His obituary in *The Times* talked of him being 'a man of depth of character, but simplicity, integrity and kindness'.[733] Where Cox had excelled in innovation and was renowned for his perseverance, McCrone made salvage a profitable business.

The 28,600-ton *Bayern,* lying at around 120ft in the waters between Houton and Cava, was the German Navy's response to the British *Queen Elizabeth*-class fast battleships. Like *Queen Elizabeth*, she and her sister ship, *Baden*, were armed with 15in guns firing a 1,653lb shell. *Queen Elizabeth's* guns could lob a heavy shell, one that weighed as much as a Mini, across 13 miles of sea. McCrone had bought the *Bayern's* salvage rights for £1,000 and set to work. Sitting on the floor, *Bayern* was listing only very slightly, around 9°, so no great issues were foreseen so far as stabilisation was concerned.

By April that year, seven towering airlocks – between 70 and 90ft high – had been constructed and bolted on to the battleship's hull. It had been decided to tow the completed towers out from Lyness as single units rather than try to assemble them on site. It must have been hard work given their weight, around 10 tons for the longest. While they were being fixed to the hull at the base, guy wires would have been bolted around the hull, the resulting mass of wires looking something like a very untidy spider's web. Once absolutely secure on the hull, compressed air was pumped in to push the water out at high pressure.

A ninety-man salvage crew worked flat out. One of the great improvements that Metal Industries brought was using the knowledge of a gas chemist, a sixty-year old called Cowan, who vouched for the safety of the air quality before the men started working. Not only did it give more confidence to the workers, it also, immediately, isolated dangerous areas right at the start.

The habits of the Flow's salvage working day started to find its way into the locals' lives in other, sometimes, curious ways. Originally from Burray, one South Ronaldsay man, Willie Budge, told of how locals knew that it was five o'clock because each day, without fail, the windows would rattle.[734] It was the salvage workers setting off a blast at knocking off time so that the silt would have settled by the next morning.

Cowan was very popular but he did not miss a trick. Gas samples would be brought up to the surface in balloons by the men working inside *Bayern*. One time, he sent a fireman back to get a sample as he was unable to go himself. The man punctured the balloon by mistake and instead of going back to get a new sample, he blew up another balloon. Cowan turned to him after analysing the sample, saying: 'You'd better get something for your breath. It's foul.'[735] He was also a member of the dance committee and used his skills to mix up some impressive alcoholic concoctions, one particularly powerful one he named 'Nelson's blood'.

Today, ghost images of the ship lie together on the floor of the Flow. What is left to tell the story is a V-shape, as though two hulls had impacted the floor side by side, bow to bow, sterns apart. In the northernmost line of the hull's V lie the four upturned turrets. The barbettes taper up in different coloured shades, which was how they appeared under powerful multi-beam sonar.*

The reason for this V is straightforward. Before the final lift there had been another. On 18 July, *Bayern* had started to rise prematurely when a heavy drainage pipe burst suddenly. Compressed air rushed into the ship's hull like a jet. *Bayern*'s bow rose so fast that it burst 10ft through the surface. And then she sank back.

The problem was that the turrets did not stay with the hull. Divers found out that she had dropped all four. They were massive, weighing a total of 2,500 tons, almost 10 per cent of her displacement.[736] Normally turret clips on the German ship would have held the huge guns in place. When interviewed in 1987, Harry Taylor said that the practice 'can't have applied to this particular ship as when she came up the turrets just stayed on the bottom'.[737]

The unexpected lift caused a number of problems. Not only had the loss of the turrets altered the ship's centre of gravity, *Bayern* had gone back down with a heavy 42° list, steep enough to put three of the seven airlocks under water. The airlocks were only made usable when additional sections were added on to them.

The list presented its own issues. According to Taylor, she had been listing at around 39° but they had managed to overcome the difficulties by using the particular design of the German ships to aid them:

> The German ships had an armoured bunker wall running right along the ship which was 12ft from the side and if you could reclaim that compartment you could get a great deal of buoyancy on that side that you couldn't otherwise have and it would give you that great leverage that enabled her ultimately to be lifted.[738]

On 1 September 1934, *Bayern* came roaring to the surface after an astonishingly fast thirty-second lift. The mixture of high air pressure and water caused a vapour spout to shoot 150ft into the air. She had come to the surface in 'one movement', something that is not usually attempted as,

---

* I've been lucky enough to see her as a guest of Gert Normann Andersen, the Danish entrepreneur, diver and maritime archaeologist who is the strength and the vision behind the new Danish Sea War Museum at Thyborøn on Denmark's North Jutland coast and he and I have become close friends. At the start of 2017, his survey ship, the S/S *Viña*, made an extensive multibeam sonar mapping of the Flow.

with the accelerated expansion of air, the control of buoyancy is immediately lost. It meant that an impressive amount of water came off her as she surfaced; in fact, a sheet of water 6ft deep. Even the Dutch tugs found themselves in danger of going under.*

The next day, *Bayern* was towed and beached at Lyness to be made ready for the journey to Rosyth for breaking up.

THE TOOLS OF MODERN MARITIME ARCHEOLOGY

Huge advances have been made over the last twenty years with the application of vast, and ever-increasing, computing power we now have at our disposal. So much so that even well-worn stories are now being reinterpreted and, sometimes, wholly rewritten.

Multi-beam sonar is one of the tools now used for both wreck search and interpretation. I have been lucky to have been on two expeditions in the last three years on one of Gert Normann Andersen's survey ships, the S/S *Viña*.

Traditional sonar works with a single ping being emitted and then bounced back from any object caught in its path. Multi-beam sonar pings between three and twenty times a second but, more importantly, collects the echo from 512 different points on each scan. The 512 data points make for extremely accurate measurements and these can be enhanced by running back and forth through already scanned areas to double up the detail.

Measurements from under the hull of a ship are only as good as the accuracy of the measuring tape. In this case, the 'tape' has to take account of a ship's roll and pitch, the depth of the water on different parts of the hull, the exact position of the ship and specific minute parts of the ship with multiple GPS points and constant reference to shore-based GPS. It is a work of enormous precision and painstaking patience.

Progress thereafter was steady. In 1935 the *König Albert*, May 1936 the *Kaiserin*, March 1937 *Friedrich der Große* and *Große Kurfürst* in 1938.† Profits were good. *Friedrich der Größe*, for example, secured £134,886 in scrap revenues.[739] Five of the ships raised between 1934 and 1938 'each averaged

---

* The new German government had brought the use of German tugboats to an end: 'It was considered an affront to German dignity' (Buxton, p. 28). The Smit company provided new tugs for *Bayern's* tow to Rosyth – the *Zwarte See*, *Witte See* and *Ganges* – at a cost of £1,650.
† It was said that McCrone filmed *Große Kurfürst* coming up and used colour film that was just coming on the market.

9,660 tons of ferrous scrap, 9,460 tons of armour, 770 tons of non-ferrous and 320 tons of sundries, totalling 20,210 tons… . The sales value of each ship averaged £126,000.'[740]

The average costs of raising these ships (*Bayern, König Albert, Kaiserin, Friedrich der Große* and *Große Kurfürst*) was just £16,185.[741]

McKenzie 'expressed strong doubts' about the last ship to be raised in 1939. The 26,700-ton SMS *Derfflinger*, purchased in March 1936, was the deepest wreck, 140ft down and listing 20.5° to starboard.* In May 1916, she had been responsible for the destruction of HMS *Queen Mary* and so to many her raising was all the more poignant. She was brought up on 25 July 1939.

War was on the horizon and the Admiralty was unwilling to have any of its dry docks tied up. They might very well be needed. That being the case, *Derfflinger* was not broken up till September 1946 and remained a sad, upside-down hull anchored at Rysa Little awaiting her final fate. A little further down by Longhope Bay, was the *Iron Duke*, lying beached following an air attack in October 1939.†

Derfflinger was towed to her wartime resting place after two of her super-firing turrets, B and C, had been removed to reduce her draught. All through the war a Metal Industries worker sat in a hut on her upturned hull. Legend has it that one evening he was listening to Lord Haw-Haw, who addressed a message directly to him. Stukas would be coming shortly, he warned in his heavy nasal voice, to bomb the Flow. Moored beside her, HMS *Iron Duke*, Jellicoe's flagship at Jutland, was very nearly sunk at anchor when, within a week of the tragic loss of HMS *Royal Oak*, her hull plates sprung open after an air attack on 17 October 1939 by three Junkers Ju 88s, their bombs landing close by.‡ McKenzie went out – while the raid was still in progress – to hold her up with tugs on each side. It would have been ironic had the German bombs hit the *Iron Dog* not the *Iron Duke*. One of the three German bombers was shot down, although only grisly pieces of the pilot's limbs – an arm in a sleeve and a foot in a boot – were ever found. A double irony, I suppose, would have been if he had been hit by machine-gun fire from the guns placed on *Derfflinger's* upturned hull. From

---

* *Derfflinger*, along with *Kronprinz Wilhelm, Markgraf* and *König* had been all purchased together for £750 each.

† Initially, *Iron Duke* had been towed ashore elsewhere.

‡ It seems clear that *Iron Duke* was moved around quite a bit during this period. Kevin Heath told me that she was beached at Lyness after she had been bombed the first time (17 October 1939). She was moved to Longhope, he said, on 29 December 1939. Maybe that was where she was moored when hit again in the second raid, the eighteen-bomber raid, of March 1940?

his house on Scapa Bay, Jonnie Miel told me that he saw the bomb plumes when *Iron Duke* was bombed.

Brief consideration was given to the idea that *Derfflinger* be used as a blockship in February 1940 as Scapa's defences had not been adequately readied before the outbreak of war – many of the Flow's entrances were still open – and her air defence was totally inadequate. It sounded like 1914 all over again. Then the Grand Fleet had taken refuge on the western coast of Scotland while the Flow's basic defences were finished.

Derfflinger eventually yielded 20,000 tons of scrap when she was broken up at Faslane on the Clyde. She had been taken under the steady hands of *Ferrodanks*'s second coxswain, Billy Dass.* Two weeks earlier, *Iron Duke* had also been broken up. She had been towed to the Gairloch 'flying the Red Ensign'.[742] There's a photograph of *Derfflinger* arriving on AFD 4 (Admiralty Floating Dock) with *Iron Duke* already in the process of being stripped down, her aft already removed and her main mast in the process of suffering the same fate.[743] It is a very sad day to see such proud ships be dismembered so ungracefully in the breaker's yard.[†]

After 1945 there was no end of scrap available and so the remaining ships stayed. On the floor of the Flow there still lie German ships; three battleships and four cruisers. The battleships are the *König, Kronprinz Wilhelm* and the *Markgraf*, and the cruisers the *Brummer, Karlsruhe, Köln* and *Dresden*. *V.83* was raised and then abandoned. Half a million tons of scrap metal had been recovered from the German Fleet – some 405,000 had been raised from the seabed of the Flow, with another 62,000 tons recovered from beached ships. It had been 'one of the greatest feats of marine salvage the world had ever known'.[744] With obvious pride, Harry Taylor concluded: 'It could not be repeated because the circumstances would never be the same.'

TOTAL SINKING, SALVAGE & WRECK TONNAGE BY SHIP TYPE

TYPE	TOTAL TONNAGE		TONNAGE SUNK		TONNAGE BEACHED		TONNAGE SALVED		WRECK TONNAGE	
	Ships	Total Tonnage	Ships	Sunk (Tons)	Ships	Beached (Tons)	Ships	Salvaged (Tons)	Ships	Remaining (Tons)
Battleships	11	285'000	10	256'500	1	28'500	9	233'400	2	51'600
Battle-cruisers	5	120'600	5	120'600	0	-	5	120'600	0	-
Light Cruisers	8	41'450	4	20'800	4	20'650	4	20'650	4	20'800
Torpedo Boats	50	43'153	34	34'513	19	13'228	31	29'925	0	-
Total	74	490'203	53	432'413	24	62'378	49	404'575	6	72'400

Source: See Appendices 1 and 2 for details of individual ships.

* Source: Fred Johnston, 23 July 2012, Kirkwall Library and Archives.
† HMS *Iron Duke* had been purchased for £8,000 by Metal Industries (Buxton, p. 44).

In the 1950s, there was further salvage, but it was minor compared to the days of Metal Industries and Cox and salvers were mainly looking for left over non-ferrous metals and some armour plate. A former employer of Cox & Danks and Metal, a diver named Arthur Nundy, established a new company, Nundy Marine Metals, but he would mainly work on HMS *Vanguard*.* In 1972 he, in turn, sold his rights to David Nichol and Douglas Campbell, who ran a short-lived company, Scapa Flow Salvage. Salvage thankfully came to an end, leaving us today's sunken memories of Scapa's history.

---

* According to Tom Muir, the Admiralty had sold *Vanguard* for scrap in 1957, but the following year consulted with the convener of Orkney County Council about the impact on public opinion if they were to sell *Royal Oak* for scrap. He completely misread the sentiment and replied that no one would care. But they did. When *The Orcadian* ran an article on the issue, there was a local outcry and the Admiralty backed down. *Vanguard* had not caught the public imagination in the same was as *Royal Oak* had done. The latter's sinking at the hands of a U-boat certainly added to the wreck's unique place in history. No salvage work was carried out and today she is a designated war grave.

13

SCAPA FLOW IN HISTORY AND TODAY

THE LAST LIVING witness of the scuttle – the last military witness – died almost a decade ago, in 2011. On 5 May that year, Claude Choules was 110 years old. None of the schoolchildren are alive but some of their voices can still be heard, on tape at the Orkney library.

All that now remains are the few ships that, despite being picked over by divers and salvers, remain under the Flow. Eight ships survive. One is the *Markgraf*, along with her sister ship, lying at 42–46m, the *König*. Both fought at Jutland. *Markgraf* now lies with her hull upturned at a depth of 147ft (45m), one of the deepest wrecks in the Flow and known to most divers as 'the jewel in the Scapa Flow Crown'. Its depth has kept it free from general sport divers because of the level of technical diving experience needed but though *Markgraf* is one of the best-preserved of the Scapa wrecks, the danger of unscrupulous scavengers is constant, even today.

In 2016 two divers were prosecuted, charged under Section 2(1) of the Ancient Monuments and Archaeological Areas Act 1979, after they had been seen coming off the wrecks, including *Markgraf*, with artefacts in October 2012. Gordon Meek, a Glaswegian, and Robert Infante, an American from New Jersey, were heavily fined – £18,000 each. The case was well-publicised and I hope will act as a strong deterrent to further acts of vandalism.

Protection of the remaining wrecks was never guaranteed. There was a point, early in the 1980s, that the Orkney Island Council (OIC) wanted salvage to continue. Technology had advanced dramatically and demand for high-quality, non-radiated steel was high. But then, thankfully, people started asking if there was not good sense in preserving the remaining wrecks to develop a new industry: dive tourism.

A number of other significant German wrecks have survived. Another battleship, the *Kronprinz Wilhelm*, lies 12–38m down, well within reach of most sport divers. Only the turrets remain from *Bayern* after they fell to the bottom of the Flow during the otherwise successful lift, and a number of light cruisers, *Dresden, Köln, Karlsruhe* and *Brummer*. And of course, there are two protected British war graves, HMS *Vanguard* and HMS *Royal Oak*. The first exploded after an ammunition fire while moored in the Flow, the second was torpedoed by *U.47*, the 'Bull of Scapa Flow', captained by Günter Prien, in 1939. On both, the human toll was high.

The last remains of the mail ship, *B.98*, can be found on Lopness, on the island of Sanday. Somehow, on 17 February 1920, she broke away when under tow. She became a welcome site for islanders. Bryce Wilson gave me a lovely memory of her in '*Island Images*':

> Come all ye wreckers come,
> *B.98*'s stranded,
> Bring all your tools along,
> Get the brass landed.
> The tugs have left her
> On the sand bank lying,
> Come Hogs and Ruggie men,
> Daylight is dying.[745]

In 2020, the renovation of what might be the last surviving vessel from Scapa Flow, the admiral's barge from the *Hindenburg,* will be completed. The *Count Dracula* was originally a gift from Kaiser Wilhelm II to Franz Hipper and became the *Hindenburg*'s admiral's barge. At the start of the Second World War, its new owner, Carl Greiner, sent his son, Alan, to take the boat over to France from Ramsgate, where she rescued 720 British and ten Belgian soldiers, including one Sergeant William Wilson. His son, David, took up the cause to restore the 35ft barge in his boatyard with the new owner, Kevin Kilkenney, who had a great uncle who was also rescued from the beaches.[746]

PROTECTING OUR COMMON MARITIME HERITAGE
While shipwrecks degrade over time through wave action, water temperature, salinity and water toxicity, salvage vandalism has become a major threat to a continued marine heritage. What are governments doing to protect the wrecks? Five main pieces of legislation help protect wrecks.

Protection of Wrecks Act, 1973 covers wrecks of historic, archaeological or artistic importance and gives them a restricted area within which diving is forbidden unless a licence has been granted by the relevant National

Heritage Agency acting on behalf of the Department of Culture, Media and Sports (Historic England, Cadw, Environment, Heritage Service in Northern Ireland or Historic Scotland). While bathing, angling and navigation are permitted within the restricted zone, Anchoring is restricted. Another section of the Act (Section II) covers sites that are potentially dangerous and these wrecks are administered through the Maritime and Coastguard Agency (MCA). In these wrecks a strict no-access policy is enforced.

The Military Remains Act 1986 safeguards the remains of aircraft and vessels that have crashed, sunk or been stranded while in military service and any associated human remains 'from unauthorised interference'. It is administered by the Ministry of Defence. Two levels of protection are foreseen (a) As a **Protected Place** covering all military aircraft sites in UK waters and individual named wrecks that sank in or were stranded on after 4 August 1914 or (b) As a **Controlled Site** are designated areas where the remains of an aircraft or named vessel sunk or stranded in military service within the last 200 years. Here diving is prohibited unless a licence is obtained from the Ministry of Defence. You can search online for 'Statutory Order Protection of Military Remains Act'. HMS *Royal Oak*, HMS *Vanguard* and HMS *Hampshire* are all protected under this Act.

The Merchant Shipping Act, 1995, Part IX requires that any object recovered from wrecks (notwithstanding whether the wreck is Protected or Designated and that a marine licence is in place if needed) are reported to the Receiver of Wreck within twenty-eight days of recovery. The Receiver of Wreck will try to identify the current legal owner and liaise with museums and heritage organisations to ascertain the heritage or historic significance of the findings. Finders are likely to be entitled to a Finders Award.

The Ancient Monuments and Archaeological Areas Act relates primarily to land-based sites and structures but has been also used recently to afford some level of protection to underwater sites. Once a site is scheduled as a 'maritime monument', public access to it, such as diving, is permitted on a 'look but don't touch basis'. It is an offence to 'demolish, destroy, alter or repair' such wrecks. The German High Seas Fleet in Scapa Flow is a scheduled site.

> **The Marine and Coastal Access Act 2009** helps protect the marine environment including heritage, via licensing and enforcement functions administered by the Marine Management Organisation. The act requires a licence for a range of activities, such as using equipment powered by a vessel's winch or crane to remove or deposit objects, using a water dredge or leaving marker buoys on site for more than twenty-eight days.

The salvaged ships' bells are scattered. Some in Germany, some still on Orkney, others in museums such as the Imperial War Museum and the National Museum of the Royal Navy in Portsmouth.

Three, at the time of writing, are still on Orkney and one more on Scotland's west coast on the small island of Eriskay, at a small church. At the time, St Michael's local priest, Father Callum MacClellan, had needed a church bell, gone to the mainland and found one of the bells from the SMS *Derfflinger* in a scrap yard in Faslane.[*] When he got back to the island, the new bell was slowly taken along the rutted track to St Michael's by McNeil and his six helpers, in a wheelbarrow. It is a long journey, however you look at it. *Derfflinger*'s bell now hangs outside the gate to the church, overlooking the small, 130-strong community of fishermen and crofters keeping vigil over the fast water around the skerries below. It is where the SS *Politician* met its fate in 1941, leaving the island 264,000 whisky bottles richer.[†] Up until the 1980s, the vigil candle cast a red light that before the causeway bridge was built was used by sailors cutting through the waters between South Uist and Eriskay as a guide.[‡]

Sadly, the bell from *Friedrich der Große*, the first bell that tolled across the waters, was damaged. The crown has been smashed through on one

---

[*] Father McCellan's (1926–2012) story was told in a BBC film about his church, *An Island Parish*.
[†] The Hebridean island of Eriskay has an important place in Scotland's history. It is where Charles Stuart, Bonnie Prince Charlie, landed in July 1745. He was carried ashore from a French ship. He is said to have turned flowers white with his touch. France, though interested in stirring revolt in the British Isles, would not go as far as sending troops. Much potential Jacobite support did not join ranks with Prince Charles as a direct result. The other wonderful association with Eriskay was that it featured in the 1949 film *Whisky Galore*, by Compton McKenzie (1883–1972). Bottles were still being brought up from the sunken cargo ship even in the 1980s.
[‡] Father Ross, who very kindly looked after me when I visited, told me that the red glow could be seen through the windows behind the altar. He and I braved strong winds as I, unsuccessfully, tried to record the bell's ringing. Even if I had mastered masking the whistle of the wind, the bell's chime was broken. On the train back from Mallaig to Glasgow, the first station I passed through was Morar. It is where my father's commanding officer, David Stirling, is buried.

side.* Stromness museum's collection owes much to one particular man, Bryce Wilson. An artist by training, Bryce became a volunteer and a museum officer in 1976. It was he who thought of putting on an exhibition about the salvage and to do so started to assemble what became the core of the collection. He was helped by the diver, Arthur Nundy, and many locals who donated artefacts from their homes. It was Bryce who started to popularise the saga of the Flow when the Dutch journalist Dan van der Vat visited one summer to write about the seal cull. The rest is history. Van der Vat's book, *The Grand Scuttle*, captured the imagination, including mine.

On Lyness, there is the bell from the *Köln*.† The bell from SMS *König Albert* made its way into private hands through the McCrone family.‡ As would be expected, a number of the bells were given back to Germany. There are two bells at Laboe, at the Deutscher Marinebund. One is the bell from the *von der Tann*, the other, that of SMS *Seydlitz*, is rung each year at Laboe on 31 May, Skagerrakstag. Another, that of *Hindenburg*, in the Armeemuseum. *Kaiser*'s bell is in Hamburg, at Peter Tamm's museum, the International Maritime Museum.§ A second bell from the *Derfflinger*, along with one from the former Flagship, *Friedrich der Große*, were presented back to Germany by Metal Industries in 1965 and after a ceremony in Faslane. Together, they were taken back to Wilhelmshaven aboard the *Schulfregatte Scheer*.

Just after the Scapa distillery but before you get to the Scapa garage is a track that leads back down to the bay. There lives an Orkney legend, Jonnie Miel and his wife, Isobel, surrounded by artefacts and memories of the scuttle, the sea and Scapa Flow. He is still going strong at, I think, ninety-two years old. He is a wonderfully generous character and I always make a point of visiting them when I am on Orkney. He looks out over the last resting place of the *Royal Oak*. During a couple of summers, he

---

* When I first visited Stromness museum, I asked about *Friedrich der Große*'s bell. The attendant had no idea of its important role on the day. Neither would visiting German tourists easily hear or read of the story. Signage – especially in German – was nowhere to be seen. The bell was found by a Kirkwall diver, John Thornton, who told me he originally gave it to the Stromness Hotel. Somehow, and he is not even certain how, it ended up in the museum. It is beside the bell of the *Dresden*, one of the few bells from the scuttle I was not privileged to record.
† When Jude Callister (Lyness Museum) and I tried to ring the *Köln* bell, however, our hearts sank. There was no tone at all, just an ugly metallic clank.
‡ It now hangs quietly in an enchanted setting – at the Somerset house of his youngest daughter, Helena, in her garden.
§ Dr Jann Witt and the president of the association kindly made one of the two bells, that of the *von der Tann*, available to bring back to the Flow for the centenary.

had worked on the salvage and once produced an enormous nut, the size of your hand. He explained it was used to secure armour plating on equally impressive bolts. The only regret I have is that Jonnie's Orcadian accent is so strong that to the untrained – myself – it is often a sadly insurmountable challenge.

After he returned to Germany, Reuter received a personal letter from the former Kaiser, who wrote: 'With your act at Scapa Flow you saved the honour of the Imperial Navy. You thereby earned the ineradicable thanks of myself, the Navy and the entire German nation.'[747]

In many ways, the words rang hollow. The Kaiser no longer spoke for Germany and the Second World War brought Reuter still more suffering. Of his three sons, two were killed: the youngest, Wolfgang, in Poland, in the first few weeks of the campaign, while the middle son, Yorck, was lucky and escaped with his life after he had been captured by the British in the Narvik operations the next year. Had Ludwig Reuter lived, he would have also suffered the death of his eldest son, Derfflinger, who died fighting the Russians in the terrible slaughter around Königsberg in 1945.

Fremantle had to defend his actions until the end of his life. As one reads his 1953 record, it is striking how he writes of the Admiralty and his C-in-C, Madden. He felt he had been left holding the baby: 'Having, rather to my surprise, had no instructions whatever either from the Admiralty or from the Commander-in-Chief as to how the Germans were to be dealt with when the Armistice expired.'[748]

Later, he went on to say that the same was the case for both Leveson and Oliver. Both had submitted detailed plans and, 'to the best of [his] belief, they had received no reply'.[749] It is quite a damning statement.

As visitors to the Flow wait at the Houton ferry terminal, there is little today that bears witness to the momentous events of one hundred years ago. Scapa Flow was once Britain's pre-eminent naval base, a sanctuary that had sheltered one of the world's most powerful navies, the Grand Fleet. For the fleeting moment of the scuttle, it became the epicentre of global focus. Nature has now reclaimed it.

BIBLIOGRAPHY & SOURCES

Arthur, Max, *The True Glory. The Royal Navy 1914–1939*, Hodder and Stoughton, 1996.

Beatty, Charles, *Our Admiral: A Biography of Admiral of the Fleet Earl Beatty*, WH Allen, 1980.

Bell, Christopher M, *Churchill and Sea Power*, Oxford University Press, 2013.

Booth, Tony, *Cox's Navy. Salvaging the German High Seas Fleet at Scapa Flow 1924–1931*, Pen and Sword Maritime, 2006.

Bowman, Gerald, *The Man Who bought a Navy. The Story of the World's Greatest Salvage Achievement at Scapa Flow*, George Harrap, 1964 (2002 Reprint used).

Brown, Malcom and Meehan, Patricia, *Scapa Flow*, Allen Lane, The Penguin Press, London 1968.

Buxton, Ian, *Metal Industries. Shipbreaking at Rosyth and Charlestown*, World Ship Society, 1992.

Chalmers, Rear Admiral WS, *The Life and Letters of David, Earl Beatty, Admiral of the Fleet*, Hodder and Stoughton, 1951.

Chatfield, Admiral of the Fleet, Lord, *It Might Happen Again. Vol. II. The Navy and its Defence*, Heinemann, 1947.

Carsten, Francis Ludwig, *War Against War: British and German Radical Movements in the First World War*, University of California Press, 1982.

Cousins, Geoffrey, *The Story of Scapa Flow*, Frederick Muller Limited, 1965.

De Courcy-Ireland RN, Captain Stanley Brian, *A Naval Life*, Max Arthur, 1990.

Epkenhans, Prof Dr Michael, *Tirpitz. Architect of the German High Seas Fleet*, Potomac, 2008.

Ferguson, David M, *The Wrecks of Scapa Flow*, The Orkney Press, 1985.

Fremantle, Admiral Sir Sydney,

———— *My Naval Career, 1880–1928*, Hutchinson and Co., No date.

———— *The Scapa Sinkings*, Personal copy, April 1953.

Freiwald, Ludwig *Last Days of the German Fleet*, Constable, 1932.

George, SC, *Jutland to Junkyard. The Raising of the Scuttled German Fleet from Scapa Flow – The Greatest Salvage Operation of All Time*, Birlinn, 1999 (First published 1973 by Patrick Stephen Ltd).

Gores, Joseph, N, *Marine Salvage*, Redwood Press, 1971.

Gröner, Erich, Mickel, Peter and Mrva, Franz, *German Warships 1815–1945 – Volume One: Major Surface Vessels*, Naval Institute Press, Annapolis, 1983.

Guttridge, Leonard F *Mutiny, A History of Naval Insurrection*, Ian Allan, 1992.

Haffner, Sebastian, *Die Deutsche Revolution 1918/19*, Rowahlt Taschenbuch Verlag, 2010 (First published 1969)

Harman, Chris, *The Lost Revolution. Germany 1918–1923*. Internationalism Socialism Series, Haymarket, Chicago, 2017 (First published 1993).

Hawkins, Nigel, *The Starvation Blockades: Naval Blockades of WWI*, Pen and Sword, 2002.

Hewison, WS, *The Great Harbour. Scapa Flow*, Birlinn, 2005.

Horn, Daniel (editor), *War, Mutiny and the Revolution in the German Navy. The World War 1 Diary of Seaman Richard Strumpf*, Rutgers University Press, 1967.

Hough, Richard, *First Sea Lord. An Authorised Biography of Admiral Lord Fisher*, George Allen and Unwin, 1969.

Jellicoe, Admiral Sir John, *The Grand Fleet 1914–1918: Its Creation, Development and Work*, Cassell, 1919.

Kennedy, Paul, *The Rise and Fall of British Naval Mastery*, Penguin 2017 (First published 1976).

Kelly, Patrick J, *Tirpitz and the Imperial German Navy*, Indiana University Press, 2011.

Kinzler, Sonja and Tillman, Doris (ed.) *Die Stunde der Matrosen. Kiel und die deutsche Revolution 1918*, Kieler Stadt-und Schiffartsmuseum, 2018.

Krause, Andreas, *Scapa Flow. Die Selbstversenkung der wilhelminischen Flotte*, Ullstein, 1999.

Koop, Gerard and Mulitze, Erich, *Die Marine in Wilhelmshaven. Eine Bildchronik zur deutschen Marinegeschichte von 1853 bis heute*. Bernard und Graefe Verlag, 1997.

Kuhn, Gabriel (Editor & translator), *All Power to the Councils. A Documentary History of the German Revolution 1918–1919*, PM Press, USA. 2012.

Lambi, Ivo Nikolai, *The Navy and German Power Politics 1862–1914*, George Allen and Unwin, 1984.

Liddle, Peter R, *The Sailor's War 1914–18*, Guild Publishing, 1985.

Lisio, Donald J, *British Naval Supremacy and Anglo–American Antagonisms 1914–1930*, Cambridge University Press, 2014.

Macdonald, Rod, *Dive Scapa Flow*, Mainstream Publishing, 2011.

Massie, Robert, *Castles of Steel*, Random House, 2003.

Marder, Prof Arthur, *From Dreadnought to Scapa Flow (FDTSF)*, Vol. 5.

McCutcheon, James, *The Ships of Scapa Flow*, Amberley, 2013.

Miller, James, *Scapa. Britain's Famous Wartime Naval Base*, Birlinn, 2001.

Morris, Jan, *Fisher's Face*. Penguin, 1996.

O'Hara, Vincent and Heinz, Leonard R, *Clash of Fleets. Naval Battles of the Great War 1914–1918*, Naval Institute Press, Annapolis, 2017.

Padfield, Peter, *Maritime Dominion and the Triumph of the Free World*, Overlook Press, New York, 2010.

Plivier, Theodor, *The Kaiser's Coolies*, Faber and Faber, no date.

Rackwitz, Martin. Kiel 1918, *Revolution – Aufbruch zu Demokratie und Republik*, Wachholtz, 2018.

Raeder, Grand Admiral Erich, *My Life*, Annapolis, 1960.

Ranft, B McL, *The Beatty Papers*, TBP, (vol. 1. 1902–1918, Navy Records Society, 1989, vol. 2. 1916–1927, Navy Records Society, 1993).

Redford, Dr Duncan and Grove, Philip D. *The Royal Navy. A History since 1900*, IB Taurus Books (NMRN) 2014.

Reuter, Vice Admiral Ludwig von, *Scapa Flow: From Graveyard to Resurrection*, 1921 (English Edition Wordsmith Publications, 2005).

Rojek, Dr Sebastian, *Versunkene Hoffnungen. Die Deutsche Marine im Umgang mit Erwartungen und Enttäuschungen 1871–1930*, De Gruyter, Oldenbourg. 2017.

Roskill, Stephen,

———— *HMS Warspite: The Story of a Famous Battleship*, Collins, 1957.

———— *Admiral of the Fleet Earl Beatty: The Last Naval Hero. An Intimate Biography (Naval Hero)*, Collins, 1980.

———— *Naval Policy between the Wars (NPBW). Vol. 1. The Period of Anglo–American Antagonism, 1919–1929. 1968 Vol. 2, The Period of Reluctant Rearmament, 1930–1939. 1976.*

Ruge, Friedrich *Scapa Flow 1919, The End of the German Fleet*, 1969 (English Edition, Ian Allan, 1973).

Scheer, Großadmiral Reinhard. *Germany's High Sea Fleet in the World War*. Casell, 1920.

Seligmann, Matthew S, Nägler, Frank and Epkenhans, Michael, *The Naval Road to the Abyss. The Anglo–German Naval Race 1895–1914*, Ashgate for the Naval Records Society, 2015.

Schubert, Paul and Langhorne, Gibson, *Death of a Fleet 1917–1919*, Hutchinson, undated.

Smith, Peter L, *The Naval Wrecks of Scapa Flow*, The Orkney Press, 1989.

Simpson, Michael, *Anglo–American Naval Relations 1917–1919*, Scolar Press for Navy Records Society, 1991.

Staff, Gary,

—— *German Battleships 1914–1918 (1): Deutschland, Nassau and Helgoland Classes;*

—— *German Battleships 1914–1918 (2): Kaiser, König and Bayern Classes*, Osprey, 2010.

—— *German Battlecruisers of World War One, Their Design, Construction and Operations*, Seaforth, 2014.

Stevens, David, *In All Respects Ready. Australia's Navy in World War One*, Oxford, 2014.

Stokesbury, James.L, *Navy and Empire. A Short History of Four Centuries of British Sea Power and the Rise and Decline of British Imperialism from the Armada to the Falklands*, William Morrow, New York, 1983.

Tampke, Jürgen, *A Perfidious Distortion of History. The Versailles Peace Treaty and the Success of the Nazis*, Scribe, Melbourne and London, 2017.

Temple Patterson, Prof A, *Tyrwhitt of the Harwich Force. The Life of Admiral of the Fleet Sir Reginald Tyrwhitt*, Macdonald, 1973.

Trask, David F, *Captains and Cabins. Anglo–American Naval Relations 1917–1918*, University of Missouri Press, 1972.

Tracy, Nicholas, *Sea Power and the Control of Trade*, Ashcroft for the Navy Records Society, 2005.

Ulrich, Volker, *Die Revolution von 1918/19*. Wissen, 2009

Van der Vat, Dan, *Grand Scuttle. The Sinking of the German Fleet at Scapa Flow in 1919*, Hodder and Stoughton, 1982.

Wilson, Ben, *Empire of the Deep: The Rise and Fall of the British Navy*, Weidenfeld and Nicolson, 2013.

Watson, Alexander, *Ring of Steel. Germany and Austria–Hungary in World War 1*, Basic Books, USA, 2014.

Witt, Dr Jann M. and McDermott, Robin. *Scarborough Bombardment. The Attack by the German High Seas Fleet on Scarborough, Whitby and Hartlepool on 16 December 1914*. Palm Verlag, 2016.

Witt, Dr Jann M. *Von Schwarz-Rot-Gold zu Schwarz-Rot-Gold. Eine Kurze Geschichte der deutschen Marinen von 1848 bis heute*. Deutsche Marinebund, 2011.

Wolz, Nicholas. *From Imperial Splendour to Internment. The German Navy in the First World War*. (FISTI), Seaforth, 2015.

Wood, Lawson. *The Bull & The Barriers. The Wrecks of Scapa Flow*. The History Press, 2009.

Woodward, David. *The Collapse of Power. Mutiny in the High Seas Fleet*. Arthur Barker, 1973.

Wragg, David. *Fisher. The Admiral who Reinvented the Royal Navy*. The History Press, 2009.

Young, Desmond. *The Man in the Helmet*. Cassell, 1963.

Christopher, John. *1918. The First World War in Photographs. The End Game*.

Archives

Bundesarchiv, Freiburg, Germany

BA-MA/RM 44/v5 *Versenkungsberichte* (*Derfflinger, Seydlitz, Moltke, Friedrich der Große, König, Dresden, Kronprinz Wilhelm, Prinzregent Luitpold, Frankfurt, Nürnberg, Emden, Bremse, Brummer, Torpedo Flotillas*). Noted as Scuttle Reports.

BA-MA/RM44/20 *Bericht* Heinemann, SMS *Köln*

BA-MA/RM44/7 *Bericht* Cordes, FdTpb.

BA-MA/RM8/1311 *Bericht* Reuter

Deutsche Marinebund, Laboe

The National Archives, Kew, London

LG/F/33/2/58 Walter Long

ADM 116/2074 Sinking of the German Fleet. Includes photographs

ADM 1/8571/296 Action to be taken re: German Fleet sinking

ADM 137/3816 Scuttling of German Fleet and instructions for Internment of such ships

ADM 1/8575/331 German Government's memorandum on sinking of German warships

ADM 1/8562/172 Disposal of Interned German ships

University of Boston, Howard Gotlieb Archival Research Centre (BUHG)

Ludovic Kennedy Papers

University of California, Irvine (UCI)

Prof Arthur J Marder Papers, University of California, Irvine

University of Cambridge, Churchill Archives (UCCA)

Sir Stephen Roskill Papers, University of Cambridge, Churchill Archives

United States Naval War College

Office of Naval Intelligence (ONI). *The Sinking of the German Ships at Scapa Flow. 9 October 1919*

Wilhelmshavener Zeitung Bildienst

Academic Works

Chusid, Edward Joseph, *The Comcurrent Conferences: The Washington Naval Conference and the Far Eastern Affairs Conference of 1922*, Masters Thesis, Eastern Michigan University 2008.

Kuehn, John Trost, *The Influence of Naval Arms Limitation on US Naval Innovation during the Interwar Period 1921–1937*, Phd Thesis, Kansas State University, 2007

MacGregor, Robert R, *Indolent Companions: The German Naval Mutinies of the First World War*, Rice University, USA 2003.

Government and Official Sources

Official State Department Series. *Foreign Relations of the United States (FRUS)*. These can be found online at digicoll.library.wisc.edu/cgi-bin/FRUS

Treaty of Versailles Naval clauses. pp. 337–351 (frus.frus1919parisv13.i0006). Volume XIII.

Political Conditions in Germany. Volume XII.

The Council of Four. Minutes of Meetings 24 May–28 June 1918. Volume VI.

Magazine Articles

Bennett, Captain Jeffrey, DSC, RN, *Scapa Scuttle.* 'History Today', Vol. 9, Iss 8, August 1959

Cavendish, Richard, *The German battle Fleet scuttled at Scapa Flow.* History Today, Vol. 59, Iss 6, June 2009

Friedman, Norman,

— *How Promise turned to disappointment.* Naval History, August 2016.

— *Analyzing Germany's Downfall*, Naval History, December 2018.

Witt, Dr Jann M, *Rote Fahnen auf kaiserlichen Schiffen. Die Meuterei der Hochseeflotte und die Novemberrevolution 1918*, Leinen Los! Nov. 2018

Newspaper Articles
Berliner Zeitung
Gerd Fesser. *Sinnlose Selbstvernichtung der wilhelminischen Armada/66 Kriegsschiffe wurden im Juni 1919 versenkt Scapa Flow – das Grab der deutschen Flotte*, 18 June 1994)
The Orcadian, Kirkwall
28 November 1919. *The German Fleet Surrender*
27 June 1929. *A Diver's Death*
The Telegraph
4 August 2017. *Dunkirk Hero's son reunited with the 'little ship' that saved him.*
Wilhelmshavener Zeitung

Radio Programmes and Recorded Interviews
Hewison, Bill, (Orkney Library and Archives, OLA) *This Great Harbour. Scapa Flow*, Radio series, Radio Scotland 1986.
Tapes OSA/AO5 463. Tape 1, recorded 16 September 1986.
Tapes OSA/AO5 464. Tape 2, recorded 29 September 1986
Tapes OSA/AO5 465. Tape 3, recorded 29 September 1986
Tapes OSA/AO5 466. Tape 4, (recording date not noted)

Ruge, Prof Admiral Friedrich. *Yesterday's Yarns* – 17 April 1997, Radio Orkney. Interviewed by Bob Mickelson. Kirkwall Library and Archives. The actual tape was lost by the Archives in 1997 and finally, after some suggestions as to where it might be found from Tom Muir, was indeed again located in 2017.
Spence, William, Lower Millfield, Stronsay. Recorded 20 May 1984. Orkney Library and Archives, TA/610.
Taylor, Harry, (OLA) employee of Cox and Danks. Recorded 25 August 1987. Orkney Library and Archives, BBC Radio Orkney Collection Tapes 451/452.
World War Series, Part 3 (WWS3). *Accounts by Henrietta Groundwater, Peggy Gibson and Maureen Heddle of the German Fleet Scuttle*. Orkney Library and Archives, TA749.

Television Programmes
Kennedy, Ludovic. *Scapa Flow*, BBC 1966. Film Editor Eric Brown and Production Assistant Patricia Meehan. Transcript in BUHG papers. *Scapa Flow*

1919. With All Flags Flying, Pelicula Films for Channel Four, 1986. Directed by Michael Alexander.
– Dr Wilhelm Deist, Historian

– Yorck von Reuter (son of Ludwig von Reuter, father of Yorck-Ludwig)
– Werner Braunsberger, SMS *Kaiser*
– Matheson, Junior Engineer (and cartoonist), HMS *Erin*
– James Roberton, Stromness Public school
– Kitty Tait, Stromness Public school
– Peggy Gibson, Stromness Public school
– Dr Barbara Marshall, Social Historian

The Battleships – The Darkness of The Future. Channel 4 documentary, episode 3. This can be found on YouTube (https://www.youtube.com/watch?v=otvrS-AYq80&feature=youtu.be)
  Peggy (here spelt Peggie) Gibson, Stromness Public school

1918. *Aufstrand der Matrosen.* NDR 2018. A docudrama by Jens Becker. https://www.ndr.de/kultur/geschichte/Vom-Kieler-Matrosenaufstand-zur-Novemberrevolution-1918,matrosenaufstand132.html

Primary Sources, Personal Interviews
Fremantle, Charles, grandson of Admiral Sir Sydney Fremantle.
Fremantle, Tom, cousin of Admiral Sir Sydney Fremantle's family.
Robertson, Morag, granddaughter of Arthur Burnett, Orkney Island Council.
Young, Helena. Youngest daughter of Robert McCrone, Metal Industries.

Secondary Sources, Personal Interviews
Burnett, Arthur

Candy, Nancy. With kind permission of John and Sarah Welburn, Orphir. *The Times*, 28 September 2003, 'Roving Eyes gets to the bottom of Scapa Flow', Nick Thorpe.

Gibson, Peggy (At the time the ten-year-old 'Peggie' Matheson of Kirkwall). Her memories were recorded in two interviews, one in the 1960s with Ernest Marwick. Interviewed 1984 by Kathryn Gourlay for Radio Orkney. In the 1997 Radio Orkney show she is mistakenly referred to as Margaret Gibson.

Groundwater, Henrietta (Mrs. William, or Rosetta) was also interviewed by Ernest Marwick.

Marwick, Willie. Worked on the salvage with Cox & Danks. Interview in Ferguson. Interviewed 1984 by Kathryn Gourlay for Radio Orkney.
Knarston, John (*The Orcadian*, 13 September 1956).

Robertson, JRT. Orkney Islands councillor for Sandwick and former provost of Stromness. Interviewed 1984 by Kathryn Gourlay for Radio Orkney.

Scott, Mrs Ivy of The Whins, Finstown, aged eighteen at the time. She died in 1984 but had written to *The Orcadian* responding to its request for her account. (Source: Ferguson)

Tate, Kitty. Married to Sandy Tait from Stromness. Interview in Ferguson.

Tulloch, John James Laird (later renamed Ian Laird Tulloch). In possession of his daughter, Mrs. Joyce Howard, Reid Crescent, Kirkwall (*The Orcadian*, 13 September 2011). Kindly forwarded to Tom Muir.

Watt, Katie. Sixth-former, aged eighteen, who lived in Kirkwall. She later worked for the Post Office as teleprinter operator.

Other Miscellaneous Sources
Cox, EF, *Eight Years Salvage Work at Scapa Flow*, The 5th Thomas Lowe Gray Lecture (Orkney Library and Archives)

Pottinger, J, *The Salving of the German Fleet. A booklet accompanying the summer exhibition*, Stromness Museum, 1974.

Exhibitions
Kiel Maritime Museum, KMM
Wilhelmshaven Naval Museum, WNM

APPENDICES

Digital resources

In addition to the appendices shown here, there are extensive digital resources available to the reader online.

Click on the QR code of search for www.ScapaFlow1919.com

Appendix 1
Destroyers Sunk, Beached and Salvaged at Scapa Flow

See pages 302–309

Sources: Reuter RM 8/1311, Ruge, pp. 163–164; George, pp. 142–145; Ferguson, p. 40; and van der Vat, pp. 219–223 (Note: van der Vat misses out *S.52* and *S.55* in his count).

Appendix 2
Battleships, Battle-cruisers and Cruisers Sunk, Beached and Salvaged at Scapa Flow

See pages 310–315

Sources: Reuter RM 8/1311, Ruge, pp. 163–164; George, pp. 142–145; Ferguson, p. 40 and van der Vat, pp. 219–223 (Note: van der Vat misses out *S.52* and *S.55* in his count).

Name	Flotilla	Tonnage (Reuter RM/8/1311)	Sunk / beached	Breaking Up	Wreck Details	Salvage Company
B.109	No.2. Flotilla	1,350	sunk	Sold 25.1.24 by Admiralty for £200 to Cox & Danks. Sold to Alloa Shipbreaking Company with G.101and G.104 for £1,800 in total.		Cox & Danks
B.110	No.2. Flotilla	1,350	sunk			Cox & Danks
B.111	No.2. Flotilla	1,350	sunk			Cox & Danks
B.112	No.2. Flotilla	1,350	sunk			Cox & Danks
G.101	No.2. Flotilla	1,215	sunk	Sold 25.1.24 by Admiralty for £200to Cox & Danks. Sold to Alloa Shipbreaking Company with B.109 and G.104 for £1,800 in total		Cox & Danks
G.102	No.2. Flotilla	1,215	beached			
G.103	No.2. Flotilla	1,215	sunk			Cox & Danks
G.104	No.2. Flotilla	1,215	sunk	Sold 25.1.24 by Admiralty for £200to Cox & Danks. Sold to Alloa Shipbreaking Company with G.101 and B.109 for £1,800 in total.		Cox & Danks
G.38	No.1. Flotilla	875	sunk			Cox & Danks
G.39	No.1. Flotilla	875	sunk			Cox & Danks
G.40	No.1. Flotilla	875	sunk			Cox & Danks
G.86	No.1. Flotilla	955	sunk			Cox & Danks
G.89	No.7 Flotilla	955	sunk			Scapa Salvage Syndicate

Year	Month	Date raised (George)	Launched	Builder	Comments
1926	Mar	27.3.26	11.3.15	Blohm und Voss, Hamburg	Tied with B.111
1925	Dec	11.12.25	31.3.15	Blohm und Voss, Hamburg	Tied with B.112. Hewison, p. 185 says raised 14 Dec. Ruge states she was dragged down by B.112 but got stuck on her mast and would not sink immediately. 1310 is, therefore, approximated
1926	Mar	8.3.26	8.6.15	Blohm und Voss, Hamburg	Tied with B.109. Had problems with bilges when trying to scuttle
1926	Feb	1.2.26	17.6.15	Blohm und Voss, Hamburg	Tied with B.110. Ruge (Ferguson, p. 9) states times as 'a little after one'
1926	Apr	13.4.26	12.8.14	Germaniawerft, Kiel	Scuttled in shallow water. Transferred to American control 17.2.20 and sunk off Cape Henry as bombing target (Buxton, p. 62 holds that arrived Charlestown 17.6.26 and commenced demolition 26.6.26)
				Germaniawerft, Kiel	Transferred to American control, sunk as a target in 1921.(Beached in Mill Bay, re: Prendergast Report)
1925	Sep	30.9.25	14.11.14	Germaniawerft, Kiel	Sunk in a storm in Nov 1925 north of Scotland (Rattray Head, Aberdeenshire) being towed to the breakers' yard
1926	Apr	30.4.26	28.11.14	Germaniawerft, Kiel	According to R MacDonald unlisted by von Reuter. Arrived Charlestown c.13.7.26 (Buxton, p. 62) and demolition commenced 7.8.26
1924	Sep	27.9.24	23.12.14	Germaniawerft, Kiel	
Cox & Danks	1925	Jul	3.7.25	16.1.15	Germaniawerft, Kiel
1925	Jul	29.7.25	27.2.15	Germaniawerft, Kiel	Tied with V.129
		14.7.25	24.8.15	Germaniawerft, Kiel	
1924	Dec		11.12.15	Germaniawerft, Kiel	Recovered by RN' (MacDonald). Raised mid-December 1924 (Beached on Fara, re: Prendergast Report)

Name	Flotilla	Tonnage (Reuter RM/8/1311)	Sunk / beached	Breaking Up	Wreck Details	Salvage Company
G.91	No.3 Flotilla	955				Cox & Danks
G.92	No.7 Flotilla	955				
H.145	No.7 Flotilla	1,034	sunk			Cox & Danks
S.131	No.6 Flotilla	890	sunk			Scapa Flow Salvage & Ship-breaking Company (Robertson)
S.132	No.6 Flotilla	890	beached			
S.136	No.7 Flotilla	898	sunk			Cox & Danks
S.137	No.7 Flotilla	898	beached			
S.138	No.7 Flotilla	898	sunk			
S.32	No.1. Flotilla	775	sunk			Cox & Danks
S.36	No.7 Half Flotilla	775	sunk		Laying at 4m (Ferguson)	Cox & Danks
S.49	No.6 Flotilla	785				
S.50	No.6 Flotilla	785	sunk			
S.51	No.7 Half Flotilla	785	beached			
S.52	No.7 Half Flotilla	785	sunk			Cox & Danks
S.53	No.3 Flotilla	890	sunk			Cox & Danks
S.54	No.3 Flotilla	890	sunk		Laying at 16m (Ferguson)	Cox & Danks

Year	Month	Date raised (George)	Launched	Builder	Comments
		12.9.24	16.11.15	Germanienwerft, Kiel	
			15.2.16	Germanienwerft, Kiel	(Beached on Hoy, re: Prendergast Report)
1925	Mar	14.3.25			George lists same date for launch and for raising. When she sank she actually came back up to the surface
1924	Aug	29.8.24 (not in George)	3.3.17	Schichau, Danzig	Scuttled in shallow water. Also raised three other unidentified destroyers. Referred to as S.31 beached on Fara (Prendergast report)
			19.5.17	Schichau, Danzig	Scuttled in shallow water. Transferred to American control, sunk in 1921
1925	Apr	3.4.25	1.12.17	Schichau, Danzig	
			9.3.18	Schichau, Danzig	Beached in shallow water. Transferred to British control, broken up in 1922 (Beached on Fara, re: Prendergast Report)
1925	May	1.5.25	22.4.18	Schichau, Danzig	Wreck lies close to S.65
1925	Jun	19.6.25	28.2.14	Schichau, Danzig	Tied in group S.32, S.36 and S.52 lie together as wrecks
1925	Apr	18.4.25	7.10.14	Schichau, Danzig	Tied in group S.32, S.36 and S.52 lie together as wrecks
			10.4.15	Schichau, Danzig	Scuttled in shallow water
1924	Oct		24..4.15	Schichau, Danzig	Scuttled in shallow water. Tied in group S.32, S.50, S.52?
			29.4.15	Schichau, Danzig	Scuttled in shallow water. Transferred to British control, broken up in 1922
1924	Oct	13.10.24	14.6.15	Schichau, Danzig	Tied in group S.32, S.36 and S.52 lie together as wrecks
1924	Aug	13.8.24	18.9.15	Schichau, Danzig	Raised twelve days after V.70
		5.6.25	11.10.15	Schichau, Danzig	Partially salvaged. Had been lying in shallow water (around 40ft) and much of her more expensive metal already stripped off by the time Cox raised her. Referred to in Prendergast Report as beached on Fara

Name	Flotilla	Tonnage (Reuter RM/8/1311)	Sunk / beached	Breaking Up	Wreck Details	Salvage Company
S.55	No.3 Flotilla	890	sunk			Cox & Danks
S.56	No.7 Flotilla	890	sunk			Cox & Danks
S.60	No.7 Half Flotilla	890	beached			
S.65	No.7 Flotilla	890	sunk			Cox & Danks
V.100	No.2. Flotilla	350	beached			
V.125	No.6 Flotilla	905	beached			
V.126	No.6 Flotilla	905	beached			
V.127	No.6 Flotilla	905	beached			
V.128	No.6 Flotilla	905	beached			
V.129	No.1. Flotilla	905	sunk			
V.43	No.6 Flotilla	830	beached			
V.44	No.6 Flotilla	830	beached			
V.45	No.6 Flotilla	830	sunk			
V.46	No.6 Flotilla	830	beached			
V.70	No.3 Flotilla	905	sunk			Cox & Danks

Year	Month	Date raised (George)	Launched	Builder	Comments
1924	Aug	29.8.24	6.11.15	Schichau, Danzig	
1925	Jun	5.6.25	11.12.15	Schichau, Danzig	
			3.4.16	Schichau, Danzig	Beached. Transferred to Japanese control, broken up in 1922 in the UK. (Beached on Fara, re: Prendergast Report)
1922	May	16.5.25	14.10.16	Schichau, Danzig	Wreck lies close to S.138
			8.3.15	A G Vulcan, Hamburg	Beached. Transferred to French control, broken up in 1921 (Beached in Mill Bay, re: Prendergast Report)
			18.5.17	A G Vulcan, Hamburg	Beached. Transferred to British control, broken up in 1922 (Beached on Hoy, re: Prendergast Report)
			30.6.17	A G Vulcan, Hamburg	Beached. Transferred to French control, broken up in 1925 (Beached on Hoy, re: Prendergast Report)
			28.7.17	A G Vulcan, Hamburg	Beached and to Dordrecht? Transferred to Japanese control, broken up in 1922 (Beached on Hoy, re: Prendergast Report)
			11.8.17	A G Vulcan, Hamburg	Transferred to British control, broken up in 1922 (George say Italian control) (Beached on Hoy, re: Prendergast Report)
1925	Aug	11.8.25	21.6.19	A G Vulcan, Hamburg	Tied with G.40
			27.1.15	A G Vulcan, Hamburg	Scuttled in shallow water. Transferred to American control, sunk as a target in 1921 off Cape Henry
			24.2.15	A G Vulcan, Hamburg	Salved by the RN'. Transferred to British control, broken up in Cherbourg 1922. (Beached on Fara, southwest corner, re: Prendergast Report)
1922			29.3.15	A G Vulcan, Hamburg	Salved by RN
				A G Vulcan,	Salved by the RN'. Transferred to French control, broken up in 1924 (Beached on Hoy, re: Prendergast Report)
1924	Aug	1.8.24	14.10.15	A G Vulcan, Hamburg	Was anchored by itself. South end of Gutter sound. According to George 'used as a salvage hulk'. It was the first destroyer raised by Cox & Danks and became a floating workshop, Salvage Unit No. 3.

Name	Flotilla	Tonnage (Reuter RM/8/1311)	Sunk / beached	Breaking Up	Wreck Details	Salvage Company
V.73	No.3 Flotilla	905	beached			Cox & Danks
V.78	No.7 Flotilla	905	sunk			Cox & Danks
V.80	No.7 Half Flotilla	905	beached			
V.81	No.3 Flotilla	905	beached			Cox & Danks
V.82	No.3 Flotilla	905	beached			
V.83	No.7 Flotilla	905	beached	Laying at 8-20m (Ferguson)		Cox & Danks

Year	Month	Date raised (George)	Launched	Builder	Comments
			24.9.15	A G Vulcan, Hamburg	Sunk in shallow water. Transferred to British control, broken up in 1922 (Beached on Fara, re: Prendergast Report)
1925	Sep	7.9.25	19.2.16	A G Vulcan, Hamburg	Part of her bridge is still in the Flow, separated in two sections
			28.4.16	A G Vulcan, Hamburg	Scuttled and beached. Transferred to Japanese control, broken up in 1922 in the UK (Beached on Fara, re: Prendergast Report)
			27.5.16	A G Vulcan, Hamburg	Beached. Sunk on the way to the breakers (Beached on Fara, re: Prendergast Report)
				A G Vulcan, Hamburg	Beached. Transferred to British control, broken up in 1922 (Beached on Fara, re: Prendergast Report)
1923			5.7.16	A G Vulcan, Hamburg	Scuttled in shallow water. Recovered by the Royal Navy. Some remains closest to the large ships (Beached on Rysa island, re: Prendergast Report)

Name		Tonnage (Reuter RM/8/1311)	Time	Sunk / Beached	Purchase Details	Breaking Up	Wreck Details
Friedrich der Große	Battleship	24,700	12:16	sunk	Sold by Admiralty for £750 to Metal Industries		
König Albert	Battleship	25,800	12:54	sunk	Sold 1.11.34 by Admiralty for £750 to Metal Industries Towed from Scapa	29.4.36 by Zwarte See *Indus* and *Ganges*. Arrived Rosyth 4.5.36. Demolition started 5/36	
Moltke	Battle-cruiser	23,000	13:10	sunk	Sold 28.8.26 by Admiralty for £1,000 to Cox and Danks. Sold to Alloa Shipbreaking Company c.3/28 for £40,000 "Towed by	*Seefalke, Simson* and *Pontos* (named as *Posen* in some literature). Arrived Rosyth 21.5.28. Demolition started 16.6.28. Finished March 1929	
Kronprinz Wilhelm	Battleship	25,800	13:15	sunk			Laying at 34m (Ferguson)
Kaiser	Battleship	24,700	13:15	sunk	"Sold 25.1.24 by Admiralty for £3,000 to Cox and Danks. Sold to Metal Industries for c £75,000 (source Buxton, p. 66)	Towed from Scapa 23.8.30 by *Seefalke, Pontos* (named as *Posen* in some literature) and *Ajax*. Arrived Rosyth 27.8.30. Demolition started 17.9.30	
Große Kurfürst	Battleship	25,800	13:30	sunk	Sold by Admiralty for £750 to Metal Industries.		
Dresden	Light Cruiser	5,600	13:50	sunk			Laying at 34m (Ferguson)
Köln	Light Cruiser	5,600	13:50	sunk			Laying at 34m (Ferguson)
Brummer	Light Cruiser	4,300	13:05:00 Ship report states 13:45) sunk				Laying at 34m (Ferguson)

Salvage Company	Year	Month	Date raised (George)	Launched	Builder	Comments
Metal Industries	1937		29/04/1937	10.6.11	A G Vulcan, Hamburg	Date of raising also given as March 1937
Metal Industries	1935	Jul	31.7.35	27.4.12	Schichau, Danzig	
Cox & Danks	1927	Jun	10.6.27	4.7.10	Blohm und Voss, Hamburg	Date of raising also given as 13.6.27
				21.2.14	Germaniaw- erft, Kiel	
	1929	Mar	20.3.29	22.3.11	Kiel DY	Sinking time given as 13:30 in Selbstversenkungsbericht.
Metal Industries	1938	Apr	29.4.38	5.5.13	A G Vulcan, Hamburg	
				25.4.17	Howaldswer ke, Kiel	
				5.10.16	Blohm und Voss, Hamburg	TIme brought forward 10 minutes to 13:30
				11.12.15	A G Vulcan, Stettin	Probably later than 13:05. Just before Köln's own sinking at 13:40. (Note Brummer first of the light cruisers to sink at 13:45)

Name		Tonnage (Reuter RM/8/1311)	Time	Sunk / Beached	Purchase Details	Breaking Up	Wreck Details
Seydlitz	Battle-cruiser	25,000	13:50	sunk	Sold 25.9.24 by Admiralty for £3,000 to Cox and Danks. Sold to Metal Industries for £64,000 (Buxton, p. 17)	Towed by Seefalke, Parnass and Pontos. Arrived Rosyth 11.5.29. Demolition started 12.6.29	
Prinzregent Luitpold	Battleship	24,800	13:15	sunk	Sold 25.6.29 by Admiralty for £1,000 to Cox and Danks. Sold to Metal Industries 2/33 for £38,000 (source Buxton, p. 69)	Towed from Scapa 4.5.33 by Seefalke, Parnass, Seeteufel and Ferrodanks. Arrived Rosyth 11.5.33. Demolition started 13.6.33	
Kaiserin	Battleship	24,700	14:00	sunk	Sold 1.11.34 by Admiralty for £750	Towed from Scapa 26.4.35 by Zwarte See, Oost See, Indus and Metinda. Arrived Rosyth 31.8.36. Demolition started 8.11.36	
König	Battleship	25,800	14:00	sunk			Laying at 40m (Ferguson)
Bayern	Battleship	28,600	14:30	sunk	Sold 3.11.33 by Admiralty for £750 to Metal Industries. (source Buxton p. 76)	Towed from Scapa 26.4.35 by Zwarte See, Witte See and Ganges. Arrived Rosyth 30.4.35. Demolition started 5.6.35	
von der Tann	Battle-cruiser	19,400	14:15	sunk	Sold 25.6.29 by Admiralty for £1,000 to Cox and Danks. Sold to Metal Industries 2/33 for £30,500 (source Buxton, p. 69)	Towed from Scapa 6.7.33 by Seefalke, Parnass, Seeteufel and Ferrodanks. Arrived Rosyth 9.7.33. Demolition started 12.7.33	
Bremse	Light Cruiser	4,300	14:30	beached			

Salvage Company	Year	Month	Date raised (George)	Launched	Builder	Comments
Cox & Danks	1929	Nov	2.11.28	13.2.12	Blohm und Voss, Hamburg	Date of raising also given as 1.11.28
	1929	Mar	9.7.31	17.2.12	Germaniaw-erft, Kiel	Date of raising also given as 6.7.31. Given that Royal Oak was back at Scapa around 14:30, this would put *Prinzregent Luitpold's* sinking anywhere between 1350 – when *Seydlitz* went down - and 1415, when *Derfflinger* joined her, and not 1330
Metal Industries	1936	May	14/05/1936	21.6.09	Howaldswer ke, Kiel	Time of sinking in Scuttle Reports, p. 286
Metal Industries	1933	Sep	01/09/1934	18.2.15	Howaldswer ke, Kiel	
	1930	Dec	7.12.30	20.3.09	Blohm und Voss, Hamburg	Date of raising also given as 8.12.30, 7th in Wiki
	1929	Nov	27.1.29			

Name		Tonnage (Reuter RM/8/1311)	Time	Sunk / Beached	Purchase Details	Breaking Up	Wreck Details
Derfflinger	Battle-cruiser	26,600	14:45	sunk		Towed to Faslane for breaking up by *Turmoil, Dextrous*, Admiralty tugs *Empire Jean* and *Empire Mascot* and MI tugs *Metinda II* and *Mentinda III*	
Karlsruhe	Light Cruiser	5,300	15:50	sunk			Laying at 24m (Ferguson)
Markgraf	Battleship	25,800	16:45	sunk			Laying at 46m (Ferguson)
Hindenburg	Battle-cruiser	26,600	17:00	sunk	Alloa bought 1,700ft long, 32ft deep quay from Rosyth dockyard in anticipation of raising *Hindenburg*	Towed by *Seefalke, Hercules* and *Hero*. Arrived Rosyth 23.7.29. Demolition started 11.9.29	
Emden	Light Cruiser	5,300		beached			
Nürnberg	Light Cruiser	5,300		beached			
Frankfurt	Light Cruiser	5,750		beached			
Baden	Battleship	28,500		beached			

Salvage Company	Year	Month	Date raised (George)	Launched	Builder	Comments
Metal Industries	1939	Aug	27.7.39	1.8.15	Wil-helmshaven DY	
				31.1.16	Wil-helmshaven DY	
				4.6.13	A G Weser, Bremen	Sinking time given as 1630 (ADM.116/2074)
Cox & Danks	1930	Jul	22.7.30	12.7.13	Blohm und Voss, Hamburg (Wil-helmshaven Bowman p.106, George)"	Original launch date (unsuccessful) was 14.6.15. Sinking time given as 1615 (ADM.116/2074)
				20.3.15	Kiel DY	Unsuccessfully scuttled and beached. Transferred to French control 11.3.20, broken up in Caen in 1926. Time taken as 1400 when Shakespeare comes back
				14.4.16	Howaldswerke, Kiel	Drafted onshore after mooring chains broke. Transferred to British control, sunk as a target in 1922
						Transferred to American control, sunk as a target in 1921
				30.10.15	Schichau, Danzig	Beached Swanbister Bay. Transferred to British control, sunk as a target in 1921 (Portsmouth 16.8.21)

Appendix 3
German Officers and Crew Killed During the Scuttle

Level of service	name	first given name	Date and place of death	Remarks
Mar.Ing.Appl.	Aumüller	Max	29.11.1918	Nürnberg
Obermachinist	Beike	Friedrich	21.06.1919	V.126. The German torpedo boat was fired upon by a destroyer and a drifter
Oberheizer	Dittmann	Hermann	21.06.1919	*Markgraf*. Also killed by a shot to the head
Machinist (Engineer Apprentice)	Eversberg	Kuno	28.06.1919	*Frankfurt*. Badly wounded when on HMS *Resolution* on the night of 23/24 June
Heizer (stoker)	Funk	Karl	21.06.1919	V.127. Wounded in the stomach and died in a lifeboat when fired upon by a destroyer and motor boat
Signalmaat (yeoman of signals)	Hesse	Hans	21.06.1919	*Bayern*. Killed by a shot to the head while on one of the life rafts
T.Mach. (Warrant engineer)	Markgraf	William	21.06.1919	*V.126*. The German torpedo boat was fired upon by a destroyer and a drifter
Obermachinist (Chief Engine Room Artificer)	Pankrath	Gustav	21.06.1919	*V.126*. The German torpedo boat was fired upon by a destroyer and a drifter
KorvettenKapitän	Schumann	W alther	21.06.1919	Commander SMS *Markgraf*. Killed by a shot in the head while displaying a white flag
Heizer (stoker)	Bauer	Karl	21.06.1919	*Kronprinz Wilhelm*. First seriously wounded and then killed after repeated shooting from a drifter

Appendix 4
Deaths on Orkney-based Ships at Jutland

Ship	Unit	Deaths
Marlborough	1BS	2
Invincible (sunk)	3BCS	1,031
Chester	3BCS	35
Calliope	4LCS	10
Tipperary (sunk)	4DF	185
Broke	4DF	47
Porpoise	4DF	2
Spitfire	4DF	6
Ardent (sunk)	4DF	78
Fortune (sunk)	4DF	67
Sparrowhawk (sunk)	4DF	6
Shark (sunk)	3BCS	86
Acasta	3BCS	6
Castor	11DF	13
Nessus	12DF	7
Onslaught	12DF	5

Appendix 5
President Woodrow Wilson's Fourteen Points

8 January, 1918:

President Woodrow Wilson's Fourteen Points

It will be our wish and purpose that the processes of peace, when they are begun, shall be absolutely open and that they shall involve and permit henceforth no secret understandings of any kind. The day of conquest and aggrandizement is gone by; so is also the day of secret covenants entered into in the interest of particular governments and likely at some unlooked-for moment to upset the peace of the world. It is this happy fact, now clear to the view of every public man whose thoughts do not still linger in an age that is dead and gone, which makes it possible for every nation whose purposes are consistent with justice and the peace of the world to avow nor or at any other time the objects it has in view.

We entered this war because violations of right had occurred which touched us to the quick and made the life of our own people impossible unless they were corrected and the world secure once for all against their recurrence. What we demand in this war, therefore, is nothing peculiar to ourselves. It is that the world be made fit and safe to live in; and particularly that it be made safe for every peace-loving nation which, like our own, wishes to live its own life, determine its own institutions, be assured of justice and fair dealing by the other peoples of the world as against force and selfish aggression. All the peoples of the world are in effect partners in this interest, and for our own part we see very clearly that unless justice be done to others it will not be done to us. The programme of the world's peace, therefore, is our programme; and that programme, the only possible programme, as we see it, is this:

I. Open covenants of peace, openly arrived at, after which there shall be no private international understandings of any kind but diplomacy shall proceed always frankly and in the public view.

II. Absolute freedom of navigation upon the seas, outside territorial waters, alike in peace and in war, except as the seas may be closed in whole or in part by international action for the enforcement of international covenants.

III. The removal, so far as possible, of all economic barriers and the establishment of an equality of trade conditions among all the nations consenting to the peace and associating themselves for its maintenance.

IV. Adequate guarantees given and taken that national armaments will be reduced to the lowest point consistent with domestic safety.

V. A free, open-minded, and absolutely impartial adjustment of all colonial claims, based upon a strict observance of the principle that in determining all such questions of sovereignty the interests of the populations concerned must have equal weight with the equitable claims of the government whose title is to be determined.

VI. The evacuation of all Russian territory and such a settlement of all questions affecting Russia as will secure the best and freest cooperation of the other nations of the world in obtaining for her an unhampered and unembarrassed opportunity for the independent determination of her own political development and national policy and assure her of a sincere welcome into the society of free nations under institutions of her own choosing; and, more than a welcome, assistance also of every kind that she may need and may herself desire. The treatment accorded Russia by her sister nations in the months to come will be the acid test of their good will, of their comprehension of her needs as distinguished from their own interests, and of their intelligent and unselfish sympathy.

VII. Belgium, the whole world will agree, must be evacuated and restored, without any attempt to limit the sovereignty which she enjoys in common with all other free nations. No other single act will serve as this will serve to restore confidence among the nations in the laws which they have themselves set and determined for the government of their relations with one another. Without this healing act the whole structure and validity of international law is forever impaired.

VIII. All French territory should be freed and the invaded portions restored, and the wrong done to France by Prussia in 1871 in the matter of Alsace–Lorraine, which has unsettled the peace of the world for nearly fifty years, should be righted, in order that peace may once more be made secure in the interest of all.

IX. A readjustment of the frontiers of Italy should be effected along clearly recognizable lines of nationality.

X. The peoples of Austria–Hungary, whose place among the nations we wish to see safeguarded and assured, should be accorded the freest opportunity to autonomous development.

XI. Rumania, Serbia, and Montenegro should be evacuated; occupied territories restored; Serbia accorded free and secure access to the sea; and the relations of the several Balkan states to one another determined by friendly counsel along historically established lines of allegiance and nationality; and international guarantees of the political and economic independence and territorial integrity of the several Balkan states should be entered into.

XII. The Turkish portion of the present Ottoman Empire should be assured a secure sovereignty, but the other nationalities which are now under Turkish rule should be assured an undoubted security of life and an absolutely unmolested opportunity of autonomous development, and the Dardanelles should be permanently opened as a free passage to the ships and commerce of all nations under international guarantees.

XIII. An independent Polish state should be erected which should include the territories inhabited by indisputably Polish populations, which should be assured a free and secure access to the sea, and whose political and economic independence and territorial integrity should be guaranteed by international covenant.

XIV. A general association of nations must be formed under specific covenants for the purpose of affording mutual guarantees of political independence and territorial integrity to great and small states alike.

In regard to these essential rectifications of wrong and assertions of right we feel ourselves to be intimate partners of all the governments and peoples associated together against the Imperialists. We cannot be separated in interest or divided in purpose. We stand together until the end.

For such arrangements and covenants we are willing to fight and to continue to fight until they are achieved; but only because we wish the right to prevail and desire a just and stable peace such as can be secured only by removing the chief provocations to war, which this programme does remove. We have no jealousy of German greatness, and there is nothing in this programme that impairs it. We grudge her no achievement or distinction of learning or of pacific enterprise such as have made her record very bright and very enviable. We do not wish to injure her or to block in any way her legitimate influence or power. We do not wish to fight her either with arms or with hostile arrangements of trade if she is willing to associate herself with us and the other peace-loving nations of the world in covenants of justice and law and fair dealing. We wish her only to accept a place of equality among the peoples of the world, – the new world in which we now live, – instead of a place of mastery.

Appendix 6
Repatriation to Germany

Number	Date	Comments
4,000	3 Dec. 1918	Source: Massie, p. 784
6,000	6 Dec. 1918	Source: Massie, p. 784
5,000	12 Dec. 1918	Source: Massie, p. 784

Appendix 7
1st Battle Squadron Battleship Assignments – Drifters and Belligerents

Ship	Assigned Belligerent ship	Assigned drifters
Revenge	South-west portion. Includes *Hindenburg* and *Markgraf*	*Cachosin, Classin*
Ramillies	Centre. *Baden*	*Cudwosin, Recluse, C.D.2., C.D.1.*
Royal Sovereign	North-east portion	*Coalsin*
Resolution		*Clonsin*
Royal Oak		*Cabalsin, Caersin, Nellie Laud*

Appendix 8
1st Battle Squadron Destroyer Actions

Spenser	*S.132, V.43*	Managed to right *S.132* and later *V.43* also towed to beach
Shakespeare	*Emden*	
Vectis	*Markgraf*	Failed to beach *Markgraf*
Winchelsea	*G.92*	Succeeded in beaching *G.92*
Venetia	*Bremse*	Slipped *Bremse*'s cable and took her in tow but the latter then capsized
Wessex	*Frankfurt*	With assistance from *Royal Sovereign* boarding party and *Classin*, was able to beach *Frankfurt* in Smoogro Bay in 4 fathoms

Appendix 9
High Seas Fleet Internment Command

Fleet Staff

Senior Officer	Kontreadmiral Ludwig von Reuter
Chief of Staff	Fregattenkapitän Iwan von Oldekop
Admiral's Staff Officer	Kapitänleutnant Lautenschlager
Flag-Lieutenant	Oberleutnant zur See Schillig
Squadron Paymaster	Stabszahlmeister Habicht
Naval Advocate	Marine-Krieggerichtsrat Lt. Loesch
Squadron Engineer	Marine-Ob stabs-Ing. Faustmann (*Markgraf*)
Squadron Surgeon	Marine-Stabarzt Dr Lange (*PrinzR Luitpold*)

Battleships

Baden	Korvettenkapitän Zirzow
Friedrich der Große	Korvettenkapitän von Wachter
Bayern	Kapitänleutnant Meißner, Hugo Dominik
Große Kurfürst	Kapitänleutnant Boer
Kronprinz Wilhelm	Kapitänleutnant Becker
Markgraf	Korvettenkapitän Schumann
König	Korvettenkapitän Junkermann
König Albert	Korvettenkapitän Böhmer
Prinzregent Luitpold	Kapitänleutnant von Reiche
Kaiser	Kapitänleutnant Wippern
Kaiserin	Korvettenkapitän Viertel

Battle-cruisers

Derfflinger	Korvettenkapitän Pastusczyck
Hindenburg	Korvettenkapitän Heyden
Von der Tan	Kapitänleutnant Wollanke
Moltke	Kapitänleutnant Erelinger
Seydlitz	Kapitänleutnant Brauer

Light Cruisers

Emden	Kapitänleutnant Ehlers
Brummer	Kapitänleutnant Prahl
Bremse	Oberleutnant zur See Schacke
Frankfurt	Kapitänleutnant Beesel
Köln	Kapitänleutnant Johann Heinemann
Dresden	Kapitänleutnant Fabricius
Nürnberg	Kapitänleutnant Georgi

Destroyers / Torpedo Boats

Leader, Torpedo Boats	Korvettenkapitän Hermann Cordes (*S.138*)
Flag Lieutenant	Kapitänleutnant Schniewind (*S.138*)
Squadron Engineer	Marine-Oberstabs.Ing. Halwe (*H.145*)
Squadron paymaster	Marine-Zahlm.d.Res. Horn (*S.138*)

I Torpedo Boat Flotilla

Leader	Kapitänleutnant Henrici (*G.40*)
G.38	
G.39	
G.40	Kapitänleutnant Henrici
G.86	
V.129	

II Torpedo Boat Flotilla

Leader	Kapitänleutnant Mensche (*B.110*)
B.109	
B.110	Kapitänleutnant Mensche, Leutnant Friedrich Ruge (officer of the Watch)
B.111	
B.112	
G.101	
G.102	
G.103	
G.100	

III Torpedo Boat Flotilla

Leader	Kapitänleutnant Steiner (*S.54*)
S.53	
S.54	Kapitänleutnant Steiner
S.55	
S.91 / G.91	Leutnant Fritz von Twardowski
V.70	
V.73	
V.81	
V.82	

VI Torpedo Boat Flotilla

Leader	Kapitänleutnant Oskar Wehr (*V.44*)
Half-Leader XI Half Flotilla	Kapitänleutnant von Bonin (*S.131*)
S.49	
S.50	

S.131	
S.132	Leutnant Lampe
V.43	
V.44	Kapitänleutnant Wehr
V.45	
V.46	
V.125	
V.126	
V.127	
V.128	

VII Torpedo Boat Flotilla

Leader	Korvettenkapitän Hermann Cordes (*S.138*)
Half-Leader XIII Half Flotilla	Kapitänleutnant Roslik (*S.56*)
Half-Leader XIII Half Flotilla	Kapitänleutnant Reimer (*S.136*)
G.89	
G.92	
H.145	
S.56	Kapitänleutnant Roslik
S.65	
S.136	Kapitänleutnant Reimer
S.137	
S.138	Korvettenkapitän Hermann Cordes
V.78	
V.83	

XVII Torpedo Boat Flotilla

Half-Leader	Kapitänleutnant Ganguin (*V.80*)
S.36	
S.51	
S.52	
S.60	
V.80	Kapitänleutnant Ganguin

Source: Reuter pp. 124–125

Appendix 10
The 'Smoking Gun'? Von Trotha's 9 May Letter to Von Reuter

Chief of the Admiralty
Berlin, 9 May 1919

No. A.III.5332
Top Secret

Sir, you have repeatedly expressed to Commander Stapenhorst the wish of the Interned ships (*Internierungs Verband*) to be informed as to their fate and the probable termination of internment.

The fate of this, the most valuable part of our Fleet, will probably be finally decided in the negotiations for a preliminary peace, now being carried on. From press news and utterances in the British House of Lords, it appears that our opponents are considering the idea of depriving us of the interned ships on the conclusion of peace; they waver between the destruction or the distribution among themselves of these ships. The British naturally raise some details about the latter course. These hostile intentions are in opposition to the hitherto unquestioned German right of ownership of these vessels, and the internment [with] which we complied on the conclusion of the Armistice only because we were obliged to consent for the duration of the Armistice, to an appreciable weakening of the striking power of the German Fleet. This assumption was freely expressed, and was not contradicted by the enemy, either at the conclusion of the Armistice or on its prolongation. We, on the other hand, have often repeated this interpretation, when we protested in February, 1919, against this unjustified internment in an enemy harbour, designating this to be a contravention of the terms of the Armistice and demanding the subsequent removal of the ships to a neutral harbour; this protest, if it is true, remained unanswered.

Sir, you may rest assured that it will be no more than the plain duty of our Naval Delegates at Versailles to safeguard the fate of our interned ships in every way, and to arrive at a solution which is in accordance with our traditions and our unequivocal German rights. In this connection, the first condition will be that the ships remain German, and that their fate, whatever turn it may take under the pressure of the political situation, will not be decided without our co-operation, and will be consummated by ourselves, and that their surrender to the enemy remains out of the question. We must hope that these just demands may retain their position in the scheme of our political standpoint in the question of peace as a whole.

I beg you, Sir, as far as possible to express to the officers and crews of the interned ships my satisfaction that, for their part, they are most eagerly nursing our most natural hope, that the interned ships will be retained under the German flag, and to communicate to them our strong desire to make our just cause triumphant. This spirit is calculated to support the German Delegates in their efforts at the Peace Conference. The fate of the whole Navy will depend upon the results of these efforts; it is hoped that they will put an end to the internment which, through our enemies breach of faith, has become so cruel, the sufferings and trials which are deplored by our whole Navy, and which will be remembered to the credit of the interned crews.

To the Commander-in-Chief of the Interned Ships,
Rear Admiral von Reuter, Scapa Flow.

Source. *Illustrated London News*, 13 December 1919. Note that the underlining is the author's. The text of the letter was published by the Admiralty on 4 December 1919 after the original had been found in von Reuter's personal safe on SMS *Emden*. The communiqué noted that the German reply of 28 June 1919 stated that the scuttling had been 'without the knowledge of any German civil or military authority' and that 'orders from the German Government failed entirely to reach Admiral von Reuter during the time when his ships were at Scapa Flow'.

NOTES

Chapter 1

[1] 'kings and generals who had shaped [Germany's] destinies through two centuries'. Friewald, p. 274

[2] 'the German Imperial Navy was subordinated…'. Witt & McDermott. P. 23

[3] 'Germany was an army with a country attached'. Friedman, *Downfall*, p. 38

[4] 'That the German unification was based on six years of success … .' Tampke, p. 6

[5] 'He was convinced of the relationship… .' Epkenhans, *Tirpitz*, p. 19

[6] *Scapa 1919*, Dr Wilhelm Deist, German Naval Historian

[7] 'a state which has sea interests or…'. Lambi, p. 75

[8] 'Those who consistently advocate the defensive… .' Epkenhans, *Tirpitz*, p. 21

[9] 'Only he who dominates the sea… .' Speech to Reichstag and Prussian Military Academy. Quoted in Epkenhans, p. 19

[10] 'aimed at emancipating the fiscal foundation…'. Seligmann, Nägler and Epkenhans, p. 1

[11] 'Geography, which Tirpitz had always neglected… .' *Ibid*, p. 402

[12] 'had depended heavily upon international trade'. Tampke, p. 45

[13] 'I realised that unless I had a Navy sufficiently strong… .' Hawkins, p. 2

[14] 'The result of this policy will be to place Germany… .' Massie, *Dreadnought*, p. 184, quoting Lord Selbourne

[15] Source: Seligmann, Nägler and Epkenhans, p. 156

[16] 'The more the composition of the new German Fleet… .' *Ibid*

[17] 'be catastrophic, in foreign waters a mere setback'. Jellicoe, *Jutland*, p. 33

[18] 'holed-up Fleet in a pre-emptive Pearl Harbour-like stroke'. Jellicoe, *Jutland*, p. 33

[19] 'get its blow in first, before the other side…'. Wragg, p. 177

[20] See Hough, *First Lord*, p. 238, and Morris, pp. 146–149

[21] 'a wanton and profligate ostentation.' Morris, p. 152

[22] 'put Britain and Germany on an equal footing…'. Jellicoe, *Jutland*, p. 33

[23] Source: Seligmann, Nägler and Epkenhans, p. 157

[24] 'in the short term…' Jellicoe, *Jutland*, p. 18

[25] 'It looked like the ratio between the British and German Fleets… .' Jellicoe, *Jutland*, p. 40

[26] 'polls in January 1907 put a halt…'. Seligmann, Nägler and Epkenhans, p. 161

[27] Source: *Ibid*, p. 279

[28] 'When the current naval policy was embarked upon… .' *Ibid*, p. 283

[29] 'The General question of whether Germany should fight England… .' *Ibid*, p. 400

[30] 'isolated, misunderstood and sometimes lonely'. *Ibid*, p. 397

[31] 'a mechanical toy'. *Ibid*, p. 398

[32] 'a weapon during the war…'. Dr Wilhelm Deist, C4, *Scapa 1919*

Chapter 2

[33] 'The soldiers, undernourished and physically and mentally exhausted, deserted in droves'. Tampke, p. 85

[34] 'scorched earth-policy'. Tampke, p. 91

[35] 'the most thankless'. Wolz, *FISTI*. p. 165

[36] 'From these arose small cells of resistance … .' Kiel Marine Museum, presentation, summer 2018, #14

[37] '*Kluft war, so dasses keener Agitation von Außen bedurfte!*' Witt, *von schwarz*. p. 55

[38] 'had a reputation in the Fleet of great

severity'. Woodward, p. 72

[39] 'The sailors, in the spirit of trade unionism... .' MacGregor, p. 12

[40] '...wobei Langweile und schlechste Menschen-führung'. Witt, *Rote Fahnen*, p. 36

[41] 'It has become a part of left-wing legend ... '. Woodward, p. 132

[42] 'very much an exhibitionist...'. Woodward, p. 81

[43] '*die mit eiserner Hand underdrückt...*'. Haffner, p. 61

[44] 'nobody wanted a revolution...'. . Woodward, p. 76

[45] 'I never thought that this could be dangerous... .' Woodward, p 76

[46] 'We knew what had happened at Wilhelmshaven... .' Woodward, p. 76

[47] '...stands up well as a reasonably accurate account of what happened...'. Woodward, p. 84

[48] 'about seven per cent of the crews of the Fleet'. Woodward, p. 86

[49] 'a short, vehement woman'. Woodward, p. 85

[50] 'that he might make rash remarks which could be used against him'. Casrten, p. 116

[51] '*beispielloser und einmaliger Vorgang...*'. Kinzler and Tillman, p. 78

[52] 'What I fear is that when peace comes all the blame will be heaped on the Navy ...' Wolz, *FISTI*, p. 169

[53] 'cloaked military strike'. Wolz, *FISTI*, p. 171, quoting Wilhelm Deist

[54] Wolz, p. 174, quoting Hipper Diary, 17 October 1918

[55] 'The note had been sent out only one week after ... .' Tampke, p. 65

[56] 'severely handicapped by lack of labour'. Tampke, p. 69

[57] See Tampke, p. 75

[58] '... might give away at the peace table what the soldiers had been fighting for...' Tampke, p. 81

[59] 'that would preclude refusal of the final Peace settlement'. Trask, p. 319. USNSF, TX File

[60] 'It would prevent us from using our strongest weapon ... .' Trask, p. 320

[61] 'The British idea of the Freedom of the Seas ... .' Trask, pp. 320–321

[62] 'You may be sure that we military men will do all ... .' Trask, p. 328

[63] '...put all his hopes for the future into U-boats...'. Woodward, p. 112

[64] 'In order to avoid anything that might hamper the work of peace... .' Woodward, p. 113

[65] 'had regained its liberty of action' Woodward, p. 113

[66] 'Lloyd George and Clemenceau vie with each other ...'. Trask, pp. 315–316. Cecil comment to Balfour, 7 October 1918

[67] 'there was by no means a close identity of interests'. Trask, p. 314

[68] 'If we are to get a fair and permanent peace... .' Trask, p. 326, Quoting Henry Hollis

[69] 'It might'. Trask, p. 337

[70] 'striving with the greatest energy to provoke...'. Marder, *FDTSF*, Vol. 5 p. 172

[71] 'from the moral point of view, a question of the honour...'. Marder, *FDTSF*, Vol. 5 p. 173

[72] See Marder, FDTSF, Vol. 5 p. 170

[73] See Trask, p. 336

[74] 'something that was never done unless a real operation was planned'. Woodward, p. 118

[75] 'It was quite clear. This was not a militarily necessary operation... .' Dr Wilhelm Dienst, *With All Flags Flying*

[76] 'mutinous dockyard workers had swarmed on board and torn down the war flag'. Reuter, p. 16

[77] '*ging wie ein Lauffeuer durch ganzes Schiffe*'. Krause, p. 148

[78] 'Not only were the crews faced with defeat and death... .' Woodward, p. 120

[79] 'requested or had been transferred to more productive duties'. Reuter, p. 15

[80] 'The men are standing by me and are showing it to me in (a) touching manner and I definitely believe I can get them through this honourably'. Wolz, *FISTI*, p. 181

[81] '*Der Kommandant des Kleinen Kreuzers Nürnberg... .*' Koop & Mulitze, p. 170

[82] '*Kadavergehorsam*'. Horn, p. 418

[83] '*Wie sie es sahen, übten sie legitime Staatsnot-wehr... .*' Haffner, p. 62

[84] '*Wir verfeuern unsere letzten... .*' Krause, p. 148

[85] '*In den vollständig dunkeln Gängen und Räumen...*'. Heinemann, RM/44 p. 33

[86] 'If we had fired into the forward battery of the *Thüringen... .*' Woodward, p. 127

[87] Wolz, *FISTI*, quoting Hipper Diary, 31 October 1918

[88] '*gaben diese auf und ließen sich schließlich wi-derstandlos festnehmen*'. Rackwitz, p. 33

[89] 'Where was Lord (sic) Jervis?', Woodward, p. 130

90 'There was no doubt that despite the greatest secrecy… .' Wolz, *FISTI*, p. 177
91 'heavy tramp of marching troops'. Kuhn, p. 9
92 'important decision which was to have fatal consequences'. Wolz, *FISTI*, p. 179
93 '*Kriegsmüden Kieler Arbeitern*'. Witt, *Rote Fahnen*, p. 37
94 Source: Rackwitz, p. 19
95 Source: Rackwitz, p. 20
96 '…were not putting an end to the war between the nations in order to start a Civil War'. Woodward, p. 140
97 'there was no impression that a great revolution had broken out'. Woodward, p. 141
98 'was able to observe the gradual rise of bestiality…'. Horn, p. 422
99 '…if the drums and bugles served any purpose at all it was to advertise the forthcoming meeting'. Woodward, p. 144
100 'it is said by his own men'. Woodward, p. 144
101 '*Plötzlich erkannten alle… .*' Haffner, p. 64
102 'the first act of SPD infiltration of the revolutionaries' ranks'. Kuhn, p. 3
103 'This bloody business must end. You must get the shooting stopped.' Woodward, p. 148
104 'We are all deeply upset over the disgraceful mutiny in the Fleet.' Wolz, p. 180, quoting Kapitänleutnant Hermann von Schweinitz. After two days, he gave up the fight, admitting, 'We are powerless, all we try, to no avail, too late.'
105 'Now at last, after many years, the suppressed stokers and sailors realise that nothing, no, nothing can be accomplished without them.' Horn, p. 418
106 'a ferocious disciplinarian, a hot-head and ardent proponent of the most extreme…'. Woodward, p. 157
107 'consider their grievances on the ship's return to Wilhelmshaven'. Woodward, p. 174
108 'We must all work together to see that the conditions of the Armistice are speedily and effectively carried out.' Woodward, p. 176
109 'reject the idea of national defence …'.. Woodward, p. 160
110 'It was the men who refused… .' Tirpitz JUB?
111 'This Navy! It was spawned by world power arrogance Wolz, *FISTI*, p. 182, quoting Ernst von Weizsäcker Diary, 5/6 November 1918
112 'A curse lies on the Navy because out of its

ranks Revolution first sprang… .' Scheer, p. 358
113 'War-weariness and hunger had already provided plenty of incendiary material … .' Woodward, p. 10
114 '*Was aber zwischen der 4. und 10. November…*'. Haffner, p. 68

Chapter 3
115 'The fate of the German Kaiser Reich was sealed in two railway coaches.' Wolz, *FISTI*. p. 183
116 Source: Ruge, p. 75
117 Kolb, p. 35
118 'France was to be weakened to such an extent … .' Tampke, pp. 48–49
119 'had received full consent with the partial exception'. Fremantle, *Sinkings*, p. 2
120 'to enable the Allies to enforce the Armistice…'. Roskill, *NPBW*, p. 73
121 'it was not desirable to risk the refusal…' Roskill, *NPBW*, p. 74
122 'Why we should be so exacting… .' Fremantle, *Sinkings*, p. 2
123 'if the Sea Power of Germany is surrendered …'. ADM 116/1825. Roskill, *NPBW*, p. 75
124 'made no inquiries in Holland, Sweden, Norway, Denmark or Spain'. Ruge, p. 48
125 Roskill, *Naval Hero*, p. 276. Also *NPBW*, p. 75. Quotes FO telegram 1378 detailing Spain's refusal in ADM 116/1825
126 *Bundesarchiv* document 5950/I, pp. 271–272, cited in Ruge, p. 48
127 'I assumed the object of the war was the destruction of German militarism… .' Chalmers, pp. 332–333
128 'admittedly assists the United States…'. Booth, p. xv
129 'I was very perturbed at the underlying tone of your letter… .' Chalmers, p. 337
130 'technical advisors', Woodward, p. 176
131 'My dramatic sense was highly developed at the moment.' Beatty to Eugénie Godfrey-Fawcett 26 November 1918. Quoted in Chalmers, p. 344
132 'The heavy fog had caused a delay… .'
133 'the strongest electric sunlights'. Chalmers, p. 344
134 'As [Meurer] stepped aboard… .' Contemporaneous description found on Ancestry.com/Rootsweb
135 'courteous in the extreme but firm as a rock'. Roskill, *Naval Hero*, p. 276. Beatty to Eugénie Godfrey-Fawcett 26 November 1918

136 'A subsequent search of the greatcoat revealed a large lump of cheese'. George, p. 17

137 See Marder, FDTSF, Vol. 5, p. 189 quoting Ralph Seymour's recollection of the meeting (Lady Seymour, Ralph Seymour, R.N., Glasgow, 1926, pp. 120–121

138 'latest type of U-boat'. Temple Patterson, Tyrwhitt, p. 209

139 'Admiral Tywhitt will guarantee their safety, but their honour … .' Temple Patterson, Tyrwhitt, p. 209.

140 'only the payment of cash bonuses of 500 Marks…'. Schubert and Gibson, p. 209

141 'voices raised on argument, coming from the open scuttles …'. Woodward, p. 177

142 'All questions were decided in his [Beatty's] favour without question.' van der Vat, p. 105

143 'to a point half way between Kirkaldy and Aberlady Bays, east of Inch Keith…'. Schubert and Gibson, p. 219

144 'in the middle of it, the Monarch buts in… '. Roskill, Naval Hero, p. 276. Beatty to Eugénie Godfrey-Fawcett, 19 November 1918

Chapter 4

145 'it won't take long. You'll be back home soon.' Karl Heidebrunn interview, Scapa 1919

146 'several hundred marks'. Wolz, FISTI. p. 189

147 'inordinate enthusiasm for the work of destruction'. van der Vat, p. 108

148 'I remember he went through our garden… .' Yorck von Reuter interview, Scapa 1919

149 'fifth child and the third son'. van der Vat, p. 109

150 'a man of action with the capacity…'. van der Vat, p. 111

151 'at one with the crew [in] that every man on this transfer voyage …'. van der Vat, p. 113

152 'The ship's band played light music… .' Woodward, p. 179

153 'In this symbolic train, Germany was leading into captivity… .' Freiwald, p. 274

154 'to prove their (ships') disarmament' Reuter, p. 28

155 'Although nothing is known officially… .' Orkney Herald, 20 November 1918

156 'die vor 3 Jahren in ehrliche Kampfe mit die mächtigsten der Feinde …'. Selbstversenkung Berichte, p. 142

157 'There was no thought in our heads… .' Karl Heidebrunn interview, Scapa 1919

158 'made their way to Wilhelmshaven, and

having heard…'. The Daily Record, 5 December 1918

159 van der Vat, p. 119. On the print that was commissioned (Der Tag), the visibility is noted as 4,500yds and the wind, 2 to 3 knots WSW.

160 'It was a beautiful day for the North Sea in November… .' Stevens, p. 358

161 Smith, p. 5

162 'a little child leading by the nose a herd of fearsome bullocks'. Brown and Meehan, p. 126, Booth, p. 7

163 Orcadian, 28 November 1918

164 'largest assemblage of sea-power in the history of the world'. van der Vat, p. 119

165 Orcadian, 28 November 1918 quoting Matrose Werner Braunsberger, SMS Kaiser

166 Source: Der Tag Commissioned chart

167 Orcadian, 28 November 1918

168 'Cardiff then turned about, "marked time" as the German ship approached… .' Brown and Meehan, p. 126

169 '…heaven conferred a certain mantle upon our shame.' van der Vat, p. 124

170 'up and loaded ready for ramming home'. van der Vat, p. 120

171 'It just needs a shot from either side to start… .' Brown and Meehan, p. 127 quoting Sydney Winsor

172 'You really had to laugh… .' Karl Heidebrunn interview, Scapa 1919

173 'Old antagonists, victors and vanquished'. Freiwald, p. 288

174 'That day hid within its bosom… .' Freiwald, p. 281

175 'high-handed'. Ruge, p. 52

176 Orkney Herald, 25 December 1918

177 Beatty, Our Admiral, p. 117

178 'reminiscent of Nelson's after the Nile'. Marder, FDTSF, Vol. 5, p. 191

179 'the Huns anchored in the form of a square…'. Stevens, p. 358

180 'more humiliating than defeat in an action at sea could ever have been'. Wolz, FISTI, p. 193

181 'the only thing is to sail into their poisonous country …', Wolz, FISTI, p. 192

182 'By all thinking persons, the part played by the British Royal Navy…'. van der Vat, p. 121

183 'nearly all the sailors wore a little red ribbon…'. Stevens, p. 360

184 'the dehumanised revolutionaries'. van der Vat, p. 108, quoting Matrose Werner Braunsberger, SMS Kaiser

185 Liddle, p. 208

186 'the stiff Prussian lieutenant'. Correspondence of Robert Surgeon Rear Admiral Robert Willan, RNRV. Kindly made available by Neale Lawson.
187 'quality of their ships and their armament'. van der Vat, p. 127
188 'keenly'. Roskill, *Naval Hero*, p. 280
189 Beatty, *Our Admiral*, p. 118
190 'the most spectacular moment in his career…'. van der Vat, p. 107
191 'The Fleet, my Fleet, is broken-hearted….' Chalmers, p. 341
192 Cavendish, *History Today*
193 'a frame of mind which can readily be understood'. Marder, *FDTSF*, Vol. 5, p. 165
194 Beatty, *Our Admiral*, p. 115
195 'It made one rub one's eyes….' Stevens, p. 358
196 'playing lively music… . They must have been just as pleased as we were…'. Brown and Meehan, p. 127 quoting Thomas Young
197 'The surrender of the German Navy was the best experience … .' Kennedy, UBHG, *Scapa Flow*, p. 11, quoting Sidney Hunt

Chapter 5
198 'failing to carry out honourably the few obligations …'. Ruge, p. 53
199 OLA Tapes OSA/AOS 464. Tape 2, Hewison
200 'In a war with Germany… .' Kennedy, UBHG, p. 5
201 'the longest distance train ever run in the British Islands and probably the most punctual'. Hewison, p. 83
202 'practically defenceless'. Kennedy, *Scapa Flow*, UBHG, Letter Malcolm Brown letter 23 January 1967, p. 3
203 'nothing should stand in the way of the equipment, Kennedy, *Scapa Flow as a Naval Base*, Notes, UBHG
204 'Probably to no place in the world did the enemy look…'. *The Orcadian*, 28 November 1918
205 OLA Tapes OSA/AO5 463. Tape 1, Hewison
206 'The German Fleet, by all accounts… .' *The Orcadian*, 28 November 1918
207 'escorted by an equal number of British destroyers'. van der Vat, p. 128
208 See George, p. 22
209 See *Orkney Herald*, Wednesday, 4 December 1918
210 'just after daybreak'. Ruge, p. 54
211 'grey November morning'. Ferguson, p. 6
212 'full of potatoes'. George, p. 23
213 'feared they would probably be "blotted out by the ship's crew on the way over"'. George, p. 23
214 'filthy and couldn't have been cleaned in weeks'. George, p. 23
215 'the bight was surrounded by treeless hills and was desolate and cheerless'. van der Vat, p. 132
216 'thoroughly frightful'. van der Vat, p. 132
217 'The lower parts of the land showed signs of rude cultivation….' Booth, p. 8
218 'Scapa tap'. Hector Matheson interview (engineer HMS *Erin*), *Scapa 1919*
219 'To the British officer, the fact that the Germans are being forced….' van der Vat, p. 133
220 'to be their home for an indefinite amount of time'. Ruge interview, *Yesterday's Yarns*, Radio Orkney
221 'sea time'. Miller, p. 15
222 Midshipman Ian Sanderson to his father, 1 December 1918, Quoted in Marder, *FDTSF* Vol. 5, p. 272
223 'The British Fleet received us with the greatest mistrust….' *Orkney Herald*, 25 December 1918 quoting *Hamburger Nachrichten*
224 'Still one does not expect to see an officer….' *Orcadian*, 19 December 1918
225 Midshipman Ian Sanderson to his father, 1 December 1918 reporting the impressions of the Gunnery Officer of HMS *Malaya*, Lieutenant-Commander Andrew B. Downes. Quoted in Marder, *FDTSF* Vol. 5, p. 271
226 'Jetsam that floated ashore….' John Tulloch memories, Courtesy Joyce Howard
227 'These I had anchored in our duck pond….' John Tulloch memories, Courtesy Joyce Howard
228 'These I anchored in our duck pond….' John Tulloch memories, Courtesy Joyce Howard
229 As a child I thought, why shouldn't they go down….' Peggie Gibson quoted in Ferguson, p. 73
230 'It is to be impressed upon all Officers and Men….' ADM 1/8571/296 Action to be taken re: German Fleet sinking. Enclosure No. 1. Atlantic Fleet submission to admiralty dated 22 June 1919 No.371/A.H.0050 based on 20 November 1918 orders
231 'It is not often that the Fleet of a great power….' Bennett, *Scapa Scuttle*, p. 535
232 'It will be seen that the British and French

Naval Delegates... .' van der Vat, p. 184
[233] 'His activities extend only to purely Church and instructional subjects.' Reuter, p. 120
[234] 'some of them did land on Hoy...'. *The Courier*, 14 January 1920 p. 4.
[235] 'were turned back by a picket boat'. *The Scotsman*, 3 December 1918
[236] 'Some of them were so near to my home... .' Tulloch, Lyness Museum, Exhibition materials summer 2016
[237] 'Then one fine day when the patrol drifter... .' Tulloch, *The Orcadian*, 23 September 2011
[238] 'were under observation the whole time', Ferguson, p. 6
[239] Smith, p. 6
[240] 'English, Geography, Mathematics and Chemistry'. Ruge, p. 62
[241] 'then we even played tag around the funnels and the bridges...'. Kennedy, UBHG *Scapa Flow*, p. 12
[242] *'und etwas wie ein Kinovorstellung...'.* Krause, p. 210
[243] 'variegated, ragged and dirty'. *Orcadian*, 19 December 1918
[244] 'hornet's nest'. van der Vat, p. 114
[245] 'Always the same comrades round you...'. Booth, p. 9. Braunsberger, a sailor on the *Kaiser*, kept a diary throughout the internment. Also interviewed on C4, *With All Flags flying*
[246] Admiral Sir Charles Madden to Jellicoe. 29 November 1919.
[247] *'Alle geplanten Befehle warden... .'* Krause, p. 224
[248] 'Engineering officers...occupied a lower social status within the officer corps than the Seamen officers.' Ruge, p, 16. (Krause, pp. 226–227. *'Besonders unbeliebtsind neben den Offizieren die Maschinisten, vermutlich, weil die von ihnen angeordneten Wartungsarbeiten den Männern nur völlig sinnloserschienen.'*)
[249] *'nachdem Reuter in einem schriflichen Vertrag...'.* Krause
[250] *'und der Heimkehrern...'.* Krause, p. 207
[251] *'unbrauchbare oder unbeliebte'.* Krause, p. 206
[252] 'took advantage of the return trip'. De Courcy-Ireland, p. 56
[253] *'Mühlenfabrikate und Teigwaren'.* Krause, p. 219
[254] 'mediocre potatoes, jam made from root vegetables ...'. Ruge, p. 62
[255] 'The entire list of articles which the ration office in Wilhelmshaven... .' Ruge, p. 70

[256] 'It was very comical.' Brown and Meehan, p. 127, quoting Thomas Young
[257] 'swarms of small fish like sprats'. Ferguson, p. 7
[258] 'smoked or fried up in torpedo oil'. Wolz, *FISTI.* p. 203
[259] 'to supplement their meat rations they carried out a few raids...'. Brown and Meehan, p. 128, quoting RC Chadwick
[260] Reported in *The Sunday Post*, 9 February 1919.
[261] 'letting off green sparks, the star whizzed on in a great arc...'. Ruge, p. 88
[262] Source: van der Vat, p. 137
[263] Source: Ferguson, p. 7
[264] 'toothache and nutritional deficiency diseases'.Wolz, *FISTI.* p. 203
[265] 'chronic intestinal catarrh...'. van der Vat, p. 138
[266] 'not clear whether he meant to convey the idea...'. *The Courier*, 14 February 1919, p. 4
[267] 'I recently received a white cabbage from Germany ... .' van der Vat, p. 137
[268] 'lively barter trade', Ruge, p. 63
[269] 'it was almost impossible to stop'. de Courcy-Ireland, p. 55
[270] 'they did not belong to the Navy and were not against establishing somewhat closer contacts'. Ruge, p. 63
[271] 'the men of the drifters cheerfully took part in the clandestine trading between ships'. Miller, p. 59
[272] 'Unfortunately, we had no contact with the islanders at all... .' Ruge on *Yesterday's Yarns*, Radio Orkney
[273] 'there were always boats out at the ships... '. *The Courier*, 14 January 1920, p. 4.
[274] Colville, Personal interview (2017)
[275] 'frowned upon by the senior German officers ...'. Brown and Meehan, p. 129
[276] 'During the last few days it has been observed from here... .' Brown and Meehan, pp. 130–131
[277] 'invented most wonderful new orders ...'. Brown and Meehan, p. 129, quoting Friedrich Ruge
[278] Arthur, p. 139. The story was reported in *The Courier*, 14 February 1919, where the object of the exchange was a bar of soap.
[279] 'That's the order of Transfer into Internment.' van der Vat, p. 139

Chapter 6
[280] 'Our downfall could only be accomplished by extraordinary means... .' Scheer, p. 359

281 'in a buoyant mood, having won a landslide victory…'. p. 102
282 'mainly young and idealistic scholars'. Tampke, p. 92
283 'had contributed little' Tampke, p. 106
284 'France and Italy were exhausted… '. Stokesbury, p. 342
285 'Only the United States and Japan remained as serious naval powers.' Ibid.
286 'the ongoing and heated discussion during that period…'. Tracy, p. 193
287 'a proven means of national survival'. Tracy, p. 193
288 'No less real because it was…' Marder, FDTSF, Vol. 5, p.179
289 'either ignored international law governing trade by neutral nations or interpreted…'. Lisio, p. 6
290 'as freedom to prolong the war…'. Tracy, p. 201
291 OLA Tapes OSA/AO5 466. Tape 4, Hewison
292 'strikes me as the advice of people who do not know what else to do'. van der Vat, p. 159
293 'thought it foolish to destroy perfectly good ships'. Tampke, p. 107
294 'I cannot consent to take part… '. Simpson, p. 486
295 'I think trade rivalry… .' Remarks to Sir Eric Drummond 23 January 1918, quoted in Simpson, p. 486
296 'many nations, great and small, chafed…'. Geddes memo, 16 October 1918, quoted Simpson, p. 547
297 'The sailors were as suspicious… .' Simpson, p. 484
298 'Nothing further need therefore be said… .' Wemyss memorandum on 'Freedom of the Seas', 17 October 1918, quoted in Simpson, p. 548
299 'leave Great Britain the absolute naval master …'. US Planning section comments quoted in Simpson, p. 545
300 'the sole naval weapon that has influenced …'. US Planning section comments quoted in Simpson, p. 545
301 'a Royal Navy with no European rival…'. Simpson, p. 485
302 'The German Fleet has ceased to exist… .' Paris, 7 April 1919, quoted in Simpson, pp. 601–602
303 'biggest politically possible share'. Scapa 1919
304 'If we, therefore, in the immediate future are to avoid… .'Ranft, Vol. II, p. 31
305 'If he wants to increase… .' Churchill to

Lloyd George, 1 May 1919, quoted in Ranft, Vol. II, pp. 35–36
306 'heterogenous combination of naval craft'. US Naval Advisory Staff memo, 7 Paris, April 1919, quoted in Simpson, p. 604
307 '…no arguments, however specious, no appeals, however seductive…'. Bell, p. 86
308 'With two navies of equal strength… .' US Naval Advisory Staff memo, Paris, 7 April 1919, quoted in Simpson, p. 605
309 'half its male population under thirty'. Tampke, p. 105
310 See Tampke, p. 123
311 'had fallen to one fifth of its pre-World War 1 value'. Chusid, p. 11
312 'dismissed the American rejection of high reparations as unprincipled and self-serving'. Tampke, p. 125
313 'incomparably the greatest Navy in the world'. Friedman. Promise, p. 28
314 'The British saw the United States… .' Friedman. Promise, p. 27
315 '…has ever maintained her commercial supremacy…'. Marder, FDTSF, Vol. 5, p. 221
316 'a man of mulish character…'. Marder, FDTSF, Vol. 5, p. 231
317 'double dose of Anglo-phobia'. Marder, FDTSF, Vol. 5, p. 231
318 'not have minded if other navies had been expanded at the expense of the British'. van der Vat, p. 159
319 'Don't let the British pull the wool over your eyes… .' Trask, p. 55 Quoting Benson to Sims
320 'There is no other Navy in the world… .' Simpson, p. 479
321 'Let us build a bigger Navy than hers… .' Wilson 24 September 1916 quoted in Simpson, p. 486
322 'Any nation which sought to equal this new American Navy… .' Lisio, p. 8
323 'Without Wilson at the helm, Congressional support for his "Navy second to none" eroded.' Lisio, p. 9
324 'the United States will continue to be…'. Simpson, p. 483
325 'The sudden, unexpected total collapse… .' Simpson, p. 483
326 'would spend her last guinea…'. Simpson, p. 489
327 'They exchanged such bitter comments… .' Marder, FDTSF, Vol. 5, p. 231
328 'It was one thing to react in that way, and another to make good the reaction… .' Stokesbury, p. 343

329 'suggested that Britain might rely upon its alliance with Japan for security'. Bell, p. 91
330 'no more fatal policy than that of basing our naval policy on a possible combination with Japan...'. Bell, p. 91
331 'Without mounting major operations... .' Padfield, *Maritime Dominion*, p. 204. quoting Kennedy, *Great Powers*, p. 386
332 'they were in no position to challenge Japan's expansion in East Asia' Lisio, p. 6
333 'most American naval planners at this time...'. Marder, *FDTSF*, Vol. 5, p. 228
334 '...as they fear the supremacy of the Japanese Navy...'. De Chair to Admiralty quoted in Simpson, p. 497
335 'A giant and a boy may fight a bigger giant... .' Bell, p. 96
336 'Surely if we all have the same size it does not matter'. Chatfield, Vol. 2, p. 5
337 'The King, Grey, Bonar Law... .' Simpson, p. 490
338 'The naval officers were quietly shunted... .' Simpson, p. 491
339 'first hope was that Germany's superior battleships would be added to the Royal Navy as the fruits of victory'. Wilson, p. 555
340 'sure that none of these German ships would fall into...'. Marder, *FDTSF*, Vol. 5, p. 264
341 'a moral lesson...of tremendous significance to the whole world'. Daniels, *The Wilson Era* quoted in Marder, *FDTSF*, Vol. 5, p. 264
342 'What spectacle could be more... .' Churchill to Lloyd George, 1 May 1919, Quoted Ranft, Vol. II, p. 36
343 'the very principle on which they had gone to war'. Simpson, p. 487
344 'President Wilson went home...a sadder, wiser and if anything a more determined man... .' Stokesbury, p. 343

Chapter 7
345 'inconceivable that in the staff meetings to which he so briefly refers...'. van der Vat, p. 140
346 'Carthaginian peace', Tampke, p. XI
347 'This is neither the time nor the place for superfluous words.' Tampke, p. 137
348 FRUS, *Treaty of Versailles Naval clauses.* p. 343
349 'the physical epitome of the stereotypical Prussian aristocrat...'. Tampke, p. 135
350 'the most tactless speech he had ever heard'. Tampke, p. 139

351 'lay like lead on the minds of the men'. Van der Vat quoting Reuter, pp. 160–161
352 'In this connection, the first condition ... ,' *Illustrated London News*, 13 December 1919. Also Wolz, *FISTI.* p. 202 although this is a slightly different translation. Published in Trotha, *Volksturm und Staatsführung*, pp. 182–183
353 'It was quite clear to me that I should be left alone entirely to my own devices.' van der Vat, p. 161
354 'had been suffering from severe digestive troubles...'. ADM 116/2074, VADM 1BS, 24 June 1919, p. 12
355 Raeder, p. 105
356 'It is grotesque that anyone should read out of this the order to scuttle the ships.' Ruge, p. 166
357 'Presumably some days will elapse... .' (ADM 1/8571/296 Action to be taken re: German Fleet sinking). Madden to Admiralty, 22 April 1919.
358 'In consequence of this omission...'. Ruge, p. 107
359 'these days in particular could bring us in particular a(n) (e)specially bitter decision'. van der Vat, p. 158
360 *Orkney Herald*, 25 June 1919
361 'celebrated with a little too much exuberance'. Fremantle, *Sinkings*, p. 3
362 'to be prepared to sink the ships if the attempt was made'. van der Vat, p. 158
363 'They are the most beaten lot I ever saw... .' Marder, *FDTSF*, Vol. 5, p. 272
364 'Certain minor occurrences and movements had been observed... .' Fremantle, p. 275
365 'Suppose the crews are detained in the transports... .' Booth, pp. 13–14
366 'In the event of the Germans refusing to sign the Peace terms... .'(ADM 1/8571/296 Action to be taken re: German Fleet sinking). Madden to Admiralty, 22 April 1919.
367 'paid no heed'. Marder, *FDTSF*, Vol. 5, p. 274
368 Fremantle to Madden, June 24 1919. 'Scuttling of the German Ships at Scapa Flow' (GT.-7674)
369 'dispatched a wireless message to the German Government...'. Ruge, p165
370 'only learned of this two-day extension from the newspapers'. Hewison, p. 127
371 'I had, however, considerable anxiety'. ADM 116/2074 VADM 1BS Report 24 June 1919, p. 11

372 'dispatched a wireless message to the German Government...'. Ruge, p. 165
373 'I have not seen the full text of the draft Peace Treaty... .' (ADM 1/8571/296 Action to be taken re: German Fleet sinking). Fremantle to Madden, 16 June 1919
374 'not received this news until the evening of the 21st'. Marder, FDTSF, Vol. 5, p. 277
375 'in an offical note'. Fremantle, Sinkings, p. 5
376 See Ruge, p. 110. It is extremely surprising to hear this. On the very day of the scuttle, when von Reuter maintained that he had been told nothing, a junior torpedo boat lieutenant is shown the headlines.
377 '...until now every date had, in the end, been extended'. Ruge, p. 110
378 'I considered whether or not I should tell the Admiral this... .' van der Vat, p. 169
379 'He [Madden] did not like this.' Fremantle, p. 276
380 'could now safely proceed to sea'. Bennett, Scapa Scuttle, p. 538
381 'until the Germans were off our hands'. Hewison, p. 128

Chapter 8
382 'warm and sunny'. Miller, p. 62
383 'Zur Sommenwende herrscht Kaiserwetter.' Krause, p. 293
384 'Die Sonne schein warm und silbergrau glitzerte die Wasserfläche des ganzen Beckens.' Scuttle Reports, Brummer, p. 401
385 To the Imperial Defence Minister, Chief of Admiralty, Chief of Baltic Station, Chief of the North Sea Station, 21 June. ADM 116/2074 VADM 1BS Report, 24 June 1919, p. 1
386 'need have aroused any suspicion'. Marder, FDTSF, Vol. 5, p. 281
387 'kept steam at five minute's notice'. De Courcy-Ireland, p. 56
388 'The Fleet was scuttled because the English gave us the possibility to do so.' Ruge interview, Yesterday's Yarns, Radio Orkney
389 'The upper flag was a white ball on a blue pennant... .' George, p. 27
390 'We had never seen anyone running on a big ship in Scapa.' Ruge, p. 111
391 'smiled and expressed his regret'. Ruge, p. 40
392 Source: Krause, p. 296
393 Knarston, The Orcadian, 13 September 1956. James Robertson interview (Scapa 1919). Hepburn, the school master, had been a colonel, not a major as cited elsewhere.

394 'sailed away very triumphantly...'. Ferguson, p. 74
395 'youthful, effervescent cargo of school-children'. Cousins, p. 5
396 'We were a bit put out but once we went... .' Peggy Gibson
397 'We though it strange... .' Cousins, p. 6
398 'warned by the teachers...'. Peggie Gibson on camera interview in The Battleships, Channel 4
399 'were to show no signs of hate or anything...'. Peggy Gibson interview, Scapa 1919
400 'because I had a great fear of them [Germans]'. Kitty Tait interview, Scapa 1919
401 'not to jeer or gloat over a beaten enemy'. James Robertson interview, Scapa 1919
402 'an excellent guide, shouting in a loud voice the name, tonnage and gun power of each ship'. Ferguson, p. 69
403 'ein seltsamer Kontrast...'. Krause, p. 293
404 'Everybody knew what they had to do. It had been prepared very well.' Ruge interview, Yesterday's Yarns, Radio Orkney
405 'set on a hair turning and lubricated very thoroughly'. Macdonald, p. 23
406 'Each water-tight compartment had a water-valve... .' van der Vat, pp. 164–165
407 'drew up their own plans to scuttle'. van der Vat, p. 168
408 'didn't trust the sea valves'. Ruge interview, Yesterday's Yarns, Radio Orkney
409 'Spindles [had been] bent'. Bowman, p. 19
410 'the seacocks appeared to have been treated with acid to prevent their being closed'. Hewison, p. 182
411 'condenser doors had been removed...'. George, p. 57
412 See McCutcheon, p. 53
413 'Owing to the cables of the destroyers... .' ADM.116/2074. Prendergast Report, p. 3
414 'mooring cables were wired down to bollards...'. Gores, p. 210
415 'all the instrument panels and especially the instruction plates in the ships ...'. Hewison, p. 184
416 'I see them. I think they're sinking their ships.' ('Ich hab's! Ich glaube, die versenken ihre Schiffe!'.Krause, p. 297
417 'Return to your ships at once. If you do not do so I will fire on you.' Hewison, p. 135
418 'The Germans must have had pigs... .' John Tulloch memories, Courtesy Joyce Howard
419 'I noticed a number of small boats pushing

off from the German ships'. Brown and Meehan, pp. 132–133

420 'the 1st division of the First Battle Squadron...'. ADM.116/2074, Report VADM, HMS *Revenge*, Scapa, p. 1

421 'until ten minutes after it had been observed...'. De Courcy-Ireland, p. 57

422 '...if the C in C preferred to accept the unsupported statement...'. *Ibid.*

423 'One hundred Royal Marines were to be landed... .' Fremantle, *Sinkings*, p. 5

424 'sight that met our gaze...'. Hugh David correspondence from HMS *Revenge*, BBC.

425 'loud and vigorous tones of single strokes...'. Reuter, p. 79

426 'too quickly, because, as a result, the British received an early warning'. Ruge, p. 114

427 'A small diamond... .' John Tulloch memories, Courtesy Joyce Howard

428 Tulloch, *The Orcadian*, 13 September 2011

429 'to wake up all the remaining ships at one stroke'. Reuter, p. 79

430 'exceedingly angry, hardly listened and really didn't understand a word [he] said'. Reuter, p. 80

431 'hard and fast on a shoal". Reuter, p. 80

432 RADM Orkney and Shetlands to VADM 1BS, 24 June 1919. ADM. 116/2074.

433 'What a damned cheek!' Ferguson, p. 70

434 'Turn back. The German ships are sinking.' Peggy Gibson interview, *Scapa 1919*

435 'We were about a third of the way through the Fleet... .' Cousins, p. 6

436 'on an even keel and some upended...'. Ferguson, p. 70

437 'We were looking at them... .' Ferguson. p. 74

438 'particularly attached'. Ruge, p. 114

439 'A German cheer... .' John Tulloch memories, Courtesy Joyce Howard

440 'wild stürzte das Wasser durch die Seitenfenster in die oberen Räume'. *König Albert*, Scuttle Reports, p. 277

441 'Leute, in einer viertel Stunde müssen wir das Schiff verlassen.' *Moltke*, Scuttle Reports, p. 189

442 'In the crew accommodation... .' Booth, pp. 88–89

443 'Wie zu einem letzten Kampfe gegen die Gewalt... .' *Moltke*, Scuttle Reports, p. 190

444 'only her keel showed at low tide'. John Tulloch memories, Courtesy Joyce Howard

445 'terrified'. Ferguson, p. 74 and OLA interviews

446 Smith, p. 9

447 *Herald Scotland*, 13 November

448 WWS3. Interview with Peggy Gibson

449 'The competition on the boat... .' Ferguson, p. 73

450 'rudely told to clear out quick'. Ferguson, p. 70

451 Knarston, *The Orcadian*, 13 September 1956

452 'I saw at least one sailor shot on the deck of one vessel... .' Cousins, p. 5

453 *Orcadian*, 26 June 1919

454 Knarston, *The Orcadian*, 13 September 1956

455 'They were really afraid for the safety of the boat   ' Kitty Tait interview, *Scapa 1919*

456 'just churning all the time. Peggy Gibson interview, *Scapa 1919*

457 'cascading up all around us'. Ferguson, p. 74

458 See *Kronprinz Wilhelm*, Scuttle Reports, p. 237

459 '...with the prescribed gear which they have had ready for days...'. Reuter, p. 117

460 'did not take similar action to that taken in Gutter Sound...'.ADM 116/2074, VADM 1BS, 24 June 1919, p. 4. Moreover, the sub lieutenant and midshipman in command of *Ramna* and *Trust-On* were praised for doing just this while the trawler *Cudwosin* was also criticised when the guards did not open fire on German crews escaping 'when the boats, on shoving off, hoisted the white flag'.

461 Tulloch, Lyness Museum, Exhibition materials summer 2016

462 'reared herself steeply into the air...'. Reuter, p. 81

463 'As she went she rose steeply into the air and then crashed downwards... .' Macdonald, pp. 26–27

464 Candy, *The Times*, September 2003

465 'so quickly that there was no time ...'. George, p. 31

466 'unser Schiff gesenkt werden, sobald der Befehl dazu vom Admiral gegeben würde.' Scuttle Reports, p. 401

467 'Alle strahlen nun vor Vergnügen, dem Engländer diesem Streich spielen zu dürfen.' Scuttle Reports, p. 401

468 'und zwar legt er sich nach Stb. Über und kenterte'. Scuttle Reports, p. 411

469 'There she lay like a monster whale... .' John Tulloch memories, Courtesy Joyce Howard

470 'Kaum war das Rieterlied verlungen... .' *Seydlitz*, Scuttle Reports, p. 178

471 'presume(d) it was surrender'. Ferguson. p. 71. From an interview with Ernest W Marwick

472 'just put on, probably for our benefit…'. Ferguson. p. 72

473 WWS3. Interview with Henrietta Groundwater

474 Knarston, *The Orcadian*, 13 September 1956

475 *Köln*, Scuttle Reports, p. 353

476 *'Befehle flogen hin und her'*. *Köln*, Scuttle Reports, p. 353

477 *'zu dieser Zeit sank Brummer'*. *Köln*, Scuttle Reports, p. 355

478 'less low in the water than other ships'. ADM.116/2074, Report VADM, HMS *Revenge*, Scapa, p. 9

479 *'hatte bereits starke Schlag-Seite'*. Scuttle Reports, p. 298

480 See *Kaiserin* Scuttle Reports, p. 285

481 See *Kaiserin* Scuttle Reports, p. 284

482 *'Doch wie wurden wir enttäusscht…'* Scuttle Reports, p. 285, *Kaiserin*

483 'That's no submarine, it's a German ship going down.' George, p. 33

484 'a large coin…'. Morag Robertson, personal correspondence

485 *Orcadian*, 26 June 1919

486 'with the German flag flying'. Reuter, p. 81

487 Tulloch, *The Orcadian*, 13 September 2011

488 'high tail it back home…'. John Tulloch memories, Courtesy Joyce Howard

489 Hugh 'Ti' David, a midshipman on *Revenge*, described seeing *Bayern* sinking in a letter home, 26 June 1919. He'e seen 'a cloud of smoke [from] bursting boilers'.

490 'The first sign we saw was the masts of a ship at a sharp angle…' Brown and Meehan, p. 134

491 'turned completely turtle and disappeared in a smother of foam;. John Tulloch memories, Courtesy Joyce Howard

492 See McCutcheon, p. 41

493 'in spite of the English sailors who had seized the vessel'. Reuter, pp. 81–82

494 Source: Krause, p. 305

495 'Obviously sinking but still afloat were *Baden*…' ADM.116/2074, Report VADM, HMS *Revenge*, Scapa, p. 6

496 Scuttle Reports, *Brummer, Machinistmaat* Gondermann, p. 411

497 'the firing dies away and is gradually silenced'. Reuter, p. 81

498 Hewison quoting a report in *The Orcadian*, 13 September 1956

499 'drifters were pulling at huge battleships …'. John Tulloch memories, Courtesy Joyce Howard

500 *'Ich habe eine freudige Mitteilung zu machen.'* *Derfflinger*, Scuttle Reports, p. 144

501 'We saw them landing on the island of Cava…' Ferguson, p. 72

502 'group of women wielding pitchforks…' Macdonald, p. 26

503 Tulloch, Lyness Museum, Exhibition materials summer 2016

504 Tulloch, Lyness Museum, Exhibition materials summer 2016

505 'spotted this boat and hastened over to order them off…'. John Tulloch memories, Courtesy Joyce Howard

506 'the island – Cava – seemed to be covered…'. Peggie Gibson quoted in Ferguson, p. 73

507 *Baden*, Scuttle Reports, p. 294

508 'rapidly making water, all WT…'. ADM.116/2074, Report VADM, HMS *Revenge*, Scapa, p. 8

509 'I went aboard (the *Baden*)…' Bennett, *Scapa Scuttle*, p. 539

510 'kept going. This work was effected…' ADM.116/2074, Report VADM, HMS *Revenge*, Scapa, p. 8

511 'cleverly manoeuvered [the *Baden*] into shallow water'. Cousins, p. 2

512 'a group of ragged desperadoes…'. BBC, Hugh David, p. 2

513 Prommersberger, *Unternehmen Albion*

514 Gröner, p. 28

515 Source: Navweapons site

516 McCall, UCI

517 *Orcadian*, 17 July 1919

518 *Orcadian*, 26 June 1919

519 'I went on board the Hindenburg when she was sinking…' George, pp. 30–31

520 *'Eine Explosion in Richtung* Hindenburg *ließ uns aufhorchen…'* Hindenburg, Scuttle Reports, p. 168

521 *Orcadian*, 26 June 1919

522 Arthur, p. 140, quoting Lieutenant Brian de Courcy-Ireland

523 'many of the clips were rusty and stiff'. De Courcy-Ireland, p. 57

524 'very nearly taking [him] with her'. Hugh David, BBC

525 *Orcadian*, 17 July 1919

526 'to sink her on an even keel to make the disembarkation of the crew more certain'. Reuter, p. 81

527 'allowed her to drift on shore'. ADM.116/2074 VADM 1BS Report, p. 3

528 'hämmern, brechstange, sägen, bohlen'. Frankfurt, Scuttle Reports, p. 389
529 'etwa noch 2 Handbreit unterkannte der Seitefenster im Wasser'. Frankfurt, Scuttle Reports, p. 390
530 'grounded in 3½ fathoms of water amidships before sinking'. ADM.116/2074 VADM 1BS Report, p. 8. The Admiralty report talked of the Classin but probably meant Clonsin
531 'leeren Beuteln, Drahtzang, Blechscheren und Brecheisen'. Frankfurt, Scuttle Reports, p. 390
532 'We had been quiet cleaning ship on Saturday morning.' Ruge interview, Yesterday's Yarns, Radio Orkney
533 'a few minutes later we saw men in one of the battle cruisers…'. Kennedy, Scapa Flow, UBHG, p 14
534 Orcadian, 26 June 1919
535 'Don't talk such tripe.' George, p. 30
536 'so near that we could read their names and see the men on them'. Booth, p. 13
537 'only see HMS Victoria …'. Margaret Gibson on Yesterday's Yarns, Radio Orkney
538 'Make for the Victoria.' Margaret Gibson on Yesterday's Yarns, Radio Orkney
539 'the most spectacular view of the Fleet sinking'. Margaret Gibson on Yesterday's Yarns, Radio Orkney
540 See Kennedy, Scapa Flow, UBHG, p. 14. See Ruge introduction in Ferguson, p. 9
541 'meatballs sizzling in the big pan'. Ruge, p. 112
542 'could comfortably step into the cutter…'. Ruge, p. 112
543 'Masts, funnels and superstructure were torn off.' Ruge, p. 114
544 'his trumpet under his arm'. Ruge, p. 113
545 'very few German ships went down with their colours…'. ADM.116/2074 Prendergast Report (050/91) p. 3
546 '…unter Feuer genommen…'. Krause, p. 299
547 'There was no question of anyone being in charge.' Reuter, p. 117
548 Orcadian, 26 June 1919
549 'half her side had been freshly painted'. Ruge, p. 115
550 'devilishly sounding, earnestly meant, and unmistakable orders…'. Reuter, p. 118
551 'He pulled the trigger…and missed….' Macdonald, p. 27
552 'of his ordering the inlets to be shut…'. ADM.116/2074 VADM 1BS Report, p. 9
553 'Exactly half the casualties, four dead and eight wounded, incurred during the

scuttling.' van der Vat, p. 176. The ninth death, van der Vat points out, occurred aboard HMS Resolution. That was Kuno Eversberg, shot the night of 23/24 June (See report in The Sunday Post, 30 November 1919). He died on 29 June.
554 '…one man shot. He dropped right out of the stern of the boat.' Hewison, p. 133. Hewison actually said 'stem of the boat' but I assume he meant 'stern'.
555 'had rightly decided that it was useless to waste…'. ADM.116/2074 VADM 1BS Report, p. 3
556 'On Fara island: S.31. S.54, V.82, S.60, V.80, S.137,… .' ADM.116/2074. Prendergast Report (050/91) p. 3
557 'the problem of what to do with the German Fleet had now been solved by the Germans themselves.' OLA Tapes OSA/AO5 466. Tape 4, Hewison
558 'In all its colourful history, and it's had plenty… .' OLA Tapes OSA/AO5 466. Tape 4, Hewison
559 Source: George, p 29
560 'thrilling experience'. The Belper News, 11 July 1919
561 'the Huns hadn't got a weapon between them'. Hugh David, BBC letter from HMS Revenge, misdated 26 June 1919
562 Source: Wolz, FISTI. p. 207. Quoting Herwig, Elitekorps
563 See The Roscommon Messenger, 28 June 1919. p. 4.
564 'a place for the wind and the birds'. Kennedy, Scapa Flow, UBHG, p. 15
565 'a pillar of water a large quantity of debris…'. The Roscommon Messenger, 28 June 1919. p. 4.
566 'every pier'. Ferguson, p. 73
567 'He was lying in bed… .' Ferguson, p. 75
568 'No, I don't think anybody was afraid… .' Rosetta Groundwater
569 'They had all raised their flags to top mast.' Peggy Gibson interview, Scapa 1919

Chapter 9
570 'personally concerned himself with the welfare of the Germans'. Ruge, p. 117
571 'dressed in their best uniforms'. AMD.116/2074 Prendergast Report (050/91) p. 2
572 'The view that the order… .' ADM. 116/2074 VADM 1BS Report, 24 June 1919, p. 13
573 Orkney Herald, 25 June 1919

[574] 'had never been seen before in Scapa Flow'. Ruge, p. 116

[575] 'articles were expressly recognised as our private property'. Ruge, pp. 120–121

[576] 'the deck surfaces were scrubbed snow-white…'. Ruge, p. 119

[577] 'loaded with extraordinary baggage, such as puppies, musical instruments…'. Ruge, p. 120

[578] 'putting his foot on the guitar and [throwing] the coat on the deck'. Ruge, p. 120

[579] '*auf nichtssagenden Gründen*', Scuttle Reports, *Kaiserin*, p. 288

[580] See Scuttle Reports, *Brummer*, p. 411

[581] 'dishevilled, wet and white as a sheet'. Hugh David, BBC

[582] '*Wassercacao*'. Kaiser, Scuttle Reports, p. 271

[583] 'to direct the salvage work on the *Baden*'. Ruge, p. 121

[584] 'morale was excellent'. Ruge, p. 121

[585] 'bolt upright'. Ruge, p. 123

[586] 'pompous speech'. Kennedy, *Scapa Flow* notes, quoting Cousins.

[587] Quoted in full, van de Vat, *The Grand Scuttle*, pp. 180–181

[588] 'The extension of the Armistice had not been communicated to him.' Ruge, p. 124

[589] Howarth, p. 168

[590] '…*der sein Wort gehalten hat…*'. Krause, p. 233

[591] 'requirements had been fully complied with'. ADM. 116/2074 VADM 1BS Report, 24 June 1919, p. 11

[592] 'roundabout route'. van der Vat, p. 187

[593] 'It was felt that as soon as she grasped what had happened… .' De Courcy-Ireland, p. 57

[594] *Orcadian*, 26 June 1919

[595] 'he'd lost two brothers in the war…'. *The Western Times*, 10 February 1920

[596] '*Ich schaffte meinen Kameraden mit größte Mühe, ohne Hilfe zu erhalten, ins Schiffslazarett.*' Krause, p. 310. BA-MA, RM 44/v5 *Versenkungsbericht, Frankfurt*, Protokol 1, Kyrielein. p. 395

[597] 'the patient's recovery was very doubtful owing to the extensive infection'. Bolton court statement

[598] 'He told me that while going to the heads… .' *Ibid*

[599] 'most of it was prompted by a feeling of panic, anger and impotence'. van der Vat, p. 177

[600] 'It serves us right… .' *The Sunday Post*, Sunday, 22 June 1919.

[601] Quoted in *Orcadian*, 26 June 1919

[602] It was typical that this manly act… .' Woodward, p. 185

[603] 'Whatever damage the act may inflict… .' Reported from Copenhagen 24 June 1919, although the newspaper's name is unknown (press cutting book at Lyness Visitor Centre)

[604] 'The German people do not understand the sea… .' *The Battleships*, Channel 4

[605] 'splashed across four columns of the paper's centre-spread'. Hewison, p. 131

[606] 'real houses and human beings, green trees and shrubs'. Ruge, p. 124

[607] 'for lack of decoration, exceeded anything we had known in Germany'. Ruge, p. 124

[608] Source Macdonald, p. 30

[609] '… as hostile crowds of off-duty soldiers, women and children spat…'. Macdonald, p. 32

[610] 'we probably would not have found the new world…'. Ruge, p. 126

[611] 'midget iron stove'. Ruge, p. 127

[612] 'troops with fixed bayonets'. *The Western Times*, 29 November 1919

[613] 'the Chancellor had even declared in the National Assembly…'. van der Vat, p. 192

[614] 'I gave no more information on my motives.' van der Vat, p. 185

[615] 'dirty, run-down transport'. Schubert and Gibson, p. 272

[616] 'fell overboard un-noticed during the night', From admiral 2ic Grand Fleet (Madden) to C-in-C High Seas Fleet, 20 December 1918

[617] 'The Law Officers of the Crown… .' (ADM 1/8571/296 Action to be taken re: German Fleet sinking). Naval Section, Paris, 26 August 1919 to 2nd Sea Lord and Deputy Chief of Naval Staff (DCNS)

[618] 'The events which have occurred and the measures thereby made necessary make it no longer possible… .' van der Vat, p. 195

[619] See *The Daily Telegraph* and *The Manchester Guardian*, 10 February 1920. Also Document 7534/V. Report by Cordes, Leader of the Torpedo Boats.

[620] 'in consideration of the fact that the man was murdered'. Naval Expenditure Emergency Standing Committee, Decision dated 22 August 1919, date stamped Admiralty 25 August.

Chapter 10

[621] 'The British were publicly indignant and privately relieved.' van der Vat, p. 183

[622] 'in consideration of the fact that the man was murdered'. Naval Expenditure

Emergency Standing Committee, Decision
dated 22 August 1919, date stamped
Admiralty 25 August.
[623] The Council of Four. Minutes of
Meetings, 24 May–28 June 1918. Volume VI
p. 659
[624] Howarth, *The Dreadnoughts*, p. 168. Letter
from Admiral Fremantle to Admiral George
P Hope

Chapter 11
[625] 'sixty-one battleships, 129 cruisers…'.
Wilson, p. 53. Redford and Grove (p. 102) give
slightly more precise numbers: 37,363 officers
and 4,000,975 men.
[626] 'well-advanced, and the other six were
about 25% complete'. Roskill, *NPBW*, p. 309
[627] 'Great Britain and France from 1919
through 1922 respected each other's…'.
Chusid, p. 13
[628] See Munson, Lt Cdr Mark. *ONI and the
Washington Conference of 1921–1922*. Centre
for International Maritime Security. Quoting
Ferris, John. *Issues in British and American
Signals Intelligence 1919–1932*. Fort Meade,
NSA Centre for Cryptographic History, 2015,
p. 44
[629] 'sunk sixty-six capital ships, more ships in
fifteen minutes than any of all the admirals of
the world in a cycle of centuries'. Lisio, p. 22
[630] '*Hood*, five *Royal Sovereigns* and five *Queen
Marys*.' Lisio, p. 22
[631] 'the Ten Year naval holiday…should be
agreed to' ADM 1/8630.Roskill, *NPBW*, p.
315
[632] '…planned and unfinished ships of the
Naval Act of 1916…'. Friedman. *Promise*, p. 30
[633] 'the British Empire will not be engaged…'.
Bell, p. 89
[634] 'The longer you can delay building new
ships… .' Bell, p. 87, quoting *The Weekly
Dispatch*.
[635] 'at the end of the ten-year period…'.
Redford and Grove, p. 105
[636] 'would result in the decay of naval ship
construction …'. Roskill, *NPBW*, p. 312
[637] 'in the manner of a bulldog, sleeping on a
Sunday doorstep …'. Lisio, p. 23
[638] FRUS, Section II, Naval Clauses, Notes to
Part V, Section II, Articles 181 to 197. Speech
House of Commons, 17 March 1920.
[639] 'what was revolutionary though about this
treaty…'. Chusid, p. 3
[640] 'the source of a new international arms
race…'. Lisio, p. 30

[641] 'could not conceive of any use of the fleet
will ever have for aviation'. Quoted from
Underwood, Jeffery S, *The wings of democracy:
the influence of air power on the Roosevelt Administration, 1933–1941* (1991), p. 11
[642] 'It was the neglected child with two
squabbling parents… .' Wilson, p. 557
[643] 'tripled its naval budget'. Lisio, p. 9
[644] 'almost twice the number of modern,
post-Jutland capital ships allowed'. Lisio, p. 32
[645] 'turned a potential ally into a potential rival
in the Far East'. Redford and Grove, p. 115
[646] 'What the Washington Conference did
accomplish …'. Roskill, *NPBW*, p. 330
[647] 'Essentially, they said that the North Pacific
area… .' Stokesbury, p. 344
[648] 'As it turned out, this is exactly what
happened'. Kuehn, p. 81
[649] 'After the Washington Conference, Navy
officers were forced to think… .' Kuehn, p. 75
[650] 'By the Washington Naval Treaty of
December 1921… .' Simpson, p. 493
[651] 'closer to 5-4-3 between the wars'. See
Munson.
[652] 'took the unusual step of protesting
publicly…'. Stokesbury, p. 345
[653] 'Distinctly inferior'. Lisio, p. 23
[654] 'The number of aircraft carriers in a Fleet
action… .' Roskill, *NPBW*, p. 310, Source:
ADM 1/8615
[655] Brassey's *Naval and Shipping Annual*, 1920–
1921. p. 132
[656] 'In its suicide, the Fleet redeemed itself in
the eyes of the nation… .' Kelly, pp. 427–428
[657] 'That Admiral Reuter and our officers…'.
Kelly, p. 428
[658] Yorck von Reuter, *Scapa 1919*
[659] 'If Singapore fell in the first two or three
months of a war… .' Bell, p. 100
[660] '…the stubborn, brutal fact remains that
the decision…'. Bell, p. 101

Chapter 12
[661] 'there can be no question of salving the
ships'. Gores, p. 211
[662] 'shipped from Orkney in herring barrels…
'. Pottinger, p. 2
[663] '£200–250 region, perhaps equal to
somewhere around £20,000 in today's prices'.
Hewison, p. 181. (Hewison was writing
around 1999).
[664] 'had never lifted a ship before, the project
was somewhat ambitious'. Cox. *Thomas Lowe
Gray*, p. 327
[665] Quoted in Hewison, p. 181

666 Courtesy the Cox Family (Quoted on Naval History-net)

667 'If he hadn't been a mixture of a genius and a mule... .' Gores, p. 214

668 'There was an explosive crack like a gun going off... .' Hewison, p. 183

669 'an artillery bombardment'. George, p. 51

670 'bent over the small pulley winches'. George, p. 52

671 'asking for trouble'. Cox, *Thomas Lowe*, p. 327

672 See Gores, p. 214

673 'unexpectedly from £5 to about £1 15s per ton'. George, p. 53

674 'sort of floating carpenter's shop'. Hewison, p. 183

675 'the quiet boys ashore'. Gores, p. 214

676 'great avenue'. Peggy Gibson interview, *Scapa 1919*

677 'to be employed as a counter weight to balance the list'. Pottinger, p. 2

678 'in the incredible time of forty minutes'. Gores, p. 215

679 'Had the fire reached the store... .' Booth, p. 53

680 'greater than any warship then in German service...'. Booth, p. 70

681 'no submersible lighting...'. George, p. 61

682 'vast submarine forest'. George, p. 61

683 'not only showed the ship's piping arrangement...'. Booth, p. 75

684 'better sealing properties than the original tallow alone'. Gores, p. 217

685 'we were trying to balance the battleship of about 100 feet...'. Cox. *Thomas Lowe Gray*, p. 332

686 'Within fifteen minutes... .' Booth, p. 80

687 '...she was now rolling so violently that one of her derricks...'. *Ibid*

688 'We'll fetch her up next spring. I've been thinking it out, and I see the idea now.' Gores, p. 218

689 'bottom up near the island of Rysa'. John Tulloch memories, Courtesy Joyce Howard. Tulloch worked as an acetylene cutter on the *Moltke* salvage working inside her once the air locks had been fitted.

690 '...it misled me, not because it was inferior work...'. Cox. *Thomas Lowe Gray*, p. 338

691 'Air pipes were embedded into the bottom valve openings... .' Booth, p. 84

692 'a choice mixture of burnt red lead, oil, paint and boiled-bilge water'. Bowman, p. 148

693 'tumbling up out of the airlock like a couple of pantomime demons ...'. Bowman, p. 148

694 Source: George, p. 74

695 'fog-like effect meant that the compressed air...'. Booth, p. 89

696 'We shouted for the men to make for the airlock... .' *Ibid*

697 See Booth, p. 85

698 'often became swollen and numb'. Booth, p. 42

699 'Inside the wreck there was a wilderness... .' John Tulloch memories, Courtesy Joyce Howard.

700 Harry Taylor, (OLA) employee of Cox and Danks. Recorded 25 August 1987. Orkney Library and Archives, BBC Radio Orkney Collection Tapes 451/452.

701 'The 'safety man' who followed each diver ...'. Bowman, p. 154

702 'like an old-time London fog ...'. George, p. 69

703 'Presently from each of them (airlocks), emerged half-a-dozen grimy men... .' Hewison, pp. 190–191

704 '... set the attendant docks rolling violently...'. Bowman, p. 160

705 'I don't know about lifebelts.' George, p. 73

706 Source: George, p. 75

707 'Alloa had insisted on purchasing *Moltke*... .' Buxton, p. 17

708 'the only battleship ever to pass beneath the Forth Bridge...'. Bowman, p. 177

709 'more than half an hour to regain control'. Booth, p. 93

710 'an improved version of the *Moltke*'. Booth, p. 96

711 'Strangers entering Scapa Flow sometimes mistook her for a small island.' George, p. 81

712 Sourced from Hewison, p. 188

713 'amid the din of hissing air and oily exhaust odour'. Booth, p. 99

714 'Twenty times she nearly right... .' Booth, p. 101

715 'It was a heart-breaking procedure as I was getting short of money.' Cox. *Thomas Lowe Gray*, p. 341

716 'proved to be the easiest of all'. George, p. 86

717 Letter WC Elliot, HMS *Vernon*, 9 September 1923

718 Letter to his wife. Herbert Hall, 2 March 1929. With kind permission of Chris Irvine

719 'natural cause'. Booth, p. 113

720 'On more than one occasion... .' Booth, p. 115

721 Harry Taylor, (OLA)

722 'the damn ship is heavier on the portside'. Gores, p. 218

723 'the biggest ship in the world that had ever been lifted'. Cox. *Thomas Lowe Gray*, p. 338
724 'disappeared in a floundering splash ...'. Bowman, p. 234
725 'as much as Cox had spent raising her'. Buxton, p. 20
726 'We saw this man floating in the oil... .' Booth, p. 133
727 'the tip of the rudder and four propellers... '. Booth, p. 136
728 Walsh, personal interview, 5 October 2016.
729 'very big boost to the Orkney economy, especially at a time of deep recession'. Hewison, p. 195
730 'as determined and forceful as Cox'. George, p. 99
731 'had a better technical understanding than Cox'. Buxton, p. 26
732 'energetic and skilful marine engineer...'. Booth, p. 28
733 'a man of depth of character, but simplicity, integrity and kindness'. *The Times*, 10 April 1982.
734 Budge, personal interview (2017)
735 'You'd better get something for your breath. It's foul.' George, p. 107
736 Source: George, p. 108
737 OLA Tape 452
738 OLA Tape 452
739 Source: George, Appendix 3, p. 138
740 'each averaged 9,660 tons of ferrous scrap...'. Buxton, p. 33
741 Buxton, p. 341
742 'flying the Red Ensign'. Pottinger, p. 12
743 See *Warship 2016*, Adrian Dodson. *Derfflinger. An inverted Life*. p. 178
744 OLA Tapes OSA/AO5 466. Tape 4, Hewison

Chapter 13
745 'Come all ye wreckers come... .' Skea, Betsy. *Island Images. Memories of Sanday*. Orkney Press 1982, p. 53
746 Source: *The Telegraph*, 4 August 2017
747 'With your act at Scapa Flow... .' Reuter, p. 23
748 'Having, rather to my surprise... .' Fremantle, *Sinkings*, p. 8
749 'to the best of [his] belief, they had received no reply'. Fremantle, *Sinkings*, p. 8

INDEX